FACES OF LABOUR

FACES OF LABOUR

The Inside Story

—◆—

ANDY McSMITH

VERSO

London • New York

First published by Verso 1996
© Andy McSmith 1996
All rights reserved

The right of Andy McSmith to be identified as the author
of this work has been asserted by him in accordance with
the Copyright, Designs and Patents Act 1988

Verso
UK: 6 Meard Street, London W1V 3HR
USA: 180 Varick Street, New York NY 10014–4606

Verso is the imprint of New Left Books

ISBN 1–85984–968–7

British Library Cataloguing in Publication Data
A catalogue record for this book is available from the British Library

Library of Congress Cataloging-in-Publication Data
A catalog record for this book is available from the Library of Congress

Typeset by M Rules
Printed by Biddles Ltd, Guildford and King's Lynn

CONTENTS

PREAMBLE

The British Labour Party would be one of the most successful political parties in the Western world if it did not lose so many general elections. It has been an enduring force for stability and measured reform. If anyone asks why mainland Britain is one of the few countries in the world to have sailed through the twentieth century free from revolution, social disintegration or political violence on any serious scale, or why Britain's poor and dispossessed have renounced such desperate extremes as fascism or terrorism, a large part of the answer is that they have always had the Labour Party through which to channel their discontent.

At the local level, the Labour Party is the natural party of government, as the late Harold Wilson once suggested it might be. It has more councillors and controls more councils than all the other political parties in Britain put together. Its strength is concentrated where it counts most – in the high-spending urban councils, some of which have budgets larger than the gross annual income of countries represented in the United Nations. There are, by contrast, large urban areas which were dominated by the Conservatives a quarter of a century ago but where they have since been wiped out. At that level, the Labour Party's greatest problems arise from too much electoral success rather than too little. There are too many cities and towns where one party holds every single seat on the local council, or commands such an overwhelming majority that it rules unchallenged by the democratic process. Yet, considering the scope for corruption, nepotism or self-indulgent schisms between rival factions of Labour councillors, the scandals that afflict Labour in local government are relatively rare and relatively small in scale. Year in, year out, Labour councillors do a reasonable job of managing schools, supervising social services, repairing roads, emptying bins and employing staff.

This obvious fact is worth repeating because the intellectual fashion of the moment is to treat the Labour Party as a hopelessly failed and out-of-date organization, trapped in its own past, part of which has been shaken out of self-destructive lethargy, a tiny little corps of professionals. A rather sour book written by a tabloid journalist named Leo McInstrey opens with the assertion that: 'The Labour Party is one of the least successful parties that has ever existed in a parliamentary democracy.'[1] Mr McInstrey is not an objective observer: he once had hopes of becoming either a political adviser to a Cabinet minister, when he was employed by Harriet Harman, or the leader of Islington Council, where he was an acolyte of Margaret Hodge. But he now regards his former membership of the Labour Party as an error brought on by a sense of guilt over his middle-class background, and appears to think that he can return to normality by writing intemperately for the *Sun*. He does, though, express in a distorted and extreme form the modernizers' view of the Labour Party: that it is worthless unless it can win enough parliamentary seats to form a government.

That is a reaction to a sequence of events which can be traced back to the 1970s, when those who were urging a radical reform of the Labour Party began from the opposing premise, that some things were more important than winning general elections. During the first half of the 1980s, the party went through a convulsion during which the purpose of its existence was fiercely debated. Then the point at issue was whether Labour was a socialist party, in the dictionary sense of the word, or not. The word 'socialist' is currently undergoing a change of meaning, but all the standard dictionaries still use the 1980s definition: that a socialist is one who believes in the common ownership of the means of production. On that definition, the manifesto with which the Labour Party fought the 1983 general election was socialist, whereas the one presented to the electorate in 1992 was not. In the early 1980s a significant proportion of the party's active membership were disillusioned by the limited achievements of the Labour governments of 1964–79, and set out to convert the party from one which managed and modernized the capitalist system to one dedicated to its peaceful abolition. The first tranche of reforms to the party rulebook in 1979–80 were introduced to that end. Many of the non-socialists in the Labour Party leadership were so sure that their cause was lost that they deserted in 1981 to found the Social Democratic Party.

The result was the débâcle of the 1983 general election, when the Labour Party's share of the national vote fell so low that it was very nearly overtaken by the Liberal–SDP Alliance. The explanation for this disaster which the whole Labour leadership accepted at the time was that voters are repelled by the spectacle of a party at war with itself, so absorbed in its internal affairs that it could not wage an efficient, professionally run campaign. It is also likely that voters looked beyond the chaotic state of party organization at the programme on offer and rejected it because socialism did not appeal to them. What seemed certain was that if the Labour Party could not resolve its own ideological conflict, its decline would continue. Some serious analysts believed that the game was already up. One contemporary study concluded that: 'The 1983 British general election succeeded in breaking the mould of British psephology . . . While the Alliance did not break the Conservative monopoly of government, it did break Labour's monopoly claim as the opposition party . . . The Labour Party has contributed to the decline in class politics in Britain by becoming a failed ghetto party. It is no longer the party of most working-class voters.'[2]

From there, the story of the Labour Party is one of slow recovery. At general elections, its gains have been principally at the expense of the former Liberal–SDP Alliance. Within five years, Labour had regained its 'monopoly claim as the opposition party', and it appeared for a time as if both the SDP and the Liberal Party were on the verge of extinction. Labour's recovery has been aided by outside events. Internationally, the changing nature of world markets and the collapse of the communist system have in effect taken socialism, as it used to be defined, off the agenda. At home, the last throw for the socialist left was the 1984–85 miners' strike, after which it was left to thrash about in an evaporating pool, unable to create a suitable environment for itself or to have any further influence in the Labour Party. The significant battles inside the party since 1985 have been less overtly political than before. They have been about turning an old organization, full of traditions and vested interests, into an efficient electoral machine and devising a menu of reforms which promise enough to entice support without threatening too much.

An equally significant factor in the party's recovery is its own resilience. Despite the demoralization and defections of the early 1980s, there was a hard core of committed party members who never gave up, and a bedrock of geographically concentrated electoral support which never deserted Labour. Even in 1983, eight million people voted for it. The trade unions never ceased to act as a reliable source of funds. At local level, the party retained control over most of the largest municipal authorities in Great Britain, including London, Birmingham, Strathclyde, Cardiff, Manchester, Liverpool and Newcastle. Its worst council election results in the late 1970s were never anything like as serious as the cull of Conservative councillors in 1994–96. One great difference between the Labour Party and the Social Democratic Party was that the latter needed instant success to survive at all. The SDP suffered a near fatal haemorrhage of its active membership after its first disappointing general election result. Two disappointing general elections and it was dead. The Labour Party endured four and continued to grow. Even in the year 1983, it was attracting new MPs to parliament of the calibre of Tony Blair, Gordon Brown, Clare Short, Chris Smith and many more. It never lost a reservoir of devotees who would drag themselves out after a defeat and carry on, undiscouraged. A large number of today's leading modernizers were involved in the Bennite rebellion when they were younger. Having decided that they were pushing the wrong political programme, they stuck nonetheless to their view that the party urgently needed to be reformed – and pushed it in its present direction with undiminished energy.

In retrospect, it is surprising how grown-up commentators so badly underestimated Labour's capacity for survival. It is inevitable that long-established political parties will undergo identity crises and periods of relative political eclipse. The test is not whether a party can avoid these crises altogether, but whether it is capable of adapting and reinventing itself as a result. The fact that the Labour Party has done so augurs well for its long-term survival. Currently, the Conservatives are gripped by an identity crisis as serious as that which hit Labour twenty years earlier, as the Tories try to decide whether theirs is primarily a party of internationalist capitalism or of the nation state. Their party is not likely to die either, for the same reason that Labour survived the 1980s: the Tories have a solid popular base concentrated in select geographical areas, and a corps of active members who will stay loyal and active through the bad times. But judged by a number of objective criteria, the plight of the Conservatives is worse in 1996 than that of Labour in 1978, yet there is less of a tendency to predict its immediate death. Even in defeat, the Conservatives command respect. There may be an unspoken class snobbery underlying the tendency to treat the Labour Party with contempt. The logic runs something like this: 'Working-class people vote for the Labour Party; working-class people are stupid; therefore the Labour Party is useless.' Actually, it is a well-organized, well-established mass political party with a depth of tradition and experience to which it has now added a formidable ability to cope with defeat and to adapt.

Just as professional football is left in the capable hands of the sort of people who believe that 'football is not a matter of life and death, it's more important than that', so the Labour Party has delegated the planning and running of general election campaigns to those who believe that there is no point to political activity other than winning general elections. That state of mind is conducive to success. To delegate so much power and influence to the modernizers was sensible though, like every sensible decision, it has a down side. The Labour Party now is increasingly run by professionals, who believe they can make direct contact with the electorate through the mass media and market research and maintain their support within the party through direct mailing and postal ballots. There is not much for the amateur activist to do any more. This bedrock of enthusiasts saw the party through its last crisis. The danger is that they may not be there next time they are needed.

One way to describe the upheaval which has taken place in the Labour Party in 1979 and what it augurs for the future would be to write a straight history. Another would be to write a biography of one prominent personality, or several. Here, I have used a technique well-known to historians since Lytton Strachey published his *Eminent Victorians*, which is to seek to capture what was distinct about a particular era through an apparently random selection of individual portraits. Strachey's subjects were by no means the most important people in Victorian England, nor the closest to the Queen.

The most common objection from those who read this volume in manuscript has been to the seemingly eccentric choice of subjects. Some eminent colleagues of Tony Blair are excluded, leaving room for people whose names mean nothing to most people. The five famous people portrayed here are not the most important members of the current Labour leadership. Blair himself is here, but such luminaries as John Prescott, Gordon Brown, Robin Cook, Jack Straw and Donald Dewar are missing. My defence is that the peculiar structures of the Labour Party mean that its most eminent leaders are not necessarily those who have the greatest impact on its internal life. A collection of profiles of famous parliamentarians would say nothing, for example, about the impact of prescriptive ideologies like Trotskyism on the party's fringes, or the social experience lying behind the trade union block vote. For that, it is necessary to take a brief interest in the failed political careers of people who are never seen on television. I hope I can get away with it.

I owe the usual debt of thanks to a great number of politicians, party members, researchers, journalists, activists and people in the publishing industry who have provided information, documents, hints and helpful comments. It would be courteous to list them all but I fear I might leave someone out. So – my thanks to all: you know who you are.

CHAPTER ONE

NEIL KINNOCK AND THE RULE BOOK: A GUIDE

Neil Gordon Kinnock never rid himself of his image as a man who had lost himself in a hopeless vain struggle to see his party elected. One of the most memorable portraits of him, disguised as fiction, is in the David Hare play *The Absence of War*, which Kinnock watched when it was first performed by the National Theatre in October 1993. Reputedly, it was a painful evening for him. The central character is a leader of the Labour Party, a captive in his office, ringed by advisers who prime him with platitudes and train him to avoid mistakes. It is said by another character that he has been reduced to a state in which the expression on his face in the television studio reads, 'Oh God, I hope I don't drop a bollock tonight.' As this strategy collapses, he is told to throw off caution and speak from the heart again; so in his speech to an election rally, he struggles to be spontaneous:

> My socialism is . . . it is concrete. It is real. It is to do with helping people. It is the way in which we go forward now to make this a country in which everyone is helped. That is what my socialism is. It is. It is an enabling philosophy. It is something by which something gets done. It is the means of doing something. That is what it is. And that is what it will be.[1]

Finally, he reaches for the comfort of a written text.

The real Neil Kinnock was never lost for words, least of all when he was speaking to the converted. There was a kind of Camelot feel to the arrival of a new, young party leader in 1983, ending a twenty-year era in which the party had been led by the generation who had entered parliament in the 1945 landslide. Now the seventy-year-old Michael Foot had been succeeded by a man of forty-one, with a strong-willed, attractive and politically sophisticated wife, who flaunted his happy home life, his good health and his love of attention. He was one of the old-fashioned breed of pre-televisual orators. He could mesmerize a crowded hall with fluent rhetoric. Arguably the finest speech he ever made was in the closing stages of the disastrous 1983 general election. It helped secure him the party leadership and is still a pleasure to read:

> If Margaret Thatcher wins on Thursday, she will be more a leader than a Prime Minister. That power produces arrogance, and when it is toughened by Tebbitry and flattered and fawned upon by spineless sycophants, the boot-licking tabloid Knights of Fleet Street and placemen in the Quangos, the arrogance corrupts absolutely.
>
> I warn you that you will be quiet when the curfew of fear and the gibbet of unemployment makes you obedient. You will have pain, when healing and relief depends upon payment. I warn you that you will have ignorance when talents are untended and wits are wasted, when learning is a privilege and not a right. I warn you that you will have poverty: when pensions slip and benefits are whittled away by a government that won't pay in an economy that can't pay. I warn you that you will be cold: when fuel charges are used as a tax system that the rich don't notice and the poor can't afford.
>
> I warn you that you must not expect work: when many cannot spend, more will not be able to earn. When they don't earn, they don't spend. When they don't spend, work dies. I warn you not to go into the streets alone after dark or into the streets in large crowds of protest in the light. I warn you that you will have defence of a sort: with a risk, and at a price, that passes all understanding. I warn you that you will be home-bound: when fares and transport bills kill leisure and lock you up. I warn you that you will borrow less: when credit, loans, mortgages, and easy payments are refused to people on your melting income.
>
> If Mrs Thatcher wins on Thursday, I warn you not to be ordinary. I warn you not to be young. I warn you not to fall ill. I warn you not to get old.[2]

It did not take Kinnock long to discover that such flowing rhetoric is impossible to maintain in a job which requires thinking hard and taking the utmost care before saying anything at all. In his first few weeks, Kinnock displayed a tendency to make rash promises on the spur of the moment, or grab attention without considering the consequences. On a day out at the races with the Labour MP, John Golding, he impulsively announced that the tax on on-course betting should be abolished. Protocol required that he should first have consulted his Shadow Chancellor, Roy Hattersley. On one of his first trips abroad, to Greece, he was impressed by the arguments he heard from the Minister for Culture, Melina Mercouri, who had been campaigning for the return of the Elgin marbles, a celebrated item of Georgian imperial loot taken by Lord Elgin from the Parthenon and housed in the British Museum. Kinnock pronounced that, 'The Parthenon without the marbles is like a smile with a tooth missing.' It has never been Labour Party policy, before or since, to return the marbles. For a few days, every reactionary bar-room wit in Britain was suggesting that perhaps Kinnock had lost his.

The next Kinnock trip abroad was to the USA in February 1984, where he met Ronald Reagan, the Defence Secretary, Caspar Weinberger, and the Secretary of State, George Shultz. He had an exchange with Shultz over the death squads in El Salvador and afterwards jovially told reporters that Shultz had 'got out of his pram'. The use of an unfamiliar phrase, which Kinnock defined as meaning 'a departure from normal, calm, diplomatic expression', guaranteed him front-page treatment, but he would pay for ridiculing a high-ranking member of the Reagan administration.

In these early days, Kinnock also agreed to appear on a promotional video for a nondescript record by the comedian, Tracy Ullman, to no obvious political benefit. Soon afterwards, during a photo-call with another actor, Bill Owen of *Last of the Summer Wine*, Kinnock was unable to resist throwing his arms around the man's shoulders and offering the cameras a rendering of 'Singing in the Rain'. He was a natural exhibitionist, who hated having to let go of his youth. When he met the singer, Billy Bragg, in the office in the House of Commons, there was a comical hiatus because Bragg, an intently serious man, wanted to discuss youth unemployment, whereas Kinnock could hardly wait to get his fingers on a guitar's strings. It might have helped if, like Tony Blair, he had been a singer in a rock group when he was young, because he seemed to envy actors, musicians and sportsmen for the glamour of their occupations. Had Labour won the 1987 general election, he would have been this century's youngest British Prime Minister, yet he wished he was younger.

Kinnock was also the physical type, who enjoyed competitive sports, enjoyed the company of other competitive, sporting types, called women 'love', and whose instinct was to settle arguments with his fists. Like many men of below average height, he wished he was taller. When he was introduced to a young and powerfully built party agent named Paul Harrington, during a televised visit to a primary school, Kinnock exclaimed: 'I wish I had his height!'

There were other days when Kinnock was provoked into physical confrontation: with a left-wing delegate to the fraught 1981 party conference who accosted him in the gents and accused him of treachery for failing to back Tony Benn; by a youth who hit him over the head with a rolled-up newspaper when he was having a quiet meal with Glenys Kinnock in an Indian restaurant near their Ealing home in 1986; and by a group of young men who, in 1991, taunted him while he was speaking to his teenage daughter on the pavement outside their home. These incidents were reported in loving detail by the tabloid press. A *Daily Express* editorial acknowledged that: 'his refusal to put up with such loutishness at least demonstrates that he has blood coursing through his veins', but added: 'Alas, it also reminds us that Mr Kinnock has a notoriously short fuse. Fine, no doubt, in the man next door. Not, perhaps, in the man at No. 10.'[3] After his fall, Kinnock commented: 'I thought people of this country would not object to having somebody normal as Prime Minister – and I think that's the majority sentiment, but of course it was represented in a not altogether friendly press as being evidence of frivolity and unfitness for office.'[4]

Kinnock also had a quick mind and an impressive memory, which he showed off shamelessly. For the first five years of his leadership, Kinnock used to give weekly private briefings to political correspondents, each Thursday evening while the Commons was sitting, when they could question him about any subject and he could demonstrate that his knowledge of it was encyclopaedic. Sometimes, he would test his audience by seeing how many of them could name all the leaders of all the main parties in the German parliament, or quote Henry V's pre-Agincourt soliloquy. He could. Journalists came away complaining that to question him was like starting a machine which had no 'off' button. Unfortunately, the more common effect of his exhibitionist attempts to be clever was to appear too anxious by half to prove himself. In one of his most famous flights of oratory, captured by the film director, Hugh Hudson, and used in a celebrated 1987 Party Election Broadcast, he asked rhetorically: 'Why am I the first Kinnock in a thousand generations to go to university? . . . Was it because they [i.e. all previous Kinnocks] were too thick?' What makes this passage so effective is that it was unscripted and heartfelt. He knew that the whisper going around smart London circles was that the thousandth Kinnock was a bit of a thicko. During the low point in his career, late in 1988, he was the target of an attack in the *New Statesman* by the academic R.W. Johnson, the nub of whose argument was that someone with the modest academic qualifications which Kinnock collected at Cardiff University was unfit to be Prime Minister. It was unfair and he resented it.

In contrast to Blair, Kinnock never mastered the television 'soundbite', the short, rehearsed phrase which could be fitted effortlessly into a thirty-second news item. Instead, he devised an unfortunate technique of expressing himself in meandering sentences, which dipped through subordinate clauses and parenthetical asides without ever losing their grammatical structure and which worsened when he was under pressure. He was warned time and again by Patricia Hewitt, his first press and broadcasting secretary, to shorten his answers. He took her advice to heart, but it seemed to desert him when he most needed to remember it. There were few by-elections he enjoyed more than the Fulham by-election in 1986, close to his Ealing home, where Labour was in the process of capturing a seat off the Conservatives in mid-parliament for only the third time since 1945; yet when he performed a question-and-answer session in front of a sympathetic public, Hewitt felt compelled to pass him a note pleading for shorter answers. As she hovered in the wings, he retorted with a covert V sign and carried on as before. On another occasion in Essex, according to a full-time party organizer present at the time, he had a two-hour question-and-answer session with the public, during which he answered just three questions. And here is the unedited reply he gave in 1989 when he was asked on *Channel Four News* for his view on a single European currency:

> No, I would not be signing up. I would have been making, and would be making now, a very strong case for real economic convergence, not the very limited version which the Conservatives are offering, so we understand, of convergence mainly of inflation rates, important though that is, but of convergence across a range of indicators – base rates, deficits and, of course, unemployment – together with a number of indexes of what the real performance of economies are. The reason I do that and the reason why that is an argument that must be won before there is any significant achievement of union is not only a British reason, although it is very important to us, it is a European Community reason. If we were to move towards an accomplished form of union over a very rapid timetable without this convergence taking

place, it would result in a two-speed Europe, even to a greater extent than now – fast and slow, rich and poor – and the fragmentation of the Community, which is the very opposite of what those people who most articulate the view in favour of integration and union really want. When I put that argument to my colleagues in, for instance, the Federation of Socialist parties, many of whom form governments in the EC, there is a real understanding and agreement with that point of view.[5]

To those who care to follow it word by word, this contains a sensible warning against rushing into monetary union, one which Kinnock repeated to rather greater effect six years later after he had moved to Brussels to be a European Commissioner.

There is no evidence that the general public was concerned about Kinnock's academic qualifications, but they did wonder why this man appeared not to be at ease with himself. Looking back on his political career after the 1992 election, Kinnock reflected that his reputation had been damaged by episodes like the public struggle with the Militant Tendency – 'imagine someone contending to be Prime Minister whose main preoccupation so far as the public could see, for twelve or eighteen months, had been wrestling with dissident elements in his own party' – and by his constant need to say one thing when he thought another, because what he thought was politically unacceptable to his own side. Asked by his interviewer, David Dimbleby, how he coped with that, Kinnock was counter-stereotypically crisp. He said: 'You give very long answers.'[6]

Kinnock never found that *gravitas* which came naturally to James Callaghan, John Smith and Tony Blair. Some of the perceptions the public had of him contradicted one another. He was thought to be a nice man, too nice to keep his mutinous party under control; or he was thought of as shallow, or simply not clever enough for the job; or he was suspected of being not nice at all, but a sinister dogmatist, bred in hardline, sectarian politics – 'a crypto-communist', as Margaret Thatcher called him in one of their last Commons exchanges before her downfall.[7] More commonly, it was thought that he had believed in something when he was young, but had abandoned all his beliefs in the empty pursuit of power. Eric Heffer, from the left, attacked him for being 'even more of a revisionist than Hugh Gaitskell'.[8] In practice, it hardly matters that Kinnock cannot have been all these things at once. The evidence from polling data is that after a promising start he became a drag on his own party. His mission to convince the public that he would be a good Prime Minister had failed.

The time when Neil Kinnock's hopes were highest were as 1985 turned to 1986, the 'soft left' was peeling away from the Bennites and rallying behind the leader, the party's shambolic national headquarters were at last being turned into an effective electoral organization with the arrival of the young Peter Mandelson as Director of Campaigns and Communications, the Fulham by-election was providing an opportunity to counter the idea that the entire London Labour Party was in the grip of the 'loony left', and the Tory Cabinet was torn apart by the Westland crisis. For a few months, it really seemed possible that a Kinnock government would soon be in power. Numerous factors, big and small, combined to prevent it.

There was a point in the Westland crisis when, faced with an emergency Commons debate on a Monday afternoon, Margaret Thatcher's confidence deserted her and she believed she might be forced out of office that very day. As Kinnock rose to speak, everyone was conscious that they were watching one of those rare days when performances in the Commons could make or break a Prime Minister. Instead of rising to the occasion with a short, sharp attack, Kinnock blustered for far too long and threw away an opportunity in a way that would haunt him for years. Alan Clark, watching in fear that his heroine might be destroyed, recorded that: 'every seat in the House had been booked, and they were all up the gangways. For a few seconds Kinnock had her cornered, and you could see fear in those blue eyes. But then he had an attack of wind, gave her time to recover.'[9] Mrs Thatcher's position was probably never at risk in the way that she and her devotees feared, so it might be an exaggeration to say that Kinnock had saved her premiership with one bad speech. Nonetheless, he missed a big chance and in doing so he further dented his own confidence.

Later in the year, Kinnock revisited Washington, subjecting himself to a humiliation which invited a contrast between Mrs Thatcher's undeniable status as a worldwide household name and his own relative anonymity on an international stage. He went because the non-nuclear defence policy which he had put together, as the only one on which the Labour Party could agree without another round of internecine warfare, was threatened from two sides. The more overt threat was from Tony Benn, Eric Heffer and the left, who were still pushing for a commitment to pull Britain out of NATO altogether, and to divert the money saved by the scrapping of nuclear weapons into social requirements like health and education rather than into conventional weapons. The more formidable opposition came from the right. Within the Shadow Cabinet, only Peter Shore's relations with Kinnock were so bad that his opposition to unilateral nuclear disarmament was more or less public, but it was very well-known that Roy Hattersley, Denis Healey, John Smith and others had opposed it until 1983, and privately had not changed their opinions.

After Kinnock had used the party conference in Bournemouth in 1985 to launch an attack on Liverpool Labour council, his standing was so high in the eyes of the right that he could face them down over defence policy. At a weekend session of the Shadow Cabinet at Rottingdean, Sussex, directly after the conference, Kinnock told them that the non-nuclear defence policy would stay and would be summarized in a document to be submitted for approval to the following year's party conference. The result was a document entitled *Modern Britain in a Modern World: The Power to Defend our Country*, launched formally on 10 December 1986, which declared that:

> The 'first use' of nuclear weapons in any conflict has always been central to NATO strategy . . . we believe that strategy to be unworkable . . . A strategy which would depend on the firing of nuclear weapons once the firing is breached is not tenable . . . we are seeking a policy of 'No First Use' of nuclear weapons by NATO and removal of all of them from Europe.[10]

As delegates gathered in Blackpool for the 1986 annual conference, Kinnock naturally expected to hear this policy attacked from both sides and particularly by government ministers. What he did not anticipate was that the US Defence Secretary would appear on British television to join in. Caspar Weinberger had agreed, with a show of reluctance, to appear on *Panorama* to warn that a British decision to close American nuclear bases might provoke an isolationist backlash in the USA which would lead to the closure of all bases, conventional and nuclear. News of the interview, which leaked out a few days early, and Kinnock's remarks in reaction to it, almost opened a chasm between the leader and the Shadow Foreign Secretary. Kinnock had said that the policy implied that Britain would not want the USA to use nuclear weapons on Britain's behalf, which was not party policy as Healey understood it. Pressed by *Panorama* on whether American opposition might force a change in Labour's defence policy, Healey muttered, 'I would doubt it, but it's not inconceivable'. After the two men had met privately, twice in one crowded day, Healey went on breakfast television the following morning to say it was inconceivable that Labour would allow the nuclear bases to stay, the more so because of Weinberger's interference.[11]

In the circumstances, Kinnock decided that another visit to the USA was the only way to limit the potential damage Labour might suffer through its non-nuclear defence policy. He was there for the first week of December 1986, accompanied all the way by a troupe of political journalists, some of whom worked for newspapers which, this close to a general election, wanted nothing but stories of Kinnock dropping gaffes or being snubbed by his American hosts. His first speaking engagement, hosted by the Mayor of Atlanta, was to a half-empty hall. His second, at the Kennedy School of Government, Harvard University, was attended by two former government officials, one of whom described Kinnock afterwards as 'dangerously articulate', while the other, who had worked for President Carter, confirmed that Labour's policy was a threat to the alleged special relationship between Washington and London. The tabloid coverage was part of the story of the trip, at least in the mind of one of the accompanying journalists, Colin Brown of the *Independent*, who wrote a graphic account of it. Unfortunately, one out-of-place sentence so angered Kinnock's economics adviser, John Eatwell, that he threatened to punch Brown on the nose at a Washington reception.

Despite these problems, next March Kinnock insisted, against the advice of his chief-of-staff, Charles Clarke, and Peter Mandelson, that he must make another visit, in order to meet President Reagan, only weeks before the general election. Before he left, Denis Healey attempted to persuade him to drop from Labour's programme the commitment to order the removal from Britain of all US Cruise missiles, claiming that 90 per cent of the party 'would breathe a sigh of relief'[12], but Kinnock disagreed. He was allowed just half-an-hour with the President on 27 March, whose press secretary, Marlin Fitzwater, emerged afterwards to claim – in flat contradiction to what Kinnock's staff had said – that Reagan had warned him that Labour's defence policy would threaten NATO and undermine the West's negotiating position in forthcoming disarmament talks. 'Angry Reagan slays Kinnock' was fairly typical of the resulting headlines. It was an unfortunate trip altogether, made worse by Margaret Thatcher's triumphal progress through Moscow a week later. Almost the only bright spot was that, this time, one of the accompanying journalists, the *Sunday Mirror*'s Political Editor, Alastair Campbell, was sufficiently annoyed to breach the normal solidarity of lobby reporters and accuse his colleagues of having been 'hell-bent on making sure that the US plot to stitch Kinnock didn't backfire . . . a cynical US plot, hatched with the help of a cynical, cowardly and corrupt Tory press'[13] – a gesture which helped Campbell enter the tight circle of people Kinnock genuinely trusted. That aside, the encounter only undermined Kinnock's own confidence in the policy of which he was the main architect, and which he would soon have to defend to the nation.

When he was not being made to suffer for retaining the views he had held as a young man, Kinnock was being ridiculed for abandoning them. It would be possible to fill pages with extracts of things which he said as a left-wing MP in the 1970s, which he contradicted during the next decade. One example will do. The most famous image of him from this earlier incarnation is a photograph of two Labour MPs, Dennis Skinner and Neil Kinnock, sitting alone in the House of Commons when everyone else had gone to the Lords for the formal state opening of parliament: the miner's son from Derbyshire and the miner's son from Wales who did not choose to rise from their seats in deference to the monarchy in its Jubilee year. A few months earlier, Kinnock had written a newspaper article describing his reactions as he watched the Coronation on television at a neighbour's house, at the age of eleven: 'It gave me my first really good look at television, my first unlimited dose of sweets and my first glimpse of a pineapple. And that, for me, was the Coronation. I was sick. It is a feeling that has stayed with me ever since.'[14] Two years earlier, when the Commons was discussing the amount paid to the leading royals via the civil list, the young Neil Kinnock observed: 'We are now considering paying an extra award to the richest woman in Britain, one of the richest women in the world . . . Those who presume to be senior executives in what I may call The Crown Limited are outrageously overpaid, some of them being relieved of tax and others getting too much for doing nothing.

I speak, of course, of the close relations of Her Majesty the Queen.'[15] Once he was Leader, he enjoyed warm relations with the Queen, and disapproved of any republican talk or disparaging remarks about royalty from his backbenchers.

It was said by the Liberal Democrat leader, Paddy Ashdown, that 'Neil Kinnock has travelled the road to Damascus so often I hear he has decided to buy himself a season ticket.' Having to reply over and over again to this accusation, which he knew to be well-founded, was another test for Kinnock's all-too-finite patience. Once, when he was challenged by a harmless backbench Conservative MP named Robert Adley, one of his contemporaries from the 1970 Commons intake, to specify one question on which he not changed his mind, the reply came straight back: 'Immediately the Honourable Gentleman and I entered the House, on the same day, I formed the view that he was a jerk, and I still hold that view.'[16] It would have sounded witty if only he had used a less coarse word than 'jerk'. Instead it came over as a crude shot at a small target.

Yet for all his weaknesses, Kinnock should in the fullness of time be recognized as one of the most successful political leaders in post-war Britain. For better or worse, he had more impact on the Labour Party than any other leader since the war. Where others of seemingly greater stature – Clement Attlee, Hugh Gaitskell, Harold Wilson, Jim Callaghan, Michael Foot or John Smith – looked down in bewilderment at the strange tribes who made up the Labour Party, Kinnock understood and was directly engaged with them. It was not a very dignified activity for an aspiring Prime Minister, but the effect of these grinding years of raging obstinacy was that he really did change the Labour Party into a more docile instrument, more respectful to its leader, more in touch with popular opinion, a party ready to be led by a social democrat like Tony Blair, who is to a large extent Neil Kinnock's creation. Scarcely a month went by without a new Kinnock initiative to turn the Labour Party into a more effective vote-gathering machine. Much of the history of the Kinnock years can be told by taking a historical guided tour through the Labour Party's rules and constitution.

SHADOW CABINET ELECTIONS

In Opposition, the composition of the Parliamentary Committee shall be the four Officers of the PLP (*the Leader, Deputy Leader, Chief Whip and PLP Chairman*), eighteen members of the Parliamentary Party having seats in the House of Commons, elected by the members of the Party in the House of Commons; the Leader and Chief Whip of the Labour Peers and one member of the House of Lords, all elected by Labour Peers.

At least four votes must be cast for women members if they stand.

On taking office as Prime Minister, the Leader shall appoint as members of his Cabinet those who were elected members of the Parliamentary Committee at the Dissolution and retained their seats in the new Parliament.
(Extracts from Standing Orders of the Parliamentary Labour Party, 1996 edition)

It is misleading to think of Neil Kinnock as a man who constantly changed his mind. He changed his mind on almost everything, but only once. Having moved from left to right, he never returned. In retrospect, it can be seen that the process began directly after the fall of the Callaghan government in 1979, in a disagreement with Tony Benn over who controlled appointments to the opposition front bench.

Kinnock and Benn were moving in opposite directions. After twelve years as a Cabinet minister, the older man wanted to go on to the backbenches to plan his next move. This was not a quixotic surrender of power. He had much bigger plans than being chief opposition spokesman for this or that. The Bennite phenomenon was something new to the Labour Party because these were radicals from the left who were seriously interested in wielding power and entered intra-party disputes fully intending to win if they could. The best known names associated with the Bennite phenomenon outside parliament, like Arthur Scargill, Ken Livingstone and Derek Hatton, were all in their very different ways actively interested in obtaining and using political power. There were also ex-ministers who had stayed in office until the last day of the Callaghan government, including Margaret Beckett, Les Huckfield, Michael Meacher and Benn himself.

Neil Kinnock, however, was from a gentler, Tribunite tradition, which believed in the House of Commons as a forum for resolving political conflict, and in the Labour Party as a vehicle for radical reform. Their high point had been the election of one of their number, Harold Wilson, as party leader and then Prime Minister. But when it became clear that Wilson was not going to execute an irreversible downward shift of wealth and power, the Tribunites did not organize themselves to challenge his authority. Some knuckled under, others rebelled by resigning or refusing to serve in his government. They did so individually, not as an organized group, as if their first and only concern was to preserve their own integrity. Frank Allaun, a long-standing, popular member of the NEC until his retirement in 1983, was proud of being the first person to resign from the Wilson government, just five months after Labour had returned from thirteen years in opposition. He had held the lowly position of an unpaid Parliamentary Private Secretary (PPS), but decided that 'as a backbencher you can say what you like, take up whatever issue you like, mix with unpopular trade unionists, MPs or journalists – and the Whips can't touch you. It is only if you are tempted by ambition for office that you are no longer free.'[18] Similarly, Eric Heffer was tempted to resign only days after his appointment as an industry minister, and did in fact quit after two years. 'I was told by one senior civil servant that Ministers were either turned or they left. I took the latter course.'[18]

The most distinguished exponent of this tradition was Michael Foot, who once observed, half in jest that, 'The sin against the Holy Ghost of the party machine was the "organized opposition", the attempt of two or three or more gathered together to make the conscientious scruples effective in action.'[19] Foot was sixty years old before he accepted his first job in government, but having done so, he served two party leaders with undeviating loyalty. When, finally, he himself became party leader, he naturally expected old opponents to treat him with the same courtesy, and was shocked by the behaviour of David Owen and the others who broke away under his leadership to form the rival Social Democratic Party (SDP). 'Why could we not behave as he had done in the past, was his unspoken rebuke,' David Owen recalled. 'We allowed you to govern when the Right was in control of the party, you are not letting us govern now that we, the Left, are in control.'[20]

Having been part of this tradition for his first nine years in parliament, holding no government office except for a brief period when he was unpaid Parliamentary Private Secretary to Michael Foot, Neil Kinnock was jolted by the fall of the Callaghan government into believing that it mattered whether or not Labour won general elections. While the Bennites were sharpening their weapons ready for the coming upheaval in the party, in which they intended to execute a dramatic shift of power away from the party leader's office and the parliamentary party towards the activists in constituency parties and union branches, Kinnock was already turning his mind to how the left and right could settle their differences and work together for victory.

When Benn decided not to compete for a place for the parliamentary committee, his intention was partly to free himself from the time-consuming task of 'shadowing' a Cabinet minister, but also to mount a challenge to one of the most important powers held by the party leader in opposition. This was the power to appoint the opposition frontbench. Although Labour MPs elect members of the Shadow Cabinet, that is as far as their writ runs. Exactly who gets which job has always been under the leader's decision. He can insult an elected member of the Shadow Cabinet by offering a low-ranking portfolio covering some obscure field of government policy, and on the same day appoint at the head of a key ministerial team someone who has never been elected to the Shadow Cabinet. Callaghan, Kinnock, Smith and Blair all did.

Moreover, all the other frontbench positions handed out to the junior members of the frontbench who 'shadow' junior ministers are in the gift of the leader, who can use them to promote the careers of loyal supporters, or to silence dissent. For that reason, the frontbench grew like Topsy during the opposition years. Originally, there were twelve elected and four *ex-officio* members of the Shadow Cabinet and about a dozen other frontbench spokesmen in the Commons. By the end, the Shadow Cabinet contained twenty-two MPs, plus peers, making it as large as the real Cabinet, while the opposition frontbench was bigger than the list of ministers. Though it was Kinnock who expanded the frontbench, which had grown to more than sixty by 1987, neither Smith nor Blair thought it expedient to cut it back. With a frontbench job went the obligation not to criticize the leader.

This would have been nipped in the bud if Benn had had his way in June 1979, when Labour MPs were preparing to elect the first Shadow Cabinet of the new parliament. Benn announced that he was pulling out, to put the case from the backbenches for a change in the rules so that all frontbench positions were subject to election. His stand was given vigorous support at that autumn's party conference by the delegate from Battersea North, Clare Short, who complained that 'the powers of patronage exercised by the Leader at present are an intolerable breach of the democratic traditions of the Party and are probably a large part of the explanation why there is a divide today between the PLP and Conference. We want to see every member of the Labour government and every Opposition spokesman elected, not appointed.'[21]

However, this was one constitutional question which could not be determined by the union block votes at party conference. The PLP makes its own rules, and for the left to succeed, they would first need the unwavering support of all left-wing MPs. Neil Kinnock broke ranks, put his name forward as a candidate and ran a vigorous campaign in which he did remarkably well for someone who had never held a government job, coming in fourteenth, directly behind Eric Heffer.

Jim Callaghan shrewdly seized his opportunity. He appointed Kinnock Shadow Secretary of State for Education, pulling him up from nowhere on to an equal footing with former Cabinet ministers. At the next PLP meeting, Callaghan brushed aside the left's clamour for elections to all frontbench positions, citing his own 'brilliant' decision to give so prominent a post to Neil Kinnock to prove that appointments could be safely entrusted to the wisdom and impartiality of the leader. Tony Benn complained in his diary: 'There is Neil Kinnock accepting an appointment from the Leader of the Party and totally undermining the left's position.'[22]

Three weeks later, the *Sunday Times* carried a rumour that the left caucus on the National Executive Committee was cracking apart, with the Bennites on one side, and Neil Kinnock, Judith Hart, Renee Short and Doug Hoyle on the other. The person most embarrassed by this story was Neil Kinnock, who would need to submit himself for re-election to the NEC by the overwhelmingly left-wing constituency party delegates to the annual conference, which is precisely why the story was leaked. The source was, in fact, Les Huckfield,[23] whose parliamentary hopes would be finally destroyed by Kinnock's personal intervention six years later. After the following Wednesday's NEC meeting, Benn recorded: 'Walked over to the House with Neil Kinnock, who is embarrassed by the account that had appeared in the *Sunday Times*. But the *Sunday Times* is right about Kinnock: he has departed from the left group on the Executive.'[24]

Callaghan's decision paid off when cheap school meals, free milk and subsidized school transport came under threat from the government's Education Bill. Labour MPs expected a pledge from their Shadow Education Minister that all the subsidies would be restored once Labour was back in office. Instead, Kinnock warned a PLP meeting in February 1980 that 'the economic situation we shall inherit' might make this an empty promise, a view opposed even by right-wing MPs like Jack Ashley and John Golding, quite apart from its effect on the left. The attack was joined by Kevin McNamara, a Tribunite who had shared a London flat with Kinnock when he first arrived in the Commons. Benn's caustic verdict was that 'he sounded just like a minister'.[25] In a different sense, that was also the view of David Owen, who was then a member of the Shadow Cabinet. He noted: 'I was pleased by his speech and did not enjoy seeing him attacked, though many on the left and right were . . . delighted to embarrass him.' Kinnock, he said was 'starting to speak as though he might one day be in government'.[26]

LEADERSHIP ELECTIONS

> The Leader and Deputy Leader of the party shall be elected or re-elected from amongst Commons members of the PLP . . . at a party conference.
> (Labour party Constitutional Rules, Clause VII(b)).

The first contest ever held under what is now Clause VII of the party constitution, which lays down that choosing the Leader and Deputy Leader involves the whole Labour Party and not only Labour MPs as it used to, stretched from April to October 1981, when Tony Benn challenged the incumbent Denis Healey for the deputy leadership. The left felt cheated of an opportunity to mount an effective campaign in the previous autumn's leadership election when Jim Callaghan retired and Michael Foot narrowly beat Denis Healey. That was the last contest under the old rules. The left had tried several times to alter the rules to allow the party outside parliament to participate. They failed narrowly in 1979, when the vote was so close that it hinged on the decision of one lonely trade union delegate from a factory on the Scotswood Road in Newcastle Upon Tyne, about whom more later. In 1980, the party conference agreed to widen the franchise, but failed to agree a new electoral system. A special conference in January 1981 agreed to create a complicated electoral college, within which the trade unions had 40 per cent of the total vote, while MPs and constituency Labour Parties had 30 per cent each. It was this which finally provoked David Owen to leave the Labour Party. Benn launched his challenge, which he announced to a few sleepy political correspondents at 3.00 am on 2 April 1982, because he suspected that the right wanted to stem any more defections to the SDP by abolishing the electoral college.

To understand Benn's action, it is important to recall that politicians had become used to fifteen years of 'swing door' politics, in which one of the two main parties took office, grappled unsuccessfully with Britain's chronic economic problems, lost support, and handed over to the other at the next election. Even after all the disasters of 1981, when every parliamentary by-election produced a massive swing to the new SDP/Liberal Alliance, which at one point commanded 50 per cent support in the opinion polls, important figures in the Labour Party, and not just the Bennites, persisted in believing that power would drop into their lap at the next election. As late as April 1982, when the Commons met in an emergency sitting after the Argentine occupation of the Falklands, John Silkin glibly described Michael Foot as 'My Right Hon. Friend the Leader of the Nation'. When Tory MPs protested that Foot was not the Prime Minister, Silkin confidently replied: 'He soon will be.'[27] He really believed it.

Benn and his supporters were also confident that Labour could win again. Their preoccupation was with what kind of Labour government it would be. Seizing the commanding height of the deputy leadership was in their view a necessary step towards forming an administration which would actually carry through Labour's increasingly radical programme.

Neil Kinnock was simply not on their wavelength. He had no strong objections to the old system of electing a leader. He had thrown himself energetically as Michael Foot's campaign manager into the last two contests, both of which had ended in unexpected success. Neither did he subscribe to the 'swing door' view of electoral politics. He was one of the first to take the SDP threat seriously, bringing delegates to their feet at the Welsh

Labour Party conference in June by denouncing the 'sycophantic' media coverage given to the 'traitors'. The Benn deputy leadership campaign therefore forced his incipient differences with the Bennites out into the open. On 25 April, without naming Benn, Kinnock made a widely reported speech on what would become a favourite theme: that by expecting too much too soon from a Labour government, the ultra-left were indulging in fantasy – 'a fantasy that insults the intelligence, invites derision, and guarantees disappointment'. Over the summer, he emerged as the effective leader of the 'plague on both your houses' tendency within the Tribune Group, who proposed to back the no-hope candidature of John Silkin in the first round and abstain in the second. He stuck to his position even after the general committee of Bedwellty constituency Labour Party voted fifty-three to eleven to support Benn. In a *Tribune* article he complained that 'by a tactically mistaken decision to contest the deputy leadership in 1981, Tony has significantly harmed the current standing and electoral opportunities of the Labour Party'.[28] The abstentions by Kinnock and fifteen other Tribunite MPs narrowly deprived Benn of victory. Yet at no time during a fraught year had he separated himself politically from the left. His differences with Benn were at this stage purely tactical and when, as votes were counted in the second round of the deputy leadership contest, and a rumour went around the Brighton conference that Benn had won, Kinnock told lobby journalists in the Metropole Hotel that he had nothing against the new deputy leader and would work with him. When, soon afterwards, Healey emerged victorious, Kinnock sought out the same journalists to impress upon them that the earlier conversation was not for publication.[29]

Kinnock's refusal to back Benn raised his standing inside the parliamentary Labour Party. He had slipped into the Shadow Cabinet, in twelfth place, when David Owen decided not to run in 1980. The following year, he shot up to sixth place, and Michael Foot proposed to promote him to Shadow Secretary of State for Industry. What Foot could not hand to him, though, was the trust and esteem of right-wingers who had served in the governments which the younger Kinnock had enjoyed tormenting.

The job Foot was offering was already occupied by Eric Varley, who refused to be moved to make way for him. Therefore Shadow Education Secretary was the only job Kinnock ever held in the party, apart from being this century's longest serving leader of the opposition. Varley later surmized that there was no future for him in a Kinnock-led Labour Party and quit at the end of 1983, creating the by-election in Chesterfield which brought Benn back into the Commons.

When that by-election was in progress, Kinnock had to make a show of supporting Tony Benn once more, judging that it was vital that Labour did not lose the first important parliamentary contest of his leadership. The public consequently saw Kinnock and Benn standing shoulder-to-shoulder in Chesterfield market square, and later with their arms raised triumphantly after they had spoken to a rally. They even exchanged some friendly words in private about Kinnock's recent meeting with President Reagan. But the next time their paths accidentally crossed, in the House of Commons, they passed each other without exchanging a word, and probably never greeted one another again. By contrast, on Tony Benn's bookshelf is a copy of the biography of John Smith, published while the latter was party leader, signed by the man himself with the words 'To My Old Friend and Mentor'. In private, Tony Blair will also speak courteously to antagonists on the left to whom he gives no quarter in public, but while Kinnock retained a residual personal affection for Dennis Skinner, which was not reciprocated, he had nothing but contempt for Benn, Heffer, Livingstone, Scargill and others. In one moment of great solemnity in the House of Commons, during the Gulf War, the Defence Secretary, Malcolm Rifkind, pointed out that Tony Benn, of course, opposed the West's involvement in the conflict, but said that having Benn on his side would not make him feel 'more secure in his arguments'. From the place where the Leader of Her Majesty's Opposition was sitting, the words 'join the club' were plainly audible.[30] Far from being too nice to discipline his party, Kinnock was a man who could take political differences very personally.

The rules governing Shadow Cabinet election survived Benn's return, and were substantially changed only once, in 1989, when the number of MPs directly elected to the Shadow Cabinet was increased from fifteen to eighteen, having risen from the original twelve years earlier, and there was a new stipulation that no ballot paper would be valid unless it included at last three votes cast for women MPs. Four years previously, there had been an embarrassment when the only woman on the Shadow Cabinet, Gwyneth Dunwoody, lost her place. There had never been more than one woman member, but in 1989 that number increased immediately to four, with Margaret Beckett, Ann Clywd and Joan Lestor joining Jo Richardson. It increased again to five when Beckett became Deputy Leader in 1992, with Clwyd, Harriet Harman, Marjorie Mowlam and Ann Taylor all elected.

Not everyone liked this reform. There was grumbling among back-bench MPs that bad habits which the party was supposed to have lost since the fall of the Bennite left were breaking out again. However, it played well with the public, who did not greatly care what the rules were for choosing Labour's frontbench, but reacted well to seeing so many women Shadow Ministers on television. In 1990, Labour was able to lead a deeply embarrassing protest when the new Prime Minister, John Major, chose an all-male Cabinet, a mistake he never repeated.

John Smith approved so much that in 1993, he agreed to tighten the ratchet one more notch, by raising from three to four the minimum number of women whose names had to be on the ballot paper for it to be valid. This produced a reaction of the tearoom, and a highly effective campaign of revenge against the women most publicly associated with calls for positive discrimination. Since they had to vote for four women, a large number of MPs deliberately 'dumped' their votes on women candidates with no real hope of getting on. Lestor, Mowlam and Taylor, who were all sceptical or hostile towards positive discrimination, did well, but Clwyd and Harman lost their seats. Thus a reform intended to increase the number on the Shadow Cabinet had precisely the opposite effect. Refusing to be taught a lesson, Smith defiantly retained Harman in her old post.

It was often suspected that Tony Blair might like to do away with Shadow Cabinet elections altogether, leaving him free to choose his own team. That would have required the support of a majority of the PLP, which was not to be had. It was one of the few ways in which backbench MPs could retain any hold over the leader. A survey by the *Observer* of a representative cross-section of 120 MPs found seventy-five in favour of continuing the annual Shadow Cabinet, thirty-four who believed they should be discontinued, and thirteen with mixed views.[31] Most of those in favour of abolition were modernizers with high hopes of a ministerial job in a Blair government.

By January 1996, though, there were indications that MPs were in the mood to call off that year's contest, allowing the incumbents to continue unchallenged until the general election. One Labour MP, John Reid, indicated that he intended to move this proposal formally at a PLP meeting. Peter Hain, an influential backbencher, also publicly supported it. Then, once again, Harriet Harman stepped into the story. Her abilities as a parliamentary performer had never been matched by any ability to make herself a favourite of the tearooms, and when it was learned that she was sending her younger child to a grant maintained grammar school in order to avoid having him educated by any school run by the Labour council in the area she represented as an MP, the reaction against her was so intense that the PLP clearly was in no mood to be deprived of its last Shadow Cabinet election.

Although all Shadow Cabinet members are guaranteed a seat in the first Cabinet formed by the incoming Labour Prime Minister, no one knows how long the rule applies. Taken literally, it could mean that the Prime Minister appoints the Cabinet he has to appoint in the morning, and sacks them again in the afternoon to appoint the people of his choice. This is not likely to happen in practice, but a number of people who have displayed the particular skills to be elected to an opposition committee may find that their Cabinet careers are over in a few months.

LEADERSHIP ELECTIONS 2: THE BLOCK VOTE

Voting in the election of the leader and deputy leader of the party shall take place consecutively in three sections:

. . . Section 3 shall consist of those delegates from affiliated trade unions, socialist societies, co-operative societies and other organisations present at party conference and . . . voting shall be by voting cards on the basis of one vote for each 1,000 members or part thereof on whom affiliation fees were paid for the year preceding the conference.

(Standing Order 5(3)(a) of the Standing Orders as amended by the January 1981
Rules Revision conference)

. . . Section 3 shall consist of those members of affiliated organisations who have indicated their support for the Labour Party . . . Voting shall take place under the procedures of each affiliated organisation and aggregated for a national total.

(Rule 5/3C5.3(b) of the Rules for Party Conference as amended by the 1993
Annual Labour Party Conference)

Two, and only two, post-war leaders of the Labour Party owed their position to the trade union block vote: Neil Kinnock and his successor, John Smith. When it was declared in July 1994 that Tony Blair had received 407,840 votes in the trade union section of the electoral college, that was a genuine figure because trade union members who had paid the political levy voted as individuals. The 4,822,000 trade union votes cast for John Smith in 1992, like the similar figure awarded to Neil Kinnock in 1983, existed only on paper as the sum of the block votes cast by general secretaries, after varying degrees of consultation with their members.

It has been said that the day the block vote died was on the Saturday after the 1992 general election, when it was common gossip that Kinnock was about to resign and John Edmonds, general secretary of the GMB, appeared on television and all but announced that the new leader would be John Smith. His haste caused waves of offence both among the left, who wanted time to find their own credible candidate, and within the Kinnock circle, where it was felt that their man was brutally shoved aside in favour of someone whose relations with the outgoing leader had been very strained. Kinnock's last important move, before he bowed out, was to persuade the NEC that they must immediately begin the process of removing the union block vote from any future leadership election. At the same time, he wanted to bring to a conclusion a decade-long dispute about the manner in which Labour parliamentary candidates are selected by their constituency parties, removing the union vote from that as well. For tactical reasons, Kinnock and his advisers believed it was essential that both reforms should go through the 1992 party conference. However, John Smith was not persuaded of the need for haste, while John Edmonds and other influential union leaders were not convinced of the case for the reforms at all. The NEC overruled Kinnock, reneged on its own decision and put the issue on hold for a year.

Then, much to the surprise of John Edmonds and of the Kinnock camp, Smith proved as determined as his predecessor to see the reforms through. He entered the arena blissfully unaware of how difficult it would be to prevail upon the unions to vote their prerogatives out of existence. The 1993 party conference produced a genuine cliffhanger, which almost destroyed Smith's own leadership. At the last minute, John Prescott had to be thrown into the breach to deliver a highly emotional pledge that the age-old link between the unions and the party would not be broken. By then, some intricate wheeler-dealing within the delegation from the Manufacturing Science Federation (MSF) had neutralized their vital vote and the reforms were passed by a tiny majority.

Although the 'traditionalists', Smith and Prescott, finally saw this one through, it was nonetheless Neil Kinnock's achievement every bit as much as it was theirs. He was the one who had spent years prevailing upon the unions that they would have to let go of some of their powers if the Labour Party was to be made electable. He had set the pace, and would have completed the task if circumstances had not required him to give up the job of managing the party, which he had done so well, because he had failed once again to convince the nation that he was a credible Prime Minster.

This story is full of twists and turns, because John Edmonds and the GMB were not always cast as the heavies. Originally, Edmonds was a 'modernizer' among union bosses, and the GMB – under its earlier acronym GMBATU – was a pillar of support for the leader. And when Kinnock was first elected, the union leaders who supported him certainly did not expect him to become the scourge of the block vote. They thought he was their boy. His term as leader had begun as it ended, with a barefaced act of presumptuousness by union barons. In their way, the barons had more reason to feel disappointed in him than Tony Benn did.

The Neil Kinnock leadership election campaign was launched on Sunday 12 June 1983 in a telephone call to the Press Association from Clive Jenkins, leader of the white collar union ASTMS, forerunner of the MSF, whose general council had met that morning. Jenkins announced first that Michael Foot was resigning, and then that the ASTMS was backing Kinnock, who thus collected 147,000 votes before a contest began. That same afternoon, the general council of the TGWU met, and the Kinnock vote leapt by a further 1.25 million, before it was even officially known that Michael Foot was bowing out. Endorsements followed the very next day from the *Daily Mirror* and *Daily Star*. Within a fortnight, Kinnock also had the backing of the print workers' union Sogat '82, the shopworkers' union USDAW, the railway drivers' union ASLEF, and the postal workers' union, the UCW, giving him a block vote totalling 3.8 million, close to one-third of the total electoral college.

Kinnock needed to get his campaign off to a flying start to get over the handicap of being the only contender without government experience. Previously, the general assumption had been that Foot would be succeeded by another senior former Cabinet minister, such as Healey or Peter Shore. Kinnock claimed years later that he was expecting Foot to continue at least until September 1994, and to be succeeded by Denis Healey, an outcome with which he would have been 'content'.[32] Nonetheless, once he was pro-pelled into a contest, he was ruthless in his determination to win, and displayed no embarrassment whatever about being handed block votes by union leaders. Shore was humiliated as the left vote disappeared from under his feet. Subsequently he was no less brutally isolated inside the Kinnock Shadow Cabinet, until he was voted off in 1987. Healey was per-suaded by Roy Hattersley that the right would have to field a younger candidate to have a chance of success, but it was soon obvious that the best Hattersley could hope for was to come in as Kinnock's deputy. In July, the Shadow Cabinet became alarmed at the manner in which union block votes were being handed out, and at the prospect that constituency party general committees would also commit their votes without consulting their rank and file. Consequently, a draft resolution was put before a meeting of the parliamentary Labour Party, urging unions and constituency parties to consult as widely as possible, but it was passed over without a vote being taken, provoking an ill-tempered exchange of words between Roy Hattersley and Michael Foot. Three of the four candidates for the leader-ship, Hattersley, Shore and Eric Heffer, all publicly urged the unions not to use their block votes without consulting their members. Only Neil Kinnock kept quiet,[33] as he collected the entire trade union vote, with the exception of the AUEW – one of the few unions which always balloted its members – GMBATU, and a couple of smaller unions, helping him to take 72 per cent of the overall vote, with Hattersley limping in at 19 per cent.

In the deputy leadership contest, the left's real standard-bearer was Michael Meacher. A large part of the old Bennite left accepted that Heffer was only a stand-in for Tony Benn, who was disqualified because he was temporarily without a seat in the Commons, and therefore hoped to secure a Kinnock–Meacher victory. Meacher, too, called for union and con-stituency parties to consult as widely as possible, but it did him no real good, because Kinnock had made no secret that he would prefer Hattersley to win, which he did comfortably.

A number of factors combined to swing the trade union movement so heavily behind Neil Kinnock. One was the urge for unity, which favoured the candidate who was neither Bennite nor of the old right. Another was the attraction of a young candidate untainted by the failures of the Wilson and Callaghan governments. He also had a working-class background which, in that particular phase of Labour Party history, was an immense advantage. At other times, of course, it has not mattered at all, in a party which has produced leaders like Clement Attlee, Hugh Gaitskell, Michael Foot, John Smith and Tony Blair. In the early 1980s, though, anti-intellectual prejudice had spread across the right and centre of the parties. Partly, it was directed personally at Tony Benn, but his apostasy was not the only cause. The right felt let down by middle-class intellectuals.

Like the left, the old Labour Party right was by no means a monolith. Essentially, it was made up of two broad strands, the larger of which was the right-wing trade unions and their political representatives. The most distinguished of the hundreds of Labour councillors and MPs who had risen through the unions was the former Assistant Secretary of the Inland Revenue Staff Federation, Jim Callaghan, whom the journalist Peter Jenkins nicknamed the 'keeper of the cloth cap'.[34] The trade union right also regarded Denis Healey as one of their own, partly because of his service as a party official in Transport House.

The other distinct group was made up of university educated intellectuals, who derived their politics from what they had read, most commonly from the works of R.H. Tawney and Anthony Crosland, rather than from the proverbial school of hard knocks. In the early 1960s, they were known as 'revisionists', in honour of Eduard Bernstein who reinterpreted the works of Karl Marx to remove their revolutionary content. Later, they became known as 'social democrats'. While the 1979 defeat hit the whole Labour Party, some parts were hurt more than others: the right was worse hit than the left, the social democrats worst of all. The latter had been weakened by personal rivalry between Crosland and Roy Jenkins, who had once been as close as Gordon Brown and Tony Blair were, prior to 1994, and discredited by the continuous half-hearted intrigues against Harold Wilson in which the Jenkins circle indulged. A large group, including Jenkins, Shirley Williams, Roy Hattersley, David Owen and John Smith, had gone seriously out on a limb in 1972 by defying a three-line whip to vote in favour of

Britain's entry into the Common Market. During the 1975 referendum campaign, Jenkins and Williams had further offended party discipline by threatening to resign if the result went against Britain's continued membership. Jenkins left parliament to become President of the European Commission in 1977, taking with him David Marquand, one of the brighter young social democrats. They were also hit by the deaths of Crosland himself and the highly respected Scot, John Macintosh, in 1977–78.

Worse than all of that was the collapse of Keynesian economics. Writing in the 1950s, Crosland had expounded an optimistic view of capitalism as a stable system, capable of producing a sustained, uninterrupted and almost painless growth in output and living standards, within which there was no risk of a 'wholesale counter-revolution' by the right. One of his more notorious comments was that 'I no longer regard questions of growth and efficiency as being, on a long view, of primary importance to socialism.'[35] By 'socialism', he meant 'a distribution of rewards, status, and privileges egalitarian enough to minimise social resentment',[36] rather than the classic definition of common ownership.

However, as early as 1967, three of the younger stars in the social democratic constellation, David Owen, John Macintosh and David Marquand had admitted that: 'Too often in the past we have been tempted to believe that economic growth would provide an automatic solution to the moral dilemma of a socialist party in an affluent society, that growth would give us equality without a fight, justice without tears. We now know that this was self-deception.'[37] By the time a Labour Chancellor, Denis Healey, had been compelled under the conditions of an International Monetary Fund loan in 1976 to cut public expenditure and introduce wage restraint, it was painfully obvious that there would be tears without justice. David Marquand confessed that 'the right didn't have . . . anything to say of a doctrinal nature in the 1970s . . . Actually they really didn't fight the battle for ideas.'[38] Many years later, the authors Peter Mandelson and Roger Liddle, the latter a co-founder of the SDP, repeated the same point:

> the mainstream leadership of the party failed to fight back. Its members had no coherent ideas to advance in opposition to the Bennite reforms, preferring instead to put their faith and their positions in the hands of those wielding the trade union block votes.[39]

In the circumstances, it is not surprising that the union bosses and working-class MPs who had risen through the union ranks started to look upon their social democrat brothers as a waste of space. Even in 1979, David Marquand felt moved to complain about what he called 'the cult of the tea-room', which held that:

> the Labour Party is or at any rate ought to be, not merely a predominantly but an exclusively working-class party: that the working class can be properly represented only by people of working-class origin who alone understand its aspirations and have its interests at heart: that middle-class recruits to the party, so far from being assets, are liabilities.[40]

Marquand, who was inspired by Tony Blair's speech on the fiftieth anniversary of VE Day to make a well-publicised return to the Labour Party, was himself on the receiving end of this anti-intellectual prejudice. One of the favourite stories of the day, which was probably untrue, concerned Jenkins' inability to pronounce the letter 'r'. It was said that after his appointment to the European presidency, Jenkins made a speech in which he declared: 'I leave without wegwet or wancour . . .' whereupon a voice from the audience cried: 'What about David Marquand?'

During the 1983 leadership contest, Neil Kinnock was ruthless in his dismissal of the SDP and the entire revisionist right, claiming that:

> Until quite recently, the main attack on democratic Socialism has come from a social democracy, once inside the party, but now outside . . . The essence of the social democrat philosophy is that the present economic system is capable of overcoming its own contradictions. This was at least plausible when it was first argued by Anthony Crosland in the 1950s . . . but the whole theoretical edifice has now collapsed.[41]

Kinnock's assertion that social democracy was 'once inside the Labour Party but now outside' was deliberately disingenuous. To quote some examples, John Smith had been part of the 1972 rebellion over the Common Market, and had considered himself a disciple of Crosland's; Giles Radice, who succeeded Kinnock as education spokesman in 1983, had been co-author with David Marquand, John Horam and others of a document entitled *What We Must Do* which was, in effect, a social democratic mini-manifesto. As recently as September 1980, a letter to *The Times* urging a series of internal party reforms had been co-signed by a clutch of future

SDP leaders and by George Robertson, a Labour frontbench spokesman on foreign affairs from 1981 until his election to the Shadow Cabinet in the 1990s. The difference between Smith, Radice and Robertson on the one hand, and the Gang of Four on the other, had come down to a single, tactical question: whether to stay in the Labour Party, or leave.

But the most important social democrat still in the party was Roy Hattersley, who had made his reputation as Roy Jenkins' political fixer, but who had gone through a painful and acrimonious parting of the ways with the formation of the SDP. Hattersley expected the right-wing vote to come to him, as the natural next in line to Callaghan and Healey. He had a rude shock when he discovered that part of the right did not see him as an ally but as another intellectual – and they had had their fill of intellectuals. They preferred the party to be led by the son of a Welsh miner, even if he had been a left firebrand until very recently.

One exponent of this kind of proletarian snobbery on the Labour right was John Golding, who was then one of the most powerful figures in the Labour Party. The link between the party and the unions was Golding's field of expertise. As political officer of the Post Office Engineering Union, he was the man who brokered the deal by which the block vote was used to break the left's control of the NEC in 1982. Once they had a majority of one, the right used it without compunction to oust the chairman of each important NEC committee. Golding himself took over from Tony Benn as chairman of Home Affairs but then, curiously, did not use his newly-won position to alter the long general election manifesto put together under Benn's supervision. On the contrary, he insisted on nodding it through unaltered and without further debate. Roy Hattersley claimed that Golding did this because he was sure that the impending election was lost, and wanted to ensure that Benn would be thoroughly incriminated.[42]

In 1981, Golding had been unstinting in delivering the union block vote for Denis Healey, whom he held in unqualified admiration. In 1983, it was assumed he would do the same for Roy Hattersley, not least by Hattersley, who invited Golding to his house, along with John Smith and others, to be part of his inner campaign team. It was an enduring shock to Hattersley when Golding subsequently declared that he was backing Neil Kinnock. A sign of how his relations with Golding deteriorated is that during his eight years as deputy leader, Hattersley made a practice of turning out to every parliamentary by-election to give the opening press conference, except one which he avoided altogether, in Golding's former seat of Newcastle Under Lyme, where the candidate was his wife, Llin Golding. Golding's opinion was that the younger MPs around Kinnock, like Frank Dobson and John Prescott, were more of an asset to the party than former government ministers, despite having voted for Benn in 1981, because they spoke with working-class accents.

However, Neil Kinnock turned into a severe disappointment for anyone who thought he would be the new 'keeper of the cloth cap'. Despite his working-class background, he completely lacked the inverse proletarian snobbery of which David Marquand had complained. On the contrary, he had the social aspirations of an upwardly mobile left-wing intellectual. His real home was in Ealing, in west London, rather than Tredegar. Though he enjoyed mixing with working-class voters, that did not necessarily stretch to their trade union representatives. John Golding, attached to Kinnock's private office in recognition of his role in the leadership election, soon felt out of place and quit parliament in 1986 to become General Secretary of the National Communications Union, successor to the POEU. Always a clever tactician, he was a poor strategist who overplayed the role of a big time union fixer, and was eventually driven out of office by his own union executive.

Subsequently, the only trade union leader who really won Kinnock's trust and was included in the inner circle of confidants was the Deputy General Secretary of the public sector union NUPE, Tom Sawyer. Having used the block vote to reach the top, Kinnock did not generally want to be surrounded by trade union vote-fixers, preferring the company of smart, youngish, disciplined university graduates. There has always been a network of mostly London-based professionals whose influence within the Labour Party far exceeds its numbers, made up of people whose political activity began in student clubs, and who gravitated into jobs as researchers or something similar, never far from the centre of power. In the 1970s, such people were visibly deserting the mainstream of the Labour Party, either for the SDP, or for the Bennite left. Ken Livingstone's GLC especially was a source of inspiration and of gainful employment for intellectuals who, a generation earlier, would have been inspired by Harold Wilson's promise of technological revolution. After 1983, there was a discernible movement among the London professionals to rally around Neil Kinnock. The progress of the Labour Co-ordinating Committee from being a Bennite ginger group when launched in 1978 by Michael Meacher and Frances Morrell, to being a vehicle for the 1990s 'modernizers' is symbolic.

The key figures in Kinnock's private office had had their political training in the National Union of Students. The most important by far was Charles Clarke, a former NUS President who joined Kinnock as a researcher in 1979 and served him right through to 1992. The son of a top-ranking civil servant, he was like the Fat Man played by Sidney Greenstreet in the *Maltese Falcon*: overweight, economic in his movements, with a pleasant way of speaking and a knack of being forever at the centre of events, calm and in control. Because he gave no interviews and deliberately discouraged press interest in himself, his importance within the machinery of the Labour Party was not widely known. But in real terms, once Kinnock was firmly established as a strong leader, Clarke was a more powerful figure than anyone but a few senior members of the Shadow Cabinet, and outranked any other paid party functionary, including Peter Mandelson or Larry Whitty, because he controlled the door to the leader's office. But his closeness to the leader was the sole source of his political authority. Once Kinnock fell, Clarke disappeared as if he had never existed. A few months into John Smith's leadership, he appeared with a visitor's pass at the 1992 annual party conference, with no role to play except to tell old contacts that he was starting up in business as a lobbyist. When he tried to visit the area reserved for journalists, he was barred from entering by a steward who did not know who he was. Later, when he was shortlisted as a possible candidate in a safe Labour seat, the view of the NEC's interviewing panel was that he was by far the most impressive contender, but the constituency party barely knew who he was. They chose a local councillor instead.

Among Clarke's other functions, he was the chief fixer who would count the votes whenever a divisive issue was due to come up before the national executive or the annual conference, and do what was necessary to ensure that Kinnock won. For four years he was assisted by Neil Stewart, another former student politician whose most direct contact with the trade union movement had been a period as an official of the Royal College of Nursing, which did not endear him to leaders of other health unions. It was part of the routine of being a mainstream member of the NEC to receive a telephone call from either Clarke or Stewart to say how Kinnock wanted his troops to vote on particular issues. They talked like people who expected to be obeyed.

John Reid, Kinnock's researcher in 1983–85, before being selected for a safe Labour seat in Scotland, was another former NUS leader. John Eatwell, now Lord Eatwell, Kinnock's economics adviser in 1986–92, was an academic who had been a student at Cambridge University contemporaneously with Clarke and Patricia Hewitt, the best-known member of Kinnock's personal staff. As one of a group of feminists associated with the National Council for Civil Liberties, who included Harriet Harman, Hewitt arrived with a reputation for being pushy. Within days of her appointment the *Sunday Times* berated her for being 'Medusa-like'.[43] She was nonetheless a major political operator and one of what later became known as the 'modernizers'. Julie Hall, the former ITN Political Correspondent who replaced Hewitt in 1989, was a political innocent by comparison.

The type of people with whom they chose to surround themselves undoubtedly reveals something about the character of party leaders. When John Smith succeeded Neil Kinnock, everyone who had worked in Kinnock's office moved out, with one exception. One reason why John Smith is now thought of as more 'Old Labour' than Kinnock or Blair is that he preferred to employ people with long track-records as political functionaries, like the former General Secretary of the Scottish Labour Party, Murray Elder, and Roy Hattersley's former aide, David Hill. The only person carried over from the Kinnock regime was Hilary Coffman, David Hill's partner, who had worked for Michael Foot.

Two years later, the leader's office was gutted a second time, and the party functionaries were replaced by professionals who had proved themselves outside politics, like Alastair Campbell, who entered into full-time politics from *Today* newspaper, and Blair's chief of staff, Jonathan Powell, the younger brother of Margaret Thatcher's devoted foreign affairs adviser, Sir Charles Powell, who came in from the British embassy in Washington. The only person who held a position of any seniority to survive was, once again, Hilary Coffman, and even she was at home thinking that she had lost her job when a call came to tell her that Campbell had insisted on re-hiring her. It was one of the many signs that there is a direct line of continuity between Neil Kinnock and Tony Blair, which was interrupted by the Smith interregnum.

THE BLOCK VOTE IN CONSTITUENCY PARTIES

The General Committee . . . shall carry out the procedure for the selection or re-selection of the party candidate . . . If this party is represented in Parliament by a member of the Parliamentary Labour Party, the MP shall be eligible for nomination for selection.

(Rules for Constituency Labour Parties (as amended by the 1979 party conference) Clause X)

all individual members registered on the national membership system with 12 months continuous membership within the territorial area of the constituency . . . shall be eligible to participate in the selection process. 4B9(b) If a sitting Labour MP with a substantial territorial interest in the constituency is nominated by two-thirds of party organisations and two-thirds of all organisations from which nominations are received, s/he shall be deemed selected without a ballot.

(Labour Party Rule Book (as approved by the 1995 annual party conference), Procedural guidelines 4B3(a) & (b) for parliamentary selections)

From the very beginning, Neil Kinnock found himself almost under siege from a politicized group of workers who believed their jobs were under threat. Later, he also had grief from the miners, but the first special interest group to camp outside his door demanding attention was the parliamentary Labour Party. The corridors of Westminster were alive with reports of eminent Labour MPs whose careers were under threat in their constituency parties, because the left was in control of their general committees, and intended to use the power available under the rules to change their MP.

Mandatory reselection, introduced in 1979, had ended the careers of at least eight sitting Labour MPs including a former Defence secretary, Fred Mulley, in the run-up to 1983. With the exception of John Sever, deselected in Birmingham Ladywood, they were all aged over fifty and had been in the Commons for more than a decade. There were perhaps half-a-dozen others who escaped deselection only by switching to the SDP. As 219

Labour MPs limped back, shell-shocked, from the 1983 general election, it appeared that the casualty rate from deselection might be even higher than in the previous round, with no less than four members of the Shadow Cabinet – Michael Cocks, Gerald Kaufman, Peter Shore and Jon Silkin – on the long list of MPs under threat. Silkin may have exaggerated slightly when he wrote that 'the common topic of conversation among those who had been in parliament for less than two weeks was their prospect of rese-lection',[44] but there is no doubt that Labour MPs were obsessively worried about it and were putting pressure on Kinnock to come to their rescue.

In London, a group called Target 87, backed by Ken Livingstone, the Islington MP Jeremy Corbyn, and the ex-MP Reg Race had a list of sixteen MPs marked down for deselection. The new MP for St Helens South, Gerry Bermingham, a signed-up member of the Campaign Group who voted for Heffer and Meacher in the leadership election, achieved the unwelcome record of being deselected only six months after his arrival, in that his constituency party general committee passed a resolution calling on him to resign with immediate effect, because of reports in newspapers and on television about his messy personal life, compounded, possibly, by regrets within the local party that they had chosen a Sheffield barrister rather than a local man. It appeared to his shocked colleagues that Labour MPs were now to be subject to instant dismissal. In April, an editorial in *Labour Forward*, which was edited by David Warburton, a senior official of GMBATU, trailed the possibility that the right might draw up its own tar-get list of MPs to be deselected. In June, Frank Field openly threatened that if his local party in Birkenhead deselected him, he would resign and fight a by-election. In those circumstances, it is very likely that he would have beaten the official Labour candidate. Party whips were also finding it dif-ficult to maintain discipline, partly because their Chief Whip, Michael Cocks, was obsessed with his own difficulties in Bristol, and partly because MPs considered it more important to be in their constituencies attending party meetings than in the Commons.

Some of the older MPs longed for a return to the Labour Party as they remembered it before it was disrupted by the militancy of the 1970s: respectful, parochial and in genteel decline. The normal constituency Labour Party, particularly in its inner-city heartlands, had a small mem-bership which was basically only interested in council affairs like house repairs, street lighting, vandalism, etc. Its ward meetings were dominated by councillors, with the women's sections waiting silently at the back to pour the tea. The local MP was not required to do much at all, except show his face on social occasions and perhaps deliver periodic reports about the party's success in the Commons and the iniquities of the Conservatives. Involvement by the MP in constituency affairs was actively discouraged, because it only interfered with the prerogatives of the local bosses. John Smith's brief leadership of the Labour Party was dogged by allegations of nepotism in Monklands Council, in the part of Scotland which he represented in parliament for twenty-four years. The Conservatives hoped to find evidence that Smith was himself in some way involved, but there was none. He had adhered to the tradition that councillors ran the council while the MP immersed himself in Westminster. To this end, many constituencies made a fixed practice of selecting their MPs from outside the region. When Tony Benn was selected for his Bristol seat in 1950, he was asked whether he would be moving into the city. He believed that it counted in his favour when he said no, having just bought a house in Holland Park.

Hand-in-hand with this parochialism went a lively mistrust of outsiders. There are stories told in several parts of the country of people trying to join their local branch but being denied admission on the grounds that it was 'full'. Full might mean 'moribund'. The membership of Brighton Kemptown Labour Party halved in 1965–69; that of Brixton fell from 1212 to 292 in 1965–70. Bermondsey Labour Party, which had had 3,000 members before the war, was down to below 400 when Peter Tatchell joined in 1978. In the old St Anthony's ward in central Newcastle there were twenty-four party members in 1983: twenty-three were pensioners, the other was a Young Socialist. A stalwart of the old right might think this was not a problem, since the voters voted Labour regardless, until it was suddenly brought home to them that they were vulnerable to the 'bedsit left': socially mobile young radicals who needed to concentrate in only very small numbers to take control of a ward or constituency party. It was not only MPs who were threatened by this phenomenon. A Labour councillor might discover that his reselection meeting – the simple, stressfree routine which he had undergone every three or four years during his decades of public service – was suddenly a nightmarish battle for survival against a polytechnic lecturer in jeans, sporting a CND badge, and backed by a dozen young people all sharing two or three addresses somewhere in the ward. But at least the arithmetic of his reselection was straightforward: he only needed to call in a sufficient number of favours, and perhaps pay the party subscriptions for a few old friends from the working-men's club, to get by. For an MP, reselection was an intricate ordeal, in which it was possible that he could have solid support from an outright majority of his party members and yet be doomed by the complexity of the Labour Party's federal democracy.

Why that should be so becomes obvious if we take an example – an extreme example, admittedly – thrown up three years into Neil Kinnock's leadership, in Knowsley North, near Liverpool, which became the first constituency party to have its right to select its MP taken away altogether. This was a quick military-style strike for which Kinnock bore the whole responsibility. No one other than close advisers like Charles Clarke was involved. The new MP, George Howarth, was selected on a show of hands in the boardroom at Walworth Road, by members of the NEC who had never met him, had never heard of him until that day, but who accepted him on the recommendation of the party leader, who had never met him either. The case is worth looking at in detail, because on the face of it there is no stronger piece of evidence that Kinnock was prepared to override the rights of local party members to purge the party of the influence of the far left.

Part of the grievance born by leaders of Knowsley North party was that they had never been allowed to choose their parliamentary candidate. The seat had been created in the 1983 boundary revision, and in the pre-election rush, the sitting MP for the now abolished seat of Ormskirk, Robert Kilroy-Silk, was imposed without a contest. Kilroy-Silk was not temperamentally suited to represent such an area, most of which was made up of spillover council estates in Kirkby and Cantril Farm, where unemployment and attendant social problems were almost as bad as the worst parts of Liverpool. Such prosperity as existed in the constituency was to be found in the rural areas, which included some attractive villages, but not quite good enough for Kilroy-Silk, who maintained his family home in Buckinghamshire and visited the seat only when constituency duties called him. He had never been able to live down the boast he made in front of television cameras just after his election in 1974, that he expected to be

Prime Minister in fifteen years. Twelve of those years had slipped by, and he was no more than a middle-ranking Opposition spokesman with a serious problem in his local party.

When he resigned from parliament, Kilroy-Silk wrote a book which was serialized in *The Times*, claiming that he had been forced to abandon a political career by conspirators from the Militant Tendency and by the supine refusal by other Labour MPs to take action. His claim was taken seriously, because there certainly was something wrong with his constituency party, but, as a matter of fact, Militant did not have an organized presence there and Kilroy-Silk's resignation was not entirely political. The original proof copy of his book ended with an upbeat promise to carry on: 'we can't afford to walk away from the fight, I can't . . . I won't'; but by the time the 'diary' had reached the bookshops, this passage had changed to 'I am resigned to oblivion and the adjustment to a new life. It can't be any worse.' He then moved into a lucrative job in television.

Having had a by-election forced on them by Kilroy-Silk's resignation, the party then had the problem of choosing a new candidate. There was no real doubt about who it would be, if the selection went ahead under party rules. Les Huckfield, the MEP for that part of Merseyside, had been a right-wing junior minister in the Callaghan government before reinventing himself as a hard-line Bennite. His personal relations with Neil Kinnock were singularly bad, from when they had served together on the NEC. As a by-election candidate, Huckfield was highly vulnerable, not least because he was the minister who had allowed Kirkby's motorcycle works to close, leaving only acres of rubble and increased unemployment, after one of his predecessors, Bob Cryer, had resigned from the government rather than sign its death warrant. He had also promised the Merseyside East European constituency party, when they adopted him as their candidate for the 1984 European elections, that he would not attempt to secure a Commons seat before his term ended in 1989. Nor did he have the confidence of most members of the Knowsley North Labour party, in so far as their opinions could be accurately gauged, but he had support where it counted, and in Knowsley North the party rules worked in a way which made sure that there was no chance that the will of the majority would prevail.

The constituency was sharply divided between wards in the run-down inner-city areas of Kirkby and Cantril Farm, which had tiny memberships and were dominated by people who had basically given up hope that the social problems these areas faced would be seriously improved by the moderate reforms which could be expected from the next Labour government, whenever that might be. There were seven of these inner-city wards, with a combined membership of just 220, all of which were backing Les Huckfield. Because every ward, however small, was entitled to three general committee delegates, that meant twenty-one votes for Huckfield. In the rural part of the constituency, there were three wards with a total party membership of 380. They eventually decided to back George Howarth. Because wards with more than 50–100 members were entitled to one extra delegate, those with 100–150 members to two extra and so on, these three wards had a combined total of fifteen. Therefore, despite representing more than 60 per cent of the members, the constituency delegates who were backing Howarth were already outnumbered by the left.

That was not all. The total voting strength on the general committee was 117, only thirty-six of whom represented local party wards. The other eighty-one were nominees of trade unions and other affiliated bodies. In theory, where there were two delegates from the same branch of a trade union, they represented a minimum of 101 levy-paying union members; where there were five, that implied a minimum of 401 members. Thus, thousands of unionized workers were represented on Knowsley North GC, but given the level of unemployment and dereliction in the area, this was not possible. Delegates came from skeleton union branches formed in workplaces which had been run down or closed down. Regional organizers, for instance, spotted that Kirkby's tobacco workers were being represented by Dave Kerr, who worked as a gardener for Liverpool Council. After his union had been persuaded to take him off the committee, he resurfaced as the representative of Kirkby Trades Council. The TGWU alone, whose regional office was heavily backing Huckfield, sent twenty-three delegates. Five came from TGWU Branch 6/522, which mysteriously had another nineteen delegates on the general committees of eight other constituencies on Merseyside, implying that the branch had at the very least 1,509 levy-paying members. Its actual membership on Merseyside was 638. Similarly, TGWU branch 6/612 had an implied membership of not less than 1,408, including at least 201 in Knowsley North, when its total membership in the region was just 263. The Militant-dominated GMBATU Branch 5 had three delegates in Knowsley North, one in Knowsley South, and twenty-four in the Liverpool constituencies, implying a levy-paying membership of at least 2,008, when the actual membership of the branch was 1,195.[45]

It was not only the left which exploited the rules in ways which were none too democratic. The EETPU had seventeen delegates on the general committee, some of whose acquaintance with the electrical trade probably extended no further than switching on a light. The manner in which George Howarth emerged as the leader's favoured candidate reflected no great credit on the party's internal workings either. Having collected soundings from regional organizers and Walworth Road staff, Charles Clarke arrived at the conclusion that no current member of the Knowsley party was sufficiently reliable, and the choice would have to be either Howarth, a former councillor who had left the area a few years earlier to become head of the Welsh TUC's Co-operatives Centre, or his father-in-law, George Rodgers, who had been MP in the 1970s for the old Chorley constituency, which overlapped with Knowsley North. Both were AUEW members, and there was no question of their competing against one another. Consequently, the only important vote taken in the constituency was when the AUEW met to decide which of the two to nominate. Abuses like these were bound to happen here and there, for as long as union delegates to general committees wielded what amounted to a block vote in the selection of parliamentary candidates. The practice was ended by John Smith in 1993.

As Kilroy-Silk was shocked to discover, MPs who allowed their constituency parties to go to rot did not necessarily get the sympathy they thought they deserved from Neil Kinnock. The right wanted to go back to a situation in which Labour MPs answered to the whips, and to the voters once a parliament, but not to their constituency party; but instead of closing the problem down, Kinnock's tactic was to open it up by having sitting MPs either endorsed or removed by a plebiscite of all party members in the constituency – the idea which David Owen had canvassed before his departure to the SDP.

Kinnock launched into this move in July 1984, apparently thinking that all he had to do was to overcome the objections of the left, who would accuse him of trampling on the rights of constituency activists. He hoped he could meet this objection through a compromise devised by his ally, John Evans, under which the one-member, one-vote system became an option open to constituency general committees if they chose to use it, rather than a universal system imposed by the centre. This compromise had almost no effect in winning the left over to what they suspected was no more than a manoeuvre to salvage the careers of right-wing MPs. It was alleged that, in reality, any contested selection contest would have to take on a one-vote, one-member system, because any general committee which exercised its right to deselect an MP without a plebiscite would be pilloried in right-wing newspapers. Kinnock's former allies in the Tribune Group sent a delegation including the veteran Ian Mikardo and the newly elected Chris Smith to talk him out of the proposal. Even Robin Cook, manager of the Kinnock leadership campaign and now the Shadow Cabinet campaigns coordinator, opposed him. The Sheffield MP, Martin Flannery, became the first to attack the new leader publicly by name, accusing him of 'lending himself to a right wing maneouvre'.

Suspicions about interference by the mass media were stoked up by the return to politics of a heavy figure from the half-forgotten past: Robert Maxwell, a former Labour MP, who was making a reappearance as the new proprietor of the *Daily Mirror*. The nation's only Labour supporting tabloid waded into the argument by publishing a front page cartoon of a demented-looking bearded party activist wielding a document on which was written the slogan 'Forward with the Lunatic Left', conveying the impression that heathens such as this were rampaging through the Labour Party.[46] This was the start of a relationship which would dog Kinnock for seven years. Maxwell was too big, wealthy and powerful to be ignored, however embarrassing his habit of walking up to the Labour leader in the presence of photographers and throwing a proprietorial arm around his shoulders, and then expecting his clumsy opinions on party matters to be treated with respect.

However, as in so many family quarrels within the Labour Party, what really mattered was not the opinions of press barons or party activists, but of the trade unions. They were not prepared to surrender the rights of constituency general committees to choose MPs. Their reason is easy to see from the Knowsley North case, where two-thirds of the votes were held by trade unions, and almost one-fifth by the TGWU alone. Frequently, union delegates were paid by their regional office to turn out to general committee meetings. When something as important as the choosing of a Labour

MP was at stake, they had to vote as they were told. In this way, regional secretaries of the big unions were able to secure seats for candidates they deemed to be suitable. This practice was so common that it was barely remarked upon unless the union boss in question was either left wing, like Arthur Scargill, or corrupt, like Andy Cunningham. Now an age-old union prerogative was being threatened by a young leader only a few months into the job. At the party conference in Brighton, in October 1984, Neil Kinnock was given a sharp lesson in who was really in charge, when the Evans proposal was voted down in the full glare of live television coverage. To complete his humiliation, that year's party chairman, Eric Heffer, called the delegate from Evans' own constituency in St Helens North to oppose the scheme, while the General Secretary, Jim Mortimer, publicly called for it to be defeated and, after it was, ruled that the matter could not be raised again for at least two years.

Afterwards, Kinnock tried to make the best of a bad result by claiming 'we won the argument, but lost the vote'. Peter Hain, of the Labour Co-ordinating Committee, did not quite put it in the same way when he said that 'the leadership handled this issue incompetently and alienating a lot of potential support for the principle of widening the franchise' – but he too was implying that the issue was not dead. Kinnock had in fact made a number of tactical errors. He had appeared to believe that his personal popularity could prevail over entrenched interest, but would find that popularity was a diminishing and unreliable asset. He had opened a campaign on two fronts: against the left in the constituency parties and the union block vote. Above all, he had failed to count where the votes were. That last mistake was not repeated. Thereafter, on every important vote, not just at the annual conference but at monthly NEC meetings, Charles Clarke had to do the rounds working out exactly who was on side and who was not, so that even when Kinnock was defeated, he was at least forewarned.

In the event, mandatory reselection did not prove as bad as had been feared. The big names – Kaufman, Shore and Silkin – all survived. There were, however, six casualties, of whom the most important was Michael Cocks. The others were a trio of London MPs, two of whom were on the left, who were replaced by Diane Abbot, Bernie Grant and Ken Livingstone, all further to the left, and two right-wing MPs from mining seats who paid the penalty for not backing the NUM fully during the

1984–85 strike, though their replacements, Ian McCartney and Joan Walley, gravitated to the soft left rather than the Campaign Group.

Cocks himself had been the beneficiary of some sharp practice by the right in the previous selection round, which ensured that he won the only safe seat in Bristol against Tony Benn, who was temporarily forced out of the Commons. In January 1986, his turn came when the general committee of Bristol South CLP voted seventy-one to fifty-six to select Dawn Primarolo. Years afterwards, Cocks' anger was undiminished despite his elevation to the peerage as Lord Cocks of Hartcliffe. 'To my knowledge,' he wrote, 'there were 22 delegates present who had associations with Militant. Had this motley crowd not been allowed to take part in the voting, I would have won and most likely would still be the sitting MP.'[47] There is no evidence of Militant infiltration on anything like this scale. Nonetheless, in the Labour Party which Kinnock bequeathed to his successors, it would be virtually unthinkable that someone as senior as Cocks could have been deselected at all.

Kinnock revisited the problem of how MPs are selected at the party conference immediately after the 1987 general election. This time, he decided not to challenge the prerogatives of the trade unions, and settled for a complicated system which satisfied no one, under which party members used a one-member, one-vote system to select a candidate, but theirs was not the final decision. The vote then went to an electoral college in which trade union and other affiliated organizations controlled up to 40 per cent of the vote.

The advantage of this system was that it enfranchised everyone, eliminating the unfair advantage formerly enjoyed by wards where party membership was tiny. Its obvious downside was that a candidate could have majority support in the constituency and yet lose the selection contest for lack of trade union backing. This happened in at least five constituencies, in three of which the NEC stepped in to force a second selection conference. Two Labour MPs were elected in 1992 without majority backing from their constituency parties: George Galloway in Glasgow and Roger Godsiff in Birmingham. The Scottish unions also rescued the far-left MP, Ron Brown, from being rejected by Edinburgh Leith constituency party the first time round, but he then self-destructed by smashing up his former mistress' flat and holding a televised champagne celebration when his trial ended. Two other MPs came back in 1992, after being rescued by the NEC from the threat of deselection. In each case, the threat came principally from the unions. They were Gerry Bermingham, again, and Frank Field, the respected chairman of the all-party Commons Social Services committee, still battling for survival against a TGWU full official based in Birkenhead. In Scotland and Merseyside, the union vote was deployed behind left-wing candidates; in Birmingham, it was used by the hard right.

Had he been leader of the Labour Party for another three months, Kinnock would have returned to the problem yet again, to make a final attempt to remove direct trade union involvement in the selection of MPs, but his resignation in 1992 handed the problem on to John Smith. Although it was John Smith who saw it to a conclusion, the conditions for this victory were set up by Neil Kinnock. Even as he moved to the right, Kinnock was never a 'keeper of the cloth cap' in the tradition of James Callaghan.

THE NATIONAL CONSTITUTIONAL COMMITTEE

Labour Party Constitution, Clause IX:
1 There shall be a National Constitutional Committee of the party to be elected at party conference . . .
2 The duties and powers of the NCC shall be:
   (a) to determine by hearing or otherwise such disciplinary matters as are presented to it by constituency Labour Parties . . .
   (b) to determine by hearing or otherwise such disciplinary matters as are presented to it by the officers of the party on the instructions of the NEC . . .
   (c) . . . to impose such disciplinary measures as . . . reprimand, suspension from holding office in the party . . . or expulsion from membership of the party or other penalty.
   (d) the decisions of the NCC in determining such disciplinary matters brought before it and imposing such disciplinary measures as it sees fit, shall be final.

The first and second years of Neil Kinnock's leadership were overwhelmed by the battle in the coalfields. During the Blackpool Labour Party conference of 1984, which marked the first anniversary of Kinnock's election, the week belonged to Arthur Scargill. While the party leader was going down to a humiliating defeat over reselection, Scargill was able to electrify delegates with his ringing claim that 'the miners' union is winning this fight and it is not only winning for miners, but for you and the entire labour and trade union movement'.[48] The old split between the 'parliamentary' and 'extra-parliamentary' left was as strong as ever. After the 1983 election, the idea of defeating capitalism by voting had lost such credibility as it had ever had. Scargill's way, pitting the massed strength of the miners and their sympathizers against the government, police and the courts, offered a quicker and more inspiring road to socialism.

The extra-parliamentary struggle spilled out of the coalfields and into town halls. The government had given itself unprecedented powers to put a legal limit on the budgets passed by elected councillors. About twenty Labour councils, including the GLC, Lambeth, Liverpool and Sheffield, believed they might be affected and were meeting to agree a common strategy. Not content with protesting or campaigning for a change in the law, they were proposing to defy it by refusing to set legally permissible budgets.

This was profoundly frustrating for Neil Kinnock. Even in his days as a left-wing rebel, he had basically believed that political issues should be resolved in parliament. Now he was leading the parliamentary party, but the arithmetic of the Commons rendered him powerless to influence or threaten the government in any way. Outside, a struggle was being waged in which his own emotions were deeply engaged, because of his family background, but it was out of his control. He disapproved of Scargill's tactic of calling the strike without a national ballot, but by the time the NUM had definitively rejected the call for a ballot, members of Kinnock's own extended family had been on strike for six weeks, at great personal sacrifice. Secretly, he gave some of his relatives financial help as the strike dragged on. Wherever he went in public, though, he could expect to be accosted by miners or their supporters demanding that he stop equivocating. The test set for him by the left was whether he was prepared to stand on a picket line, which he did for a few hours months after the strike began. Some of his immediate advisers, by contrast, were warning him to do less, rather than more, that might identify him in the public mind with Arthur Scargill. During one of the rare Commons debates on the miners' strike, Kinnock was more eloquent in support of the miners than his political adviser, John Reid, thought wise. Afterwards, the two had a sharp exchange back in his suite of offices. On top of the political pressures, Reid was exhausted by having to commute from his family's home in Scotland. As Kinnock left the room, Reid almost blacked out.

Meanwhile, the Conservatives and the tabloid press set Kinnock the test of satisfying them that he had unhesitatingly and unreservedly condemned the occasional violence on the picket lines. Of course, he never passed. In all, he complained years later:

> It was a very, very large diversion . . . and a year out of the job that we should have been doing in the renovation of policies and the appeal to the country. It obscured just about anything else and totally preoccupied both the movement and the general public . . . I could be frequently represented, and was, as someone who is weak, who was diffident, who was controlled by sentimentality rather than the welfare of the nation, and so on.[49]

When the miners marched back to work, Kinnock knew that his own fortunes would take an upward turn. There was one last kick to be delivered by the dying struggle in the pits. At the Bournemouth party conference, in October 1985, Kinnock made an unusual break with precedent by speaking twice in one week, the second occasion being in answer to a motion from the NUM that a Labour government would review the cases of all miners jailed for alleged picket-line violence during the dispute, reinstate those sacked for their part in the strike, and reimburse the NUM and all other unions for money lost through fines and sequestration. Despite Kinnock's warning that 'it would be utterly dishonest now for this party to give such an undertaking . . . that somehow people can come into conflict with the law and one day, sometime in the future, the cavalry will ride in in the form of a Labour government and pick up the tag . . . [because] even if we said it was going to happen, nobody would be convinced',[50] Scargill carried the day. It was almost the last occasion on which Neil Kinnock suffered so personal a defeat at the conference, and its impact was much muted by other events that same week.

In fact, the miners' defeat had taken the wind out of every form of extra-parliamentary resistance to the government. One by one, the Labour councils which had been defying the law capitulated, the last to fall being Liverpool, which set a rate on 14 June, and Lambeth three weeks later. At the same time, the Bennite left split in two. The process took place over several months in the summer and autumn, and was hardly noticed as it was in process, but the schism was deeper and more lasting than the previous one in 1981. The catch word for those who split away was 'realignment'. Rather implausibly, they claimed not to be retreating or changing their politics, but simply executing a tactical manoeuvre by striking up an alliance with Neil Kinnock to achieve victory at the next general election. The most important figures in this realignment were David Blunkett, Tom Sawyer and Michael Meacher, whose conversion gave Kinnock a working majority on the NEC. Curiously, Ken Livingstone was also identified with the realignment, having had a head-on confrontation with the ultra-left on the GLC, led by his deputy, John McDonnell, who opposed setting a legal rate. So was the newspaper *Tribune*, after Nigel Williamson had replaced Chris Mullin as editor; and the influential pressure group, the Labour Co-ordinating Committee, with which Robin Cook and Peter Hain were closely associated. The big catch the realigners hoped to make was Benn himself. However, as it became obvious that Benn was a lost cause, the realigners made a somewhat improbable claim that he had abandoned the Bennite cause, to which they were remaining true.

They could make this claim because all that the realigners were saying, for the time being, was that the 1983 election manifesto was as far left as the party could go. Benn and Eric Heffer were pushing for a policy of withdrawal from NATO, which had never been in any Labour election manifesto. Calls for a general strike in support of the miners were never taken up by the NEC, because Tom Sawyer, for instance, thought the idea was hopelessly unrealistic. The realigners also wanted an end to the traitor-hunting and name-calling denunciations which had been part of the language of the left. In short, they wanted to work with Neil Kinnock. In offering cooperation, they expected concessions. The first practical test arose when the NEC came to choose a General Secretary to replace Jim Mortimer, who was retiring. The candidate of the 'realigned' left was Larry Whitty, a GMBATU official. The right preferred the General Secretary of the Scottish Labour Party, Helen Liddell. For the last time ever, Neil Kinnock and Tony Benn were on one side of a division with Roy Hattersley on the other, to secure the job for Whitty. Thereafter, Kinnock exacted one concession after another from his new allies, giving very little in return.

The very act of putting up an ideological boundary fence on the port side implied that there were people whose ideas were so far out that they were not welcome in the Labour Party. The point was made in Patrick Seyd's article: 'There is a strong feeling that Militant and other organised Trotskyist groups within the party cannot be left unchallenged. Tony Benn does not acknowledge enemies on the left . . . The new left still adheres to an outright rejection of expulsions, but will not be swayed any more by talk of "witch-hunts" from taking Militant and other groups on in ideological and political debate.'[51] Through that small breach in the solidarity of the former Bennite left, Kinnock shrewdly drove a very large bridgehead.

In July, there was a closely fought by-election in the Tory-held seat of Brecon and Radnor, in mid-Wales, where, according to a MORI report published in the *Daily Mirror* on polling day, Labour was poised to win comfortably. In fact, the Liberals took the seat by 559 votes, with the Conservatives driven into third place. In the final stage of the campaign, Kinnock's press secretary, Patricia Hewitt, made an unexpected appearance in the constituency. Why she was there became obvious as the votes were counted. She commandeered a pass into the count and, as it emerged that Labour had lost, briefed the assembled journalists that the setback was to be blamed personally on Arthur Scargill and Tony Benn: Scargill for a speech urging the next Labour government to reimburse the NUM for its sequestered assets, and Benn because he had recently called for the nationalization of the land, and had introduced a private member's bill in the Commons which would have extended an amnesty to all miners imprisoned during the strike.

It was an early sign that, even before the arrival of Peter Mandelson, Kinnock was developing a personal machine able to conduct some aggressive briefings against rivals inside the party, with more foresight and effect than had ever been done on Michael Foot's behalf. Not everyone within the Labour Party machine was pleased with Hewitt's intervention, which invited journalists to write up the by-election as a setback for Labour despite a remarkable increase in the party's share of the vote. A few days later, the new General Secretary, Larry Whitty, gave a private briefing to industrial correspondents in London, making no attempt to blame the left for throwing away the Brecon by-election. He told them that Walworth Road had been forewarned about the offending Scargill speech, although there had been no advance notice of Benn's private member's bill.[52]

Kinnock's next move was riskier and braver. In a diary which I was keeping at the time, the entry for 29 September 1985, the opening day of the Bournemouth conference, notes that:

> Kinnock is determined to go up front, taking on the NUM on the question of retrospective legislation to reimburse their funds sequestered by the courts. He is facing almost certain defeat, but apparently thinks this price worth paying for the praise he will get for 'taking on extremists'. Immediately before today's NEC meeting, he was singing to himself. All the Kinnock camp is outwardly calm.

The next paragraph but one irrelevantly records that 'Joan Lestor and Barbara Castle were at dinner together, on the next table, reminiscing about some woman politician who, they say, is living in the past.' Irrelevant, except that where a couple of thousand Labour party members are confined together for a week, all sorts of historical memories are thrown up about past industrial struggles in the coalfield, the hunt for communist fellow travellers in the 1950s, all of which stood in the way of what Kinnock wanted to achieve. He was lucky even to be able to secure for himself the job as the NEC speaker in the miner's debate, in order that he could handle the issue personally. He first needed to win a majority on the NEC, which he accomplished only at the last minute when Michael Meacher reluctantly put loyalty to the leader before solidarity with the arrested miners.

Two days later, Kinnock delivered his leader's annual conference address, a peroration through the unemployment statistics, the Conservative record on health, education and the social services, the evils of nuclear weapons, the struggle against apartheid, the need to win the next election and – just as it appeared that he must be drawing to a close – a sudden reference to the Militant-influenced Liverpool city council, whose brinkmanship had driven them to temporarily lay off thousands of employees:

> I'll tell you what happens with impossible promises. You start with far-fetched resolutions. They are then pickled into a rigid dogma, a code, and you go through the years sticking to that – out-dated, misplaced, irrelevant to the real needs – and you end in the grotesque chaos of a Labour council, a *Labour* council, hiring taxis to scuttle round a city handing out redundancy notices to its own workers.[53]

For a moment, as the impact of his words sank in, it appeared he must lose his audience, the larger part of which had come prepared to vote against him. One of the first on his feet was Derek Hatton, sitting among the constituency delegates to Kinnock's right, who shook his fist and shouted 'liar' repeatedly. On the platform, the great bulk of Eric Heffer rose and walked off, followed out by a scramble of camera crews and journalists. His first words, outside, were 'Where's Doris?' as he looked bewilderedly around for his devoted wife. No one noticed that another member of the platform party, the Young Socialist delegate to the NEC, Frances Curran, also stood up and walked off. Tony Benn, who had been listening from the back, slipped away unseen. In other parts of the hall, the scattered abuse was drowned in a rising wave of applause as delegates demonstratively rose to their feet in Kinnock's support. Heffer swept past the folk singer, Billy Bragg, who was applauding the fact that the leader had at last 'come off the fence'. It was the moment when Kinnock seized the initiative.

The executions were a long and messy business, opening with a farcical NEC meeting in February, at which Militant supporters mounted a demonstration on the pavement in Walworth Road while Derek Hatton and Tony Mulhearn waved from an upstairs window, giving the impression that they had taken over the building, and the NEC meeting was aborted on a technicality. On legal advice, eight NEC members who had formed an enquiry team which visited Liverpool were denied a vote in the hearings, seven members who were opposed to expulsions – Tony Benn, Eric Clarke, Frances Curran, Eric Heffer, Joan Maynard, Jo Richardson and Dennis Skinner – walked out, leaving behind less than half the committee, so rendering it technically inquorate.

The next time, the NEC voted through a change to their own standing orders to ensure that the hearings could begin. They dragged on for a year, twice forcing Neil Kinnock and Roy Hattersley to miss Prime Minister's Questions: the only occasions in eight years when both men were absent from what is usually the highlight of the week in the Commons. Derek Hatton boycotted the NEC meeting which was called to deal with his case, claiming to have business in Liverpool, and was expelled without a hearing. Eight expellees turned up to appeal at the Blackpool conference in October, but then declined to go to the rostrum, so the expulsions were confirmed in their absence. The case of Felicity Dowling was delayed so long that her appeal was heard, and rejected, at the Brighton conference on

30 September 1987, fully two years after Kinnock's Bournemouth speech. Unlike Hatton and others, she spoke in her own defence, claiming: 'I am guilty indeed of fighting for socialism; and, expel me or not, I shall go on with that fight: but believe me, you cannot expel ideas from this movement.'[54]

That was not the conclusion which the NEC drew from the whole protracted exercise. The political costs involved were judged to have been well worth the resultant benefits. The main cost came from the cumbersome machinery for carrying through expulsions. Under the old system everyone had a right of appeal. Anyone expelled by their constituency party could appeal to the NEC but where, as in this case, the action was initiated by the NEC, the only body which could hear an appeal was the annual conference. That was all changed under a rule brought in as Hatton and Co. went out, creating a directly elected, eleven-member National Constitutional Committee, which initiated no disciplinary action but acted as the final court of appeal in every case. At the same time, the power to expel members was removed from constituency parties: only the NCC could pass sentence, but constituency parties could initiate proceedings against any known Militant members in their midst and an increasing number were willing to do so. One example was Newham North East, where Militant had been building up its strength. In one raid, the local party picked off seven, including Andy Bevan, who had been an official at Labour's national headquarters for fourteen years, all of whom were duly expelled by the NCC. In Bevan's case, the irony was that he had already left Militant. While he was secretly a member of its Central Committee, the Labour Party paid him a decent salary and allowed him to hold a sensitive job. After he had split with them, he was made redundant and expelled.

The NCC first met in February 1987. In its first four-and-a-half years, it heard 251 cases and expelled dozens of party members, 107 of whom were expelled on the specific charge that they were members of the Militant Tendency, without ever attracting any publicity. Removing or disciplining recalcitrant party members had become a painless routine.

THE BY-ELECTION PANEL

Where a parliamentary by-election occurs, the NEC shall take whatever action may be necessary to ensure that the vacancy is contested by a duly endorsed Labour candidate.

(a) The NEC shall each year elect a by-election panel consisting of eight of its members to initiate and oversee such action and deal with other matters delegated to it.

(b) ... Whenever possible nominations shall be sought from organisations entitled to send delegates to the general committee of the party, such nominations to be submitted to the by-election panel who may require the constituency party concerned to adopt a particular candidate or select a candidate from a number of such nominees.

(National Rules and Procedures of the Labour Party, 4A.16)

Guy Barnett, Labour MP for Greenwich, died suddenly over the Christmas break in 1986, putting the party in the inconvenient position of having to defend one of its own parliamentary seats only a few months before a general election. Almost as soon as the process of choosing a candidate had begun, rumours began to circulate that the result could be a disaster reminiscent of the Bermondsey by-election four years earlier, when the dramatic loss of a central London seat had presaged a general election defeat. Guy Barnett had been one of the London MPs named by Target 87 as vulnerable to deselection, and had in fact come uncomfortably close to being deselected, an ordeal which, some said, had contributed to his early death. His opponent had been Greenwich's representative on the Inner London Education Authority, Deirdre Wood. During the budget crisis in the last year of the GLC, when Ken Livingstone was challenged from the ultra-left by his deputy, John McDonnell, Wood had been one of the handful who voted with McDonnell to defy the law by not setting a rate. In due course, she was selected to fight the Greenwich by-election, and went down to defeat after a virulent press campaign which forced down the already depressed Labour vote and encouraged a huge tactical switch by Conservative voters, to secure victory for the SDP candidate, Rosie Barnes. It was bad enough to lose any Labour seat a few months before a general election; to do it in London, close to where all the national news media had their headquarters, was a disaster of epic proportions.

After the Greenwich defeat, it could be said that two 'traditions' grew up to explain why it took place. For most outside commentators, and for the larger part of the Labour Party, the explanation was straightforward: Labour chose a hard-left candidate and the voters rejected her. That opinion was shared by Neil Kinnock, who was appalled when the Greenwich party obstinately chose to run Deirdre Wood again as their general election candidate only months after the by-election. Two years later, he was prepared to countenance a deal with David Owen, who had approached him through an intermediary to offer his personal endorsement of the Labour Party in the 1992 election, which he would not himself be contesting, if the party would run no candidate against the two remaining SDP MPs, Rosie Barnes and John Cartwright, in Greenwich and Woolwich. By the time Owen had made a second approach, by a different route, Deidre Wood had indicated that she did not want to make a third attempt at the seat and the Greenwich Labour Party had selected a new candidate, Nick Raynsford, winner of the 1986 Fulham by-election. This time, Owen was met with a blunt refusal.[55] In fact, he gave his endorsement to the Conservative Party in 1992.

The left, naturally, has an alternative explanation: that to try to prevent Wood from being selected in the first place, the party machine spread innuendoes about her which failed to prevent her selection but destroyed her as a parliamentary candidate.[56] Gossip was indeed spreading about her as the selection process was under way, principally from fellow members of the ILEA who did not like her, and members of the Greenwich Labour Party who resented the attempt to deselect Guy Barnett. The selection conference itself was secretly taped and the tape passed to a journalist. It was only months since the NEC had imposed a candidate in Knowsley North, and Wood's supporters were in real doubt as to whether they would be allowed to select her.

However, the accusation that this was a deliberate operation from the centre is untrue. In London, councillors and party activists who think they know how to interpret the leader's wishes can find their way to representatives of the national media without going through the party's head office. To Neil Kinnock and those who advised him, Deirdre Wood was a name they were hearing for the first time. Having no opinion of her, they asked those who knew. Gerald Kaufman, for instance, sought out the opinion of Jeremy Beecham, leader of Newcastle city council, who knew almost everyone there was to know in local government, and spoke well of her. The Labour MP Chris Smith, a former Islington councillor, also defended her. The former GLC chairman, Illtyd Harrington, took the trouble to visit Peter Mandelson in Walworth Road to allay fears about her. The picture that emerged by word of mouth was not a hard-left ideologue, but a well-meaning local councillor, more driven by emotion than by philosophical thought, who could nonetheless be trusted to defend party policy faithfully. Furthermore, it was clear that, in contrast to Knowsley North, the constituency party was democratically run and a majority appeared to support her candidature. The head office of NUPE, Deirdre Wood's union, indicated that they would lend logistic support to the campaign if she was adopted, but the offer might not apply for another NUPE member who was in the running, the former MP Reg Race. When Mandelson was informed that she had been selected, his private reaction was that the local party were probably right not to let themselves be frightened out of making the candidate of their choice by press coverage.[57] Frank Dobson, who acted as Deirdre Wood's minder during the campaign, defended her even after her defeat.

When she met Neil Kinnock privately just after her selection, with only one other person in the room, Wood disarmingly opened the conversation by saying: 'I promise I won't drop you in it,' to which his reply was, 'It is not you, love, it's those bastards out there,' – meaning a hostile Tory press. He advised her to play to her strengths, because 'you have done something in your life, you're a mother, you've brought up children on your own, you're a councillor: what have they done? – Nothing.'[58] By now, Kinnock's animus to journalists from the tabloid press was such that he did not even credit them with being able to raise families. Wood thought her rapport with Kinnock was such that after her defeat, she seriously expected a call from his office to tell her that it was not her fault, and was terribly hurt when none came. But just as circus acrobats are reputed to turn and walk away when one of their colleagues is injured, so a politician as intent on winning as Neil Kinnock has a horror of associating with losers.

For obvious reasons, a by-election candidate associated with the left wing of the Labour Party is more vulnerable to a centre candidate like Rosie Barnes than one from the right. The Greenwich by-election occurred at a time when years of relentless press reports about 'loony left' London councils had begun to take effect. In fact, the old myth about *Baa Baa Black Sheep* being proscribed as racist actually came true midway through the campaign, when an educationally backward child was sent home by a nursery nurse in nearby Islington for singing it. What had happened was that the nurse had read somewhere that this was council policy. When the council leader, Margaret Hodge, found out she instantly ordered that the child be reinstated and the offending staff member was disciplined. The next morning, Glenys Kinnock was at a nursery in Greenwich, joining in a hearty rendering of *Baa Baa Black Sheep*. Some of the suspicion that the Labour Party had abandoned its traditional supporters in pursuit of esoteric trendiness was nonetheless visited upon the hapless Deirdre Wood. But even that explanation of the defeat in Greenwich must be treated with caution, because the local council was relatively popular and well-run, when compared with London boroughs like Lambeth or Southwark. Early in the campaign, it was singled out for praise by the head of the Audit Commission, Howard Davies, for having its finances under control. There being no large Black or Asian population in the borough, racial politics were not a major local issue.

A more simple and basic explanation is that Wood was a victim of straightforward character assassination. She was selected on a Saturday morning. The following Monday's *Daily Mail* featured two pages about her private life, revolving around the fact that she was living in comfortable style with a man who had been a militant shop steward during the 'Winter of Discontent' and was not the father of her children. She was also tubby and in her first encounter with the national press, she repeatedly refused to disclose her age, eventually settling for 'forty-ish'. This contrasted with the exemplary home life of the smartly turned out Rosie Barnes. The *News of the World* dug out Wood's birth certificate, proving that she was actually forty-four, and ran this discovery across two pages, under the heading 'Deirdre's Big Fat Lie'. Subsequently, the same newspaper uncovered the fact that her mother had turned her father out of the house for being a violent drunkard, and considered whether to expose her as a callous daughter who shunned the old man. It was at this point that Wood's increasingly desperate campaign managers decided to counter-attack. A *News of the World* writer was invited to the campaign headquarters to interview Wood. When he arrived, he discovered that a camera crew and the rest of the press corps were already there, and he was expected to perform noble deeds in front of them all. He literally turned and ran, whereupon the whole pack set off in pursuit, including a fleet-footed BBC cameraman. Stopping at the first telephone box, our hero tried to ring his news desk to describe his misfortune, but the phone was out of order. When the pack returned, minus the *News of the World*, a lachrymose Deirdre Wood gave an impromptu press conference, in which she relived her grim working-class childhood.

Later in the day, David Montgomery, editor of *News of the World*, rang the BBC, demanding in vain that the footage of his reporter should not be shown, because the newspaper had been unfairly lured into a trap by the Labour Party. A plaintive editorial the following week echoed the same theme. Unfair or not, it almost ended the media persecution of Deirdre Wood. Only the next morning's *Sun* carried on intrepidly with yet another story about her personal life. An editorial in the *Daily Mail* described the sight of her in tears as 'pathetic' and called for an end to the smears which they had themselves started. Even the *Daily Express* paid tribute to the Labour Party organization for turning over the mighty *News of the World*. However, the damage was already done. Most of Greenwich's voters had not heard of Deirdre Wood until the campaign began, since when they had been deluged with information and disinformation about her life, conveying the impression that she was not respectable. Her defeat is evidence that what the Americans call 'negative campaigning' works.

It was too close to a general election for the Kinnock leadership to react to a disaster in the now traditional manner, by altering the party rules to prevent it from happening again. That turned out to be an expensive omission, because within less than two years, there was a by-election which produced an even worse result than Greenwich.

It originated, ironically, from the perennial feud within the Conservative Party over Britain's role in Europe. Mrs Thatcher suspected the Tories' own nominee as EC Commissioner of having gone native in Brussels, and insisted on replacing him with her former Cabinet favourite, Leon Brittan. She also insisted that Labour's nominee be recalled, lest he become the senior British commissioner. Consequently, Kinnock was obliged to name a successor, and chose the former Secretary of State for Scotland, Bruce Millan. It was generally viewed as a good appointment, except for the one drawback that when an MP quits parliament to take a better paid job, his party usually does badly at the consequent by-election. However, since Millan's majority in Glasgow Govan was 19,509, there was no apparent reason to fear that Labour could lose the seat.

The first warnings were heard in September, when it was known that the local party was likely to choose Bob Gillespie, an official of the print union, Sogat. He was a traditional left-wing socialist. As a militant union leader, he had personally offended Robert Maxwell, owner of Scotland's largest selling newspaper, the *Daily Record*. Maxwell threatened to order his editor in Glasgow to campaign against a Labour victory, until he was persuaded by his advisers, Joe Haines and Helen Liddell, that he would be damaging his own interests if he were seen to be handing victory to the Scottish Nationalists.

Labour's position in Scotland looked unassailable, with fifty out of seventy-two of the country's MPs. But all this voting power meant next to nothing when there was no Scottish assembly, and England had overwhelmingly voted Tory. The SNP had therefore given Labour's contingent the telling nickname, the 'Feeble Fifty'. They had also decided to field the best campaigner they had, the former Labour MP Jim Sillars, who was married to Margo MacDonald, winner of a celebrated by-election in the same constituency twenty-one years earlier. Sillars was able to tear to shreds the basic Labour case, that the interests of Scotland were best served by waiting for another general election and hoping that by then the English would have improved their voting habits.

Like others on the left, Gillespie sympathized with those who were saying that on principle they would refuse to pay the iniquitous poll tax which was to be introduced to Scotland the following spring. Of all the issues threatening to tear the Scottish Labour Party apart, that was the single most contentious. The line that Donald Dewar, John Smith, Gordon Brown and others were taking was that Labour councils would have no choice but to collect the tax, however reluctantly, and no one should be encouraged to break the law by not paying it. But even a figure as senior as Robin Cook was ambivalent. One MP, Dick Douglas, was provoked to leave the Labour Party over this issue and join the SNP, which had no compunction about encouraging poll tax protestors to take direct action by refusing to pay, in the hope of making the tax unworkable. This issue alone would have made Gillespie an awkward choice to defend Labour's policy of compliance against a determined SNP campaign.

Unfortunately, Gillespie had other weaknesses. For example, he had the words 'Hong' and 'Kong' tattooed on his fingers, one letter to each finger, which set tremors through Labour party officials. Also, when put alongside Sillars, he seemed to have a weak grasp of the more complex political questions. The turning point of the campaign was a televised debate between the main candidates, which Sillars succeeded in dominating throughout. At one point, he cruelly asked Gillespie for his opinion on 'additionality'. This is the principle that certain categories of regional subsidies granted by the EC have to be additional to, rather than a substitute for, state funding by national governments; given the Conservative aversion to state subsidies, there were documented incidences in which they had refused to take the money on offer from Brussels, depriving Scotland of a source of funds. Unfortunately, the word 'additionality' did not mean anything to Gillespie, who was made to look as if he was out of his depth. As Labour's campaign bus toured the constituency the following morning, dismayed MPs standing on the top deck could see voters removing Labour Party window stickers, to put up SNP material instead. Labour lost by 3,554 votes, the worst by-election result since 1983.

This plunged Kinnock into the worst depression of his entire leadership. Between then and the Christmas break, he came closer to quitting than any other time during his leadership. He actually threatened to quit during one angry meeting in his office with three Shadow Cabinet members, Robin Cook, Frank Dobson and Derek Foster, plus his PPS Adam Ingham, and Charles Clarke, though there were differing opinions among those present as to how seriously he meant it. He himself denied that he was genuinely on the point of going, and during the Christmas break his spirits rallied.

As usual, a crisis produced a rule change to prevent its repetition. For every parliamentary by-election after Govan, potential candidates have had to appear before a panel of NEC members and Walworth Road staff, who cross-examine them to judge whether they would be able to withstand the kind of intense media attention which might be in store for them. Only after they have been cleared by the panel can they go on a shortlist to appear before the constituency party general committee.

It was at once suspected that this panel would be used as a means to bar candidates on political grounds, a suspicion which was soon proved to be well-founded. The first celebrated controversy blew up after the resignation of the Vauxhall MP Stuart Holland. Vauxhall was a stronghold for radical activists from the party's unofficial Black sections. The front-runner for the seat was Martha Osamor, a Nigerian-born, left-wing former deputy leader of Haringey council, who was under investigation because of alleged irregularities in the accounts of various council-funded voluntary groups of which she was treasurer. The NEC panel refused to allow her on the shortlist. While they were about it, they also barred every other Black nominee except the television journalist Wesley Kerr, who withdrew his name. The general committee of the Vauxhall party then refused to accept the panel's shortlist, and the panel therefore completed the selection, choosing Kate Hoey. In the subsequent by-election, on a reduced turn-out, she increased Labour's share of the vote.

Other decisions, in subsequent by-elections, attracted less attention, but demonstrated that tolerance had taken second place to the will to win. Crispin St Hill, a West Indian who had fought the hopeless seat of Mid-Staffordshire in the 1987 general election, was denied a place on the shortlist in the same seat three years later, for a by-election which Labour stood a chance of winning and where, in fact, because of the poll tax, there was the best by-election result Labour had had since the war. In Bootle, a former researcher for the previous MP Allan Roberts, was barred purely because he was an 'out' gay, living with a prominent Labour councillor. In Wallasey, a marginal Tory seat adjoining Birkenhead, where Frank Field had been saved by the NEC from deselection, the panel was sent in without the pretext of a by-election, because the selection procedure had been delayed and a general election was imminent, to bar the front-runner Loll Duffy, a former member of the now-proscribed Socialist Organiser grouplet, allowing Angela Eagle, a 'soft-left' trade union official, to take the seat instead. In Hemsworth, in the heart of the Yorkshire coalfield, the panel barred the local miners' leader, Ken Capstick, after the death of the sitting MP George Buckley. When the death of Buckley's successor, Derek Enright, caused another by-election, another leader of the Yorkshire NUM, Steve Kemp, was also barred. In both cases, the decision was purely political. Brutal though this system is, had it applied earlier, it would have saved poor Deirdre Wood from a trauma which soured her life.

THE 20 PER CENT RULE

(a) In the case of a vacancy for Leader or Deputy Leader, each nomination must be supported by 12.5 per cent of the Commons members of the PLP. Nominations not attaining the threshold shall be null and void.

(b) Where there is no vacancy, nominations shall be sought each year prior to the annual session of party conference. In this case any nomination must be supported by 20 per cent of the Commons members of the PLP.

(Rules for party conference: Rule 5: Election of Leader and Deputy Leader/3c5.2)

The final days for nominations for the post of leader and deputy leader following the resignations of Neil Kinnock and Roy Hattersley in 1992 almost degenerated into farce. In the deputy leadership stakes, five MPs expressed an interest, but mathematically it was impossible that they could all run, because of a rule which said that each nomination had to be signed by a minimum of 20 per cent of the parliamentary Labour Party, and no MP could nominate more than one candidate. Even after Bernie Grant and Ann Clwyd had dropped off the bottom of the list, a crisis developed: Bryan Gould did not have the necessary number of signatures on his nomination paper either, and could only compete by appealing to MPs who nominated Clwyd to switch to him. First, though, he had to go to the party officers, Larry Whitty and Joyce Gould, for a ruling on whether this was allowed, because strictly an MP could nominate only one candidate. They gave him the ruling he wanted, but word reached the rival camp of John Prescott, who used the information without mercy to give the impression that Gould was the outsider, while the real contest was between Prescott and Margaret Beckett. That was borne out by the eventual result, in which Gould picked up only 10 per cent of the vote.

This was nothing compared to the monumental embarrassment which might have hit the party after John Smith's death in 1994, when Tony Blair collected nominations from 57 per cent of the PLP. Luckily, the NEC had had the foresight to amend the rule while John Smith was alive, lowering the threshold for a contest triggered by death or resignation to 15 per cent, and both John Prescott and Margaret Beckett narrowly scraped on to the ballot papers. Had the 20 per cent rule still applied, there would have been no contest, and the election in which nearly a million people participated, giving Blair his exceptional claim to legitimacy, would have been aborted. It was all because of a rule whose original purpose was to stop Tony Benn from challenging Neil Kinnock every year – or, to put it differently, to ensure that every candidate was as serious as John Prescott.

The Labour Party awoke after a late night on 12 June 1987, knowing that the general election result had been far worse than they had ever foreseen. Instead of a Kinnock government, which thousands of party activists had imagined was within reach, they had five more years under a Conservative government with another vast majority. This time, the comfort of blaming a badly conducted campaign was not an option. By general consent, Labour had run its best campaign for a generation.

The view from the left was that the party had done well where it fielded socialist candidates brave enough to put their views clearly and forcefully, and had faltered where it lost its nerve. The best evidence in support of the left's case was in Merseyside, where two years of the highly publicized Militant dispute had had no obvious detrimental effect on the result. Eric Heffer was understandably keen to make sure everyone knew that his own majority in Liverpool Walton was up from 14,000 to 23,000, a swing of 11 per cent. Loll Duffy, the Marxist candidate in Wallasey, was equally ebullient: 'We got Labour's highest ever vote in Wallasey, and we . . . doubled Labour Party membership . . . The people of Wallasey had a clear choice: it was either Toryism or socialism They came over in their thousands to Labour as they did in other areas where a clear socialist alternative was put before them.'[59]

Actually, anyone looking for a direct correlation between the result in a given area and the politics of the local party is in for a difficult time. The swing to Labour had been uniform across Merseyside. Sworn enemies of Militant, like Frank Field in Birkenhead and George Howarth in Knowsley North, did as well as the left. Yet in nearby Hyndburn, the second most marginal Tory seat in Britain, the Conservative majority jumped from 21 to 2,200. In London, there was a predictable drop in Labour support in Brent and Tottenham, where Labour borough councils had been beset by political controversy, but the vote went up in Lambeth, which was becoming a byword for everything that was bad in Labour local government. The probable explanation is that horror stories about Lambeth council had a muted impact in the borough itself, where dustbins continued to be emptied and a basic level of service kept ticking over, but that they eroded Labour's support in slightly more prosperous neighbouring boroughs like Lewisham, where there was no local history of wild militancy, but the Labour vote fell. Similarly, stories about Liverpool council would appear to have had a more damaging effect on Labour's support in rural Cheshire and Lancashire than on Merseyside.

Neil Kinnock was in no doubt that Labour had lost because it appeared to be threatening the new-found prosperity of people of lower middle-class and skilled working-class voters who were feeling the benefits of an economic boom. He announced that 'democratic socialism has to be as attractive, as beckoning and as useful to the relatively affluent and the relatively secure as it is to the less fortunate in our society'.[60]

Until now, despite the appearance that the Labour Party had been moving to the right since Kinnock became its leader, there had been few substantial changes to party policy. The 1987 election manifesto had contained far less prescriptive detail than the one four years earlier, but was not substantially different. After the 1987 defeat, Kinnock resolved that there would have to be a genuine overhaul, to which end he launched a policy review, accompanied by a slightly absurd exercise called 'Labour Listens' in which frontbench politicians were sent around the country to hear the opinions of the sort of people who turned out to sparsely attended public meetings to air them. The pivotal figure in both exercises – the one, inconsequential, the other, fundamental – was Tom Sawyer, who took over the chairmanship of the NEC Home Policy Committee.

Meanwhile, there was no immediate sign of a shift to the right among the slightly enlarged group of Labour MPs who returned after the general election. On the contrary, what appeared to happen was that the old right, embodied in the Manifesto Group, was obliterated, while the Tribune Group, which had once been Aneurin Bevan's parliamentary base, swept all before it. Throughout the 1983–87 parliament, the Manifesto group held a majority of places on the Shadow Cabinet, while barely a quarter of the members at any time had voted for Kinnock in the leadership election. These 'Kinnockites' – Robin Cook, John Prescott, Michael Meacher *et al.* – were the more junior members of the Shadow Cabinet with little or no government experience and not always on good terms with the leader. Consequently, the most important roles on the frontbench were taken by the senior members of the Manifesto Group: Roy Hattersley, Denis Healey, Gerald Kaufman, John Smith and John Cunningham.

But in 1987, the highest votes went to three Tribune Group nominees: Bryan Gould, John Prescott and Michael Meacher. The Tribunites Robin Cook and Bob Hughes, who had been ousted in 1986, were re-elected, and four others – Gordon Brown, Frank Dobson, Jo Richardson and Jack Straw – were elected for the first time. All the casualties were on the Manifesto Group slate, whose strength was halved. Except for Bob Hughes, who was ousted a year later, making room for Tony Blair, and the unpredictable Denzil Davies, the 1987 line-up proved to be remarkably durable. Nine of its twelve elected members stayed on to serve in Tony Blair's Shadow Cabinet in 1994, the others having either died or retired voluntarily. The first to lose his seat in a Shadow Cabinet election was John Cunningham in 1995.

However, the Tribune Group was no longer the left-wing ginger group it had once been. On the contrary, it had expanded to take in more than half the parliamentary Labour Party, and contained at least four separate political strands. One part was no longer politically distinguishable from the Manifesto Group, except that it was made up of slightly younger MPs, less scarred by the battles of 1979–83, and 'Kinnockite' rather than 'Hattersleyite'. One new MP privately described his astonishment on arriving at his first Tribune meeting: 'I couldn't believe it – there were people like Gordon Brown, Tony Blair and Nick Brown, calling themselves "left"! They're the new right.'

Next, to their left, were those like John Prescott and Robin Cook, who had backed Kinnock for leader in 1983, who had accepted the expulsion of Militant and much else as regrettable necessities, but thought that Kinnock was in danger of delivering too much to the right. One of Tribune's first meetings was dominated by an argument over tactics for the forthcoming Shadow Cabinet elections. Robin Cook and John Prescott, with past experience of the effectiveness of the Manifesto slate, were prepared to strike a bargain with Campaign, under which Tribune members would be encouraged to vote for certain Campaign nominees like Tony Benn and Stuart Holland, in return for the far-left's support for the Tribune slate. That was fiercely opposed by Jack Straw, Gordon Brown and Tony Blair, who said they would rather not be elected at all than reach the Shadow Cabinet with Campaign Group backing.

Another group, including Jo Richardson, Margaret Beckett and Clare Short, maintained joint membership of the Tribune and Campaign Groups, but were ready to cooperate with the Shadow Cabinet and to accept frontbench responsibilities. Their dalliance with the Campaign Group did not last long, however, and they merged with Prescott and Robin Cook into the next 'soft left'. Finally, there were a few Tribune members like Ken Livingstone, who were not, in practice, going to cooperate with Neil Kinnock, but were looking for allies outside the Campaign Group. Further to the left, increasingly entrenched in isolation, was the hard core of Campaign.

It soon became apparent that the days when Kinnock needed to worry about the Bennite left as a serious threat to his authority were over. The only source of internal opposition that he needed to worry about for the rest of his tenure as leader was from the 'soft left' who, in line with William Blake's maxim that opposition is true friendship, sincerely regarded themselves as his friends. These were people who agreed that Labour's economic programme was going to have to offer something other than a return to state control, who agreed, reluctantly, that unilateral nuclear disarmament might have to be abandoned, but believed that too much of the radicalism which made the Labour Party distinct was being thrown overboard with happy philistinism. They had, however, no organizational structure, no recognized leader, no platform, and only a hazy agreement on tactics. The three pre-eminent personalities were Bryan Gould, Robin Cook and John Prescott. Their strategy, essentially, was to stay on side, participate in the policy review and try to keep Neil Kinnock's ear. The first to break ranks was John Prescott, with a bold move which in the medium term established him as the leading personality on the 'soft left'.

Volatile, courageous, hard-working and accident prone, Prescott is variously thought of as a gift to the Tories because his heavyweight scowl and aggressive manner frighten voters; or an asset to Labour, because he has a down-to-earth bluntness and because, in a party founded to secure representation of working men in parliament, he is the most successful example of a politician whose working life began in a manual job.

There is an old newsreel of Prime Minister Sir Alec Douglas-Home having a meal aboard ship on his way back from Australia; the ship's waiter attending to him was a young John Prescott. He went to sea at seventeen, a bright boy with no obvious career prospects. His childhood, in Wales, was probably a touch more prosperous and settled than the early years of David Blunkett or Margaret Beckett, but was marred when he failed the 11-plus, and was sent to Ellesmere Port Secondary Modern school, which must have been a humiliation for someone whose father was a signalman, a skilled worker a cut above the run of general workers, and a magistrate. Much of his adult life seems to have been spent trying to catch up on the education he lost in his teens. His first political experience was as a militant shop steward in the National Union of Seamen, whose leaders decided to get him out of their hair by arranging for him to go to study economics and politics at Ruskin College, Oxford. He subsequently went on to Hull University. As a twenty-eight-year-old student, he contested his first parliamentary seat in 1966, and sat in the gallery of the House of Commons to hear Harold Wilson denounce the 'tightly knit group of politically motivated men' leading the first national seamen's strike.

Things happen when Prescott is around. If any member of the Shadow Cabinet is going to be caught speeding on the motorway, or bringing camera equipment through customs without valid receipts, or swearing on television, it is probably going to be John Prescott. He is well known to have a short fuse, and when carried away he is liable to trip over his own words, saying things which taken literally make sense – a failing of which he is well aware and which only adds to his irritation. Interviewed on Radio 4's *The World at One* programme about the aftermath of the Lockerbie bombing, he once exclaimed: 'People died on that aircraft, and they want to know what happened!' On another occasion, when being interviewed for TV-AM by its then Political Editor, Adam Boulton, he fluffed his lines, let out several expletives, and asked for the interview to be re-recorded. Alas, it was a live interview. There was nothing Prescott could do but apologize to the viewers, keep a straight face and carry on.

At other times, Prescott has let loose his real feelings about political events, momentarily forgetting how, for high-profile politicians, walls have ears. Three months before the 1987 general election, he berated the former Prime Minister Jim Callaghan for criticizing Labour's defence policy, choosing to do so, unfortunately, in the tearoom of the House of Commons, within earshot of Tory MPs who gleefully relayed what they heard to the press. It was not the only tearoom conversation of his which found its way instantly into print. There was another occasion, in the same room, in which, provoked by something which the Tory MP Phillip Oppenheim, son of Baroness Oppenheim-Barnes, had said in the Chamber, Prescott told him to go back to his rich mother. In January 1996, after journalists had broken the news to him that his Shadow Cabinet colleague Harriet Harman was sending her younger child to grammar school, he made some very unguarded comments about her to an ITN camera crew, while the camera was switched off. He was furious because he had not been forewarned. ITN staff leaked to newspaper journalists that he had called Harman a 'fucking hypocrite', though he denies it, claiming he had said nothing worse than 'I am not answering questions about that bloody woman,' but it hardly mattered.

Sometimes, there is reason to believe that Prescott uses his own reputation for making unguarded remarks to achieve calculated political ends. For example, interviewed for the TV documentary *The Wilderness Years*, Prescott accused Mandelson and other unnamed spin doctors of having had 'an extraordinary influence beyond what should have been exercised'. Between recording and transmission, Mandelson had been appointed Shadow Minister of the civil service, and a member of Prescott's own frontbench team. Prescott therefore demanded that his remarks should not be broadcast, a request which he must have known was sure to be both turned down and leaked to newspapers. By protesting, he acquitted himself of the charge of having wilfully and publicly attacked a member of his own team; by protesting ineffectively, he reminded Labour Party members of what his relations with Mandelson were really like, which could only improve his popularity.

In a similar vein, he entered both the party election contests of 1992 and 1994 declaring himself to be a 'traditionalist' when being a 'modernizer' was all the rage, and the best guarantee of sympathetic press coverage. He was not being naïve, nor even particularly straight. Those who knew him well knew him as a closet 'modernizer', who in due course put his prestige behind all the important modernizer causes from the curbing of the block vote to the abolition of Clause Four. But Prescott knew that within the Labour movement, there were votes to be had from being called a 'traditionalist'.

Sometimes, things happened to him which were just not his fault, like the story of the misnamed 'Ship of Shame', which I know all about because I was on board at the time. On 27 July 1985, the *Sun* had a front-page story alleging John Prescott had hired a boat for a floating celebration to mark the start of the summer break, during which there had been a fracas with a guest who complained that there was no vegetarian food on board, and which was said to have culminated with a young female reveller staggering topless on to the House of Commons terrace in the early hours of the morning, to vomit over the parapet into the Thames. As is sometimes the case with *Sun* exclusives, fragments of truth had invaded the story. Prescott really had organized a party on the Thames and had had a sharp exchange with a young vegetarian, who subsequently sent him a gracious letter of apology. And a female really had disgraced herself later in the night, but she was reportedly a guest at an entirely separate party, given by a researcher working for another member of the Shadow Cabinet. Consequently, it would not have served the Labour Party's interests to protest and establish the truth, and the innocent Prescott had to endure an undeserved season of stories in *Private Eye* about his virility.

These incidents can obscure the fact that Prescott is a shrewd, hard-working political operator who studies his subject thoroughly and plays to his own strengths. As a young MP in the 1970s, he hardly ever spoke in the Commons other than on his specialist subjects of conditions at sea and trade union law. Even when he opened out into more general subjects, for instance to defend socialism as a superior system to the private ownership of capital, he invariably built his arguments from observations on the industry which he knew from personal experience. He held views which were common on the Labour left at the time, for example 'my party is committed to owning and controlling the means of production. That is what we are here for',[61] or 'anyone who has studied the history of the trade union movement knows that trade unions have constantly had to fight against the law . . . I think there can be justification for breaking the law.'[62] In his field, he soon became an authority recognized and respected even by ministers in the Heath government. A junior Energy Minister, Peter Emery, paid tribute to him in 1974 as a 'renowned expert' on safety on North Sea oil rigs.[63]

It was his knowledge of maritime law which made Harold Wilson decide to appoint him to the Council of Europe in 1972, and three years later to the then unelected European Parliament, where he was leader of the Labour delegation in 1976–79. Given the number of zig-zags which the Labour Party performed over European policy in the 1970s, there was no need for its leading spokesman in Brussels actually to have been a lifelong European. Prescott had campaigned for a 'no' vote in the 1975 referendum, but accepted defeat and declared soon after his appointment that 'it is not conceivable that we shall leave the Community'.[64]

In 1979, James Callaghan appointed him an opposition spokesman on transport. He alternated between specializing in transport or employment for most of the following fifteen years, until he became deputy leader of the Labour Party without ever having held any of what are considered the big frontbench portfolios. Several Cabinet ministers who found themselves opposite him made the mistake of underestimating him. The luckless Paul Channon, the old Etonian scion of a famous political family, was routinely worsted by Prescott, until he was sacked by Mrs Thatcher and replaced with Cecil Parkinson, who thought Prescott was crude and cack-handed, and once called him a 'vulture' for allegedly trying to make political capital from the Lockerbie tragedy. Parkinson had not realized how carefully Prescott checked his lines with bereaved relatives before saying anything about any major transport disaster. On this occasion Jim Swire, who had lost a daughter over Lockerbie, came publicly to Prescott's defence, saying that he spoke for the relatives. Prescott was still there when Parkinson bowed out.

In the days that followed his achievement of a strong second place in the 1987 Shadow Cabinet election, Prescott became increasingly restive as the door to the leader's office opened, one after another, to colleagues who had collected fewer votes than he had, but not to him. Suspecting that the most important jobs were being filled first, he bombarded the leader's office and the whips' office with angry telephone calls. His suspicions were correct. The four most senior jobs in the Shadow Cabinet had been held before the election by the quartet of Roy Hattersley, Denis Healey, Gerald Kaufman and John Smith. With only Healey bowing out, there was room at the top for just one new entrant, who was going to be Bryan Gould. Kinnock had an exasperating time dealing with the defence spokesman, Denzil Davies, who believed he was due for promotion. By the time an irate Prescott marched into his office, the leader had no patience left to deal with him tactfully. Prescott was appointed Shadow Secretary of State for Energy, and came away feeling insulted. He hinted soon afterwards to the Labour Editor of the *Observer*, Robert Taylor, that he might run for the deputy leadership of the party.

For someone with Prescott's political contacts, there would be no problem about collecting sufficient names for a valid nomination. At that time, he needed only a dozen MPs to back him. Rather, his problem was political: how to explain why, as a loyal Kinnock supporter, he was upsetting the unity of the party and mounting a challenge to an incumbent with whom neither he, nor Kinnock, had any clear political differences. A variety of motives were attributed to him at the time, from simple pique to a personal grudge against Roy Hattersley dating back twelve years to the 'cod war' between Britain and Iceland, when John Prescott had courageously taken the part of Icelandic fishermen – a course with obvious risks for a Hull MP – and had been accused of being 'neither sensible nor honourable' by the then Minister of State at the Foreign Office, Roy Hattersley.[65]

Prescott's real motives appear to have been a product of personal ambition and serious concern about party organization. So much of Neil Kinnock's energy had been absorbed in managing the party that he had hardly had time to be a parliamentary leader. For that purpose, Hattersley was not a natural deputy. He, too, was principally a parliamentarian, with less understanding of the Labour movement than either Kinnock or, come to that, John Prescott, who announced: 'The deputy leader . . . has a central role to play in turning the party outwards . . . travelling the country, building the party and leading the way in creating a mass modern dynamic party . . . It cannot be done by someone who also has to carry a heavy parliamentary portfolio.'[66]

This was a profoundly sensible proposal, in the abstract. Ever since the post of deputy leader was invented in its present form to assuage the hurt feelings of Herbert Morrison after he had unexpectedly lost his seat on the NEC in 1952, no one had seriously addressed the question of what it was for. Morrison's grandson, Peter Mandelson, is among those who have suggested that it should be abolished outright.[67] If the deputy was to deputize while the leader was away, it would have been sensible to appoint someone whom the leader could trust, but, traditionally, the post was filled by heavyweights like George Brown, Roy Jenkins and Denis Healey, who were not deputies but rivals with their eyes on the leader's job.

John Prescott's scheme of converting the deputy leader into a party manager made sense in that no other member of the Shadow Cabinet would want to be taken out of parliament into full-time party activity, because they must annually remind fellow MPs to vote for them. Robin Cook attributed the loss of his Shadow Cabinet seat in 1986 to his being a full-time campaigns coordinator with no role to perform in the Commons. A deputy leader, by contrast, needed support in the party at large and could afford to devote time to it. Since 1992, the successive deputy leaders Margaret Beckett and John Prescott have in fact carried out the function Prescott suggested they should.

However, it was never likely that Neil Kinnock was going to look at the issue in the abstract. His only concern was the immediate consequences of a challenge to Roy Hattersley, especially one which might succeed. Kinnock's own relations with his deputy had started out badly but improved with the passing of the years. By now, although he did not think of Hattersley as a friend, he had ceased to think of him as a threat and was prepared to defend him against all comers. Around this time, Bryan Gould – who appeared then to be the leader's closest political ally – made soundings to see if Kinnock would like him for a deputy. He received a blunt refusal. It was the start of Gould's political descent. To remove the deputy leader, in a campaign which would necessarily drag out for several months, was not a simple administrative action. The drama would be played out on prime time television, providing a spectacle of disunity and giving the impression that the party was shifting to the left. Furthermore, having sacked the deputy for not being the best possible party manager, the party might then have turned its attention to the obvious fact that Kinnock was not their best parliamentary performer either, and that a Kinnock–Prescott leadership was not the sort of 'balanced ticket' which allowed both the main wings of the party to feel they were represented at the top. However loyal Prescott claimed to be, it is likely that a Prescott victory in 1988 would have destroyed Kinnock's leadership.

In December 1987, John Prescott had a private meeting with correspondents from Sunday newspapers, to whom he gave a detailed exposition of how and why he would run a deputy leadership campaign.

Anxious not to appear to be going behind Kinnock's back, he did it in the presence of a party official, who took detailed notes and passed them directly on to the leader. The result was a shouting match in the leader's office, in which Kinnock made it clear that if Prescott went ahead with the challenge his life was going to be made as miserable as it was in Kinnock's gift to make it. It was a classic clash of similar temperaments: hot-tempered, self-opinionated, authoritarian and determined to overcome a perceived educational disadvantage to play in the political big league. Afterwards, Prescott complained in private that Kinnock was the sort of man who believed that the only quality which mattered was the courage to speak his mind, a criticism he could equally have directed at himself. He also remarked, on more than one occasion, that he and Kinnock were alike in that they each believed that anyone who was not for them was against them. In that vein, his first act on leaving Kinnock's office was to ring the official caught in the middle of his duel to pass on some of the aggravation he had been put through by Kinnock. I know, because I was that official. 'Kinnock's nark' was one of the epithets that hurtled down the telephone line in my direction.

Over Christmas, Prescott was heavily lobbied not to run. Rodney Bickerstaffe and the seamen's leader, Sam McCluskie, secured a face-saving promise that the role of the deputy leader would be debated at the next party conference. On 20 January 1988, Prescott made a formal announcement that the race was off. However, the day ended with more ill feeling than it began. As Neil Kinnock listened to a summary of Prescott's remarks, he had visions of the next day's newspapers reporting that Roy Hattersley would be stripped the following autumn of his portfolio as Shadow Home Secretary to concentrate on party matters, in line with the Prescott plan. Kinnock immediately issued a press release saying that 'my view on the idea of excluding a deputy leader of the Labour Party from a major parliamentary portfolio is well known: I'm completely hostile to it, like, I think, just about everybody else in the trade union and labour movement.' Prescott's humiliation was completed by a tour of the press gallery by Peter Mandelson, Hilary Coffman from Kinnock's office, and Hattersley's adviser, David Hill, who gave the story the required spin: that Prescott had been forced to climb down without any concession from the leader. The purpose of the exercise was to stop any challenge either from him or anyone else. It left Prescott with an additional grievance and it did not work, because there were others beyond the reach of heavy-handed persuasion.

Late in January 1988, Tony Benn delivered a speech at a day school for Nottinghamshire miners which must rate as one of the most comprehensive attacks on a Labour leader ever delivered by a fellow Labour MP. Although Neil Kinnock was not named in it, it was aimed at him, directly and unmistakably, and showed the depth of the division which he had opened with old allies on the left.

Point one of Benn's ten-point indictment was the 'consistent failure' to support strikers like the miners and the printers sacked when Rupert Murdoch moved his newspaper operation to Wapping; two, the 'repudiation' of surcharged Liverpool and Lambeth councillors and others who wanted to put councils in conflict with the law; three, 'the mounting attack on socialist ideas and socialists', as instanced by expulsion of Militant's leaders; four, 'the abandonment or watering down of basic policies which have long been agreed at successive conferences'; five, the shift of influence away from the NEC, the trade unions and party conference.

Six complained of the 'almost total subordination of the NEC and party staff to the Leader's office, which now exercises its power in an increasingly authoritarian and intolerant manner, often showing contempt for those who express dissent, or even seek an open democratic debate about important issues'. Seven rubbished the 'Labour Listens' campaign for conveying 'indecisiveness and weakness'. Eight alleged that the party had effectively been taken over by 'pollsters and public relations people'. Nine was 'the growing suspicion that the real strategy that is being followed by the leadership may be to prepare the party, slowly, for a possible coalition with some merged Liberal–SDP grouping after the next election' and, finally, ten was 'the nagging fear that if this process is not soon checked, and reversed, the Labour Party might actually go into a terminal decline, or be so weakened as to be virtually unelectable'. These criticisms, claimed Benn, 'are by no means confined to the left, and are expressed widely throughout the party, leading to a great deal of disillusionment and demoralisation'.[63]

The next move was a personal *credo* which Benn submitted to the NEC in February as an early contribution to the forthcoming policy review.

It was voted down, but it served as a manifesto for Benn's leadership campaign. His policies included unilateral nuclear disarmament, a tax regime which would 'radically reduce' the gap between rich and poor, an implied commitment to absorb private hospitals and clinics into the NHS, the takeover of public schools and some private housing by local authorities, a ban on all blood sports and, centrally, 'the common ownership, under democratic control and management, of the commanding heights of the economy, the land and all the companies which dominate our industrial system'.[69]

Before this ambitious programme could even begin, Benn needed the backing of the Campaign Group, some of whom were reluctant to have him challenge Kinnock, because the only foreseeable outcome was heavy defeat which might weaken the left's bargaining position. About one-third of the Campaign group's membership opposed the exercise. There was also a shortage of volunteers to run for the deputy leadership alongside Benn. Ken Livingstone, who had recently been elected to the NEC and was serving on one of the economic committees conducting the policy review, declined. Audrey Wise, who was also approached, pleaded a prior commitment, having been elected national president of USDAW. Eventually, the left fielded Benn and Eric Heffer, both former government ministers, both over sixty, both losers in earlier contests.

It was only the second time since the war that there had been a challenge to an incumbent Labour leader. The previous one, twenty-eight years earlier, had resulted in short-term humiliation for the challenger, but was the making of him in the long term: he was Harold Wilson. The 1988 election also had a contestant who emerged bruised and apparently weakened, only to gain in the long term. A week after Benn and Heffer declared that they were going to force a contest, John Prescott announced he would challenge after all. The year 1988 had already been shaping up to be a bad one for Neil Kinnock and Roy Hattersley. Now they faced six months during which they had to hold the old 'dream ticket' together.

Britain was at the peak of an economic boom, with interest rates low, income tax cut and house prices soaring. The recklessness of the Chancellor, Nigel Lawson, would have to be paid for later; for the time being, it was doing the government nothing but good, as is shown in two MORI opinion polls taken a year apart:

	Conservatives	Labour	Lib Dems	SDP
November 1987	50%	38%	12%	
September 1988	50%	36%	8%	4%

As the people who wielded influence in the Labour Party read opinion polls such as these, week after week, they asked themselves whether all the loyalty they had paid to Kinnock and Hattersley had honestly been worth it. Opposition to Kinnock was, indeed, not confined to the left. The year began with an editorial in a newsletter called *Forward Labour*, a mouthpiece for the centre right edited by a GMBATU national officer, David Warburton. He complained, in words that Benn echoed a month later, that 'the distance between the leadership and the rest of the movement is, at best, rather sad, even surprising. At worst it is demoralising.' Almost at once, GMBATU's General Secretary, John Edmonds, put some distance between the union and Warburton, by shifting him to a less sensitive job. Even so, it was a bad beginning to a bad year.

With everything else going wrong, Kinnock's Commons performance opposite Margaret Thatcher at Prime Minister's Questions deteriorated from a peak which had never been outstanding. On 17 May, for instance, he tackled her on the question of interest rates, which Nigel Lawson had just cut for the third time since his expansionary budget. Having elicited from her that the move was intended to lower the value of the pound on world money markets, he rose again to ask, in wooden tones:

> I am, and I am sure everybody else is, interested to hear the Prime Minister draw attention to the three cuts in interest in the past two months. Two months ago I asked her whether she would intervene or use interest rates to bring down the pound and she said that intervention 'would lead to inflation' and interest rate action could not deal with the matter because it would not be in the 'interests of inflation' to do so.[70]

More than eighty words expended, no sign yet of a question, and the Labour leader seemed to think that the government wanted to act 'in the interests of inflation'. The slip, actually, was not his: he was accurately quoting Mrs Thatcher's own words, and making a serious point about the apparent difference in her policy of maintaining a strong pound, and that of Lawson, who was covertly keeping sterling in line with the

Deutschmark, but Kinnock sounded for all the world like someone who was reading out lines he did not understand. He was drowned in jeering and barracking, rescued by the Speaker, and then floored by Thatcher's icy reply that 'I don't think the Right Honourable Gentleman is entirely the master of his subject.'

Things grew worse as the Labour Party underwent one of its periodic convulsions over defence policy. Privately Neil Kinnock had decided that his last visit to the USA was a débâcle he never wanted to repeat, and that he could not therefore fight another general election on a policy of unilateral nuclear disarmament. The next logical step was to shove the policy through the review process, where it could be decommissioned and reshaped into something that was pro-disarmament but not unilateralist. Unfortunately, two of the four biggest trade unions affiliated to the party, the TGWU and NUPE, were committed to the CND position by their own annual delegate conferences. Together, they controlled 12 per cent of the total votes in a leadership election, and by June there was a very real possibility that their votes would go to John Prescott. The only solution was to confine defence policy to stage two of the review, which would begin in 1989, and in the meantime remember that careless words from Kinnock could cost Roy Hattersley the deputy leadership.

On 5 June, Kinnock gave an in-depth television interview, in which he was predictably questioned on the nuclear issue. He replied – so he claimed – 'very plainly':

> I don't think there is a need to insist that it is all go it alone . . . It doesn't have to be something for nothing. The fact is now it can be something for something . . . It is already clear that bilateral, reciprocal missile for missile reductions between any part of the West and the Soviet Union has been on for some time . . . So the idea that there is a something for nothing thrust that can be made is now redundant. There is something for something. I've put it very plainly.[71]

In case it was not plain enough for political journalists watching the programme, Patricia Hewitt and Peter Mandelson rang round to emphasize the significance of Kinnock's repeated use of the phrase 'something for nothing'. What was in Kinnock's mind was a prospect of a deal, first preferred by President Chernenko and since confirmed by Gorbachev, that if Britain rid itself of nuclear weapons, the USSR would voluntarily decommission a section of its nuclear arsenal equivalent in size to Britain's. According to the scathing calculation of Conservative politicians, this amounted to 3 per cent of the Soviet nuclear firepower. Nonetheless, it was 'something for something'.

Without referring to the defence issue directly, Kinnock hinted in a speech later in the week that a momentous change was about to be made to party policy, when he told a rally in County Durham:

> Policies change: principles are permanent – so permanent . . . that those who hold them deeply are not afraid to submit them to . . . the test of getting them into power and putting them into effect . . . It's the difference between having a dream to strive for and just being a dreamer.[72]

For one member of the Shadow Cabinet, it was altogether too much. Denzil Davies was one of the cleverest men in the Labour Party: as a bright Treasury Minister, he had been admitted to the Privy Council as its youngest member, at the age of thirty-nine. It was said that he had been one of the few Labour ministers who really understood the tax system. It was a fact that for several years in succession he had been the only person elected to the Shadow Cabinet without being on either the Manifesto or Tribune Group slates. He had handled the defence brief competently since the first year of Kinnock's leadership. But he was restless: in the 1987 Shadow Cabinet reshuffle, he had demanded the job of Shadow Foreign Secretary, had been offered three other jobs, all of which he turned down before being returned to his old post at defence. He was resentful at having to take orders from a Welshman who was younger, less experienced and academically a great deal less well-qualified. He was also going through a painful divorce and acquiring a reputation for unreliability. He had recently sued the BBC successfully after the comedian, Jasper Carrott, made a pointed joke about why Davies had missed his turn to sum up in a late night debate after spending part of the evening in the House of Lords bar.

At about 1.00 am on the night of 13/14 June, the Political Editor of the Press Association, Chris Moncrieff, was awoken at home by a telephone call from an emotional Denzil Davies, who announced: 'I am fed up with being humiliated. Kinnock never consults me on anything.' Moncrieff was so taken aback that he dropped his pen and, in trying to retrieve it, painfully banged his head. Nonetheless, he was able to take down what was clearly a resignation statement. As a precaution, he then rang Peter

Mandelson, the thought having crossed his mind that Davies either might not remember the conversation in the morning, or not mean it. However, Mandelson was left in no doubt that the Shadow Defence Minister was clear-headed and determined to persist with his act of political suicide.

Tony Benn had undertaken not to attack Kinnock personally, but the language in which he expressed himself was routinely insulting in its implications. He claimed, for example, that the 'entire Establishment' was backing Kinnock and Hattersley, not because they wanted a Labour government but because they wanted to ensure that 'it would be quite harmless if it did slip into office'.[73]

After the Davies incident, Kinnock went heavily into the attack, with Benn as his main, unnamed target. He accused his opponents of 'promising miracles . . . and believing that socialism will someday be able to call up cataclysm and bring the people fleeing to its side', and of taking 'the Jericho approach – the strategy by which labour Joshuas simply offer enough critique of the market system and enough promises of dramatic remedies with enough born-again passion, and the walls of scepticism and capitalism come crashing down together'. As to the attacks on him, they were 'Nothing personal – perish the thought – but the campaign for the Leadership has, sadly but foreseeably, to some extent become what George Orwell called the game of "fee, fi, fo, fum, I smell the blood of a right-wing deviationist".'

Referring to the nuclear issue, Kinnock complained that the 'deviation hunters' were on his back at a time 'when changing East–West relationships both validate our case and facilitate the new opportunities of getting rid of weapons systems and, by that process, getting a reduction in others' weapons systems'[74] – another seemingly unmistakable hint that he was in pursuit of 'something for something'. In a speech to a Fabian Society conference that same weekend, he said 'strategy' was up for review, while the 'objective' of Labour's disarmament policy would be unchanged. The question left unanswered was whether unilateral nuclear disarmament was a 'strategy' or an 'objective', but clearly one reading of the speech was that unilateralism was a strategy and world disarmament the objective. The leader's staff briefed journalists that this was his definitive position on the defence issue, until stage two of the policy review twelve months into the future.

Unfortunately, the new Kinnock position turned out to have a shelf-life of only three days. The following Monday, he had lunch with the Editor and senior staff of the *Independent*. The journalists came expecting an 'off-the-record' conversation and assumed they would have to use subtlety to steer it to the awkward topic of defence. Instead, Kinnock sprung two surprises before they had finished their soup. A telephone call from his office that morning specified that the conversation would be 'on the record', because Kinnock was annoyed by the way the newspaper had reported a previous lunchtime conversation with them, citing him as an anonymous source. The next, equally welcome, surprise was that Kinnock dived straight into a discussion of defence policy without waiting to be asked.

What followed bore little relation to the comments which had driven Denzil Davies to resign. All talk of bilateral relations and 'something for something' was gone. Instead, he condemned nuclear weapons as a waste of money, which would be better spent on conventional arms. 'In terms of our defence interests, it would be better for us not to be nuclear dependent.' A Labour government would decommission Trident without an enforceable guarantee from the Soviet side that they would reciprocate, he said, 'because the Soviets want it as least as much [as we do] . . . for very strong practical reasons'.[75]

In that case, what was the point of setting a hare running about 'something for something' disarmament in the first place, provoking an extraordinarily damning Shadow Cabinet resignation – the only one of Kinnock's entire leadership?

In retrospect, there is no doubt that what Kinnock wanted to do was to abandon unilaterism, as he in fact did a year later. Meanwhile, there were short-term considerations he was forced to take into account. Most alarmingly, there was the risk that the TWGU block vote, which alone was worth about 8 per cent of the electoral college, might go to John Prescott. There was a proletarian feel to the Prescott campaign, which was being managed by Dick Caborne, a former Sheffield steelworker, and Peter Snape, an ex-railwayman, which meant that it did not pick up some of the intellectual support which might have been available, but it was playing well with the powerful union delegations. In June, the TGWU executive overruled its own General Secretary, Ron Todd, who had publicly committed the union to backing Kinnock and Hattersley. That was probably on Kinnock's mind as he ate his own words at the *Independent* lunch.

Given the power of the big union leaders, the only way out of the nuclear dilemma was to harness one of them behind some kind of compromise resolution which would have a chance of slipping through the autumn conference undefeated. Consequently, the GMBATU General Secretary, John Edmonds, was in and out of the leader's office, finalizing the wording of a resolution which backed disarmament by unilateral, bilateral or multilateral means.

Late in June the *Independent* ran a story quoting the opinion of an unnamed trade union leader that the Labour leader was suffering a bad bout of depression. This set off front page stories in the *Sun* and the *Daily Mail* that the moody Labour leader was on the verge of quitting. Mood swings were certainly one of Kinnock's weaknesses, and he later looked back on this time as the worst period of his leadership.

In the circumstances, Neil and Glenys Kinnock must have been looking forward to their long-planned four-day trip in mid-July to the front line states in southern Africa as a relief from the grinding frustration of domestic politics. Instead, the occasion went into Westminster folklore as another occasion when Kinnock tried to play the world statesman, with disastrous effect. Long afterwards, saying the word 'Zimbabwe' in the presence of a certain type of Tory MP had the same sort of effect as saying 'bottom' in a nursery. On 18 July, the Speaker of the House of Commons had to rebuke them for reducing the proceedings of parliament to a farce with the string of Zimbabwe jokes which animated Questions to the Secretary of State for Wales. A sample, from Tony Marlow MP: 'If a patient were to present himself to the health service in Wales with steam coming out of his ears, can you assure us that there are facilities for dealing with this complaint?' All this sprang from an incident on Sunday night, when the plane which was taking the Kinnocks and accompanying journalists from Mozambique to Zimbabwe was diverted and kept waiting for an hour on a military base. Journalists alleviated the tedium by having a singsong, with Neil Kinnock unwisely joining in, before the unnecessary delay got the better of his temper, and he had an angry exchange with a Zimbabwean lance corporal, telling him he was 'for the bloody high jump'. The next day, he received a formal apology from Zimbabwe's President Mugabe; but the image of a future Prime Minister singing songs in a military hut before rowing with a semi-educated soldier was exactly what part of the popular press needed to justify the expense of sending a correspondent on the trip. The ridiculing of the Kinnocks carried on for days. It was obviously still on Neil Kinnock's mind in October, when his speech to the annual conference ended with a long and unscripted passage about what he had seen in Africa.

In his absence, Roy Hattersley handled Prime Minister's Questions in the Commons. The trouble with Hattersley – it was often said at the time – was that he had lost the motivation to make full use of his considerable gifts. However, the threat of losing his position to John Prescott had temporarily cured his *ennui*. He had not worked so hard for years as he did during that summer, and his performances at the Despatch Box were first-class. He made such a fool of Margaret Thatcher that he was able to throw back her own jibe, accusing her of not being the mistress of her own subject. Unfortunately, his success only emphasized the shakiness of Kinnock's performance. The newspaper commentator Edward Pearce, who had originally been one of Kinnock's most avid fans, turned on him: 'You cannot fail in the Commons and succeed in politics . . . If Neil Kinnock is deemed to be failing by his parliamentary colleagues, then he is failing. And indeed that is the general verdict . . . the leader is simply not up to it.' He forecast that the leader would soon 'come to understand the artificiality of his position', and resign. This diatribe might have been unremarkable, except that it was published as the cover story in the Labour-supporting *New Statesman & Society*.[76] At the end of July, Radio Four listeners were invited to phone in with their opinions on the question of the week: whether the Labour Party could hope to win a general election with Neil Kinnock as its leader. To ensure balance, the programme's compere, Nick Ross, divided the calls equally between those who defended Kinnock and those who thought he was useless. This was generous because by now, the proportion of voters telling the opinion polls that they thought Kinnock was doing a good job had fallen below 30 per cent.

In the end, the TGWU voted for Hattersley rather than Prescott, ensuring that the incumbent deputy leader sailed comfortably home, while Kinnock himself collected 88.63 per cent of the vote against Tony Benn (slightly less than the margin of victory which John Smith achieved over

Bryan Gould four years later). That was as much loyalty as could be wrung out of Ron Todd that week. On Tuesday evening, after Kinnock had given what was meant to be a triumphal leader's address to conference, the TGWU leader upstaged him with a speech to a Tribune rally which included a categorical promise that his union would never retreat from its policy of unilateral disarmament, and some fairly direct comments about Kinnock's new Labour Party:

> Nye Bevan is spinning in his grave as the last vestige of controversy, of political opinion, of socialist content, is ground out of the election literature, in favour of glossy pink roses, a sharp suit, and a winning smile.[77]

Later in the week, the resolution so carefully crafted with help from John Edmonds was defeated, with the TGWU voting against it. That provoked another day of damaging headlines, but those who knew the Labour Party well were more impressed by the narrowness of the defeat than the result itself. It fell by 3.277 million to 2.942 million, a majority of just 335,000. Three small unions with a combined vote of 203,000 had switched at the last moment, including the Post Office engineers, who had had to rush six of their fifteen delegates back to London for urgent pay talks. Those who read the runes could see that the Labour Party's policy of unilateral nuclear disarmament had only a year to run. It was, in fact, laid to rest at the Brighton conference in 1989.

The summer would have been so much simpler if only Benn and Heffer could have been stopped from putting up their challenge in the first place. At the time, the Campaign Group had around thirty-six members, although forty-one MPs eventually voted either for Benn or Heffer, or both – the most eccentric vote being that of the Scottish MP Dick Douglas, who voted Benn for leader with Hattersley as his deputy, before defecting to the SNP. If only there had been a threshold somewhere higher than forty-one, neither would have been able to stand and Prescott would then presumably not have gone ahead with his challenge either. Perhaps even the disaster of Denzil Davies' resignation could have been avoided.

However, with nothing to lose, some of Benn's supporters were seriously urging him to run again the next year, and presumably each year after that, to keep socialism on the party agenda. Neil Kinnock himself was reluctant to introduce a rule change whose only immediate effect could be to fortify his own position, but his supporter, John Evans, did not hesitate. The rule was rewritten so that any challenger must have his or her nomination signed by at least 20 per cent of the parliamentary Labour party, which at that time meant forty-six MPs, just enough to stop Tony Benn from doing it again.

CLAUSE FOUR

The Labour Party is a democratic socialist party. It believes that by the strength of our common endeavour we achieve more than we achieve alone, so as to create for each of us the means to realise our true potential and for all of us a community in which power, wealth and opportunity are in the hands of the many not the few; where the rights we enjoy reflect the duties we owe and where we live together freely, in a spirit of solidarity, tolerance and respect.

(Labour Party Constitution, Clause IV)

In January 1989, after the Govan by-election had reduced Neil Kinnock to a state of gloom even worse than the previous June's, the party's fortunes suddenly turned. It began with the government's reforms to the health service, which many feared was a prelude to nationalization, and continued with the privatization of water, the poll tax, and the Conservative Party's internal differences over Europe, until the fall of Margaret Thatcher in November 1990.

In this quiescent period, Neil Kinnock allowed his CND membership to lapse, the Labour Party became more European than the Conservatives, and fully committed to British membership of the European Monetary System, and one day the party's seventy-year-old commitment to socialism, in its classical sense of 'the common ownership and control of the means of production' passed away in its sleep. Exactly when is a moot point. The policy document agreed by the 1989 party conference, *Meet the Challenge, Make the Change*, contained a strain of socialism just visible to the naked eye, in that it committed a Labour government to controlling 51 per cent of British Telecom and taking back into public ownership the water companies and other privatized utilities, subject to 'the situation we inherit in each case and on the constraints of finance and legislative time'.[78] The following year's main policy document *Looking to the Future* had a more decorative front cover, and marginally less in the way of socialist content, with only three industries – telecommunications, water and the national grid – heading back to the public sector. In August 1991, when the government announced the sale of another tranche of British Telecom shares, Labour dropped its commitment to renationalize the company. One commentator, Peter Kellner, heralded that as the moment when 'British state socialism died'.[79]

By then, it was certainly gone from Neil Kinnock's breast. The man who, when running for the party leadership eight years earlier, said that 'it is inconceivable that we could transform this society without a major extension of public ownership and control' now asserted that the 'huge majority of the Labour party' never believed in wholesale nationalization at all, 'but they were the tunes of glory that were coming out. Well, we've stopped that nonsense.'[80]

Actually, there was one symbolic act to be completed before a Leader could truly say that he had 'stopped that nonsense', which was to rewrite Clause Four of the 1918 party constitution, which referred to the common ownership of the means of production. That was Tony Blair's boldest and riskiest act of party management. Nevertheless, Blair is not the man who 'ditched socialism', as is sometimes suggested. He made public what had become an accomplished fact under Neil Kinnock.

The 'democratic socialist' moniker which appears at the front of Tony Blair's version of Clause Four is also an inheritance from Neil Kinnock. In a lecture Kinnock delivered in June 1983, as a candidate for the party leadership, he gave the name 'democratic socialism' to his evolving set of beliefs, where previously he might have thought the adjective unnecessary or even tautological. He suggested, in a passage already quoted, that 'democratic socialism' had been fighting a war on two fronts: against social democracy and against an undemocratic 'hard left', but even in 1983, Kinnock was maintaining that the battle with the social democrats was over, because they were now outside the party. By implication, within the party the leader had no enemies to the right.

The term 'democratic socialism' was routinely used by others in the Kinnock circle, like Gordon Brown and Tom Sawyer. In 1988, Kinnock set out to define what it meant, in a document entitled *Democratic Aims and Values*, which he co-wrote with Roy Hattersley. It betrays Hattersley's influence from the opening sentence onwards, which equates democratic socialism with a genuinely free society, in which discrimination on the grounds of class, sex, age, race, colour or creed have been eliminated. It includes a foreword attributed only to Kinnock:

> We are democratic socialists. We want a state where the collective contribution of the community is used for the advance of individual freedom. Not just freedom in name, but freedom that can be exercised in practice . . . Just as it is the duty, the privilege, of the strong to help the weak, so it is the duty of the free to help those across this planet who are oppressed . . . freedom can have no boundaries.[81]

The Blair version is rather more socially conservative. Instead of generally being free, which might be thought to include the freedom to be bone idle, people in Blair's vision of the future are to have 'the means to realize their potential', and their 'rights' will be offset against 'duties', but apart from that important distinction, the two visions of 'democratic socialism' are fundamentally the same.

Another distinction between the two leaders is that Kinnock continued to look upon the SDP's action in setting up a rival party as a betrayal, however much he closed the distance between his beliefs and theirs. It was left to Blair to create an atmosphere in which former SDP members were openly welcomed back to the bosom of their former party and in some cases to positions of responsibility. According to Mandelson and Liddle, 'Blair does not carry any animus towards those who defected to the SDP . . . He felt as little sympathy with the old right in the party, with their reliance on unattractive local-machine politics and deal-making and fixing votes with trade unions, as he did with the left.'[82]

It was also left to Blair himself to make the bald statement to a group of 600 business leaders in Birmingham that 'in other European countries the Labour Party would be called the Social Democratic Party, in some countries the Democratic Socialist Party – the values are the same'.[83] In the contest with the Bennite left and the old right, the social democrats had won.

CHAPTER TWO

THE LONG TRUDGE OF TED GRANT

Left-wing politics is strewn with the names of politicians who said one thing in their youth and another in middle age. Not Ted Grant, who sprang into British politics like Mars, fully armed with the thoughts of Leon Trotsky. He remained for nearly seven decades without equivocating or retreating from the certainties he had adopted in his adolescence. If, as Aldous Huxley claimed, 'consistency is contrary to nature', then there was something unnatural about Ted Grant, but for about twenty years he was the main intellectual inspiration of the official youth wing of the Labour Party.

It is not known that he was ever born Ted Grant at all. He came from Germiston, near Johannesburg, in South Africa,[1] and probably changed his name when he left his native country in his late teens. A paper presented to the War Cabinet in April 1944 by the Home Secretary, Herbert Morrison, described him as 'aged thirty' which would put his year of birth as 1913 or 1914. No other details of his family background are available, but it seems to have been bleak. There is no evidence that he ever formed an emotional attachment at any time in his long life. Given the adulation he was capable of inspiring in the young, he could have abused their trust, in the manner of his old comrade and rival, Gerry Healy, whose obituary by Brian Behan observed that 'seventy-six women in all were asked to embrace the erect forces of Healyite labour,'[2] but Ted Grant had no vices, no visible weaknesses at all, except jelly-babies, gobstoppers and low-grade cowboy films. At the end of his working day, he retired alone to a small flat to listen to Bach and Beethoven. He began his morning by taking exercise. Roger Protz, who was briefly a comrade of Ted Grant's in the 1960s, said: 'Unlike

Gerry Healy, he had absolutely no charisma. Grant looked like a tramp, always wore a dirty raincoat from which old copies of the *FT* bulged, and looked as though he slept under a hedge.'[3]

At the age of eleven, this lonely boy came under the influence of Ralph Lee, an activist in the recently formed South African Communist Party, who introduced him to the works of Bernard Shaw, H.G. Wells, Maxim Gorky, Jack London, and then gradually on to the hard stuff, Marx, Engels and Lenin. Too young to join the Communist Party, Grant was already a Marxist when, in 1928 or 1929, he encountered an even more illicit and exhilarating stimulant which had recently begun circulating in Johannesburg: copies of an American Trotskyite newspaper, *The Militant*. Here he and Lee together first encountered Trotsky's critique of the Stalinist bureaucracy, which was already banned in its country of origin and virtually unobtainable in most parts of the world. The boy could only have just reached the age of puberty when he sampled it. It came to him not as an interesting set of ideas to be compared with other thoughts from other thinkers, but as a body of received truth, a set of scientific principles which could be interpreted and translated correctly or incorrectly into a modern setting but could never be dated or disproved. Becoming one of the first Trotskyites on the African continent would reinforce his isolation from respectable white society, and exclude him even from the limited companionship of the little Communist Party, yet the best part of his adult life was to be spent exhorting adolescents to take up the same ideas through a newspaper of the same name, so we can assume the experience was seminal.

In the early 1930s, Ralph Lee was expelled from the South African CP, and became a leading figure in the tiny Workers' International League, taking his teenage protégé with him. They were involved in a strike by black laundry workers, but on reflection, they had to accept that South Africa's black proletariat was too small to be the spearhead of a revolution. Europe beckoned, with its millions of factory workers lacking only strong and principled leaders to lead the world revolution. The WIL had made contact with a little Trotskyite group in Great Britain, which had sent copies of its newspaper, *The Red Flag*. Half a dozen of the South African comrades decided to transfer operations to Britain. Lee's young protégé arrived in London in 1933 or 1934, using the name Ted Grant, in the company of a fellow South African who changed his name on arrival to Sid Frost. They had travelled by boat, stopping off for a week in Paris to meet Trotsky's son, Leon Sedov. Grant never met the Old Man himself.

Trotsky was at this time urging his British followers to join the Independent Labour Party which had disaffiliated from the Labour Party in 1932, though British Trotskyites were increasingly taking the view that there was more point in being in the Labour Party itself. In 1936, Trotsky relented. Grant dutifully joined the ILP on arrival and was still a member in March 1935. Soon afterwards, he transferred to the Labour League of Youth. In 1938, there had been an internal rift among the Trotskyites working inside the Labour Party, which may have been connected with Ralph Lee's recent arrival from South Africa. A group of nineteen, including all the South Africans, plus Gerry Healy and a Scottish seaman named Jock Haston, broke off to form the WIL. The charismatic and extroverted Jock Haston was the WIL's main organizer.

The WIL may have been tiny, but its ambitions were not small and it was not afraid to stand alone. At that time, the British Communist Party was looking for a Popular Front with the Labour Party and ILP. One of the WIL's first acts was to republish Trotsky's polemic on the Spanish Civil War, with an introduction by Ralph Lee and Ted Grant, explaining why this policy was, in effect, a betrayal. Here, in an essay published in 1938, we find the themes that Grant would still be hammering out half a century later. An economic crisis was imminent, as indeed it would be imminent for the next thirty-five years, until Grant finally convinced himself that it had begun. It would be worse than the depression of the early 1930s, and would put an end to the comparative passivity of the British workers, creating an historic opening in which it would be possible for the workers to seize power, provided they were led with the same courage and insight shown by the Bolsheviks in 1917. There was no hope of such leadership coming from the communist party if it was busy snuggling up to the Liberals, the Labour Party and all manner of other organizations which would take fright when the crisis came. Consequently, 'the working class has need, above all, of a party, once more a party, again a party'.[4]

At this point, the prospects were not promising for the little WIL. It not only had no following among the workers, it was not even recognized by the Fourth International which Trotsky had launched in France in September 1938. They also had to cope with the bitter hostility of the communists, who almost anywhere else in Europe would have set about killing them. A frisson of scandal ran through their small community when Ralph Lee's South African wife, Millie, deserted him to move in with Jock Haston. Lee returned to South Africa alone in 1940. He was expendable, Millie was not; most of the WIL's paltry funds came from her mother, who ran a hat business in South Africa. This fact was duly recorded at Scotland Yard, who had an informer within the WIL Central Committee, whose identity has never been revealed.

Even so, the tiny group picked up scattered recruits. When Ted Grant made his first recorded visit to Liverpool in 1938, he came upon a network group of thirty-five to forty Trotskyites grouped around Liverpool Trades Council who had organized their own float for the May Day march, consisting of a huge plywood tank on a horse-drawn wagon, with the slogan: 'Not a man, not a gun for imperialist war'.[5] He persuaded one of them, an eighteen-year-old named Jimmy Deane, to join the WIL and organize a Liverpool branch. Deane is now the acknowledged founder of the Liverpool Militants.

The advantage the Trotskyites enjoyed after the Soviet Union's entry into the war was that they alone, apart from the pacifists, were not committed to the war effort. Where there was industrial unrest, they backed the strikers against the government, against the management, the official union leadership, the Labour Party and the Communist Party, believing that the class war was not to be suspended on account of a military contest between capitalist states. It was a strike by shipyard apprentices in the Tyneside which suddenly lifted the tiny WIL out of obscurity and into the unwelcome attention of the authorities. The strike itself was neither political nor anti-war. Some of the apprentices actually wanted to go to the front. What made them down tools was the fear that they were about to be taken out of the factories and sent as 'Bevin boys' down the mines. Roy Hadwin, who was secretary of the Junior Workers' Committee during the strike, said: 'All this talk about Trotskyites – I never saw them. It's quite clear in my mind.'[6] However, the strike spread sufficient alarm for the Home Secretary, Herbert Morrison, to report to the Cabinet and for four leaders of the WIL, Jock Haston, Ann Keen, Heaton Lee and Roy Tearse to be arrested and charged with illegally abetting a strike. The three men were jailed, but were subsequently released on appeal. Suddenly, the little group was big news. Journalists crowded into their London headquarters at 265 Harrow Road, where Millie Lee gave an impromptu press conference beneath a large portrait of Trotsky. In Newcastle, the local Conservative-supporting newspaper, *The Journal*, issued a thunderous denunciation: 'They are "Trotskyites" – an ill-conditioned clique with an ideological spite against Stalin, and therefore against the Russian renascence, and in favour of chaos.'[7]

This success was all the more unexpected because, until 1939, there were no active Trotskyites on Tyneside. The first was an optician named George Brown, who left the Communist Party on the day the Soviet Red Army entered Poland, and organized the first WIL branch in the region. He did not stay long. He joined the army in 1941, returned with more mainstream opinions, and disapproved when his daughter, Audrey, started going to political rallies on Newcastle Town Moor, and listening to rabble rousers repeating the views her father once held. Audrey Brown is better known under her married name, Audrey Wise, the Labour MP for Preston.

In his place, the WIL sent in an organizer named Bob Shaw, with instructions to concentrate on recruiting members of the local ILP, many of whom sympathized with the striking apprentices. This was a change of tack from before the mid-1930s, when Trotskyites abandoned the ILP for the Labour Party but, as Ted Grant had explained in a long article written in 1942 optimistically entitled *Preparing for Power*, virtually all political activity had been suspended within the Labour Party because of the war, making it 'almost automatic' that radicalized workers would gravitate towards the ILP. Here we see the first written evidence of the 'entryist' tactic which Grant doggedly pursued for the rest of his life, as he urged that a 'great part' of the WIL's political activity must be devoted to establishing itself inside the ILP.[8]

Shaw accordingly struck up a close link with the ILP's energetic young full-time organizer on Tyneside, T. Dan Smith. When Jock Haston visited Newcastle in 1942, he took Smith under his wing and 'taught him everything he knew about organizing', and for a time what was effectively a WIL cell made a passable job of taking over the Tyneside ILP from within. The tactic was blown by a visit from Ted Grant, in 1943, who was by now convinced that:

> We are in a pre-revolutionary situation. With a correct policy we can gain a good springboard for a great leap in influence in the coming period . . . the WIL has made substantial if modest gains . . . Yes, comrades, we definitely assert that the workers are *beginning* to challenge the right of capitalism to continue as the system of this country.[9]

In these exciting circumstances, time was too short to waste on building bridges with members of the ILP. Grant stayed at the home of Ken Skethaway, an ILP member, and when members of the Newcastle East ILP assembled there for a meeting, with T. Dan Smith in the chair, Grant informed them that they belonged to a fake, reformist organization, that its leader, John Maxton, was 'slinking back to the Labour Party', and that its sister party, the Partido Obrero de Unificacion Marxista (POUM), had betrayed the revolution in Spain. One member of his audience, Barney Markson, was so incensed that he demanded that no more Trotskyites should be invited into the region as guest speakers. Markson was then expelled from the ILP as a troublemaker. He appealed to the leadership in London, who sent a team headed by a future Labour MP, Bob Edwards, to investigate. The commission reinstated Markson.[10] A follow-up investigation resulted in a group of Trotskyites, including Dan Smith and Ken Skethaway, being expelled from the ILP at its 1945 conference.

Having precipitated this, Grant was unfortunately unable to be of any assistance during the strike itself. He missed all the excitement, according to a contemporary report in *The Journal*, because he was away on a walking holiday in Leicestershire. The story perfectly illustrates the problems of entryism. If the entryist is to achieve his mission, he must persuade members of the host party that their leaders are contemptible and their policies lukewarm; but by standing up and saying so, the entryist exposes himself and his supporters to possible reprisals.

Dan Smith, who liked Haston but never warmed to Ted Grant, broke with them in 1947, joined the Labour Party, and in the 1960s became a legendary figure as Newcastle's charismatic and corrupt city boss. His reputation was revived posthumously in 1996, when he appeared thinly disguised as a fictional character in the television drama, *Our Friends in the North*. Ken Skethaway, who is reputed to have slept with a portrait of Lenin above his bed, was an important figure on Newcastle city council when Smith was its leader, but was never involved in corruption. Unlike

Smith, he stayed with Ted Grant and was the only known Militant on Tyne and Wear county council at the time of its abolition in 1986. By then, he was so well-known and well-liked in Newcastle Labour Party that every attempt to take action against him for his adherence to a banned organization floundered.

In 1944, the WIL merged with a rival Trotskyite group the Revolutionary Socialist League (RSL), which had begun as the larger of the two organizations, and was the one which Trotsky himself had recognized as the British section of the Fourth International. During the early part of the war, polemics flew between them in the traditional Trotskyite manner. The issue was whether young working-class males should avoid the draft. Unlike the pacifists, WIL members neither encouraged others to evade the draft nor refused to go into uniform themselves, although a core managed to avoid military service by one means or another. One young recruit, Frank Ward, was discharged from the RAF early in the war for his political activity. Ted Grant was drafted into the Pioneer Corps in 1940, but had the 'good fortune' to break his skull in an accident and be invalided out for the rest of the war. Thus passed the one occasion when he might have been torn from the Trotskyite ghetto in which he spent his entire adult life, and he was left free to edit the WIL newspaper *Socialist Appeal,* and trade insults with the RSL. He accused them of interpreting Lenin's slogan 'revolutionary defeatism' so literally that they were in effect siding with the Third Reich. The RSL accused the WIL of being covert 'defencists'. The apprentices appeared to respond better to the Grant line. The fact that it commanded a modest working class following enabled the WIL to pull off what amounted to a reverse takeover, with Jock Haston emerging as General Secretary of the newly-formed Revolutionary Communist Party and Ted Grant as editor of its main journal.

For the only time in the century, all Britain's Trotskyites were united in one organization, sufficiently large to be the subject of a report to the Cabinet, and for the government seriously to consider banning it. Even then, there was an evident disagreement on tactics. While Haston and Grant had pulled their supporters out of the ILP, there was still a minority, led by Gerry Healy, doggedly holding on to their Labour Party cards waiting for normal political activity to resume. That, though, was a small matter. The big question was whether war would be followed by revolution.

On that, they were all so convinced that despite the risk of arrest, they began collecting all the weapons they could find to create a small arsenal at their Harrow Road headquarters. On VE day, most of the RCP membership was in Neath, where Jock Haston was standing in a parliamentary by-election. Under a wartime agreement, none of the main parties stood against one another during the war, thus opening out the possibility of fringe candidates scoring impressive votes or even winning seats. The RCP had opportunistically decided to take advantage of what proved to be the last by-election before the 1945 general election. As Germany surrendered, the supposed vanguard of the impending revolution were traipsing from door to door giving out leaflets. One survivor recalled: 'Every house had the radio on as Churchill was speaking, so we heard his speech in snatches as we went from one house to another. Almost every family was getting out their best tablecloth. But we were unaffected. We lived in our own, closed world.'[11] Despite the absence of a Liberal or Conservative candidate, Haston collected only 1,781 votes and lost his deposit.

Always there was the search for new recruits. Soon after the war, Grant visited Hertford and sought out a young building worker who was chairman of the Hertfordshire County Communist Party Committee, because his published writings had suggested that he might be open to Trotskyite ideas. The startled communist was inclined to turn him away, but invited him into the front room, accepted some papers and pamphlets, but did not join. He was Eric Heffer.[12] On another occasion, a similar event caused Grant to be out late in the streets of Birmingham. The police arrested him for being unable to give a satisfactory reason of why he was there. Fortunately there was a Trotskyite hairdresser named Percy Downing who was able to come and vouch for him. (For some reason, there was more than one hairdresser in the movement, and the reasons Trotskyites had such awful haircuts, allegedly, was that when the comrade hairdresser was drunk he would cut everyone's hair for free.)[13]

Gradually, over several months, it dawned on the little band that the economy was refusing to follow the course charted out in Grant's scientific forecasts. In 1946, he acknowledged the start of an unforeseen post-war boom as industrial capacity which had been destroyed or damaged by the war was brought back into production, but he was in no doubt that it would be the prelude to a new crisis:

Events may speed up or slow down the processes but what is certain is the height-ening of social tension and class hatreds. *The period of triumphant reaction has drawn to a close, a new revolutionary epoch opens up in Britain. With many ebbs and flows, with a greater or lesser speed, the revolution is beginning.* The Labour govern-ment is a Kerensky government . . . the revolution will probably assume a long, drawn-out character but it provides the background against which the mass revo-lutionary party will be built.[14]

Within Trotskyite circles, these sentiments marked him out as a pessimist. Gerry Healy and others either disputed that there was a boom at all, or that its character would be 'drawn out'. All agreed on the urgency of creating a mass revolutionary party, in theory. In practice, they tore the little RCP apart with doctrinaire feuds which divided British Trotskyites for the rest of the century: behaviour which defies rational explanation.

By 1947, the party was so short of money that one member, who was recruited to the RCP on Tyneside that year at the age of seventeen, recalled setting out to leaflet a Wallsend council estate at a time when no new leaflets were available, so they had to make do with a batch dating from before the war, disputing the evidence from the Moscow show trials. As the group leader stood at the end of the terraced street with a loudhailer, the party members knocked on doors, and handed over the news that 'Trotsky is Innocent'. One housewife asked: 'Where is he, like – in Durham jail?'[15]

In 1950, the RCP disbanded and its members joined the Labour Party. Some, like Jock and Millie Haston and T. Dan Smith, had genuinely given up on revolutionary politics. One ex-RCP member, Syd Bidwell, went on to be Labour MP for Southall in 1966–92. Frank Ward was later Information Officer at the Labour Party's Walworth Road headquarters. His widow Ann journeyed from girlhood Trotskyism, through a period as part of the right-wing Labour leadership of Southwark Council, to membership of the mid-1990s feminist pressure group, Emily's List. For Haston, there was an important practical step to be taken as he renounced revolutionary politics for ever. He decided to hand in the guns still stored at 265 Harrow Road. As a precaution, he contacted Scotland Yard to forewarn them that the guns would arrive at Paddington police station. Unfortunately, there were two police stations in Paddington and Scotland Yard notified the wrong one. At the right one, the desk sergeant was startled by the arrival of an excitable Scot who had brought along a pile of weapons big enough to fill two taxis.

For most of the rest of his life, Haston worked as a lecturer at trade union colleges. When Frank Chapple and his allies ousted the communists from control of the electricians' union, the EEPTU, which they then steered over to the extreme right of the trade union movement, they needed someone to run their college at Esher who could be trusted not to fall under the influence of the communists. In that respect, no one was more trustworthy than a reformed Trotskyite. In the late 1960s, young electricians who had started reading *Socialist Worker* for the first time were a bit startled on arriving on courses in Esher, eager to lecture their elders on revolutionary Marxism, to discover that the middle-aged tutor could recite Trotsky's works backwards and knew exactly who was who inside the ultra-left.

In 1972, Haston fell out with the EEPTU over Chapple's refusal to open up all senior union posts to election rather than appointment, and switched to the GMB; but according to the EEPTU's official historian: 'just before he died; he attended a celebration at Esher . . . where he held a cheerful conversation with Frank Chapple and told the current national officer for education that he wished he'd never left.'[17] His extraordinary life came to a quick and tragic end when, characteristically, he stood up to speak at a meeting and struck his head against a plank from which a nail was protruding.

The decision to disband the RCP was a personal sacrifice for Ted Grant because he lost the room above the party's headquarters, which he had called home, and had to move into a caravan in Dalston. All the same, he approved of the disbanding, but not because he was renouncing Trotskyism. He reverted now to his old belief that the way forward was to infiltrate a larger workers' party. The ILP, though, had failed to expand in the manner in which he had predicted, leaving him and others of like mind with no choice but to join Gerry Healy's group in the Labour Party. Healy, however, was already displaying paranoid determination to keep control, and set about expelling those who threatened his supremacy. The remnants of the RCP split into three. The largest, led by Healy, was detected and proscribed by the Labour Party and became the Workers' Revolutionary Party, which disintegrated when Healy's sexual excesses were exposed in 1985. Another fragment, led by Tony Cliff, became the International Socialists and later the Socialist Workers Party. The third, which remained in the Labour Party partly because it was too small to be detected, was led by Ted Grant.

Grant stayed on in London, bringing out a magazine called *The Socialist International*. In 1955, due to a quarrel between Healy and the Fourth International, Grant and his group were able to become recognized as the British section. They took the name Revolutionary Socialist League, with Jimmy Deane as the first General Secretary. In 1957, the RSL launched a new newspaper, called *Socialist Fight*, which was written, typed, proofread, retyped and sometimes even duplicated by Ted Grant. Throughout this bleak decade, when he was short of money, friends and a permanent address, he never allowed himself to doubt that a potentially terminal crisis in capitalism was imminent. In 1960, at around the time when the Prime Minister felt able to tell the nation that 'you never had it so good', Ted Grant prophesied:

> Whatever the exact date, it is absolutely certain that the unprecedented post-war boom must be followed by a period of catastrophic downswing, which cannot but have a profound effect on the political thinking of the enormously strengthened ranks of the Labour movement.[18]

The only part of the world where the RSL had a following capable of influencing even a small corner of the Labour Party was in the Liverpool Walton constituency, where the Deane family – Jimmy, his mother and two brothers – were based. Walton stood out as a 'fortress of the left' in a city where the moribund party organization was dominated in Tammany style by Bessie and Jack Braddock. Hitherto, all the people who had been important in Grant's political life had either drifted away or would prove to be ineffectual. In Liverpool in the 1950s, he was for the first time able to draw recruits who would stay for decades and would be capable of operating effectively as the organization became large enough to attract national attention.

In 1952, Liverpool Walton had the youngest constituency Labour Party Secretary in the country, in sixteen-year-old Pat Wall, who was also running the local youth magazine *Rally*. When Wall was summoned before the NEC thirty-four years later, he admitted to having been active in Militant up until it was proscribed in 1982, a full thirty years' membership. Although the NEC accepted his story that he had severed his link then, allowing him to be elected Labour MP for Bradford North in 1987, the breach appears to have been more tactical than political.

After Wall was called up, the energetic Laura Kirton took over as CLP Secretary and, in 1954, Grant was almost adopted as their parliamentary candidate. But the vote was tied and the imminence of a general election enabled the regional office to impose a candidate of its choice. Grant's supporters accepted this setback without complaining, and their influence in Walton continued to grow. New recruits to the Walton youth section included Keith Dickenson in 1957, Terry Harrison in 1958, Peter Taaffe in 1960 and Tony Mulhearn in 1963. Harrison, a boilermaker by trade, was secretary of the Apprentices' Committee on Merseyside during the 1960 strike by 100,000 young engineers. The contest to be Walton's candidate in the 1959 general election was between Woodrow Wyatt and an RSL supporter named George McCartney. McCartney easily won the selection, but the Tories held the seat until 1964, when it was won by Eric Heffer.

The Militant – for Youth and Labour was launched as a weekly newspaper in 1964, copying the name of the American Trotskyite publication which had first inspired Ted Grant (although he would have preferred the name *Forward*), with Taaffe as Editor and Ted Grant as Political Editor. At the age of fifty, with three decades of political activism behind him, Grant had finally embarked on the project which would make his reputation. He appears to have gone into it uneasily, fearing that *Militant* would be like so many other left-wing publications: launched in a burst of amateur enthusiasm, only to hit financial and production difficulties just as the supply of volunteer labour dried up.

However, in Peter Taaffe, Grant had found his most valuable political partner since Jock Haston's apostasy. One of six children of a sheet-metal worker from Birkenhead, Taaffe was a capable organizer whose experience in Liverpool had taught him that the way into the Labour Party was through its youth organization. He was sent south to edit *Militant*, with a promise of a £10 weekly wage and somewhere to stay. Like the crisis of capitalism, these benefits did not materialize when expected. He was compelled to sleep on the floor of a flat in Balham, but was evicted after a small split in the tiny RSL, and then had to live illicitly in the office which *Militant* was renting over a bookshop run by the ILP, who would have evicted him if they had caught him there.[19]

Despite this disjuncture between theory and practice, *Militant* had also been launched at a fortuitous moment. The election of the Labour government had raised the political awareness of working-class youth, raising hopes which it was unable to fulfil, providing a large pool of radicalized and disillusioned adolescents from whom Militant could find recruits. At the same time, the political climate inside the Labour Party had changed. A reaction had set in against the proscriptions and expulsions of the Gaitskell years. By adopting the cover name of the Militant Tendency, and claiming to be no more than informal groupings of the like-minded, inspired by the ideas expressed in their newspaper, the RSL was able to expand and operate unhindered for the whole of the 1970s. By 1969, Grant was able to give up his night job as a telephone operator to join Taaffe and Keith Dickenson as a full-time employee of Militant, with his own office at its Hackney headquarters.

One of Militant's first successes outside its Liverpool redoubt was in Brighton, where two students at Sussex University, Alan Woods and Roger Silverman, set themselves up as *Militant* sellers as early as 1964. The University remained a strong base for Militant, and it was because of that that a Militant candidate was adopted to run for Brighton Kemptown in 1983. Clare Doyle, the only woman among Militant's top leadership in the 1980s, and Lynn Walsh, who became assistant editor of *Militant*, were both from Sussex University. Roger Silverman and his brother, Julian, the sons of the well-to-do Labour MP, Sydney Silverman, brought a substantial amount of money into the organization after their father's death in 1968. Alan Woods rose to be Roger Silverman's deputy in Militant's international division and was one of the few who stood by Ted Grant when the final rift came in 1992. He came from Swansea, where Grant and Taaffe paid a visit in 1968, laying the basis for what would be another important recruiting centre. In October 1980, for example, Ken Smith, who went on to be Militant's press spokesman, chaired a meeting in the college refectory, at which Rob Sewell, full-time Militant organizer and half-brother of Andy Woods, debated with a member of the NEC before an audience of 150 students. The NEC member was Neil Kinnock.

In London, the Militant Tendency began to take hold in some of the solid Labour seats in the economically depressed dockland areas on the eastern side of the capital. Party organization was rudimentary, partly because local party bosses behaved as the Braddocks had in Liverpool, keeping membership low to minimize the risk that they could be challenged within their own power bases. Because Militant's most active members were young and not yet settled, they could move them into bedsits in areas they chose to target.

Despite these limited successes, Ted Grant had very little to show for his four decades of political activism. There were two other competing Trotskyite organizations: Gerry Healy's Workers Revolutionary Party, and the newer International Marxist Group inspired by the Belgian Marxist, Ernst Mandel, plus Tony Cliff's neo-Trotskyite Socialist Workers Party, all of which were bigger and better known than the tiny, secretive RSL. Grant regarded them with contempt. Healy and Mandel had been guilty of 'fundamental theoretical incapacities' since 1945, while the idea that Cliff had been expounding since 1948, that the USSR was not a socialist but a 'state capitalist' society was 'artificial' and 'totally incorrect'. Grant's science told him that the communist economies would never collapse under the weight of their internal contradications, because 'there can never be a slump in an economy which is state-owned'.[20] During Tony Benn's first brief conversation with him, at a fringe meeting at the 1973 LPYS conference at Skegness in 1973, Grant asserted that 'there is no one else in the world who follows Trotsky correctly'. He struck Benn as being 'really a theological leader, a teacher by instinct'.[21]

The contempt was mutual. Those who were not familiar with the Labour Party Young Socialists or with the Liverpool Walton Labour Party treated the sect as being too tiny and inconsequential to matter, even in the relatively small world of Britain's revolutionary left. David Widgery's classic book on the far left in Britain, published in 1976, did not even mention Grant's name, and referred to Militant only twice in passing, to ridicule it. His inaccurate prophesy was that Militant would find 'the protective covering of the Labour Party actually becoming absorbed by a process of political osmosis, on to their own surface'.[22]

Those who encountered it often judged it to be hopelessly out of fashion. The middle-class radicalism of the 1960s and 1970s had thrown up movements and ideas which were not accounted for in the works of Trotsky, most notably the feminist and gay rights movements, the campaigns against racism, the shop stewards' movement, the environmentalist movement and CND, none of which fitted into Ted Grant's scheme to build the revolutionary party in time for the next crisis of capitalism. It appears that there were arguments inside the organization before Militant took any line on social issues of this kind at all, with younger leaders prevailing over Grant, but even then, they arrived to the cause late, giving themselves a reputation among other left-wing groups for being downright reactionary. Grant was, for instance, opposed to the organization of autonomous women's groups in the 1970s, just as in the mid-1980s, Militant staged a demonstration outside an NEC meeting at Labour Party headquarters in support of the leadership's refusal to recognize separate Black sections.

Even on questions whose importance was obvious even in the mental world of Ted Grant, his analysis never strayed from the premise that all history is the history of class struggle. Because Militant, like the Liverpool Labour Party, had its main social roots in that city's Catholic community, it was taken more seriously by Catholics across the water than any other organization to the left of the Labour Party. Catholic politicians knew what Militant's Irish policy was and they were appalled that it should give only half-hearted support to the Troops Out movement, believing that if the British army went, it should be replaced by a trade-union-based workers' militia. To Catholics, this sounded like a call to rearm the dreaded B Specials. This was one of the few issues on which Militant's line was regarded as helpful by the Labour Party leadership. Just as Trotsky had been sarcastically opposed to bomb-wielding Russian populists and anarchists, the Tendency was adamantly hostile to the IRA. They urged republicans to apply to join the Labour Party.

Andy Troke, a member of Dulwich Labour Party for many years, was recruited in 1972 to Militant at the age of sixteen, but left five years later. The approach came about a year after he joined the Young Socialists, when he was invited for a drink with the branch Chairman:

> He started off talking about revolutionary organisations working within social democratic parties and how they kept themselves and their ideas together within the organisation, and he said an organisation existed called Militant – actually, he was more specific, he said the Revolutionary Socialist League. I was astounded. It was a total shock, because I was young and rather naïve. He gave me *British Perspectives*, and asked me to read it. He gave it me in a brown paper envelope. And I read it.

Very soon, Troke was making visits to the Deptford Engineers Club, for meetings of what was then the south London branch of the RSL. Not yet a member, he had to wait in a bar while the 'comrades' had their business. He was then allowed in with other 'contacts' for the political session, which was usually about twenty people packed into a crowded room listening to Ted Grant or whoever was the guest speaker raising his voice to compete with the trains on the London–Dover line.

After six months, Troke was initiated into membership The price was high. He was still a schoolboy, but he was earning £3–£4 by working in an off-licence on Fridays and Saturdays. He had to hand over fully 50p, 10 per cent of his income. He was also required to sell fifteen to twenty copies of *Militant* every week to fellow members of the Dulwich Labour Party and a round of people he knew well enough to call on personally. In Militant parlance, regular buyers of the newspaper were 'contacts', members of the organization were 'comrades', full-time organizers were 'sellers'. The organization to which they belonged was neither a party, nor a faction, but a 'tendency'. The excitement of entering this secret organization with its private coded language and apocalyptic ideology more than made up for the demands it put on him.

> It was like the Secret Seven, being involved in who to approach and who not to approach. At that time, Militant was a very tight organization in terms of secrecy. There was a very strong peer-group pressure once you were inside, like the Masons or the Plymouth Brethren, which ultimately I bucked against, because I didn't like people telling me what to do.
>
> There was an RSL branch meeting once a week, usually a Wednesday. There would also be what we called the London Aggregate, which used to be in the Old Red Lion, Islington, about once a fortnight. I was never on the branch committee, but if you were, that was once a week as well. Also, there used to be general Readers' Meetings about once a month, which used to be advertised in *Militant*. It was very much a religious thing: You'd be asked to bring your fruits to the meeting, so if you had a contact you had been working on, you'd bring him as an offering.
>
> It's like somebody who has been through a religious period. You look to either Trotsky, Marx, Lenin, Engels or Ted Grant or Peter Taaffe and you have got the rationale for why people are reacting this way or that way. And obviously, everyone else is illogical, because you have got the right view. I believe there was a great deal of that type of thinking: we were the chosen few. We had the right ideology. People like *Tribune*, who were at that time Militant's main opponents, didn't know where they were going – nothing. We were the right ones.[23]

After several years, having seen his peer group break up as friends became disillusioned and quit, Troke began to suspect that Militant had become 'self-fulfilling', the real purpose of its existence was to raise the money to pay the full-time workers to keep the organization going. He tried in vain to raise issues like race and nuclear energy at branch meetings. Later, when he took a social science degree as a mature student, he was grateful for all the Marxist methodology which Militant had instilled in him, although it did not alter his view that what he had been taught was dogma constructed to bind the group together rather than to give its individual members a real understanding of the world outside.

One of the cardinal rules of membership, always, was to deny the organization existed. The line was succinctly expressed by Lynn Walsh, in his unsuccessful appeal against expulsion from the Labour Party:

> Militant is not an organisation, it is not subsidiary or ancillary to any organisation outside the party . . . Militant was proscribed as a result of an entirely one-sided inquiry which acted on McCarthyite reports and poison-pen letters from self-appointed snoopers.[24]

Yet this little, friendless, dogmatic, secret sect managed to break out from the ghetto of ultra-left politics to become, for a time, the largest organized force to the left of the Labour Party anywhere in England. The first reason for their success was the shrewd decision to concentrate their efforts on the Labour Party's moribund youth organizations. While the party recognized that it had to have a youth movement, the overall impression is that no one at that time was the slightest bit interested in how to attract the young to politics, apart from Militant. In the Yorkshire region, for example, the full-time officer with responsibility for youth in the late 1970s was Bert Twigg. A story is told that a group of young people once applied to set up an LPYS, whereupon they received a visit from Bert Twigg, who lectured them on the evils of Militant, an organization of which they never heard. Their curiosity aroused, the youngsters contacted Militant, who sent a full-time organizer along to recruit them. At one LPYS conference, a booklet was on sale entitled: 'What Bert Twigg has done for the LPYS', and a companion volume: 'What Bert Twigg is Going to do for the LPYS'. Both contained nothing but blank pages. Grant, by contrast, knew how to inspire the alienated young. Tony Benn observed:

> He has got a tremendous influence over young people. Listening to him speak, he is absolutely rational, logical and analytical up to a certain point and then he just goes over the top and keeps talking about 'the bloody settlement that the capitalists are preparing for the workers'.[25]

In 1972, the Labour Party enacted a well-intentioned reform by creating a seat on the NEC for a representative to be elected directly at the LPYS annual conference, thus ensuring that there would always be someone under the age of twenty-five on the executive. The unintended result was that for more than a decade and a half, Militant in effect had a reserved seat, giving its leaders valuable access to private NEC documents. During 1972–73, the group grew rapidly. It had 397 members in March 1973, and 464 in July.[26] One member, Ray Apps, put himself forward as a candidate for the constituency section of the NEC in 1973, and collected the votes of eighty-one CLPs, fifty more than the previous year. The only time that was ever bettered by a Militant candidate was when Pat Wall collected 103 votes in 1982. The following year, the party introduced a practice of publishing how CLPs' votes had been cast, and no more Militant candidates thought it worthwhile to run.

There was a temporary embarrassment in spring 1974, when it was discovered that the first representative, Peter Doyle, was twenty-seven. He had to surrender his seat to Rose Degiorgio, from the West Midlands, who would later play a substantial role in the expulsion of Militant supporters from the party. Militant's Nick Bradley took the Young Socialist seat back off Degiorgio in November 1974, giving the left narrow control of the NEC, which it retained for eight years.

In 1975, the Labour Party's National Agent, Reg Underhill, became sufficiently alarmed by the trickle of reports reaching him from the party's predominantly right-wing organizers about the spread of Militant to obtain the NEC's consent to submit a report on it. Underhill's report arrived in November 1975 which, by accident or design, caused the specific question of Militant to be raised alongside the long-running saga of the Cabinet Minister, Reg Prentice, who was threatened with deselection in his Newham North-east constituency. It was manifestly untrue that Prentice's problems were caused by infiltration of the Labour Party from the left, although Militant had a small presence in the seat, but the publicity provoked by Prentice had stimulated the first press interest in Militant, including the leak to the *Observer* of a letter written more than a decade earlier by Roger Protz, whose career took him through several revolutionary organizations before he found his niche in the Campaign for Real Ale, describing what early meetings of the *Militant* editorial board were like:

> We told Grant that he was hopelessly factional and sectarian, [and] that his attitude would strangle *Militant* . . . He began screaming and shouting, threatening that I had no rights at all as I wasn't active in RSL, hadn't 'proven' myself, etc.[27]

Despite this glimpse into how Grant treated dissent within his own organization, he and Militant were protected by a profound reluctance of anyone who had been on the left in the 1950s, to open a new round of proscriptions and expulsions. Even Harold Wilson, who gave a rambling speech in Prentice's defence, thought it relevant to mention that he had opposed removing the Labour whip in the House of Lords from Bertrand Russell. The NEC voted sixteen to twelve to do nothing. Most of the sixteen, who included Michael Foot and Barbara Castle, would have known almost nothing about Militant. They certainly did not know that it was produced by a secretive Trotskyite group who charged schoolchildren a tenth of their income to join. The two members who were well-informed, Eric Heffer and the Young Socialist delegate, Nick Bradley, spoke vigorously against expulsions.

Late in 1976, the Militant issue blew up unexpectedly, in a way which could be said to have finally put the Militant Tendency on Britain's political map, when Andy Bevan was appointed Labour Party National Youth Officer. He had joined Militant in Swansea in the late 1960s, becoming chairman of the LPYS in 1972–73 and one of the Newham party activists involved in the attempt to remove Reg Prentice. On the day he arrived to work at Transport House, he had to walk past a demonstration by his new colleagues, who objected to his appointment. It provoked a new round of press interest in the Underhill Report, and calls from both Jim Callaghan and the now-retired Sir Harold Wilson for action against entryists, but it was not, as it might seem, a calculated provocation by a left-dominated NEC. The job interviews had been conducted by two right-wing trade unionists from the NEC and the General Secretary, who chose Bevan because he was patently the best applicant. The staff protest was not over Bevan's Trotskyism, but in defence of pre-entry closed shop agreements.

Within a few years, Bevan was sufficiently popular among his peers to be elected chief shop steward, to fight a threatened round of job cuts which followed the 1983 election defeat. He was eventually prevailed upon to take voluntary redundancy in 1988.

The effect of Bevan's appointment was to widen the rift between the party leadership in parliament and the national executive. The left on the NEC became involved only to block what they regarded as an attempt to remove Bevan on purely political grounds. They answered the Prime Minister's call for an end to left-wing infiltration with a resolution, proposed by Eric Heffer, deploring a 'calculated campaign' to open a 'frenzied witch hunt'.[28] Early in 1977, Underhill was able to prevail upon the NEC to set up a sub-commission to re-examine his neglected report. The members were Foot and Heffer from the left, and Tom Bradley and John Chalmers from the right, plus the General Secretary, Ron Hayward. Though he was now deputy leader of the party, Foot's attitude to expulsions was still guided by his own experience of the Gaitskell years, when he lost the party whip. Hayward also objected to expulsions, and though he regarded Militant as a harmful sect 'with its own organization and policy . . . which is determined outside the structure of the Labour Party',[29] he thought it was too small to be worth jettisoning a deeply held principle.[30] Their report went no further than suggesting a political education programme and recruitment drive to counter Militant's influence over the LPYS. Realistically, there was no prospect of executive action against Militant while the left controlled the NEC.

Not only had the organization made inroads into the Labour Party, but in the world outside it seemed that the crisis which Ted Grant had been predicting with such certainty for more than thirty years had begun. The miners' strikes, the oil crisis and the emergence of Margaret Thatcher as leader of the Conservative Party in opposition were all symptoms. In September 1977, in a work confidently entitled *The Crisis in British Capitalism*, Grant was once again to use his unique grasp of scientific Marxism to see into the future. He predicted an 'inevitable' split between the right under Thatcher and Keith Joseph and 'so-called' moderates like James Prior. He added:

> This split in the ruling-class party of big business – which will be patched up and papered over for the moment – is an indication of the beginnings of a revolutionary crisis in Britain.[31]

Despite this, he forecast that the approaching general election would bring Margaret Thatcher to power, and that her government would begin the 'bloody settlement' with the trade unions which Benn had heard him forecast several years earlier. Preparations were already in hand, with CS gas, riot shields and other paraphernalia in store. The outcome would be a general strike 'possibly within one or two years', which would force a general election and put a left-wing Labour government in power. After that:

> The militarists will risk all and take to arms to crush the labour movement even if it means civil war. The social crisis of Britain will be protracted. It will end either in the greatest victory of the working class achieving power and the overthrow of the rule of capital, with the installation of workers' democracy, or a military police dictatorship which will destroy the labour movement and kill millions of advanced workers, shop stewards, ward secretaries, Labour youth, trade union branch secretaries and even individual members of the labour movement.[32]

In the troubled period of the late 1970s and early 1980s, this grim prognosis was more convincing to the young working-class or polytechnic-student audience at which it was aimed than in the previous decade. By 1982, no less than eight known Militant supporters had been adopted as parliamentary candidates around the country: four in Liverpool, the others in Bradford, Brighton, Coventry and the Isle of Wight. Bradford North CLP had chosen Pat Wall, who was a popular trade union leader in the city, and in the process had deselected the sitting MP, Ben Ford. All eight candidates were endorsed by the NEC before the right took control in October 1982, though in the event, boundary changes deprived Terry Harrison, Derek Hatton and Tony Mulhearn of seats to contest, and the Labour Party's poor performance in the 1983 general election meant that only Terry Fields, a Liverpool fireman recruited to Militant during the 1977 FBU strike, and Dave Nellist, were elected.

By then, there was a change in the atmosphere on the party left, with new voices being heard on the 'soft left', of past or current student activists too young to have experienced the purges of Gaitskell, but with direct experience of the intolerance and dogmatism of Militant. They knew perfectly well that Militant's claim to be no more than an association of like-minded newspaper readers was nonsense, and that it was a party within a party, which met separately, raised its own funds for itself, employed full-time organizers, published its own literature, maintained its own premises and pursued its own strategy. Key phrases had been heard too often, coming from too many mouths, for listeners to believe they were hearing anything other than a rigid political line laid down by a disciplined organization. As one observer put it:

> You are at a meeting and someone with a fake Liverpool accent makes a speech demanding the nationalisation of the principle 253 monopolies. Well, what's wrong with that? Why is everyone groaning? You'll soon see. Half a dozen other people stand up and make the same speech, with the same fake accent and the same curious hand movements. Are they clones? No, you have just met the 'Militant.'[33]

For instance, Jack Straw, who had been President of the National Union of Students in 1969–71, and subsequently Political Adviser to Barbara Castle, whose Blackburn seat he had inherited in 1979, was convinced that dealing with Militant was a precondition for winning the next general election. In 1983, the left-dominated Blackburn CLP was the first to expel any of its members for belonging to Militant, after a local party member, Michael Gregory, owned up to taking part in Militant meetings.

Furthermore, Michael Foot was by now desperately concerned not to give any more Labour MPs cause to defect to the SDP and, much as he found expulsions personally distasteful, was prepared to strike against the Tendency. The recently appointed General Secretary, Jim Mortimer, was tied by personal friendship and political affinity to Michael Foot, and was prepared to accommodate him, despite having himself been expelled from the Labour Party in 1952–56 for his membership of the British–Chinese Friendship Association.[34]

Moving against the Militant Tendency proved extremely difficult in practice, because of a warning given early on by Peter Taaffe that his side was prepared to defend itself in court if necessary. On legal advice, the NEC voted in December 1982 to proscribe Militant, the first such action since the formal abolition of the Proscribed List in 1973. The Foot–Mortimer strategy after that was to cut off the head of the organization, leaving its young adherents a chance to remain in the party and hopefully mend their ways. The following February the NEC voted nineteen to nine to expel the five people identified as the Editorial Board of *Militant*: Peter Taaffe, Ted Grant, Keith Dickenson, Lynn Walsh and Clare Doyle. After thirty-three years, Ted Grant's membership of the Labour Party was over.

He, and his four colleagues, had a chance to appeal to the annual party conference in Brighton in September 1983. This provided him with one of the largest audiences he had ever addressed in almost half a century of political activism, and undoubtedly the most important. He might have risen to the occasion by summarizing the beliefs which had motivated him through his life and using his unique position as Trotsky's only true interpreter on earth to forecast the great events of the coming years. Instead, he complained petulantly that the social democrats had been allowed to organize within the Labour Party before they left to form the SDP, and about the fact that the NEC had made its decision to expel him on the day before the disastrous Bermondsey by-election. The only scientifically-based forecast he offered was this:

> There is no way you can succeed in these expulsions. We will be back. We will be restored, if not in one year, in two or three years. At every trade union conference, at every ward, at every GMC, at every shop stewards' committee meeting this question will come up and we will be back.[35]

He was, of course, wrong as usual. Still, there appear to have been some people in the conference who were moved either by his speech or by the length of his party membership. The vote to expel him was carried by 4,972,000 to 1,790,000. Interestingly, the number of votes cast to expel him was noticably less than any of the other four. The explanation of this fact is bizarre. Frank Chapple, leader of the EETPU, which occupied the far right of the Labour Party and would shortly be expelled from the TUC, entertained a soft spot for Grant, possibly because of the service which Grant's old comrade, Jock Haston, had performed for the electricians' union, and withheld the EEPTU block vote, confident that Grant would be expelled without it.[36]

He was expelled, but by no means finished. His stature among the young was, if anything, enhanced by what appeared to be political persecution. My own first encounter with Ted Grant was at the LPYS conference of 1984, where he arrived bearing a press pass, as the Political Editor of Militant. He could be seen in cloth cap and tweed jacket, with his thinning hair brushed forward over his forehead, walking slightly flat-footedly about the hall, a great bundle of papers under his arm, and with a preoccupied scowl which created what seemed to be a permanent vertical ridge on his brow, above the thick-set spectacles. I was told that in the ladies toilet, someone had written 'Ted Grant is a hero', whereupon a second hand had inserted the word 'mega', and another hand had added yet another 'mega'. Some months later, I was in a crowd which included a Militant sympathizer who entertained us all with very funny impersonations of leading figures in the Labour Party, including a superb take-off of Tony Benn; but when he was asked for his rendering of Ted Grant, his mood suddenly changed and he informed us that someone who had suffered so much for his principles should not be ridiculed.

Militant was in its heyday. In May 1983, a left-wing Labour group took control of Liverpool city council, quickly turning its Deputy Leader, Derek Hatton, into a national celebrity and giving the little organization the prestige of direct confrontation not just with the official Labour Party leadership, but with the government too. Membership rose from less than 2,000 in the late 1970s to 6,000 in 1984 and 8,000 in 1985. The instructions went out to supporters that no one was to leave the party in protest against the February expulsions of the five leaders. The policy of entryism took precedence over individual feelings. Even in the latter part of 1986, when Hatton had joined the casualty list, the line was maintained and Militant acquiesced in the removal of Hatton, Mulhearn and Felicity Dowling from the positions they held within the Labour group on Liverpool council rather than risk having others expelled for supporting them. When a candidate was imposed by the NEC in the Knowsley North by-election late in 1986, Militant solemnly announced they would work for a Labour victory in the seat when other activists in the area were boycotting the campaign.

In May 1986, the organization's presence in Newcastle Upon Tyne paid a dividend when Militant supporter John Macreadie was elected General Secretary of the Civil and Public Services Association. His support came principally from the huge DHSS office in Newcastle. The election was subsequently rerun, and he lost the General Secretaryship, but became a Deputy General Secretary. Another Militant supporter, Phil Holt, was emerging as the dominant figure in the left-led executive of the National Communications Union, which was able to force out the incumbent, John Golding, in 1988.

For a group of Trotskyites to be wielding real power in one of Britain's largest cities and two large public-sector trade unions, in addition to having a stranglehold over the Labour Party's youth organization, and the open support of two MPs, was unprecedented in British politics. Even in his exile from the Labour Party, Ted Grant could afford to be pleased with himself. In December 1986, he forecast: 'Militant will become the majority in the Labour Party and the unions and it will transform society during the course of the next decade.'[37]

There was, however, a cloud on his horizon. In his long life, Ted Grant had never stepped outside the tiny world of Trotskyite sects. He had no experience of parliament, of town halls or even of the trade unions. He had never been a particularly active member of his local Labour Party branch. In the circumstances, it was almost inevitable that the organization he had created would slip out of his control. Inside and outside the organization, it was becoming increasingly clear that the real leader of Militant was not Ted Grant, but Peter Taaffe. As early as 1986, Grant was complaining that he was not receiving the number of invitations to speak from the platform at Militant meetings that he was used to. Derek Hatton, who was temporarily the public face of Militant, acknowledged a political debt to Tony Mulhearn, who had recruited him to the organization, and to Taaffe as 'the man at the helm', of whom Hatton wrote: 'I have never known such a clear thinker, or such a tactical genius.' He mentioned Ted Grant only in passing, as a 'long-standing inspirational figure,' who was 'a significant influence at all times'.[38] It was Taaffe and Mulhearn who lent on a reluctant Hatton in 1986 to let go of his position as Deputy Leader of Liverpool council for the greater good of the organization.

One of the great joys of being in a tiny, self-enclosed organization is that it allows its members to believe whatever they choose, confident that reality is not going to intrude. But Militant was now a large organization with a substantial income. In November 1986, it hired the Albert Hall for a rally enlivened by laser beams and attended by 5,000 of the faithful, and correspondents from all the serious daily newspapers. With this at stake, Militant had to look critically at Grant's scientific predictions, to see what their effect might be on thousands of young followers. He was now over seventy, and was being expected for the first time to make his science reflect the 'actually existing' world.

When the stock exchange crashed in October 1987, Grant believed it was the start of the crisis of capitalism which he had been predicting for four decades. He calculated that within six months there would be a depression on the scale of 1929. Ominously, he was overruled by other members of the editorial board of *Militant*.[39] When Iraq invaded Kuwait in August 1990, Grant saw at once that a Vietnam-style conflict was looming, which would last six months to two years. Dipping back into his own experience of the start of another war fifty years earlier, he produced the slogan: 'If there is conscription, we have to go with the workers into the forces and fight.'[40] Again, he was overruled, when others refused to believe that there would be conscription, or a protracted war, or that there would ever be mass resistance to US action against a regime like Saddam Hussein's.

When the 1988 Labour Party conference decided not to support a campaign of mass disobedience by encouraging supporters to refuse to pay the reviled poll tax, it left a gap to the party's left which Militant jumped in to fill, by launching the nationwide Anti-Poll Tax Campaign, which encouraged mass non-payment. However, there is nothing in the works of Leon Trotsky about non-payment of poll tax. To Ted Grant, the emphasis which Militant gave to the issue was a disturbing sign that the organization was engaging in 'activism' for its own sake instead of concentrating its energies on correctly interpreting the Old Man's theories. He urged that, to protect their positions, two remaining Militant MPs, Dave Nellist and Terry Fields, should pay their poll tax. He was again overruled and Fields became the only MP jailed for non-payment of the tax.

During 1991, Grant's relationship with Taaffe and the core of Militant's leadership deteriorated rapidly, spurred on by uncontrollable events which were making it impossible to hold to the 'entryist' tactic. Militant's rise had been halted. Expulsions had reduced its influence over Liverpool council. Ten out of seventeen broad-left members of the CPSA executive were removed in one sweep in the May 1988 elections. Soon afterwards, eight Newcastle Militants were expelled from the union. The number expelled from the Labour Party was approaching fifty. Andy Bevan had been dislodged from his job at party headquarters. The rules of the LPYS were being revised to deprive Militant of the NEC seat.

The only bright spot was the success of Militant's poll-tax campaign. Tommy Sheridan, a Glaswegian who was not even born when Grant and

Taaffe founded Militant, became the best-known anti-poll-tax campaigner outside parliament and, like Fields, went to jail for non-payment. The campaign inspired what was called the 'Scottish turn' when, in April 1991, Militant's leaders agreed in principle to establishing their own organization outside the Labour Party. From his cell in Saughton Prison, Edinburgh, Sheridan was elected to Glasgow council in 1992, running as the candidate for Scottish Militant Labour.

In 1990, sixteen Liverpool councillors were suspended by the NEC for voting to break the law by refusing to set a poll tax – an offence no different from that which dozens of Labour councillors had committed with impunity five years earlier. The action handed leadership of the city over to Harry Rimmer, one of the so-called 'sensible four' who had broken the whip by refusing to vote for an illegal budget in Derek Hatton's day. In the following year's council elections, several wards had candidates imposed by the NEC, whereupon six former councillors barred by Labour stood as broad left candidates. Five of the six were elected, implying that the left had more popular support in Liverpool than Labour's national leadership had previously supposed.

In 1990, there had also been a closely fought contest to decide who would be the next Labour candidate in Liverpool Walton, where the sitting MP, Eric Heffer, was dying of cancer. It was narrowly won by Peter Kilfoyle, who had been appointed party organizer in Liverpool in the wake of the 1985 inquiry, with a brief to expunge Militant influence. His rival, Lesley Mahmood, sent a stream of complaints to head office about the unfairness of someone being allowed to enter a selection contest when, as party organizer for the city, he had been in control of the membership list. When Heffer died, Kilfoyle was jeered by other mourners at his funeral. Mahmood decided to run against him as the Real Labour candidate, and Militant's leaders made the portentous decision to give her public backing. The outcome was that Kilfoyle won the election, although Mahmood scored an unusually high vote for a fringe candidate; and everyone who could in any way be linked to her campaign was automatically expelled from the party. Until now, the party machine had been careful not to devalue the action against Militant by using it as an excuse for expelling other left-wingers not linked to the organization. There is, however, anecdotal evidence that the veritable massacre which followed the Mahmood campaign took out some innocent bystanders who were so annoyed that they refused to appeal.

Two other incidental casualties were the Labour MPs Terry Fields and Dave Nellist. Hitherto, the party had lived with the illogicality of having two MPs known to be associated with Militant, an offence for which dozens of others had been expelled. Fields maintained a careful neutrality during the Walton campaign, but not careful enough to save him. His successor as Labour MP for Liverpool Broadgreen was Militant's old enemy, Jane Kennedy. In 1992, Nellist and Fields both ran as independents and picked up thousands of votes. Nellist was only 1,351 votes short of holding on to Coventry South East. Their support, plus the 6,287 votes cast for the Scottish Militant Labour candidate, Tommy Sheridan, in Glasgow Central, implied that the despised Trotskyite sect had reached a size in which it was capable of sustaining political life outside the Labour Party. Inside the party, it was dead. By Militant's own count, 219 members had been thrown out of the Labour Party by August 1991.

As it became clear to Grant that Taaffe and others intended to bring Militant out into the open as a separate political party, he felt compelled to act. In September 1991, he and the loyal Andy Woods, who had been replaced as Editor of *Militant International Review* by Lynn Walsh, circulated a letter to members in London, warning that 'A clique exists at the top level of the organisation; that this clique, operating outside the formal structures of the Tendency, has usurped the functions of democratically elected bodies; that enormous damage has been done by Zinoviest methods pursued by the clique.' Moreover, 'At this very moment, full-timer and CC members are being required to show their loyalty – not to the organisation, but to this leading group.'[41] For many years Grant and Woods, like other Militant supporters, had claimed there was no organization, let alone a CC, or Central Committee.

Within that previously non-existent Central Committee, Grant was in a minority of forty-six to three, his only other ally being Woods' half brother, Rob Sewell. This arithmetic was repeated at a Militant conference in Bridlington, in October 1991, where 93 per cent voted in favour of a document drafted by Taaffe and others which effectively abandoned entry-ism until the day when a radicalized Labour Party welcomed back those it had expelled.

One item of business remained. Just as the Labour Party had been forced to decide what to do about an organized Trotskyite group operating inside it, the new Militant organization now had within it a dissident group which, instead of bowing to majority decisions, proposed to launch a rival publication to argue the case for entryism. A statement by the editorial board of *Militant* noted – in words which defy satire – that:

> They now have their own small premises, and their own staff, and are raising their own funds. This is a clear split from Militant. Those supporting a rival publication cannot be regarded as Militant supporters. We regret that Ted Grant has split in this way.[42]

So, at the age of seventy-eight, Ted Grant was expelled from the organization to which he had devoted his life, leaving him powerless and almost friendless in his flat in Islington. But loneliness held no terrors for him. Most of his life he had been alone, fortified by the certainty that in the end he would be proved right, provided only that there was a revolutionary party adhering to the correct principles laid down by Lenin and Trotsky, to seize its opportunity when the crisis came. He had dedicated almost fifty years to building that party, and now it had rejected him.

CHAPTER THREE

THE SHOPPIE ON THE SCOTSWOOD ROAD

A shop steward from Tyneside named Jim Murray once held the future of the Labour Party in his hands. It was he who decided that sitting Labour MPs should face mandatory reselection, thereby sending a score of mostly undistinguished political careers to an early grave. He played no small part in deciding who would control the contents of the 1983 election manifesto, Jim Callaghan and Michael Foot or Tony Benn. Yet he also effectively killed Benn's only chance of becoming leader of the Labour Party. He was therefore to a large extent responsible for the election of Michael Foot. Apart from that, he never found an effective outlet for his immense gifts and spent a long career in honourable pursuit of impossible objectives. Power was placed in his hands by sheer fluke.

Three important reforms which the Bennite left wanted to make to the Labour Party constitution were given their first serious run at the annual party conference in Brighton in autumn 1979, before the main confrontation at Blackpool a year later. In Brighton, Jim Callaghan gave his first address as Leader of the Opposition. It was a plea for good behaviour, tolerance and loyalty to the old way of doing business, devoid of vision or political content. He was given a standing ovation and, for most of the week, his advice was ignored.

On Wednesday, the delegates voted by 4.008 million to 3.039 million to introduce a mandatory reselection procedure in Labour-held parliamentary seats. The result provoked audible groans from the enclosure where the MPs sat like defendants at a mass trial, as they saw themselves having to reapply for their own jobs to the hostile and left-dominated general committees of their constituency parties. The issue would bedevil four successive party leaders, until John Smith resolved it fourteen years later.

On Thursday, there was an even more direct challenge to Jim Callaghan's authority, when a delegate named Stuart Weir raised the issue of who ultimately controlled the contents of the general election manifesto. It was a well-known story that prior to the 1979 general election, Callaghan had personally vetoed a manifesto promise to abolish the House of Lords, which was supported by the NEC and which a substantial part of the Cabinet also favoured. Because the constitutional issue posed by Weir had not been considered before, it could not be settled immediately, but there was a majority of about a million in favour of putting it on the following year's agenda. The vote implied that even if someone other than Tony Benn succeeded Jim Callaghan as party leader, the next election manifesto would be heavily influenced by Benn, in his capacity as chairman of the NEC's Home Affairs committee.

It is easy to forget the shock these two votes caused in 1979, because they were eclipsed by yet more dramatic events in 1980 and 1981; but at the time, it was unprecedented for the leader of the Labour Party to be defeated on issues of such magnitude, in the full glare of television cameras. One of Callaghan's principal qualifications for the high office had been his rapport with the union leaders, who controlled 90 per cent of the voting strength at annual conferences. Any of the three biggest unions, the TGWU, GMBATU, or AUEW, had a block vote larger than the combined votes of all the constituency Labour Parties in England, Scotland and Wales. The TGWU vote had been unreliable since its General Secretary, Arthur Deakin, died while giving a May Day speech in Leicester in 1955, without first arranging for a suitable successor; but the votes of the other two giants and a handful of medium-sized unions had been sufficient to ensure that the leader could be challenged but never defeated on the conference floor on any matter as serious as these. In 1979, it became shockingly obvious that the block vote had gone native. The relationship between the Labour Party and the big unions would never be the same again.

Yet, curiously, in that same week the Bennite left unexpectedly lost on the very issue about which they cared most. A pressure group called the Campaign for Labour Party Democracy had been organizing maneouvres for several years in the hope of bringing about a change in the system for electing the leader of the Labour Party, throwing the franchise open to unions and constituency parties, rather than restricting it to Labour MPs. To the former Foreign Secretary, David Owen, and others, this idea was more sinister than anything else on the left's agenda, because it raised the spectre that when a future Labour government was coping with industrial unrest like the previous year's 'winter of discontent', the Prime Minister himself could be directly challenged by a nominee of one of the trade unions involved, but, out of the three constitutional reforms under consideration, this was the one which did most to enhance trade union influence and therefore, on the face of it, the one most likely to be voted through. Yet it was defeated by 3.033 million to 4.009 million.

Benn himself was not too downcast. He foresaw that the left would be able to come back the next year, having secured the block votes of a few more of the middle-sized trade unions, and they would win. What he could not foresee was the critical importance of timing. It would take fifteen months for the party eventually to set up a new system for leadership elections. By then Callaghan had resigned and Michael Foot was installed as the last Labour Party leader to be chosen by his parliamentary colleagues alone. The anticipated ideological prizefight between the heavyweights, Tony Benn and Denis Healey, was fought out vicariously in a contest for the deputy leadership in 1981.

Others noticed the odd symmetry in the voting. On two out of three big organizational questions, the left had had around 4 million votes, while 3 million backed the leadership. On the other occasion, the figures were almost exactly reversed. It did not take long to work out the reason: the AUEW had a block vote of 928,000 which had shifted from one side to the other. The whole future of the Labour Party had been controlled by the delegates from just one union.

Then it emerged that the thirty-four-strong AUEW had been split almost precisely down the middle. It contained seventeen delegates on the left, sixteen on the right, and one floater. When the one loose delegate voted with the Bennites, they won eighteen to sixteen, and tomorrow belonged to the left. Where he supported the right, the delegation was split seventeen to seventeen and the union President exercised a casting vote. The President was a right-winger named Terry Duffy, who had just taken over from the newly ennobled Hugh Scanlon, the Marxist who had dominated the union and the TUC for more than a decade. When Duffy used his casting vote, the forces of moderation won. Consequently, all the big conference decisions hinged on the vote of that one uncommitted AUEW delegate, whose name was Jim Murray.

His case is interesting because it demonstrates that the 'block vote', which may sound like a solid inanimate lump of voting matter, is the product of human experience, prejudice and sometimes even reasoned argument. Murray himself was a rare and interesting individual. He proclaimed himself to be a syndicalist in the tradition of Tom Mann, a turn-of-the-century union leader whose influence had been largely forgotten since the Russian revolution. A kind of syndicalism has always pervaded the Labour Party. It had always been considered right that the Party's internal affairs should be controlled by officials whose only real experience was in negotiating wages and working conditions; but this practice was usually defended on short-term, practical grounds. Union leaders pointed out that they were the people capable of raising the money needed to keep the Party going, and that they were a bulwark of hard-headed common sense against the wilder elements in the constituency parties. They did not construct a whole political and economic philosophy around the idea that all power should be devolved to the elected representatives of industrial workers. Jim Murray did.

His reason for refusing to play his part in helping Tony Benn become the next Labour Party leader was unconnected with the usual objections to Benn's 'extremism'. He regarded Benn's record as Minister for Industry as one of the few creditable episodes from the previous Labour government, but he did not trust Benn personally because he did not trust leaders generally. There were no top-down solutions in Murray's political philosophy. Everything depended on industrial workers becoming politicized and organized at their workplace under the leadership of lay activists drawn from the shop floor. Political parties and trade union bureaucracies were no more than a back-up service to be called on in moments of crisis, but otherwise to be treated with suspicion because of their innate tendency to interfere and subordinate the working class to their own institutional interests. His life was a noble and ultimately futile attempt to live by principles drawn directly from personal experience. Almost nothing now remains of his life's work, except the reputation he left behind on Tyneside. Joyce Quin encountered him about four years before his death in 1989, when he was unemployed and in failing health. She said: 'He was amazingly well thought of. He was, really, a working-class hero, because he was so articulate, and self-educated. He was a very independent, radical socialist.'[1]

Her admiration for him is coloured by gratitude, because one of the last services he performed for the Labour Party was to support Ms Quin's adoption in 1985 for the safe Labour seat of Gateshead East, where he had lived since 1961. The Militant Tendency had been concentrating its strength in the seat for several years, moving full-time organizers into Gateshead bed-sits, to secure the seat for one of its supporters, Malcolm Graham, a shop steward in the nearby Ever Ready factory, who has since broken with Militant. His main rival was Dave Clelland, leader of Gateshead council, who had served his time as an apprentice at the same factory as Murray. When the redrawn Gateshead East constituency was created by the boundary changes in 1983, Militant made a tactical decision to back Bernard Conlan, the incumbent from the old Gateshead East seat, knowing full well that he was a product of the AUEW's right-wing machine with a poor attendance record at the Commons and a home far away in Cheshire. They calculated that Conlon would soon retire, giving their man a better chance next time. In 1985, the AUEW divisional office perversely came to Militant's aid by refusing to nominate Clelland, on the grounds that he was too left wing. Graham appeared now to have a clear run. He in fact led on the first ballot, and his supporters had a victory celebration organized for the night. Joyce Quin did not appear to be a serious contender, since no safe Labour seat in the north east of England had adopted a woman candidate since 1945, and there had been no women Labour MPs in the region since 1950. However, she narrowly won. She herself did not realize how narrowly until she walked back into the selection meeting after the result had been announced.

In his life, Murray had opportunities to be either an MP, a civic leader or a trade union baron, but had never seized any of them. He had never been sufficiently single-mindedly devoted to getting on in the world. He brought the same sort of attitude into the Labour party: he was all in favour of there being a Labour government, but never looked to a general election victory as the be-all and end-all of political activity. Honourable, loyal to the community into which he was born, steeped in trade union tradition, and yet afflicted with a love of books and the company of intellectuals, he was what we would now call 'old' Labour.

Soon after Murray's death, unity suddenly broke out in the northern regional Labour party as every party activist, left wing, right wing, old Labour or New Labour combined against a common enemy: the staff at the party's Walworth Road headquarters who had devised a cost-cutting proposal to close the regional office on Tyneside and merge the Northern and Yorkshire regions. At the Brighton conference in 1994, Jim Murray's widow, Pat – a party member of over forty years standing and a long-serving Gateshead councillor – led the charge on behalf of the aggrieved northerners, suggesting to the national treasurer that if he wanted savings he should 'seriously consider getting rid of some of the Armani-suited yuppies down there, with the phones they were using . . . because they could not be bothered to cross the floor of the Conference room in case they damaged their Gucci shoes'.[2]

Jim Murray had one stroke of luck in the timing of his birth, on 22 September 1929. Although his widowed mother had to raise him and four other children on her own in a two-room house in Gateshead during the depression, his father having died when he was six, at least when Jim left school, it was during an interlude when Tyneside was not blighted by unemployment. The war had created both a labour shortage and a massive demand for the output of the shipyards and heavy engineering factories. So, term having ended on a Friday, Jim Murray and his fourteen-year-old classmates went to queue at the Labour Exchange on Monday, and were all handed jobs:

> It was just given to you, like. It was a bit like a lottery, going into the dole on a Monday morning. He would shuffle among the cards he had from companies wanting to set on labour, and, you know, from the lottery, he would draw a card and that was your career fixed for the rest of your life.[3]

The idea of a career that was fixed 'for the rest of your life' turned out to be optimistic; but it seemed secure at the time. The boys were soon made aware of the power of the unions, which were not only recognized but institutionalized. They were signed up as soon as they arrived by a branch secretary who controlled the rations of tea and sugar and had no compunction about slipping a little extra to his members. Thus Jim Murray joined what was then the Amalgamated Engineering Union. (It became the AUEW after merging with the foundry workers, and then the AEEU after a merger with the electricians' union, the EETPU.)

Murray arrived in time to witness the wartime strike by Tyneside apprentices, who had been alarmed by rumours that they were to be sent as 'Bevin boys' down into the mines. During his break Murray would literally run out of the factory, with other boys, to stand at the back listening at the apprentices' meetings. He had been taught to respect the Labour Party and the unions by his mother, who used to allow her front room to be used for party meetings and told him that his late father had been a union official. But here he learned that neither the Party, nor official union leaders, nor even the Communist Party supported the strike; the only outside help was coming from a small and mysterious group of 'Trotskyites'. His first impression, therefore, was that the official institutions of the Labour movement had become institutionalized and were not to be trusted. That was reinforced twelve years later, after he had completed his apprenticeship and a stint in the merchant navy, and joined Gateshead Labour Party in 1954.

Gateshead is one of the oldest Labour strongholds in the country. An ILP candidate, John Johnson, was elected its MP as early as 1904, with Liberal backing. The council has been continuously under Labour control for decades, but the local party had been split in 1949 by the decision taken in London to expel the sitting MP, Konni Zilliacus, as a communist fellow traveller. It was not a view shared by Stalin's police, who would have arrested him if they could have got their hands on him, for his links with Yugoslavia's President Tito. These same police had tortured Hungarian and Czechoslovak communists into confessing that Zilliacus was a British spymaster. At the 1950 general election, he scored a respectable vote running against the official Labour candidate. He was later allowed back into the party, and was MP for Manchester Gorton from 1955 until his death in 1967.

The affair left Gateshead Labour Party in a sorry state. As often happened in the Labour heartlands, the local organization had been allowed to run down by a right-wing establishment fearful of any further infiltration by the left. A few years earlier, there had been an arrangement locally that would be unthinkable in today's Labour Party: the Gateshead district

Labour Party and trades council had a joint committee, which meant that communists, Trotskyites and others did not need to infiltrate the Labour Party by stealth to influence it from inside: they could be elected under their own colours through the unions. This was ended by fiat. Gateshead Trades Council ceased to exist. The Tyne District organizer of the AUEW, a former member of the ILP named Len Edmondson, disapproved and defiantly affiliated the Gateshead branches of the union to the Newcastle trades union, where delegates could continue to mingle with the Marxist left. In the circumstances, the decaying Gateshead Labour Party was glad of a recruit from an engineering factory, and almost at once they found Murray a safe seat on Gateshead council, which he held for about nine years. Edmondson, whose home is close to the ward Murray represented, remembers him as an exceptionally good councillor. In a town where almost no one went into higher education, and the privileged teenagers were those with apprenticeships, Councillor Murray vigorously objected to the very low discretionary student grants Gateshead awarded to its tiny number of university students, and succeeded in having them increased.[4] This quick success made no great impression on him. In fact, it was after becoming a party activist that he 'really found out the meaning of helplessness'.[5]

However, Murray had found a more rewarding outlet for his energies by changing jobs, commuting across the Tyne river to the Vickers plant in Elswick, on the Scotswood Road, in Newcastle. This was an old and famous factory. Two entire communities on the west side of Newcastle Upon Tyne had been built by the Victorians to house the 70,000 workers employed by engineering factories along the Scotswood Road. There was Elswick, near the river bank, for the unskilled, and further up the hill there was Benwell, where the skilled workers and their families lived. Another important service which capitalism provided was the fifty pubs along the Scotswood Road, the last of which, the evocatively named Hydraulic Crane, closed in the late 1980s. Vickers, a Leeds-based armaments firm, had acquired the Elswick factory from the family of its founder, the Victorian entrepreneur William Armstrong, after the war. With it came a long, unbroken trade union tradition. It was the site of the twenty-five-week strike of 1871 at which, for the first time in British industrial history, the unions secured a nine-hour working day. The management recognized the shop stewards as legitimate representatives of the workforce as early as 1913, years ahead of most engineering employers. The chairman of the factory's trade union committee, or works convenor, Roy Hadwin, was an important figure in Newcastle: a city councillor, a future Lord Mayor and a friend of the legendary T. Dan Smith.

Soon after Jim Murray arrived as a fitter in the variable speed gear shop, there was an incident which confirmed his belief that this interlocking network of Labour Party and union dignitaries on Tyneside had degenerated into an idle élite. Vickers decided to move the variable speed gear operation to Weymouth, removing 400 jobs from Tyneside, with a knock-on effect on others. As one of those whose job was disappearing, Murray naturally looked to the union and the Labour party to put up a fight. He lobbied his MP in Gateshead, Harry Randall, who agreed to raise the issue in parliament. Mysteriously, nothing happened. Randall later told Murray privately that he had been warned off by Ted Short, an important figure in the Labour Party who would rise to be its Deputy Leader, before his name was also dragged embarrassingly into the limelight in the corruption scandal which followed T. Dan Smith's arrest. Short brusquely reminded Randall that there are certain informal rules about how MPs conducted their business, one of which was that they did not interfere in matters concerning one another's constituencies without prior agreement. The factory was in Newcastle Central, Short's constituency. As this homily was delivered, Roy Hadwin sat by, saying nothing.

The incident convinced Jim Murray that a corrupt and supine Labour establishment was virtually conspiring with the capitalist class at the expense of working men. He never forgot or forgave. More than a quarter of a century later, he referred back to this as the beginning of the destruction of west Newcastle's engineering base. 'We for twenty-five years were telling everybody, telling MPs, Labour MPs, telling the Labour-controlled city council what Vickers had in mind; they didn't believe us, they believed Vickers but of course to their chagrin we were right.'[6]

However, at the time, there was still no shortage of jobs for skilled men. Murray was himself transferred to the die-shop at Vickers Elswick, a bed of militancy where very soon he was plunged into a ten-week strike over pay rates, during which he was elected secretary of the strike committee and subsequently a shop steward. He was also engaged in head-on conflict with

Roy Hadwin. In general, it was a bad idea to be simultaneously fighting management and a well-entrenched and politically well-connected union boss, but Murray was convinced that Hadwin had not only sold out the workforce in the variable speed gear workshop, but was now sabotaging the pay claim in the die-shop. At a heated factory meeting, he recklessly called Hadwin a liar to his face and threatened to have him expelled from the union. Hadwin, as might be expected, has a version of this story which is very different to Jim Murray's. He claims that he was in the middle of a delicate negotiation with Vickers management under which the die-shop would have expanded to become the nucleus for car manufacturing, reducing the factory's dependence on the arms trade. This was wrecked, so he claims, because Murray's obstinate militancy forced the wage rates up in the die-shop, making the whole plan uneconomic. Whatever the truth of it, the dispute was sufficiently serious to involve the AEU district committee, who ruled in Hadwin's favour and made Murray apologize. Sentiment on the shop floor, however, was running in Murray's favour.

Not long afterwards, Roy Hadwin received an attractive offer to join T. Dan Smith in a business venture. Having become city council leader in 1960, Smith had abandoned his former career as a painter and interior decorator to enter the exciting world of public relations, a strange new phenomenon in a region where the Labour establishment did not really need to battle for hearts and minds as the votes came in by the barrow load. Dan Smith was one of the modernizers of his day, a spin doctor who helped second-rate politicians sharpen their public appearances, and put architects and builders in contact with councillors who controlled huge budgets but knew very little about the construction industry. It was a time when councils were demolishing slums and constructing homes at lightning speed. High-rise blocks were the height of fashion. Newcastle city alone completed 3,000 new council homes in the year 1966–67. A whole new town sprung up in Peterlee, county Durham, under Smith's personal stewardship. With working-class slum dwellers receiving their first introduction to indoor bathrooms and toilets, it seemed unimportant that some of those involved were accepting money, holidays and other gifts which were technically against the law. Hadwin entered this world as a relative innocent. He was soon earning a wage a long way above that of a Vickers fitter. He also rose to be Lord Mayor of Newcastle in 1969–70. Then an architect named

John Poulson went bankrupt, and his creditors hired a barrister who demanded explanations about unexplained items in his accounts. Poulson, Dan Smith and the most powerful union leader in the North East, Andy Cunningham, went to jail. Hadwin was relieved to escape with a suspended sentence and a £600 fine. Like Smith, but unlike Cunningham, he had not been accepting bribes, but disbursing them. He maintained that he had been driven by a sincerely held belief in modernized council housing. Years later, he reflected: 'They called me the bent Lord Mayor, but I don't even own my own house.'[7]

Meanwhile, Jim Murray stepped into the convenor's job which Hadwin had vacated. Aged only thirty-two, he had every reason to believe he could find his own road to success without being sucked into the corruption of the north east's Labour establishment. Two previous convenors in the same factory had gone on to be national presidents of the engineering union. In an early indication that he was heading the same way, he was elected president of the union's Tyne district committee. In an arrangement more common then than it is now, the employers allowed him to leave the shop floor to be a full-time union representative paid by the company. In the privacy of his convenor's hut, Murray was able to indulge the taste for book learning which he had first acquired as a twelve-year-old, when he spent his part-time earnings as a butcher's boy acquiring second-hand books in Newcastle's Grainger Market. He worked his way through an eclectic sample of the modern classics: Upton Sinclair, E.M. Forster, Malcolm Lowry, Somerset Maugham, Olive Schreiner and Robert Tressell, until he was able to mix easily and on equal terms with intellectuals. He was also allowed to roam across the factory, making contacts everywhere. His eyes were opened to immense size and complexity. There were forty to fifty separate workshops servicing different markets: a hot metal forge, a foundry making castings, an old naval gunshop, a small toolroom where skilled men turned out dies and punches, workshops turning out car body dies, or deck machinery for ships, and printing presses. There were also eight different classes of canteen, ranging in quality from the Directors' dining room, through separate canteens for office staff or for factory foremen, down to the one where the shopfloor workers ate, and ten different classes of toilet. The factory employed 15,000 unionized members, in twenty-six separate unions. About 2,000 were women workers, many of them young, for whom a young, clever and good-looking works convenor was an object of some interest, notwithstanding the fact that he was married with children. There were separate unions for the leatherworkers, brass moulders, steel workers and so on. An industrial dispute of some form or another was virtually a weekly event. Every one required Jim Murray's attention. He was in many ways the most important person in the factory.

It was as far as he got. The rest of his active life would be spent witnessing the gradual dismantling of this paradigm of Victorian England. He was the works convenor for over twenty years, until Vickers closed the Elswick factory. By then, he was seriously ill. He never held another steady job.

From this resumé, we can see how Murray came by the political beliefs that illuminated his life. None of the established structures of the Labour movement were wholly to be trusted: neither the Labour Party under its Gaitskellite leadership nor subsequently under Harold Wilson or James Callaghan, nor the official trade union hierarchies, nor Labour-controlled city councils, nor even an organization which purported to be revolutionary, like the Communist party. All had their own narrow institutional interests, which they put before the interests of the working class. But the industrial working class itself, properly organized at the point of production by disinterested political activists, was a force to be relied upon. Murray considered himself to be in the tradition of Tom Mann, founder of the Industrial Syndicalist Education League in 1910, who believed that if industrial workers were properly organized, they could 'bring about such changes as they desire in society by direct action without the intermediation of any other institute'. Mann considered that any political activity, like running for parliament, was a waste of time, and concentrated on trying to organize a general strike, beginning in the docklands in 1912. Murray did not go that far. There being no realistic prospect of bringing the state to its knees through a general strike, Murray kept a foot in the Labour party, without really believing that party political activity could achieve real results. Like most left-wing Labour party activists of his generation, he had been inspired by the oratory of Aneurin Bevan, who left an abiding image of what it was like to make progress through the political system: you might begin as a lodge secretary in a Welsh mining village and at that stage think you had achieved power, but 'there was no power there; and he became a Member of Parliament, a member of the government, and every time he got to this position, you know, power was vanishing round the corner'.[8]

In that spirit of pre-ingested scepticism, Murray set off to become an MP. His best hope was Gateshead West, where the incumbent MP, his friend Harry Randall, had decided to retire in time for the 1970 general election. As one of the region's leading trade unionists, and a former councillor, born and brought up in the constituency, he was widely expected to win the nomination. Unfortunately, he had made an enemy of Andy Cunningham, the powerful and corrupt leader of the region's largest union, the GMWU, who threw his support behind the head of a London market research company named John Horam, who narrowly beat Murray. Horam went on to become the only MP in recent British history to sit in the Commons as a member of three political parties. He defected from Labour to be a founder member of the SDP in 1981, lost his seat in 1983, switched to the Conservatives, and returned as MP for Orpington in 1992, serving as a minister under both James Callaghan and John Major.

Murray, meanwhile, ran in Louth against Jeffrey Archer in 1970, and in Carlton, another hopeless prospect for Labour, in February 1974. Had he put his mind to it, he could surely have obtained a Labour seat later in the decade. The engineering union has a long tradition of taking promising activists off the shop floor, training them in public speaking and other skills in political life, and sending them to the Commons as union-sponsored MPs; but running for parliament was not really socially acceptable behaviour in the intellectual milieu in which Jim Murray moved. In the late 1960s, after he had given up his seat on Gateshead council, he became intrigued by the student protest movement, which was bringing Leon Trotsky back into fashion. From 1968, he was a member of the Nottingham-based Institute for Workers' Control (IWC), founded by Ken Coates, a former miner turned university lecturer who had been through a brief Trotskyite phase. Murray's decision to stand as a Labour candidate earned him a formal expulsion from the International Socialists, a neo-Trotskyite group which later changed its name to the Socialist Workers Party. There is a mystery here, because he adamantly denied ever having belonged to the organization in the first place, but the comrade who moved the resolution to expel him has a clear memory of doing so, and he must be telling the truth because, unlike Murray, he later became a Labour MP.[9]

The songwriter and singer, Alex Glasgow, who was only occasionally active in the Labour Party, was persuaded to go canvassing for Jim Murray and was inspired to write a song called the Socialist ABC, about the alphabet 'my Daddy taught me', in which 'B's for the Boss who's a Bastard . . . T is for Trotsky, the hero', and the pay-off line is:

> For Daddy's no longer a union man, and he's had to change his plea.
> His alphabet is different now, since they made him a Labour MP.[10]

Even in the early 1970s, the 'culture of betrayal' was setting in on the Labour left. It was assumed that any Labour MP who was not already sucked into the establishment before being elected would be soon afterwards.

In 1971, Alf Robens, a former Minister for Labour in the Attlee government, was appointed Chairman of Vickers. Lord Robens was well-known on Tyneside, having been Labour MP for Wansbeck and later Blyth, in Northumberland, for fifteen years. There were unrealistic hopes on the shopfloor that, as a Labour man, he would look after the workers, and his arrival produced a false optimism that he would also go out of his way to halt the rundown of the Scotswood Road factories. In fact, inevitably, it intensified. The car body die-shop closed. Printing presses were moved out to Leeds. None of these events inspired much protest from the workforce generally, who gratefully accepted what seemed like generous redundancy terms and found other work. The numbers of lost jobs were not big enough at any one time to alarm the national trade unions either. Generally, only the shop stewards objected. Murray therefore settled into what became his life's work: to try to create a shop stewards' movement uncorrupted by the self-interest of political parties or union bureaucracies, yet large enough to act as a brake on investment decisions made by the distant managements of multinational companies.

He was helped by the return of a Labour government in 1974, with Tony Benn as Secretary of State for Industry. Labour's manifesto had promised a National Enterprise Board and planning agreements between the government and Britain's 100 largest companies. This provided a bobbin around which to weave two possibilities: a company-wide combine of shop stewards from all the main Vickers factories around the country, and a regional network of stewards from all the Tyneside factories owned by the large manufacturing companies.

The Tyne Conference of Shop Stewards came into being at a meeting in Newcastle in January 1975, organized by Jim Murray. It maintained a flimsy existence for two or three years. Regional union officials were naturally hostile to it because, had it succeeded, it would have threatened their authority; but its real weakness was that it depended on the Industry Department being an oasis of radicalism in a weakened and divided government. Other than Benn's Industry Bill, there was no obvious reason for its existence. When Benn was shifted out of the Industry Department in 1975 and replaced by Eric Varley, Tyneside's incipient shop stewards' network started to wither away.

The Vickers Shop Stewards Combine Committee was a sturdier creation. It was founded in Leeds in autumn 1974. It met quarterly and was able to perform a genuine service for union leaders in individual factories who had been arguing over pay and other benefits in ignorance of comparative rates paid by the company elsewhere. Information circulated between shop stewards through the Combine quickly opened their eyes to anomalies like the fact that wages for a 'time-served' fitter at different Vickers plants varied from £41.50 to £50 a week, and that some provided their workforce with pensions schemes, non-contributory sickness benefits and extra paid leave, while others did not.[11] Two years later, inflation had widened the gap, in favour of the factories where the union organization was strong enough to extract the extra pay necessary to protect living standards. Thus in July 1977, a skilled worker doing piecework in the Vickers Elswick factory was collecting a weekly wage of £71.27. His colleague at the Vickers plant in Leeds Water Lane, doing exactly the same job, was being paid £62.00.[12] The Combine at least made shop stewards conscious of these disparities and was able to make some progress towards 'levelling up' pay and other conditions.

In 1976, when workers at Vickers Crabtree, in Gateshead, went out on an eight-week strike in opposition to a proposed wage cut, disguised as a bonus scheme, the Combine was able to make the strike effective by 'blacking' the factory in every other Vickers plant and by collecting money for strike funds throughout Tyneside. Emboldened by this success, shop stewards in Vickers Scotswood brought their factory to a halt the following year, demanding that they be paid the same rates as the workers in the Elswick workforce. They extracted a pay rise of around 22 per cent.

To enthusiasts, it seemed that the Vickers Combine and others, especially the celebrated Lucas Aerospace Combine, had the power to tame the multinationals and compel them to behave responsibly towards the communities from which they recruited labour. A book published in 1979 about the Vickers Combine looked forward optimistically to the prospect that this could be the embryo for a 'saner (and ultimately more rational) way of organizing society'.[13] In January 1980, representatives from twenty different Combines held a meeting in London organized by the Lucas Shop Stewards Committee. Jim Murray returned from it in a state of euphoria which seemed to cancel all the disappointments he had suffered in his career so far. He saw it as the resurrection of syndicalism as Tom Mann had expounded it, before it was polluted by the Russian revolution. 'This first get together of Combines can be the first step towards the development of a real international working-class movement . . . The next meeting may hopefully be the beginnings of founding the Industrial Parliament which Tom Mann argued for and which the TUC in no way represents.'[14]

This was achieved by shop stewards organizing themselves without permission or approval from their own union bosses, and despite the parochialism of their own members. There were craft rivalries to be broken down. Murray often had to answer to fellow engineers who could not understand why he, as a skilled man, would interest himself in the welfare of unskilled labourers, even from the mighty General Workers Union. The craft consciousness of time-served fitters, however, was as nothing compared with the boilermakers, the highest paid manual workers on Tyneside. They refused to be represented on works committees. When the Scotswood workers struck in 1977, the eighty-odd boilermakers at the factory carried on working until the strike was over, then threatened to bring the factory to a standstill for the second time, to ensure that their pay increased proportionally to everyone else's, lest the social gap between them and other workers should close. (These problems were partially solved when the engineering union absorbed the lower-paid foundry workers into its membership, changing its name from the AEU to the AUEW, and later when the Newcastle-based Boilermakers' Union merged with the General and Municipal to form the cumbersomely-named GMBATU, which has since become the GMB.)

In addition, there were the inevitable regional hostilities to be broken down. 'While the people analysing the situation saw the necessity of national action to stop one plant closing down, the reality was that the bloke working away in a corner of a factory in – let's say in Crayford or in Swindon – couldn't see what the fact that people up in Newcastle were losing their jobs had to do with him. He couldn't see how it affected his interests and in some cases it might benefit his interests because the work, some of the work, was going to come to him.'[15]

Later in life, Jim Murray came to accept that there were some significant holes in the makeshift democracy which he and his fellow shop stewards had tried to introduce into their workplaces. In theory, those who attended meetings of the Vickers Combine or the Tyne Shop Stewards were reporting back to the workers who elected them. In reality, it was not likely that large numbers of factory workers, their minds numbed by the monotony of assembly-line jobs, cared very much what their shop stewards talked about among themselves. Those who travelled to Leeds for Combine Committee meetings would generally report back to other shop stewards in their factories, but what the stewards then did with this information was up to them.

Contributing to the self-conscious élitism of the shopfloor activists was a curious demographic fact that a disproportionate number of Tyneside's militant shop stewards came, as Murray did, from Roman Catholic families. For about twenty years, he was a lapsed Catholic, though when he felt death approaching he went back to the church. Lapsed or not, the Catholic shop stewards were, he claimed, more successful than the communists at persuading their members to strike, because they were free from any suspicion of being involved in any 'red' plot; although they endured a severe clash of loyalties when the regional TUC called a one-day strike against the Wilson government's attempt at industrial legislation, *In Place of Strife*, and inadvertently timed it to coincide with the feast of the Assumption of the Blessed Virgin Mary.[16]

On reflection Murray came to think of the movement to which he devoted such energy as a 'club of the politically conscious'.

> There was still this feeling that shop stewards, convenors, were moving a kind of inert mass in the way that was best for them, you know. I suppose you had this feeling of justification in achieving what you were after, like, but not necessarily getting everybody involved in achieving this. Now that was probably a mistake.[17]

That was later. At the time, Murray believed that working-class people in general were too nice and too placid to defend their own interests, while their recognized leaders – the Labour politicians, councillors and full-time union officials – had been bought off. The future rested on the shoulders of self-motivating, self-organizing political activists.

During the 1970s, the Engineering Section of the AUEW went through convulsive arguments over its internal system of democracy, arguments which foreshadowed those that overtook the Labour party. It was a power battle between three main political factions, of which the weakest was the one with which Murray was aligned, the Bevanite 'soft left'. It had achieved some successes in the 1960s, for instance, by securing the election of Len Edmondson to the élite executive council in 1966, but generally it was caught between two formidably efficient election machines: the traditional right and the Communist Party. Hugh Scanlon owed his position to communist support and, as he became more right wing in office, he was at least loyal to his roots in one respect: his contempt for any soft notions about being accountable to his members. For example, a majority of AUEW delegates to Labour's 1978 annual conference had supported the principle of mandatory reselection. Scanlon disagreed, and when it came to the vote, he failed to put in a ballot slip, pleading that he had been confused by the procedure. He had a track record of behaving as if the AUEW block vote were his personal property.

That year, Scanlon retired. It had been generally anticipated that his successor would be Bob Wright, the union's talented 'soft left' Assistant General Secretary, who was accustomed to negotiating with Cabinet ministers; but he was beaten by Terry Duffy, the union's West Midlands district organizer. For the left within the union, and indeed for the Labour party left, this was seriously bad news. Though they had been annoyed by Scanlon's authoritarian behaviour, they at least respected him for his intellect and his stature as a national political leader. To many of the old hands, the AUEW had provided a passport to self-respect and upward social mobility. Union activism was a form of self-education which pulled them up the social ladder. Not content with having a skilled trade, they were self-educated, too, a self-conscious labour aristocracy now finding themselves led by a president who prided himself on being no cleverer than the average working man, who was a poor public speaker who seemed to wallow in his own limitations. 'He never read anything,' one of his former colleagues complained. At the special conference in January 1981, where the Labour party finally settled on a new electoral college for choosing a party leader and deputy leader, it was Duffy's tactical ineptitude which caused the unions to have 40 per cent rather than a third, of the vote. His union considered that even 33 per cent was too much and abstained, handing victory to the left. In his speech, Duffy expressed regret, saying: 'I wish that I could extricate myself from the problem that we have put in a vote that is of no avail.' A barracker in the audience suggested he 'extricate himself' by resigning, sending Duffy soaring to the height of his oratorical powers: 'I have been elected, which in our union is the highest court in the land! Ordinary lads and lasses who go to clock in at factories, who measure whether I should be leader or not! It is obvious that no matter of my logical persuasion is going to make you change your mind.'[18]

His cloth cap image and calculated deference has meant that it is little appreciated what a significant figure Duffy was in the trade union movement in the early 1980s. In the previous decade, Scanlon's name had invariably been linked with that of Jack Jones of the TGWU. They were assumed not only to be the most powerful figures in the trade unions, but among the most powerful men in the country. This is because of their position on the centre left: theirs were the vital unions which had to be won over if any piece of industrial legislation was to be made to work, or the party leader was to avoid defeat at party conference. Under Duffy, the AUEW went out of the news bulletins because it was never in open conflict with either the government or the Labour leader. It was the block vote which Neil Kinnock or John Smith knew they could count on, and consequently the limelight transferred to the unions in the centre of the spectrum, like the GMB under John Edmonds. The one moment of drama came near the end of Duffy's life, in 1985, when the AUEW risked expulsion from the TUC by accepting government funds to subsidize its internal ballots, under a piece of legislation which the other TUC unions proposed to boycott. There appeared to be a real risk of the TUC splitting, with the AUEW, the outlawed EETPU, and other renegades like the Nottinghamshire miners forming a separate association, until the TUC engaged in eyeball-to-eyeball confrontation with Duffy, and backed down. On the day of his death, Neil Kinnock described him as 'blunt, irascible, not always easy to agree with, but as honest as the day is long'.[19] More than any other union leader, he was the one who halted the TUC's leftward drift and hauled it into compliance with government legislation.

Duffy's rivals within the union soon discovered that he had staying power. He had been a boxer for a brief time, between his army service and his apprenticeship, and even if he had one too many blows to the head, he at least knew how to stay on his feet and fight back. The ground on which he chose to fight the left was on union democracy. The engineers had always prided themselves on running one of the most democratic unions in the TUC, and made all the important full-time union officers subject to election, years before it became compulsory under government legislation.

However, in a precursor to the battles Neil Kinnock fought in the Labour Party, left and right fell out over whose democracy it was. As a member of the Rules Revision Committee, Jim Murray was involved in what he believed was, in essence, an 'activists' democracy' in which leaders were made to account to those who had seen them in action and were in a position to judge them. In effect, he wanted those at the top to have to answer to the shop stewards in the middle, while they were to answer to their workmates. Terry Duffy believed in direct democracy, in which the union president answered directly to the rank and file, over the heads of activists if necessary.

This crystallized into an argument over whether elections for union leaders were to be conducted by postal ballot, which were expensive but likely to maximize turn-out, or workplace ballots, which by their very nature eliminated from the franchise the apathetic mass who did not turn out to union meetings. Murray was vehemently opposed to postal ballots. He suspected that union elections would be effectively hijacked by the mass media. The average union member, filling in a ballot slip in the privacy of his home, would have no other 'form' guide than to back the candidates who were given a good press. The outcome he feared was 'the running of the union by its activists' would be 'destroyed'.[20]

To an extent, his predictions were fulfilled. The right-wing machine in the AUEW was well-connected with selected journalists, for whom the union's elections were a sufficient novelty to be worth covering in detail in national newspapers. Their intervention opened up a weakness in the union's left, that they had advanced far ahead in a direction in which their members might not want to go. Any shop steward like Murray who entered into discourses on what Tom Mann had written in 1910 had obviously put daylight between himself and the average metal basher. Terry Duffy, by contrast, always thought and talked like the man on the Wolverhampton workbench. During his leadership, there were recurrent instances of highly articulate left-wing candidates being beaten by less imposing figures on the right, including the contest to succeed Duffy, when Bill Jordan, a right-winger from a Birmingham secondary modern, beat the clever Scottish communist, Bill Airdrie. In 1977, Len Edmondson retired from the union's all-powerful seven-man executive, creating a vacancy in the north of England. The run-off was between Jim Murray, and Harold Robson, from Teesside. Since most of the vote was on Tyneside, Murray was front runner, until the columnist Woodrow Wyatt urged *Sunday Mirror* readers not to vote for him on the grounds that he was pro-communist. Upmarket engineers were given the same advice by Bernard Levin, in *The Times*. He lost.

This argument between an 'activist's' democracy and a 'membership democracy' echoed through the Labour Party in the 1980s. Mandatory re-selection was a deliberate attempt to transfer power from MPs to the activists in their constituencies, and Murray had no hesitation in supporting it. He knew that general committees of constituency parties were liable to be dominated by union representatives, allowing powerful regional secretaries to control the selection of MPs. That was part of the reason why he believed in reselection: it gave local party members an opportunity to rid themselves of union placemen. Had someone come up with a refinement which removed the power of trade union regional secretaries, it is quite likely he would have supported that as well. He was not a great admirer of the union block vote. He was scathing about left-wing unions, like the communist-dominated TASS, whose leaders never submitted themselves to election but used their block vote to compel the Labour Party leader to do so. He always found it laughable that so much power was put into his hands during one frenetic week in autumn 1979.

However, on the issue of how to choose a party leader, Murray stuck to the same principle that leaders should account to the 'activists' who are in daily contact with them – in this case Labour MPs. He understood very well that in voting the way he did, he was leaving an immense obstacle in front of Tony Benn, but he was not a great admirer of Benn's. Like many older union activists, he remembered exactly which Cabinet ministers had supported Barbara Castle's *In Place of Strife*. He also thought that Benn should have resigned from the Cabinet when he was shifted from the post of Secretary of State for Industry in 1975, to continue the fight on behalf of the shop stewards' committees he had helped call into being, instead of leaving them to wither under the unsympathetic Eric Varley, and then emerging four years later to do a 'hatchet job' on the government of which he had been a member all along.[21]

However, Murray's basic reason for not supporting the left had nothing to do with personalities. Unlike most of the delegates, who were caught up in an unfolding power struggle, he was thinking strategically into the future. In the AUEW, he had witnessed the election of a strong left-wing leader, who had then become a law unto himself and a menace to internal democracy. His view was that a change in the method of electing the Labour Party leader would not made the holder of that office more accountable. On the contrary, the leader would be beyond anyone's reach. He would not have to account to fellow MPs, because they would have lost the power to sack him, while a challenge from outside would be impossible in practice. 'If we have to have leaders, let's have as many as possible, not just one Leader,' he pleaded.[22]

This argument may yet have its day, when it becomes a left-wing cause to cut the leader down to size by putting his job at the mercy of Labour MPs, but in 1979–81 their standing was so low that left activists did not believe they were capable of anything so bold. As the delegate from Newcastle Central constituency put it at the special conference in January 1981, 'The impotence of backbench MPs is well-known to many of us, so to suggest that the MPs will have to control in some way the Leader who is put forward is a myth that we ought to stamp on right now.'[23] The delegate's name, for the record, was Marjorie Mowlam.

For someone associated with the left to vote in a way which was likely to hand the leadership to Denis Healey seemed like treachery, and it was to a traitor's welcome that Murray returned to Tyneside amid rumours that he had been in some way bribed or bought off. The *New Statesman's* correspondents, Patrick Wintour and Francis Wheen, reported that:

Murray murmured an explanation about the primacy of the reselection issue, and the views of local Tyneside members. But he was less than forthcoming about the two hours of talks he had with Duffy in Newcastle last week. It appears that one of Duffy's more persistent questions had been 'What do you want to do in the union?'[24]

That provoked a reply from Murray so gratuitously offensive about Duffy that he surely killed any chance there might have been that he would ever be offered a full-time union job, even if there had been one in Duffy's gift. The 'two hours of talk', he claimed, had in fact been 'a forty minute slanging match in a Newcastle bar' in front of a crowd of engineering shop stewards. For good measure, he insulted the two *New Statesman* journalists for being part of a 'Bloomsbury/Hampstead/Holland Park' cabal, identifying himself with Tom Mann, James Connolly, the leader of the Lucas Aerospace shop stewards, Mike Cooley, and others 'who have viewed with equal suspicion the bourgeois in the movement, both right and left'.[25] Privately, he complained of feeling like Prometheus having his liver plucked out. More generally, he defended himself against the charge of disloyalty with the argument that 'More damage has been done to society and humanity by leaders who pushed policies through by a mixture of patronage and threats than by any individual who argues against a trend because of personal conviction.'[26]

Murray's rift with the Bennites was, however, no more than an irritant when compared to the real threat to everything in which he believed, posed by the collapse of heavy engineering on Tyneside. Before the crisis began to bite seriously at the end of the 1970s, his standing as a shop steward was protected by his ability to secure good wages and working conditions for the workforce at Vickers Elswick. As the job losses gathered pace, his reputation suffered from his inability either to stop the management running down its investment, or the men from seizing the attractive short-term option of a redundancy pay-off. In 1977, Vickers announced the closure of the Scotswood plant, its second biggest on Tyneside. Despite Stuart Holland being brought in to do a 'social audit' which demonstrated that the overall cost to the community, in knock-on job losses, increased social security payments and lost income tax, was comparable to the cost of subsidising Vickers to keep the factory open, it closed.

This failure added to suspicions that had been voiced by trade union members for years that Murray moved in another mental world, different from the one inhabited by Tyneside metal workers. The people who most admired him tended to be middle-class radicals, who were delighted to come upon a shop steward from a large factory who was at ease in their company. The feminist writer, Hilary Wainwright, described him as 'sometimes shamelessly sexist, but full of contradictions . . .He was at home equally in his convener's cabin at Elswick and the magnificent building of the Literary and Philosophical Society, and had either haven sold Newcastle Scotch Ale he would never have needed to look elsewhere.'[27]

Connections like these, and his hair – which in middle age began to creep over his collar – caused him to be known to other trade unionists, behind his back, as the 'hippy shoppie'. Roy Hadwin, his predecessor at Vickers, is predictably scathing about him, calling him 'shallow' and 'clever, but not competent', and suggesting that Murray's obvious enjoyment of female company had made him suspect in the masculine culture of Tyneside's shop stewards. 'He was leftie. He was like T. Dan Smith – he started to believe in his own myth. But he was a good Catholic,' he said.[28] The Labour MP John Evans, a contemporary of Murray's who was convener on one of the Tyne shipyards, who had no personal motive for joining Murray's detractors, remembered him as 'rather a Bohemian character', adding, 'I think for that reason he was not entirely trusted. It was thought that his heart was not in it, and his backbone was not in it. You needed hard men to be conveners on the Tyne in those days, because the bosses were bastards.'[29]

On the other hand, it would be hard to find a living witness who knows more about the engineering union on Tyneside in the 1950s, 1960s and 1970s than Len Edmondson, who was Tyne District secretary in 1953–66, until his election to the national executive council. He believes that Murray sacrificed the chance of becoming a major player within the AUEW when he resigned from the lay post of district president in the 1970s, in protest at the union's increasing willingness to accept redundancy deals rather than follow his strategy of organizing company-wide and using its industrial muscle to prevent closures. Edmondson said: 'He was a good convener and a very good member of the national committee. He always put forward a very sensible, logical argument in support of any resolution which he had to support and I thought he had a very good approach within the framework of the union. He always knew which questions were worth taking and whether he had a good case. I thought his only mistake was to resign from the district presidency. I said that he should not resign, and I thought he would have been appointed a full-time official if he had stayed in office.'[30]

In 1979, Vickers Elswick was hit by disaster from a wholly unexpected quarter, when the regime in Iran was brought down. In the previous decade, the factory had narrowed the variety of its operations until almost its only activity was turning out Chieftain tanks. The main buyer had been the Shah's army. Soon after the revolution, Murray visited revolutionary Iran and made contact with the Fadayeen, the main secular opponents of the Shah; but that did not resolve the problem that without a market, the factory could not survive. The one remaining customer was the military regime in Nigeria, whose demand for tanks was insufficient to sustain a factory the size of the old Elswick plant. It shut early in 1982, and part of it reopened on a site at the far end of the Scotswood Road, conveniently located in an enterprise zone which provided tax advantages for the company. Passing motorists could identify it by the full-scale model of a Chieftain tank mounted on a sloping pedestal outside. Murray speculated that it was put there for the 'impulse buyer'. He had, meanwhile, lost the will to fight. He was fifty-two and already suffering from the painful kidney problem which eventually killed him. Like thousands of other Tyneside engineers in his age group, he would never find a full-time job again. It was a straightforward demonstration of the limitations of syndicalism. He had discovered that – to quote a favourite chant of the 1970s demonstrators – 'the workers united could never be defeated' if and only if capitalism required their labour. As unemployment spread, and the pattern of employment altered, destroying the old centres of militancy and the collectivist experience which gave rise to them, the power of militant shop stewards or of unionized labour of any kind was disappearing.

Their passing in one sense simplifies the way for New Labour, because the shop stewards' movement was a vigorous lobby for 'producer' interests, from which New Labour is determined to keep a certain distance. One of Tony Blair's first public undertakings upon assuming the party leadership was to reassert that the trade unions could expect 'fairness but not favours' from his government. Among other things, that means that the legal immunities which enabled the unions to impose a closed shop will no longer exist. Another simplification is that in Murray's day, to establish a company-wide Combine for the workers in every plant in Britain was difficult enough; to achieve it Europe-wide would have been practically impossible. Under a Blair government, that would be accomplished effortlessly through the European Social Chapter, which guarantees Europe-wide representation on works councils for workforces above a specified size. The very fact of it being achieved through collaboration takes away any syndicalist potential the works council may have had.

However, a much bigger problem which is still unresolved is whether communities are to be protected from the catastrophe of mass unemployment caused when a large employer decides to shift its investment somewhere else. The Blairite slogan of a 'stakeholder' economy suggests that large companies will have unstated responsibilities to the communities from which they draw their workforces as well as to their shareholders. How that is to be translated into practical effect is not known, at the time of writing. The syndicalist method of using the industrial muscle of unionized workforces to hold together economically vulnerable communities failed, but it is not yet apparent that New Labour can produce a better solution.

CHAPTER FOUR

THE BLIND MAN FROM SHEFFIELD

He was, in his way, the most successful local government leader of the second half of the century. He was never as celebrated as the GLC leader Ken Livingstone, nor did he ever dominate Sheffield in the way that Jeremy Beecham controlled Newcastle Upon Tyne, but no one from any political party used local government to launch a career in national politics more successfully than David Blunkett, since Herbert Morrison moved from the London County Council to the War Cabinet in 1940. This is all the more remarkable because in the greatest crisis of his career, Blunkett led Sheffield to the brink of a disaster from which his own career might never have recovered. He then paused and stepped back.

There was a similar pattern to his contribution to Labour's self-renewal in the 1980s. No upheaval, like the expulsion of Militant or the renunciation of unilateral nuclear disarmament, was complete without an incident involving Blunkett looking for a formula which would somehow embrace the leader's new position without entirely abandoning the old. Never quite satisfied with the wording of any resolution, he became known as the Great Amender. After an emotive confrontation, after Blunkett had established anew that he was not to be taken for granted or pushed around, he would usually give in. He was argumentative, stubborn, troublesome and emotional; no one was harder to win over, except for the intractables like Tony Benn or Dennis Skinner, but he was persuadable. When Blunkett gave in, the cause was a very long way to being won. The most sensitive political topic of Tony Blair's first eighteen months as opposition leader was education. He and his Shadow Education Secretary collided several times; at a crucial moment, Blunkett openly opposed Blair over the treatment of the would-be parliamentary candidate Liz Davies; but when it counted, he stood up to an angry conference hall and delivered. A relieved Tony Blair became the second party leader to appreciate the importance of having Blunkett on his side.

Blunkett is also well capable of getting things disastrously wrong. The campaign against rate-capping, his first big test as a national figure, was a spectacular failure, whichever way it is viewed. His attitude to Militant was deeply contradictory and unpredictable. In his first job on the frontbench, he was the driving force behind an ill-chosen policy on a replacement for the poll tax which snarled the careers of two members of the Shadow Cabinet. His device of a Foundation School, Labour's current way out of the political dilemma posed by Grant Maintained Schools, looks like little else but a device to avoid confrontation. Overall, he is an example of someone who has made the political journey from the Bennite left in the early 1980s to the social democratic centre in the 1990s. He was more intimately tied up with the Bennite left than any member of the current Shadow Cabinet apart from Michael Meacher, but unlike some who were only half in the Benn camp at the time, his break with them has been complete. He gives the impression of arriving at a political position by 'feel' rather than cold analysis. In contrast to his former colleague, Bryan Gould, who could not settle anywhere between perfection and failure, Blunkett has the resilience of someone who can make bad judgements, run himself into a cul-de-sac, turn round and start again. When other Labour politicians are finding that the shock of being in government is more than they can handle, Blunkett can be relied on to settle into ministerial office and cling on limpet-like through all the storms follow.

As is well-known, Blunkett was born blind, because of a rare genetic mismatch between his elderly parents. His attitude to this condition is to treat it as an 'inconvenience' rather than a disability. Sometimes an opponent might think Blunkett is using his blindness as a psychological weapon to win an argument; he appears not to be conscious of doing it. As an ambitious young delegate to annual party conferences, he had no scruples about making use of the fact that he could not see the red light come on when it was time for him to wind up his speech. He has, on occasions, fought ferociously on behalf of other political activists inconvenienced by physical disabilities. For instance, when an Islington councillor suffering from cerebral palsy was deselected by the left in November 1989, Blunkett exploded and sent a furious letter to Neil Kinnock, the Shadow Environment Secretary, Bryan Gould, and the party's Local Government Officer, Gordon Prentice, claiming that the 'ultras deselected him for not carrying out the "purist" line . . . It does illustrate the lengths to which some of the less reputable members will go.'[1] But he never put himself forward as a spokesman for the blind or the disabled. He demands to be treated as a player in the political game, subject to the same rules as others. There was one occasion when he stood up to intervene in a heated parliamentary argument, and could not find the dispatch box from which frontbenchers normally speak. One or two Conservative MPs started jeering at him as he fumbled for it; others looked as if they disapproved of their own colleagues' behaviour; but Blunkett ignored it, as if ridiculing an opponent's blindness was part of the normal parliamentary knockabout. It would simply be foreign to his nature to suggest that anyone should pull their punches on him because he cannot see, and it would annoy him if anyone else suggested it on his behalf.

This 'inconvenience' has, after all, been with him always. In everyday conversation, Blunkett talks as if he were sighted; for example, if someone approaches him to tell him the contents of a document, he is likely to thank them for letting him 'see' it, though in fact he sees only enough to tell the difference between intense light and pitch dark. In the evenings he cannot tell whether the room he is in is lit or not. This condition compels him to observe a strict daily routine. He must be accompanied everywhere by a dog which must be fed and exercised at given times. A parliamentary ritual as fixed as the Speaker's procession is that of David Blunkett going out on to the green below Big Ben, behind the main gates into parliament, to let his dog have a run. Others easily forget that the dog is not a pet but a part of his life, as vital as a limb. In restaurants, for instance, other diners might think it is a kindness to offer the animal a titbit when, on the contrary, it could be seriously disruptive to a guide dog which has been strictly trained to eat only at fixed times.

There was an occasion when a pool of foul water mysteriously appeared in the Member's Lobby in the House of Commons, and someone jokily suggested that the culprit could be Blunkett's dog, a rumour which found its way into a newspaper diary. The idea that a dog does not appreciate the social disgrace of pissing in one of the citadels of power might be funny to someone else. To Blunkett, it was an insult. He compelled the Commons authorities to establish that the real cause was a leaking flower box in a room above, and then extracted an apology from the offending newspaper. After all, if it was thought that his dog was not housetrained, that too could seriously affect Blunkett's social life, such as it is.

Apart from having to deal with the usual inconveniences of occasionally missing his way and colliding with an unexpected obstacle, Blunkett is forced into a kind of isolation in an environment which thrives on gossip and where a person is often judged by the amount of illicit information they can glean. As he passes through the Members' Lobby, where politicians and political journalists meet and plot, Blunkett cannot tell who else is there, cannot catch anyone's eye or steal up to them to exchange confidences, and because he is busy giving orders to his dog, others are reluctant to approach him. If they do, he has to be warned if there is a third person in the vicinity who can overhear.

Not knowing who is in the room can land a politician in difficulties. There was an occasion, for example, when details of a private meeting of Labour MPs were leaked. It was immediately noticed that the list of people who were present contained one omission; one member of the Shadow Cabinet had arrived late for the meeting, and had sat in without speaking. Immediately, suspicion as to the identity of the leaker fell upon the one person present who would not have been able to see his colleague sitting silently at the table.

There are logistical implications to being a blind politician. He is in a profession which lives on words, some spoken, but most of them written down in the mountains of documents which pass daily through the Commons. If he goes to a committee meeting, Blunkett has to familiarize himself with all the relevant documents before it begins, while others can go in unprepared and skim through documents when someone else is speaking. He needs an extensive support staff to help with the practical problems of ingesting so much information. Annually, when MPs vote on their own salaries and office expenses, a special clause is inserted to award David Blunkett an office allowance 50 per cent larger than anyone else's.

Blunkett has a recollection of beginning to see things in infancy which he cannot make out now; but a much more striking fact about his childhood

is that he did not realize he was different from other children until the trau-
matic day when, as a four-year-old, he was delivered by his parents to a
boarding school for the blind.

Everything about the circumstances of his upbringing suggests that fate
did not intend him to make a success of his life. He was, for all practical
purposes, an only child. Though his parents had children by previous mar-
riages, all his various step-brothers and sisters and his half sister had left
home by the time he was old enough to recognize them. His mother was
forty-three and his father fifty-five when he was born in June 1947. He was
brought up in a two-bedroom council house in the Longley district of
Sheffield. Arthur Blunkett was a foreman at the local gas works, who died
an agonizing death when the younger Blunkett was twelve, after falling into
a vat of boiling water. Though the accident was down to the carelessness of
another employee, the East Midlands Gas Board refused to compensate the
family on the grounds that they had not suffered any lost earnings because
he was working past the normal retirement age. The case dragged on for
two years, during which Blunkett and his mother endured extreme hard-
ship. He wrote later:

> Those who have never experienced real poverty are all too often very sentimental
> about it and about poor people in general. I have to smile at this and think: if only
> you knew what it was like, you would know all about aspirations and expectations,
> and why it was that, in the community in which I grew up, escaping the poverty
> trap and achieving success were the key aims.[2]

There were no appropriate day schools for blind children in Sheffield, so
Blunkett was sent away as a boarder at the age of four to the Manchester
Road School for the Blind, where he shared a dormitory with nine other
frightened, homesick little boys. He was allowed a parental visit one
Saturday per month, and a visit home one weekend a month. At the age of
twelve, soon after his father's death, he went on to another boarding school,
the oddly named Royal Normal College, in Shropshire. This was the only
time in his life until his election to parliament at the age of almost forty that
he lived outside his native Sheffield. The school did not place great emphasis on academic achievement or instil dreams of fame and fortune in its
pupils: its purpose was to teach them self-sufficiency. At the end, Blunkett
was offered a choice of three training schemes: as a capstan lathe operator

in a sheltered workshop, a piano tuner, or a commercial course as a Braille shorthand typist, which he took. His first job, obtained with help from the Royal National Institute for the Blind, was as clerk and typist with his father's former employer, the East Midlands Gas Board.

However, Blunkett was already self-motivating and, despite his later claims that he was shy in the company of others of his own age, he was already displaying a pushiness, a will to be the centre of attention, and an interest in politics. He joined the Shrewsbury Labour Party at the age of sixteen, and although he was never profoundly religious, as a teenager he was a Methodist lay preacher. He made his first television appearance at the age of only twenty, as an outraged viewer, after he had been sitting with his mother who was shocked by the portrayal of naked bodies lying in a morgue. The producers of a talkback programme had invited him down to London to appear on the programme on the strength of an irate telephone call, unaware that he was blind, until he turned up at BBC Television Centre with a white stick. 'I did not need to see their faces, I could actually feel the sheer bewilderment, nay horror,' he recalled. 'Here was a young blind man about to appear on their programme to comment on the filming of naked bodies which he could not possibly have seen.'[3] It is Blunkett's firm view that you do not need to see something to make a balanced judgement of it.

By sheer self-exertion, Blunkett managed to work his way through night school to obtain a place to read politics and modern history at Sheffield University, where his tutors included Bernard Crick, who was head of politics, and Roydon Harrison, Professor of History. This was the late 1960s. Other students were joining revolutionary organizations, or getting stoned to rock music; but Blunkett was having to learn a discipline which would stay with him for life. His tap-tapping on a Braille typewriter as he took notes during lectures was a distraction to other students, and consequently he was allowed to tape them. While other students were enjoying free time, he was alone in his room, transcribing his tapes, with the result that he remembered his lectures better than anyone else in the audience. He also stolidly persisted in turning out to dreary meetings of his ward Labour Party. In 1970, at the age of only twenty-two, he was elected to Sheffield Council, in a safe Labour seat which he held for eighteen years. He took his council work intently seriously, in spite of the formidable logistical problems confronting him. Councillors are fed huge quantities of documentation, most of it written in the specialized language of senior council officials in which – for instance – instead of saying that the 'sun shone through the skylight' an officer's report might record that 'high level fenestration ensured good general daylighting levels'.[4] A conscientious councillor must absorb mountains of this indigestible information, in addition to meeting electors in regular surgeries, attending party meetings and turning out to civic functions, for no more reward than a modest daily attendance allowance. Most are driven by boredom, incomprehension or laziness to the fringes of the council, so that decision-making is left to the senior officers and a tiny inner core of leading councillors – a situation which suited the inner core very well.

It is unlikely that the Sheffield city leaders saw the arrival of a lone, young blind man as any threat to their power base. Even if he had wanted to read the incomprehensible officers' reports which are the key to understanding how decisions are made, he would not be able to. He was a useful figure to have hovering outside the corridors of power, making speeches on behalf of the disabled, and acting as a harmless exhibit to demonstrate that neither youth, nor a working-class background nor a physical handicap were a bar to service on Sheffield city council. But anyone who thought he would settle into an innocuous support role underestimated Blunkett's cussed determination. It was as a young councillor that he established the logistical support system he will need for as long as he is in public life. Other Labour MPs sometimes grumble about his anti-sociability, because he seldom mixes in the tearoom or stops for a drink in the bar. What they may not appreciate is that when others are enjoying a quiet evening, Blunkett is usually locked away alone in his office, listening to tapes and dictating. Every document or letter sent to him has to be conscientiously read out on to a tape, except a few of the most important, which are transcribed into braille. He answers every letter by dictating a reply and leaving it on a tape where a secretary can find it and transcribe it in the morning.

Blunkett's blindness compelled him to develop a superior memory, so that while other councillors would turn up to meetings having glanced at the papers beforehand and would surreptitiously study them as the meeting progressed, Blunkett had already committed their contents to memory and could quote sentences from numbered paragraphs without a downward glance. Even so, he was disadvantaged by the old officers' habit of producing last minute supplementary reports which would be put in front of councillors as they entered the committee room. He was also doing what passed for a full-time job, as an Industrial Tutor at Barnsley College of Technology. Fortunately, the college was more understanding about his taking time off for council activities than a private sector employer might have been. He also married in 1970, and his first son was born in 1977. By 1982, he was the father of three boys.

Blunkett's blindness helped him in subtle ways to make progress through the political jungle. It brought media attention. He was able, for example, to turn his first visit to the Houses of Parliament as an obscure young councillor into a national event, when his guide dog, Ruby, was barred at the door; the resulting protest, orchestrated by the Guide Dogs for the Blind Association, brought a change in the rules governing the Palace of Westminster. It also gave him a certain psychological advantage over opponents. Those who have sat in committee meetings with him have experienced the Blunkett tantrum. When it appears that he might not get his way, he can threaten to storm out of the room or worse, and the first instinct of everyone around him is to placate him and try to meet him half way. If he was not blind, he might be accused of bullying.

Having discovered that Councillor Blunkett could be dangerous, the civic bosses decided that the best course was to promote him quickly. He was enlisted on the most important committees, the Executive and Policy Committees. In 1973, he was elected to the newly created South Yorkshire county council, which came into existence under the 1974 reorganization and was abolished twelve years later. There, too, he served on the key Policy and Executive Committees. In May 1976, at the age of twenty-seven, he became chairman of Sheffield's Family and Community Services Committee.

Parts of the Sheffield Labour Party also looked kindly on his ambition to be an MP. He was one of the youngest candidates in the general election of February 1974, although he was fighting the hopelessly Tory seat of Sheffield Hallam, where he picked up only 27.2 per cent of the vote. Possibly because it was a Tory seat, the Hallam constituency party was more left-wing than others in Sheffield and was more dominated by middle-class public sector employees, like Blunkett's former lecturer, Roydon

Harrison. Blunkett's big break nearly came when the MP for Penistone, Jack Mendelson, died in 1978. Penistone was then Blunkett's home constituency, consisting of the council estates from what is now Sheffield Hillsborough, and part of Barnsley. It was so solidly Labour that the party had held on to it even in the 1930s. Blunkett entered the selection contest, and missed by only one vote – a disappointment which was probably the best piece of disguised good fortune he has ever had in his political life. If he had succeeded, he would have enjoyed eleven months as a backbench MP on the government side, followed by the best part of eighteen years as an opposition MP, without accumulating any more experience of being in charge of anything, and without becoming a figure of any consequence in the Labour Party outside parliament.

Local tradition at that time worked against a native of Sheffield becoming an MP for the city. Local constituencies habitually chose their MPs from outside and encouraged Sheffield's brightest talents to go out and seek their political fortunes somewhere else. Thus Roy Hattersley, who was a Sheffield councillor at the age of twenty-five, first stood for parliament in Sutton Coldfield before finding a safe Labour seat in Birmingham. This had two great advantages. First, by pulling in upwardly mobile outsiders and handing them safe Labour seats, the city increased its chances of being represented in Labour governments. A good example was Fred Mulley, MP for Sheffield Park 1950–83, a labourer's son from Leamington Spa who rose to be Defence Secretary in the Callaghan government. At the same time, it left the civic bosses firmly in charge, undisturbed by MPs with a working knowledge of the city. According to a 1967 survey, 'the demands made upon the Member of Parliament by his constituency party in Sheffield are slight, and unlikely to offend his conscience. Loyalty is given to the man and there are very few attempts to influence the policy he will follow.'[5]

Although it was known even then as the Socialist Republic of South Yorkshire, and seemed to take pride in the reputation, Sheffield city council was in fact controlled by stalwarts of the traditional Labour right: high spenders, with a strong sense of civic dignity, happy to do deals with the public sector unions, loyal to the party's national leadership and hostile to any left-wing radicalism. Its most famous representative was Enid Hattersley, a coal-merchant's daughter who was Lord Mayor of Sheffield in

1981–82, and who was the feared mother of a Cabinet Minister. The council leader, George Wilson, defected to the SDP in the early 1980s, though he was out of place there. Like most of Sheffield's leaders, he belonged in the old right-wing tradition that the council delivered the goods for a supine and grateful working class, and honoured its civic leaders. One of the most famous incidents from these years was when the official Mace Bearer was sacked because he had become such a well-known character in the city that he was acknowledging the applause of the crowd and in other ways upstaging the outraged city Mayor.

During the 1970s, however, the rumbling changes within the Labour Party which would culminate in the Bennite rebellion were beginning to be felt in Sheffield even under the Heath government. Stimulated by national events, educated recruits were joining the party and rising relatively quickly to positions of influence. The practice of choosing outsiders as MPs was breached when the redrawn Sheffield Hillsborough constituency selected a local headteacher, Martin Flannery, who had been in the Communist Party until 1956 and was well-known in the area as a party and union activist. Much more seriously, in neighbouring Brightside, the constituency for which Blunkett would eventually be elected, open conflict broke out between the incumbent MP Eddie Griffiths and the party's general committee, which resulted in a rare example of an MP being deselected. The conflict was essentially about union militancy and extra-parliamentary protest. Within the constituency party, opinion was running high against incomes policies in any form and in support of the miners' action in 1972, the direct challenge to Heath's industrial relations court mounted by the AUEW and other unions, and the refusal by councillors in nearby Clay Cross urban district to obey parliamentary legislation by increasing council-house rents. Griffiths supported none of these, being a convinced believer in parliamentary sovereignty. He was also under attack for being an outsider, a former industrial chemist and worker–director of the nationalized British Steel Corporation whose involvement in constituency affairs was considered too infrequent. He complained to the *Sheffield Morning Telegraph* that 'the Brightside party's thinking seems to be that unless you have a cloth cap, a muffler and a boilersuit, you are not fit to be a Labour MP'.[6] Even in these fraught circumstances, the Sheffield Brightside party observed one local tradition, by going outside Sheffield to find a new MP in Joan Maynard, leader of Yorkshire's agricultural workers' union, whose formidable looks and undeviatingly left-wing views earned her the nickname 'Stalin's granny'.

Within Sheffield Council, a group of Young Turks began to challenge what they regarded as the paternalism of the old leadership. After Blunkett, the most important of the younger generation was Clive Betts, a Cambridge University graduate who joined the council in 1976 and succeeded Blunkett as council leader in 1987. Altogether, no less than five of Sheffield's younger left-wing councillors went on to become MPs, the others being Jimmy Boyce, Helen Jackson and Bill Michie.

The unpopularity of the Callaghan government, which was driving the Labour Party to the left, speeded up the process in another way because, by about 1977, the Labour Party was unable to win any elections outside its heartlands, and was losing council seats all over Britain. By the end of the decade, that had been reversed and Labour was picking up council seats it had not held for years, introducing waves of new and predominantly left-wing councillors who had no compunction about ousting long-term civic leaders. The best-known example is the Greater London Council. Before the May 1981 council elections, the Labour group was down to twenty-eight councillors led by Andrew McIntosh, the Managing Director of a Market Research Company whose leadership had the personal endorsement of Michael Foot. After the election, the Labour Group was fifty strong, back in control of the council, with Tony Banks and Paul Boateng among the new intake, and with Ken Livingstone as their new leader.

In Sheffield, the takeover by the left came a year earlier, when David Blunkett was elected leader by the enlarged Labour group returned during the May elections. The new city leaders self-consciously tried to break with a long paternalist tradition in which Labour councils gave the working class what was believed to be good for them without seeking their opinions or encouraging their participation. They set out to encourage community groups, tenants' groups, trade unions and local Labour parties to participate. The health warning which New Labour would attach to this sort of exercise is that if councillors are not careful, they open themselves to being unduly influenced by local interest groups like the town hall unions or radicalized party activists, and in their enthusiasm for nuclear free zones and other exotica, forget that most of the public are passive users of council services who only want their bins emptied on the right day and repairs carried out efficiently. However, in the early 1980s, what Sheffield embarked on was highly innovative because it was unusual for council leaders to ask anyone at all for their opinions, other than senior council officers and, in Sheffield's case, the District Committee of the Confederation of Shipbuilding and Engineering Unions, which wielded immense influence in the Sheffield Labour Party.

For instance, the manner in which manifestos for local election councils were drawn up was radically changed. In the past, this had been an exercise free of politics. A few councils would compile a list of the recent achievements of the various council departments and invite electors to vote for more of the same. Now the District Labour Party (DLP), a committee on which sat representatives of each of the city's constituency Labour parties, became involved in the task of drawing up long, elaborate manifestos, which required the creation of six Manifesto Working Parties. Instead of relying on the mighty Confed, the DLP's principal link with the unions was through Sheffield Trades Council, to which the public sector unions began affiliating in larger numbers, so that the AUEW was soon overtaken by the white collar council union NALGO as the union with the largest number of trades council delegates.[7] The 1983 local manifesto for Sheffield was fifty-nine pages and 25,000 words long. After the election, it was formally adopted by the Policy Committee as council policy, and the Manifesto Working Parties continued to function as monitoring groups to ensure that council departments were carrying it out. As an extra means of ensuring that Labour councillors took the manifesto seriously, the DLP was given control over the candidates' panel. No one could stand for the council as a Labour candidate unless they had been nominated to the panel by a local party branch and interviewed by the DLP executive. Sitting councillors had to be renominated and interviewed. Because this happened gradually over several years, rather than in the one spectacular leap forward executed by the GLC in 1981, the changes created less friction and produced fewer hair-raising newspaper stories.

In a Fabian pamphlet published in 1983, Blunkett set out what he regarded as the four basic aims of Sheffield's new left-wing administration. The first was local industrial sector plans, including planning agreements between the council and private employers and the channelling of public money into socially useful projects which would create jobs to reduce Sheffield's unemployment. To this end a new Employment Department was created at Sheffield city hall to establish training centres, improve safety at work and other practices, and to support local unions campaigning against redundancies. By 1986, the department had a staff of more than 100 and an annual budget of £5 million.[8] One of the enterprises attracted to Sheffield was the National Union of Mineworkers, whose new President, Arthur Scargill, wanted his headquarters out of London and closer to the coalfields. The deal struck in 1983 included grants of £500,000 from Sheffield and from South Yorkshire county council, plus £20,000 more from the city towards the cost of employing twenty workers, £1,000 per job created.

The second was to reduce the relative size of the private sector economy by building up Sheffield's direct labour force and encouraging the spread of worker cooperatives. The third part was a critique of the welfare state, which Blunkett claimed was no more than a distribution system to compensate for inequalities, and should be transformed into a means of preventing inequalities and encouraging the deprived to participate in shaping their own lives. Finally, he argued that council staff could not be neutral specialists, but should be required to have a commitment to the council's objectives.[9]

The first two parts directly reflected the Bennite national economic programme, just as the huge length and prescriptive detail of the Sheffield manifesto reflected the document which Labour put before the country's electorate in 1983, with such memorably disastrous results. Blunkett now defends the job-creation programme for its 'psychological' impact in restoring 'morale and motivation' in a city where 50,000 jobs were lost in three years. 'It gave the feeling that there was an effort being made to protect people from what was a calamity for the whole community,' he claimed.[10] The overall cost was enormous: Sheffield rates were hiked up by 41 per cent in 1980 and 37 per cent in 1981, yet the city continued to vote Labour. Clearly, no government list of councils whose rates needed to be capped by law was likely to exclude Sheffield.

The last point on Blunkett's list has alarming overtones. Labour has spent a generation in opposition trying to combat the politicization of the civil service by Conservative ministers, and any Labour council leader who proposed to demand political commitment from town hall staff in the late 1990s would be rapidly disowned by the party's parliamentary leaders. However, almost the entire section on the welfare state could have been written by a modernizer in the Labour Party of Tony Blair.

Although Blunkett was a Bennite radical on economic issues like state intervention in the economy, he was never part of what came to be caricatured as the 'trendy' left, with its emphasis on positive discrimination and on 'race and gender' as opposed to 'class' issues. It was not until 1986, fully five years after the GLC, that Sheffield Council established its Women's Unit. In that same year, Blunkett became so agitated by the activities of some London councillors that he risked throwing away precious votes in the annual NEC elections by composing a polemic against the 'trendy' left, in which he remarked in passing that: 'I am not prejudiced against gays and lesbians but there is no point in trying to delude myself that I feel anything but revulsion at the idea of touching another male.' He also said:

> Probably one of the most annoying and patronising aspects of trendy Left politics today is the way some people simply trot out the groups which they believe deserve their benevolent positive action. People are lumped together rather than understood as individuals, who at one moment fall into one category, and at another fall into none. So we checklist our own sincerity by talking about women (of course not a minority), gays, lesbians, blacks and, if we remember, the disabled . . .
>
> Perhaps the daftest of all are those politicians or pressure group activists who irritate the bulk of the population beyond measure by suggesting or inferring that, instead of reflecting the variety of lifestyles, cultures and interest in our community, we should go so far as to repress the norm in order to avoid the promotion of one lifestyle above that of another. As someone with a handicap . . . I would no more expect phrases such as 'blind as a bat' to be eliminated from usage, than 'blackboard'. I also expect the bulk of our entertainment and cultural expression to reflect the fact that the majority of the population is heterosexual.[11]

Almost a decade later, Blunkett used the pages of the *Daily Mail* to deliver a similar diatribe about Islington councillors who had allegedly allowed 'paedophiles, pimps and drug dealers' to victimize children through misguided opposition to homophobia and racism:

> I have been plagued by political correctness all my life . . . On the council, it began with simply changing the names of things . . . There was the ridiculous suggestion that words such as 'manhole' were no longer acceptable . . . My personal experience is similar. I am blind. It is a simple enough word for an obvious enough fact. Yet

people want to call blindness anything but blindness . . . The puritanism that is part of political correctness seeks to instil guilt about simple, guilt-free things.[12]

On occasions, Blunkett has been prepared to go out on a limb and accept the consequent political damage in order to defend what he regards as acceptable social norms, when others in the Labour Party think he is being reactionary. The best-known example was that he was among a very small number of Labour MPs to vote against lowering the age of consent for homosexuals to sixteen. During the passage of the 1990 Human Fertilisation and Embryology Bill, he tore himself away from his immersion in Labour's alternative to the poll tax to set out what he believes are the rights and wrongs of artificial insemination and scientific research on human embryos. Rather reluctantly, he accepted that embryos could legitimately be used for research within the first fourteen days, and that insemination might be an acceptable antidote to infertility under specific conditions, which did not include the insemination of single or widowed women. 'Child bearing is not a right. It is part of the unfathomable life force. That is why man and woman together must take responsibility for the well-being and love of the child,' he stressed.[13]

In the early 1980s, the Bennite left managed to be astonishingly united despite its underlying differences. So far as the Labour Party at large was concerned, Blunkett was a young Bennite in charge of a major city council. When he travelled to Brighton in 1983, as Sheffield Hillsborough's constituency party delegate to Labour's annual conference, the record shows that he cast his constituency vote exclusively for the 'Bennite' candidates in the NEC and leadership elections, including Michael Meacher in the contest for the deputy leadership, with two deviations: like many others on the left, he backed Neil Kinnock rather than Eric Heffer for leader, and in the NEC elections, in the best tradition of pushy young politicians, he voted for himself.

But what was he doing standing for the NEC anyway? At the time, the left had a highly developed system for filling the seven NEC places reserved for nominees of constituency parties. The list of candidates favoured by the network of Bennite pressure groups was published annually in *Tribune* and on leaflets handed to each confused constituency delegate as they arrived for the annual conference. In 1982, six out of seven names on the

Tribune 'slate' were elected. The only member to get back on without Tribune's support was Neil Kinnock, who had been struck off for his failure to support Benn in the Deputy Leadership contest. In 1983, Kinnock no longer needed to run, and the popular CND veteran, Frank Allaun, had decided to retire. Tribune's two candidates for the resulting vacancies were Michael Meacher, who was in the news because of the Deputy Leadership contest, and the little known London MP, Norman Atkinson. Blunkett spotted an opportunity and went for it. Having persuaded Sheffield Hillsborough Labour Party to nominate him, he rounded up a few friends to help and wrote to the secretary of every constituency Labour Party in the country to promote himself. He emphasized the importance of having someone from local government on the NEC. Thus Blunkett won a place on the NEC at the first attempt, whereas there were others who had had to try every year for more than a decade before succeeding. Moreover, it was the first time for thirty-five years since the departure of Harold Laski that one of these places had been taken by someone who had never been an MP.

This meant that in addition to his sporadic appearances at Barnsley College of Technology, where he was still on the payroll as an Industrial Tutor, and what amounted to a full-time job leading Sheffield Council, Blunkett had now committed himself to travelling to London several times a month, accompanied by his guide dog, to find his way around a strange city in which he had no regular place to stay. He also had three sons aged between six and one. It is not entirely surprising that his marriage ended in divorce soon afterwards.

Blunkett was immediately given the chairmanship of an NEC committee. Until this time, councillors had played almost no role in national Labour Party politics, but now, as local government became more politicized, it was beginning to be appreciated that they wielded real power in a way parliamentary leaders did not. No one else on the NEC had ever been the employer of several thousand staff and controller of an annual budget equivalent to £400 million at 1996 prices, as Blunkett was. His arrival on the NEC was the occasion to create a new Local Government Committee, which he was the only person qualified to chair. From the start, therefore, despite being identified with the Bennites, Blunkett was offered the opportunity to be one of the big players in the national executive, which was then a much more significant force in party affairs than it was by the 1990s.

Blunkett was also invited to the private meetings of the left caucus, which at that point included eleven of the twenty-nine members of the NEC. Almost at once, he reacted against it. For eight years, the NEC had been irreconcilably polarized between the two factions. Both held their separate caucus meetings and went into the NEC itself without the slightest intention of holding a constructive discussion or seeking compromise. Confrontation, followed by competitive briefings to the journalists circling outside, were the order of the day. Blunkett supported the Bennites, but he had arrived by his own efforts and was irritated to discover that they treated him as if his vote belonged to them.

Two other members of the Bennite caucus were also finding its demands irksome. Michael Meacher was the one in the most difficult position, because he owed his NEC place to the backing of radicalized constituency activists and his membership of the slate. But he was also a member of the Shadow Cabinet. Such was the estrangement between the PLP and the active Labour Party that there was a short period when Meacher was the only person who succeeded in being elected to the NEC and Shadow Cabinet simultaneously. In parliament, he held the vital job of Shadow Health and Social Security Secretary, and was the front man for the party's main political campaign of the year. In February 1984, two members of his team, Frank Field and Max Madden, had claimed the distinction of being the first Shadow Ministers sacked by Neil Kinnock for failing to follow the party whip. To function at all in his parliamentary role, Meacher needed to cooperate both with the leader and with a right-wing dominated Shadow Cabinet. When NEC meetings were on, he was expected to join in a policy of systematic confrontation.

Tom Sawyer, then the Deputy General Secretary of the public sector union NUPE, was in a similar position to Blunkett. He supported the Bennite left, but was not beholden to them for his position on the NEC. He had been a union organizer for most of his working life, having switched careers in his mid-twenties after becoming an engineering apprentice at fifteen, but he had the curiosity and many of the mental attitudes of an intellectual. His south London home was stuffed with books on labour history collected over the years. As with Blunkett, it jarred when Sawyer discovered that his vote seemingly was at the disposal of a caucus.

After a few months, Blunkett and Sawyer both stopped going to caucus meetings. There was no public break involved. Neither, at this point, renounced any opinions they had held in the past. Like Kinnock's original rift with Benn, it was a semi-private affair which became public in dramatic circumstances almost two years later. For all that, it was personally quite painful. They had both revered Tony Benn from a distance and could not bring themselves to share Kinnock's personal antagonism towards him and the other Bennites. This was at a time when the miners' strike was dominating British politics. Because the NUM was based in Sheffield, the city councillors were used to dealing with Scargill and knew him well. Blunkett and Sawyer both believed that the miners were fighting a just cause. They admired the fortitude of the mining communities, they believed the Labour Party and the unions could have done more to help, but they were aghast at Scargill's tactics. The break came into the open at the NEC meeting at the opening of the 1985 annual conference, when the proposal to pledge the Labour government to reinstate sacked miners was narrowly defeated. This was when Michael Meacher's break with the Bennite caucus became final.

However, the issue that forced both Blunkett and Sawyer into open confrontation with old allies on the left was not the miners but the dry-sounding issue of how to finance local government. The council leaders of the 1980s were in no position to build grandiose municipal centres or other monuments which they could name after themselves as their predecessors had done in better times. A generation of seemingly limitless growth, when local government expenditure rose at twice the rate of expansion in the economy generally, had ended painfully. The proportion of Britain's Gross National Product consumed by local councils rose from 9.8 per cent in 1951 to 18.6 per cent in 1975. Two-thirds came from taxes raised nationally, through the Rate Support Grant awarded annually by the government, which functioned like an annual wage round. Each year, Labour and Conservative councils alike would submit inflationary budgets, which were ritually beaten down by officials at the Department of Environment, so that council leaders could complain that they were being forced to provide a poorer service than they would wish, at a higher cost to local ratepayers.

It was a Labour government which struck the first real blow against local government finances, in the wake of the oil crisis and the IMF loan. In

October 1976, Anthony Crosland, as Secretary of State for the Environment, told municipal leaders in a speech at the Manchester Free Trade Hall that 'the party's over'. His successor, Peter Shore, began the ruthless business of cutting the proportion of council spending borne by central government, reducing it from 66.5 per cent to 61 per cent. He anticipated that it would stop at about that level, but Conservative secretaries of state kept pushing it steadily down by around 2 per cent per year, until the poll tax débâcle forced them into retreat in 1991. In 1978–79, rate support grant totalled £12,226 million; by 1985–86, it was down to £8,489. To illustrate the effect, imagine a council whose budget in 1978–79 was £100 million, of which £61 million came from government grants and £39 million from ratepayers. Seven years later, its budget would need to be £160 million merely to keep up with the inflation of the early Thatcher years, but by now the central government grant had fallen to £74 million. Therefore, £86 million must come from the rates, an increase far above the rate of inflation. These are only illustrative figures, making no allowances for regional variations or the distinction between domestic and industrial rates. The general point is that councils were forced either to reduce their budgets, or impose enormous rate increases.

It was never intended that the effects should be felt equally by all councils. The purpose was to bear down heaviest on a small number of mostly Labour-led councils who were considered to be high spenders. While the total grant was being cut, the government also changed the system for distributing it. Every council was assigned a 'grant-related expenditure assessment' which, in simple language, was the amount central government thought it should be spending each year. If a council's budget went above its assessment, penalties came into play, to the extent that an extra £1 million spent cost the ratepayers £2.2 million.

Experienced councillors who remembered the futility of confrontation between Labour councils and the Heath government over council rents were inclined to shrug their shoulders and say that ultimately power lay in Westminster, and the lot of Labour councillors was to make the best they could of a bad deal. However, there was a new breed of councillors about. This was partly because of the general shift to the left in the Labour Party, but also because it is traditional that electors use local elections to punish the government rather than choose the legislators who will make the best job of emptying their dustbins. Consequently, having lost a great many council seats in the late 1970s, particularly in the elections of May 1977, Labour was recovering them very quickly. There were a lot of new left-wing Labour councillors and even where the Labour group was dominated by the right, it was difficult to discipline them. Anyone expelled from a Labour group for voting against cuts in a budget only had to appeal to the NEC Organization Committee, chaired by Eric Heffer, to be sure of a sympathetic hearing.

Since some councils would not cut budgets voluntarily, and the voters refused to punish them in the polling-booth for overspending, the government decided to move into a new phase by making it illegal to set an oversized budget. The process, introduced in 1984, was known as 'rate-capping'. A formula worked out in Whitehall imposed a ceiling on certain council budgets, leaving the councillors with the unpalatable choice of making cuts or breaking the law. Precedents for defying the law were not encouraging. All the members of tiny Clay Cross urban district council, including Dennis Skinner's brother David, were personally surcharged and disqualified for refusing to raise council rents in line with legislation passed by the Heath government. An attempt by Lothian council to take on the government over an item of Scottish legislation in 1980 had ended similarly. The same had happened to councillors in Poplar, in London's east end, before the war.

However, for many of those directly involved, including David Blunkett, the attack on local democracy implicit in the Rates Act was so serious that it made civil disobedience morally justifiable at the very least. In his view, this was the first time in a century that a government had undermined the right of local communities to govern themselves through the ballot box. Conservatives disputed this on the grounds that local democracy had become a fiction; the rate burden fell hardest on the business community, who had no vote, while large numbers of voters in local elections paid no rates. This was the argument which justified the subsequent creation of the poll tax and the uniform business rate. To Blunkett, it was 'social fascism'.[14] In October 1983, he warned Labour's annual conference darkly that 'if this labour movement does not stand up and fight on this issue . . . then I am afraid we will be wiped out as a Labour Party, because local government is the only place where Labour representatives are taking up decisions about the well-being and lives of ordinary people.'[15]

The Rates Act became law and the first hit-list of eighteen councils was published in July 1984, in the excitement generated by the start of the miners' strike. In that same month the new Labour administration in Liverpool succeeded in squeezing extra money from the government after a protracted confrontation in which Labour councillors threatened to break the law by setting a rate which they knew to be too low to cover their budget. The drama had inspired an unusually high turn-out at the May 1984 elections in Liverpool, and an impressive increase in the Labour vote. The government was officially said to have conceded an extra £20 million; Liverpool's Finance Chairman, Tony Byrne, claimed the real amount was £90 million. Either way, it raised the hopes of left-wing councillors that confrontation could achieve results.

The government obviously hoped to deal with the rate-capped councils singly. A procedure was laid down by which they could apply for 'redetermination': or, in other words, plead for mercy. However, none of the original eighteen rate-capped councils availed itself of this facility – not even Portsmouth, which had the peculiar distinction of being the only Tory council ever to be rate-capped. With that partial exception, the government found itself confronted with an unexpectedly united front. The very fact that rate-capping was impending had inspired a large number of councils to move quickly to protect themselves as soon as it was known that Labour had lost the 1983 general election. Their first meeting was held in Sheffield in June 1983. From that emerged a National Campaign Unit. Subsequently, seventy councils contributed to a London-based Local Government Information Unit, of which David Blunkett was chairman.

In July 1984, seventeen of the rate-capped councils, and nine others which were in conflict with central government, met in Sheffield for the second time. London was heavily represented, by the GLC, the ILEA and no less than eight rate-capped boroughs. Liverpool was not rate-capped, but was contesting the level of its support grant. The metropolitan county councils, like the GLC, were facing abolition. Liverpool councillors wanted the others to emulate their example by 'deficit-budgeting'. Suspecting that this carried a more immediate threat of surcharge than the tactic on which all eventually agreed, the majority settled for a common tactic of not setting any rate until they had jointly forced the government to concede.

This show of unity put the government in a position where they might have to disqualify and surcharge hundreds of councillors rather than the handful caught in the Clay Cross or Lothian affairs and send in government administrators to run the affairs of large parts of London and several provincial towns and cities, at a time when it was locked in a confrontation with the miners. However, unity was only superficial. The running had been made by Ted Knight, leader of Lambeth council, an ideologically driven former Trotskyite, who had never cut his ties with the Workers Revolutionary Party to which he had belonged in his youth. Knight wanted the councils to defy the law and confront the government, to open up a new front in the industrial struggle being waged by the miners. But the call of the class struggle was not what stirred the leaders of, say, Basildon council, who had a budget to set in 1985 under conditions which the government had made extremely difficult, and they wanted a solution which would do minimal damage to council services on their patch. Under Knight's 'blockbusting' tactics, according to Blunkett, other council leaders adopted the tactic 'cautiously and uneasily' – a caution 'based on uneasiness, not careful deliberation'.[16]

There was also the ambiguous attitude of the Labour leadership, who supported the campaign against rate-capping in principle, but did not approve of illegality, whether practised by the miners' union or by Labour councils. Neil Kinnock told the party annual conference that a Labour government would want to use the law to redress grievances, outlaw discrimination and nationalize economic assets. He warned: 'We cannot sharpen legality as our main weapon for the future and simultaneously scorn legality because it doesn't suit us at the present time.'

These tensions were given a public airing as the conference debated an NEC statement entitled *Defence of Local Democracy, Services and Jobs,* whose principal author was David Blunkett. It urged that 'no individual council should be expected to stand in resisting government policy' and that 'Labour local authorities should not act as agents for central government even if the resulting budget is out of line with government policy.' This was obviously open to different interpretations, and in an excited gathering dominated by the presence of Arthur Scargill and striking miners, most speakers preferred to read it as a call to civil disobedience. To the Liverpool Militant leader, Tony Mulhearn, it meant 'breaking laws designed by the Tories to defend their class'. NUPE leader, Rodney Bickerstaff, turned to Kinnock, sitting on the platform behind him, and said: 'Neil, we do not scorn legality, but we do scorn the spiteful and unjust laws brought in to bind our unions and destroy our services.' In the law-and-order camp they preferred to rest their argument on tactics rather than principle. Thus John Edmonds of GMBATU: 'We mustn't destroy that unity by trying to outdo each other in ideological purity'; and the Shadow Environment Secretary Jack Cunningham: 'If we elevate these issues simply to one of a question of the law, we will be playing the battle on Mrs Thatcher's ground. That would be one of the biggest errors for us to make.'[17] Cunningham was more explicit at a lunch in the parliamentary press gallery on 16 November, when he declared: 'Virtually everything Labour has achieved has been achieved by using the law, by governing in Parliament. Any odd hint that parliamentary government can or should be changed other than through the ballot box is unacceptable. Labour in Parliament cannot hint at, incline towards or acquiesce in illegality as a policy in local government.' Blunkett, characteristically, came down resoundingly on both sides of the argument simultaneously:

> In the last year, we have had tremendous support for the recognition, the old recognition, that socialism will not come from parliamentary action alone. Socialism will come from the fight in the trade unions and in the community . . . We are standing up and fighting for those basic tenets of democracy which people gave all for. So, let us not be afraid of offering ourselves as elected members in the struggle ahead. Let us not pretend that breaking the law is the objective, because it is not. Being martyrs is not what we seek. Martyrs fail. We intend to succeed.[18]

By November, the warning signs were there: the miners' struggle was plainly not going to be settled without a long winter of attrition; Patrick Jenkin, the Environment Secretary who had capitulated to the Liverpool councillors, had been fortified by the appointment of a new Minister for Local Government, Kenneth Baker, who had no intention of giving ground. If Baker is to be believed, he was covertly encouraged by Jack Cunningham, who privately tipped him off that the Labour Party leadership had no intention of standing by Derek Hatton, and intended to let Ken Livingstone and other 'loony left' London council leaders 'twist in the wind'.[19] Blunkett conceded later that this might have been the moment to do a deal with the government,[20] but the mood was still defiant. In London, 100,000 workers in the threatened boroughs and the GLC came out on a one-day strike. John Austin-Walker, leader of Greenwich council, declared: 'The time for fudging is over. We should learn the lesson from Liverpool – we can win!'[21] What was more embarrassing to Blunkett was that a Sheffield councillor, Jimmy Boyce, expressed very similar sentiments at the 1984 party conference, saying: 'Comrades, there isn't law and order in Britain, there is no such thing. What we get in Britain today is the whims of a dictator . . . Liverpool gave us a lead, let's build on that lead, let's smash this mob before they smash us.'[22]

By February, there were signs that the councils might be making headway. Patrick Jenkin at last agreed to see a delegation, headed by Blunkett, and there were concessions for Haringey, Hackney and Leicester councils. Leicester was required to make a 32 per cent cut in its proposed rate, rather than 56 per cent. On 6 March, designated as Democracy Day, police estimated that 70,000 were out demonstrating in London.

But the weakness of the campaign was that while it was relatively easy to motivate unionized council staff whose livelihoods were at stake, the mass of working-class people who depended on their councils to house them, educate their children and provide a safety net against economic disaster, were unmoved. The agreed tactic was that every affected council would convene on 7 March, ostensibly to set a budget, but should adjourn *sine die*, in the hope that this could give them a technical defence in law. As the day drew nearer and the warnings from council legal officers became more urgent, hundreds of Labour councillors had to ponder their individual circumstances and consider whether the struggle was worth the loss of office and financial ruin. There was an outbreak of by-elections as councillors quietly quit their seats to take themselves out of the line of fire. The majority remained at their posts, but the difficulties for council leaders in holding them together increased.

One complication was that the risk was not equally spread. For a London borough, or a district council like Leicester or Basildon, there was no precise legal deadline by which a rate had to be set, although any council which left it until after the end of the financial year on 31 March was taking a risk; but the legal position was quite plain for a county council which collected a rate in the form of a precept on the district or borough councils within their boundaries: by law, they must set a rate by 10 March. It was not therefore possible for hundreds of councillors to go over the edge together. A couple of hundred from just four of the authorities involved – the GLC, ILEA, South Yorkshire and Merseyside, three of each were on the verge of abolition – would become lawbreakers by default ahead of the rest. Blunkett consequently agreed that the four should pull out of the joint protest while the others continued. South Yorkshire and Merseyside concurred, but word came back from down south that the political atmosphere in the London Labour Party made it impossible for the GLC to back down gracefully.

Actually, the ILEA leader, Frances Morrell, had decided by now that the protest was doomed and that the best hope for London's state school system was the return of a Labour government. On 7 March, much to the surprise of other councils, the ILEA set its precept. Basildon, the least militant of the Labour councils on the rate-capping list, pulled out on the same day. Hackney council also acted decisively, but with the opposite effect. Instead of adjourning, it voted not to set a rate. Fifteen other councils voted for delay.

Three days later, the GLC, riven as it was by a dispute between Ken Livingstone and his deputy, John McDonnell, also caved in. Blunkett blamed that débâcle on McDonnell and the ultra-left, whom he accused of perpetrating a 'propaganda disaster'.[23] Brent followed later in the week.

In Sheffield, Blunkett and other councillors had done their best to build up a popular campaign against cuts in the city budget. The first target was the council's own workforce, large numbers of whom had almost no idea what rate-capping meant or implied. The town halls were encouraged to put that right. Shop stewards were allowed time off, at the council's expense, to convene small question-and-answer sessions at council worksites. By February, about 28,000 of the council's 33,000 staff had been at one of these meetings. However, come the 'Democracy Week' demonstration on 7 March, councillors could not help but notice that nothing like that number turned out. The unity of the Sheffield Labour Group was extremely fragile. Right-wing councillors did not want to lose their seats or be personally surcharged, and were kept in line only by the advice of legal officers that they were not immediately at risk. Those who showed the greatest real enthusiasm for a confrontation, the 'all-or-bust-brigade' were shop stewards, local party members, and workers in some of the council-funded community groups, who were not personally at risk. Under this pressure from outside, the council met four times in two months without setting a rate. A three-and-a-half hour meeting of Sheffield district party on 30 April was dominated by an argument over whether the council should revert to the Liverpool tactic of setting a deficit budget, or deliberately defy the law by refusing to set a rate rather than continuing to defer the decision. A majority opted for illegality. With that, unity melted away. The largest of the manual unions involved, GMBATU, opposed the step and lobbied councillors to set a rate. The teaching unions, and one of the six Sheffield constituency Labour parties, were also opposed. During an eight-hour council meeting on 7 May, the Labour Group split in public, and a minority moved a proposal to set the highest rate permissible under the new legislation, which was carried with Conservative and Liberal support, by thirty-eight votes to thirty-seven, with ten abstentions. The split was a defeat for Blunkett, who had tried to hold the group together. But in the long run, the twenty Labour rebels did him a service by enabling him to escape surcharge and disqualification, and he never displayed any wish to be involved in an illegal campaign again.

Like other councils, Sheffield now entered an era of creative accounting, in which the ingenuity of finance officers was directed into extraordinary paper transactions which enabled the council to claim that it was within its assessment without actually cutting costs. This continued until 1987, as councils gambled on a Labour government to pull them out of their difficulties.

Meanwhile, with Sheffield out, only eight London boroughs and Liverpool continued their defiance of the government, with diminishing sympathy from the official Labour leadership. Islington, under Margaret Hodge, capitulated at the end of May, despite its predominantly left-wing Labour majority. After Greenwich backed out on 8 June, only Liverpool and Lambeth remained. They too caved in eventually – Liverpool on 14 June and Lambeth on 3 July – but too late to save themselves from disqualification and personal surcharge. It was this which took Derek Hatton, Ted Knight and others out of local government. Their departure was not universally mourned.

The collapse of the rate-capping revolt, coinciding with the return to work of the last of the striking miners, was a turning point in Labour Party history. Blunkett did not mince words about it: it had failed and should not be repeated, though he mitigated that stark verdict by claiming that if the councils had not challenged the Rates Act in the way they did, no one outside local government would have known of its existence. In that they had 'lifted awareness and consciousness', but 'we simply cannot go over the same ground in order to fail again'.[24]

An immediate consequence was a split in the Bennite left. One of the first portents of this was a remarkably well-informed article right at the start of the rate-capping revolt by Patrick Seyd, whom Blunkett knew well as a politics lecturer at Sheffield University, giving rise to the suspicion that Blunkett was partly responsible for its appearance. The piece, provocatively entitled 'Bennism Without Benn', heralded the emergence of a 'new left', more accommodating to Neil Kinnock's leadership than the Bennites, naming Blunkett, Michael Meacher, Tom Sawyer, Margaret Hodge and others as being on one side of a new divide with Tony Benn, Eric Heffer and Dennis Skinner on the other. The names and the facts were all accurate, though they were marshalled to support the questionable proposition that this 'new left' was the authentic continuation of the Bennite tradition, which others were abandoning. Seyd approvingly quoted the 'new left' editor of *Tribune*, Nigel Williamson, as saying: 'I don't think we have changed our basic politics. Circumstances have changed.'[25]

It would be hard to sustain this claim that the 'new left' had not shifted its position. The Bennite strategy had been to bring pressure on the leadership by direct action outside parliament, to transfer power within the party away from the parliament to the activists in the party and the unions, and to recognize no enemies on the left. The rate-capping episodes had convinced Blunkett and others that the likes of Derek Hatton, Ted Knight and John McDonnell were their ideological opponents, although at this stage they believed in defeating them politically rather than administratively, by expulsion. As part of their accommodation with Neil Kinnock, Blunkett and others were willing to see power drift back towards the Shadow Cabinet, for instance, through the creation of a new Campaign Strategy Committee, a joint committee of the NEC, the Shadow Cabinet and the trade unions. Finally, and most significantly, there would be no more instances of a political figure like Blunkett proclaiming that 'socialism will not come from parliamentary action alone'. The Labour Party's appetite for extra-parliamentary struggle was spent. For at least the next decade, its only tactic was to win elections.

Meanwhile, the party's autumn conference faced a call from Derek Hatton to send councillors back into the fight again, to risk another round of disqualifications and personal surcharge. Blunkett addressed the conference on the morning after Neil Kinnock's dramatic attack on the 'grotesque chaos' of Liverpool council, and at the end of a bad-tempered debate during which Hatton had directly challenged Kinnock to 'come to Liverpool, look through the books, and if you can show me any other option where jobs are safe, then fine, we will do it'. It was not a genuine offer. Neither side wanted reconciliation, but Blunkett, typically, wanted to make one last attempt to reunite the two sides. He unexpectedly proposed that the NEC take up Hatton's challenge and send a commission in to examine Liverpool's finances to see if any way could be found for the city to keep its budget within the legal limit without sackings. In return, he wanted Hatton to withdraw a call for industrial action in support of the surcharged councillors. From the rostrum he called out, 'Will you do that? Will you do that, Derek?' But he was unable to see Hatton's reaction. As Tony Benn recalled it: 'There he was, this Christ-like bearded blind man, standing on the rostrum appealing to Derek Hatton . . . Hatton, who is a bit of a smart alec, ran towards the rostrum in his neat suit.'[26] Part of the Liverpool contingent could be heard shouting 'no', as Hatton demanded the floor, the smarter ones having realized that it was a trap. In the heat of the moment, the conference chairman, a luminary of GMBATU named Neville Hough, almost came to their rescue, because he disliked Hatton so much that he refused to turn a microphone on for him, and called to him: 'Are you making a contribution? Is the answer yes or no? Yes, thank you very much,' whereupon the hall erupted in applause.[27]

The episode had come as a complete surprise to everyone in the hall: delegates, journalists, observers, Derek Hatton and the Liverpool contingent, and not least to Neil Kinnock, who had distinctly mixed feelings about it. He walked up to Blunkett to whisper in his ear: 'You're bloody good at skating on thin ice,' to which Blunkett replied, 'I didn't realize how thin it was.'[28] Patricia Hewitt's private reaction was more direct than Kinnock's. She thought Blunkett had spoilt the impact of Kinnock's speech the previous day, and feared that the investigation into Liverpool's finances would end in rotten compromise, but the gallery Blunkett was playing to was the 'soft left' whose feelings about Liverpool were very mixed. The general unpopularity of Hatton and the Militants was offset by a belief that Liverpool council had been doing its best in a city which had been exceptionally badly hit by recession. The city's nominal leader, John Hamilton, who was up in the spectator's gallery without a delegate's credential, was a Liverpudlian equivalent of Michael Foot, a mild-mannered veteran who had once been expelled from the party by the right and was now being treated with contempt by the left. Hatton described him as a 'tired little old man who had clung on to power no matter what'.[29] Blunkett's interference made a large number of activists less uncomfortable about the choice that was being forced upon them.

A commission duly went into Liverpool, consisting of Maurice Stonefrost, the GLC's former Comptroller of Finance, and three other finance officers. The Stonefrost report revealed that the city's finances were in a serious state, and recommended a 15 per cent rate increase, a cutback in the ambitious house-building programme and other austerity measures. The Liverpool councillors rejected him, and Hatton, Tony Mulhearn and the finance committee chairman, Tony Byrne, arranged a new deal which included borrowing £30 million from Swiss banks. This merry march into deeper debts hardened opinion against them. It was at this point, for instance, that John Edmonds, general secretary of GMBATU, called for expulsions, a significant move because the leader of the town branch of GMBATU, Ian Lowes, was a known Militant, who was now in effect being abandoned by his own union leadership.

Blunkett went up to Liverpool on 4 November, to a rally of the Liverpool Labour Left, where he and other speakers urged that the report be implemented. The atmosphere was highly emotive and, for some, frightening. In situations like these, Blunkett claims there is a real advantage to being blind: 'I'm not susceptible to visual intimidation. It has to be verbal or physical to work on me, and since the cameras were there they could not do that. But I could feel John Hamilton physically shaking next to me. It was one of those moments that you never want to go through, but it was seminal. It was when the left outside Militant decided that it was prepared to take them on.'[30]

It has always been the charge laid by Kinnock's enemies that he launched the assault on the Liverpool Militants purely as a propaganda exercise, to win himself some respectability. There is obviously an element of truth in this. Kinnock's own image-makers decided that the extract from his Bournemouth speech already quoted should feature in the celebrated Kinnock video released as a political broadcast twice over during the 1987 general election. Nonetheless, when an organism as complex as the Labour Party turns itself around to expel from its own ranks the deputy leader of one of Britain's largest councils, there is inevitably something deeper going on than simple public relations. Fundamentally, the party was beginning to redefine itself through a Spinoza-like process of stating what it was not. A new consensus was forming around the idea that the party could not play host to hostile entryist groups with their own distinct organization and ideology.

Once Kinnock had made the opening move, the people whose opinions now mattered most were the leaders of the 'realigned' left. The old right would obviously support Kinnock, their only criticism being that the purge he initiated was too modest in its scale. Conversely he was obviously not going to win over what remained of the Bennite left. Crucially, he needed to win over ex-Bennites. On the NEC, which was where the action was concentrated, his most important supporters were Michael Meacher, David Blunkett and Tom Sawyer. In the next stage in the drama, Sawyer moved into the central position. It was Sawyer who first suggested that a team of eight NEC members should set off to Liverpool in December 1985, to investigate complaints of infiltration and intimidation by Militant – and because of the delicate arithmetic involved, he was the most important member of the commission.

There were a variety of reasons why different individuals rejected the Bennite idea that Labour had no enemies to the left. In Sawyer's case, it was the direct experience of having used trade union militancy as leverage to try to force a change in government policy – Labour government policy, in his case – which had worsened rather than improved the pay and working conditions of his union members, by helping bring Callaghan down and a hostile Conservative administration to power. Moreover, Liverpool council's treatment of its own employees demonstrated that the left, in power, was capable of bullying and exploiting workers. A few years earlier, when Sawyer was a regional union official, it had all seemed very different.

In the north-east of England, where Sawyer's career began, the backbone of the Labour Party establishment was the union then known as the GMWU. The union, the regional Labour Party and County Durham were dominated by Andy Cunningham. Sawyer' NUPE was smaller and newer than the GMWU, but was competing on the same patch of ground for the same groups of members. Roy Troughton, who preceded Sawyer and Rodney Bickerstaffe as NUPE's northern regional secretary, was on occasions ejected from meetings by the police after the other unions had disputed his right to negotiate. Therefore, while the GMWU was a stronghold of the right, the northern regional committee of NUPE was like a soviet, made up of the Bennite left of the Labour Party and an assortment of revolutionaries. However, NUPE was different from the craft unions in the print, motor or coal industries, even when they all shared a reputation for militancy. Its members were less skilled, less well-paid, more scattered and more socially mixed. The majority were women. They were the people who did the drudge jobs in local councils and the health service: the cleaners, porters, caretakers, etc., and who were immediately hit when the Callaghan government resorted to wage restraint. It did, however, have a democratic tradition like the AUEW's, and was the only other important union to ballot all its levy-paying members during the 1981 deputy leadership contest. Benn's campaign team complained that the ballot forms were not accompanied by any advice from the union executive, a majority of whom supported Benn, but otherwise could not object when, despite the views of the union leaders, its 600,000 block vote went to Denis Healey. Every region of the union turned in a majority for Healey, except the north, where Sawyer was Benn's campaign manager.

In Liverpool, there was the same rivalry between the same two unions, but the political line-up was radically different. The GMBATU was Militant's main union stronghold, particularly GMBATU branch 5, which organized the city council gardeners and the uniformed security guards from the Static Security Force, known colloquially as Hatton's private army. Staff who objected that jobs in these areas were being handed out as political favours, or who believed they had been harassed for not following the council policy, or were opposed to the left's call to strike in opposition to government-imposed spending cuts, took their complaints to NUPE. As Militant's leaders Peter Taaffe and Tony Mulhearn recorded: 'In most local authorities, there is one union which tends to act as a refuge for those workers who are not prepared to engage in struggle. In other areas this role had been sometimes fulfilled by the GMBATU. In Liverpool the roles were reversed.'[31] Jane Kennedy, who worked in an old people's home and was secretary of one of the town hall branches of NUPE, became a particular target of Militant's hostility, and is alleged to have been spat at and abused at meetings. When she appeared at the Bournemouth conference, to attack from the city council leadership on the day after Kinnock's speech, NUPE provided her with an escort of London dustmen all week to deter Militant supporters who might consider accosting her.

Tales like these, from his own union members, set Sawyer on a political course which would culminate in him taking Larry Whitty's place as general secretary of the Labour Party nine years later. The NEC team had four members from the left and four from the right, plus Larry Whitty, who generally shared the left's distaste for expulsions and other sanctions. According to an unpublished memoir by the railwayman's leader, Charlie Turnock, three members of the team – Turnock himself, Neville Hough of GMBATU, and the future Speaker Betty Boothroyd – were looking for a mass execution, with as many as seventeen city councillors and forty-seven members of the Liverpool district Labour Party expelled. When this was put to other members of the team, it was met with a 'ghastly hush'.[32] Two, Margaret Beckett and Audrey Wise, had gone to Liverpool determined to oppose any expulsions, and treated the whole subject of Militant as 'taboo'. On their return, they submitted a separate minority report. Two, Eddie Haigh of the TGWU and Tom Sawyer, wanted a 'damage limitation exercise', harsh enough to reinforce Neil Kinnock's authority, but not so harsh that it would alienate potentially sympathetic figures like John Hamilton and tear apart the Liverpool Labour Party. Tony Clarke, of the post office workers' union, called for compromise. This presented Sawyer and Haigh, and particularly Sawyer as the stronger personality, with an effective veto of the final contents of the report.

Once the team was in Liverpool, they had no difficulty in agreeing that there was something odd about the way the city's Labour Party ran its own

affairs. Unusually, political life did not centre on the parliamentary constituency parties, but on the Liverpool district committee and its executive.
Other cities had district party committees, but typically they were shell
organizations which did no more than supervise the selection of candidates
and the contents of the manifesto when council elections loomed, while the
constituencies discussed national politics and, crucially, handled members'
subscriptions and other funds collected locally. In Liverpool, the district
party committee dealt with issues as diverse as Northern Ireland, Nicaragua,
nuclear weapons, calls for the resignation of the General Secretary of the
TUC, and the defence of Militant. This concentration of political power in
the Liverpool district party was not new. It was the means by which the
right, under Bessie Braddock, had maintained control in their heyday.
Militant had taken it up and refined it by turning the 'open' meetings held
under the old regime, where all party members were admitted as visitors,
into 'aggregates', where any party member who turned up was allowed to
vote. The aggregates took on a life of their own during the city's budget crisis, with six held between 5 September and 22 November 1985, when the
district party organization was suspended on orders from the NEC. They
were often called at short notice, with the obvious result that the people
most likely to turn up were the city council staff from union branches like
GMBATU branch 5 whose officials were on the grapevine. There were also
reports of members of the Static Security Force standing at the door, in uniform, checking membership cards. It was alleged that those who dissented
from the prevailing political line were verbally abused, although the enquiry
team conceded that all allegations of verbal intimidation are hard to sub-
stantiate. The votes taken at aggregates were regarded as binding on all
Labour councillors. Three of the five officers of the DLP, the Chairman
Tony Mulhearn, Vice-Chairman Terry Harrison, and Secretary Felicity
Dowling, were long-standing members of Militant.

The team returned with a series of recommendations for reforming the
Liverpool party, and a list of candidates for expulsion. Sawyer and Haigh
had agreed to ten names, including Hatton, Mulhearn, Harrison, Dowling,
and the secretary of GMBATU branch 5, Ian Lowes. There were six more
names which four team members wanted to include. One, Harry Smith,
was in fact hauled up before the NEC, where his evidence provided so
much entertainment that the charges against him were dismissed, it being

axiomatic that no one could be a member of a Trotskyite sect and have a sense of humour.

Although the resulting expulsions were a psychological watershed, resistance to the idea of settling a political dispute through expulsions did not disappear overnight. Even those who accepted it when applied to distant figures from Liverpool had their own Militant supporters whom they knew as colleagues and tried to protect. In Blunkett's case there was Paul Green, a Sheffield councillor who lived in Sheffield Attercliffe, which was the local stronghold of the Labour right. The local party pounced on him before the Militant enquiry had even begun and expelled him, whereupon he appealed to the NEC, where Blunkett fought hard to protect him, saying that he had never done any damage to the party or promoted a separate political programme. The vote to expel him went through the NEC by fourteen to thirteen, after a rancorous argument in which Benn told Blunkett that this was his fault for allowing the 'witch hunt' to start, while Kinnock accused Benn of suffering from an 'hallucination'.[33]

Afterwards, Blunkett had to prevail upon the Labour group on Sheffield council to accept the NEC's authority and exclude Paul Green from the group, and won that by a majority of only four. Ten years after the event, Blunkett regarded his expulsion as an unnecessary act of vindictiveness against a minor player. 'He was just a simple hard-working councillor who never pedalled the Militant line; but a bunch of unreconstructed righties in Attercliffe decided they wanted a purge. It shows that when you start something, you cannot control the zealots.'[34]

By voting for expulsions, Blunkett made public his rift with the left. It was formalized during 1986, when the Campaign Group drew up its slate for the seven constituency representatives on the NEC. Having reached the NEC without the help of the slate, Blunkett had been co-opted to it in 1984. In 1985, he topped the poll at only the third attempt, ending Benn's extraordinary record for having come first for eleven years in succession. Consequently, it was not very likely that he was going to be removed in 1986, even without Campaign backing. Actually, Campaign's decision rebounded comically on them. Having added Tam Dalyell to the slate, in recognition of his one-man campaign over the sinking of the *Belgrano* during the Falklands War, they succeeded in getting him on to the NEC, but at the cost of seeing Eric Heffer ousted. Dalyell's incorrigible individualism meant he repeatedly used his vote against the left, and was dropped from the slate after less than a year. Blunkett, meanwhile, topped the poll again. He stayed in the top place for eight years, until Neil Kinnock, as ex-leader, beat him in 1992.

In the meantime, Blunkett secured the safe Labour seat of Sheffield Brightside, where the sitting MP Joan Maynard had retired. While others arrived in the Commons in 1987 shell-shocked by the scale of Labour's defeat, Blunkett presumably did not, because he had seen it coming. Rather embarrassingly, he had blurted it out only three months before the election to a journalist who was interviewing him for *Woman's Own*: 'If I had to put my last £5 on the election, out of evangelical faith I'd put it on Labour, but my head tells me I might end up starving.'[35] When his remark was broadcast on the front pages of most of the anti-Labour tabloids, along with other indiscreet remarks about Kinnock being relatively isolated in the Shadow Cabinet, Blunkett flatly denied having said it, but it has an authentic feel to it, as if he had momentarily forgotten that he was talking to a journalist.

Despite that, Blunkett made a flying start in his new role when he was the first of the 1987 intake of MPs to make his 'maiden' speech. Indeed, he was only the second Labour MP to address the new parliament at all, following directly after Neil Kinnock – another small advantage accorded to him for his blindness. He warned that in Conservative Britain, normal democracy was being superceded by the democracy 'of the bank balance and of the privilege that comes with wealth and property' and that 'if the symptoms of the present decay of inner city areas are not allowed a democratic outlet, the government will inevitably be forced into even greater authoritarianism in order to suppress those symptoms'.[36] After that, his parliamentary career went into a nosedive. Five months passed before he made his second speech and, after that, his return was slow. Both of the celebrated municipal leaders, Blunkett and Ken Livingstone, appeared to suffer from a well-known problem – that new MPs who have made their reputations before their arrival are not made welcome and usually encounter a thick barrier of jealousy and mistrust.

However, the distinction was that Livingstone's problem was political: having gravitated to the 'realigned left' during the 1985 rate-capping débâcle, he could not make up his mind in 1987–88 whether to make a break with the shrinking Bennite left or aspire to lead it, and ended up hopelessly isolated with only his celebrity status to keep him going. Blunkett's problem, by contrast, was predominantly personal. For the first time since his teens, he was having to go through the domestic upheaval of establishing a second home outside Sheffield. He also had to fight for special facilities to be able to function as a working MP inside the overcrowded House of Commons. Other new MPs were allocated a table in a corridor with a telephone and told that they should think themselves lucky, but Blunkett obviously needed a room of his own, and an extra office allowance to cover the cost of having all his documents either dictated on to tapes or transcribed into Braille. It was a slow business. After six months, a special resolution granted him an office allowance 50 per cent above the normal rate. On top of that he fell ill. First he had to have his gall bladder removed in November, and a few months later he contracted viral pneumonia. It was at this point in his life that he and his wife decided to separate, after seventeen years. Then in May 1988, his guide dog, Teddy, who had been with him for nine years, collapsed and two months later had to be put down, while Blunkett accustomed himself to a new dog, Offa, who had to learn her way around the House of Commons, a task which even humans find challenging.

No sooner had he absorbed these shocks in his personal life than Blunkett's personal relations with Neil Kinnock, which had never been entirely smooth, went rapidly downhill. This was in the summer when the issue of unilateral nuclear disarmament came on and off the menu according to the political pressures of the moment. Here, Blunkett's path and Tom Sawyer's diverged. Sawyer was now chairman of the Home Affairs committee, Benn's former powerbase, and a driving force behind the post-1987 policy review, which he steered tactfully through that year's autumn conference by hinting ever so discreetly that it was time to give the word 'socialism' a different meaning from the one set out in the dictionaries:

> We have to reach a generation many of whom have never experienced the community of the Labour heartlands or the solidarity of trade union membership . . .
> Socialism was not born just out of a concern for the deprived and the dispossessed, but from the everyday experience of ordinary working people . . . Socialism grew out of applying simple values to practical everyday problems: equality, fairness and freedom. Socialism is a stand against discrimination of all kinds: a respect for the

individual, yes, and for the environment; a belief that a test of a civilised community is to share wealth, to care for those who on their own would be poor, or sick or weak. It has never been locked into an unchanging programme.[37]

Having once committed himself to the process, Sawyer made it his business to deliver what the party leader wanted from it, on defence policy as on any other issue. He was held back by his own union's public commitment to unilateralism. In May 1989, he went to a meeting of NUPE's executive to oppose his own General Secretary, Rodney Bickerstaffe, who had been his closest colleague for years, even before they had moved to London to take up the two most senior positions in the union, and delivered the union's 600,000 block vote, ensuring that the policy devised by Gerald Kaufman and Neil Kinnock went through that autumn's conference. Sawyer's relationship with the party leader became so close that a rival trade union representative on the NEC remarked privately that 'He would have sold his granny for Kinnock.' Figuratively that may be true; but unlike shadow ministers in the Commons, or those who aspired to become Labour life peers, Sawyer was not beholden to Kinnock in any way. He had simply made up his mind that if another general election defeat was to be avoided, Kinnock's authority must be upheld.

After Kinnock's resignation, he found that he had nothing like the same rapport with the new leader. A novice in party management, John Smith did not seem to be aware that Sawyer was a big player, and scarcely bothered to consult him as he embarked on the risky enterprise of trying to persuade the trade unions to vote away their own power to use their block votes. Consequently, it was Sawyer who came out with the slogan 'No say – no pay', which seemed to confirm his estrangement from the new regime. In this period, NUPE completed a merger with the white collar union NALGO and the health union COHSE, to create the country's biggest union, Unison, which began its existence with a General Secretary and no fewer than five deputy or assistant general secretaries, all male, and a policy of promoting women to as many senior posts as possible. Looking ahead, Sawyer saw no worthwhile future for himself either in the union or the party, and decided to retire early. Then Smith died, and those who had been on the inside track in Kinnock's day were back in again.

By contrast, Blunkett now had an interest in keeping on the right side of Neil Kinnock, in order to advance on to the front bench in parliament, yet he gave the leader a great deal more trouble during the course of the policy review, particularly on the question of nuclear disarmament. He believed that abandoning unilateral nuclear disarmament would be wrong in principle and would open up a rift in the party. Having made that his sticking point, Blunkett did his best to be helpful to Kinnock in every way he could, but that was not how his actions were viewed from the leader's office. There, not to put too fine a point on it, they thought he was a nuisance. The deterioration of Blunkett's relationship with Kinnock is documented in a series of unpublished letters from one to the other. Blunkett has his copies stored away on a disc somewhere. The copies which reached Neil Kinnock are in the Kinnock Archive in Cambridge University.

The trouble started as early as June 1988, when Kinnock gave his notorious television interview, in which he appeared to reject 'something for nothing' disarmament. That week, shortly before Denzil Davies's resignation, Blunkett wrote to Kinnock, warning that there was going to be a 'great débâcle' at party conference if he persisted with this line. However, he lowered the chances of his warning being taken in the spirit in which it was intended by issuing a public statement on the same day, declaring that, 'If an unnecessary and devastating split in the Party is to be avoided, the Leader needs to make it clear that his words were not an abandonment of his long-standing commitment on which so many of his allies have placed their trust.'[38] Two weeks, one Shadow Cabinet resignation and one lunch with journalists from the *Independent* later, Blunkett and other 'allies' thought they had won the leader back into the unilateralist fold. Blunkett and Kinnock spoke privately on the day before an NEC meeting about a resolution Blunkett was putting to the NEC that 'reliance on such weapons of mass destruction cannot contribute to the effective defence of our country'. To Blunkett, the meaning of his resolution was plain: no more British nuclear weapons, no more NATO nuclear weapons on British soil. He thought Kinnock agreed and that he was helping to clear matters up. However, after the meeting, he heard that Patricia Hewitt had been briefing journalists that Kinnock regarded the resolution as irrelevant to any future reassessment of party policy. Off went a furious letter to the leader's office, complaining that he was made to look 'a complete idiot' and enquiring whether 'I am really wasting my time' trying to act as a bridge between the leader and the 'soft left'.

The same story was played out in May 1989, when the NEC had had a two-day session to agree the policy documents which were to be presented to that year's conference, including *A Power for Good*, the report of the foreign policy review group, meticulously put together by Gerald Kaufman. On the morning before it was to be debated, Blunkett saw Kinnock in his office early in the morning, and came away aware that the leader now had a secure majority on the NEC, with or without Blunkett, and would be able to get the document unamended. He believed, naïvely, that it would be carried in a way that salvaged the feelings of old unilateralists, with all the emphasis on continuity rather than the stark break with the policy which Labour had embraced for the past decade. Later in the day, Blunkett called together a convention of five of the 'soft left' NEC members – himself, Margaret Beckett, Robin Cook, Jo Richardson and Clare Short – and tried unsuccessfully to get them all to agree to back an amendment imposing a timetable for the scrapping of Trident. However, the NEC meeting was dominated by a dramatic speech from Kinnock in which he declared that he was not prepared to subject himself ever again to the humiliations he had experienced in Washington as he tried to explain Labour's policy to a 'totally uncomprehending' audience. He ended on an up note by proclaiming that new opportunities for disarmament were opening up in the world, and pledging that a Labour government would work 'unstintingly' to bring about dramatic progress.[39]

It was magnificent, but very different from the conversation Blunkett had had in the leader's office the previous day. The press coverage, predictably, focused on the departure from unilateralism rather than the undying commitment to world disarmament in the latter part of the speech. Blunkett suspected that that was deliberate. He sent another angry letter to Kinnock complaining that 'someone, somewhere, is promoting the idea that there is a sea change in views rather than a reappraisal and updating.' He believed it was being done by spin doctors, on the leader's instructions. The feeling that Kinnock had not been straight with him, saying one thing in private conversation and another at the semi-public forum of an NEC meeting, lingered. Blunkett said:

> At the May 1989 NEC, Kinnock made a brilliant speech, but it didn't touch me at all. Not that it wasn't a good argument. It was. It simply meant that nobody could ever trust him again. I had been trying to be helpful, arguing that we could use

Britain's nuclear weapons in multilateral discussions. As a 'first strike', let's divest our-selves of nuclear weapons. To kick start the process, let's be the first in. At the start of the correspondence, Neil Kinnock reassured me, and he continued to reassure me until directly afterwards, when Gerald Kaufman wrote an article saying, in effect, that we had completely ditched the unilateralist nonsense which he had never believed in. So we went into the 1992 election committed to pay for a fourth Trident. That is the issue on which I fell out with Neil Kinnock, and never fell back in.[40]

So, when did Blunkett perform his *mea culpa* and renounce the 'unilater-alist nonsense' left over from his Bennite days? The answer is that he never did. As a shadow minister, he observes the collective discipline which requires him not to dissent from party policy; but one job he is never likely to hold in a Blair government is that of Secretary of State for Defence, because he remains 'unreconstructed' in his hostility to nuclear weapons.

The issue that saved him from floundering in semi-obscurity on the opposition backbench was the poll tax. In retrospect, this attempt to reform local government finance was such an unmitigated disaster that it seems obvious that it was going to hurt the Conservative Party and heap political benefits on Labour. However, this was not how it appeared in 1988, as leg-islation went through to introduce the tax in Scotland first, to be followed in England and Wales a year later. At that time, it was well within the bounds of possibility that the Labour Party would greet this political gift as it had over rate-capping four years earlier, by embroiling itself in such an emotive and simplistic argument about whether unjust laws should be enacted or defied that it would never be able to turn outward and open an effective attack on the government.

The 1988 annual conference was dominated by a stand-up argument over whether the Labour councils should impose and collect the new tax, and whether supporters should be encouraged to pay their poll tax bills, or whether the Scottish Labour Party should attempt to lead a mass campaign of civil disobedience, with Scottish MPs setting an example by not paying their own poll tax. The Shadow Scottish Secretary, Donald Dewar, a solic-itor by profession, naturally wanted no part of an illegal campaign, but even someone as senior as Robin Cook was ambiguous on the subject, declining to answer when asked if he had or would pay his poll tax. Other Labour MPs were subsequently taken to court for non-payment, and one – Terry Fields – went to jail.

There was a price to pay for not calling for civil disobedience, especially in Scotland, where a gap opened up to the left of the Labour left, into which rushed the Scottish Nationalists and the newly created Scottish Militant Labour. One Labour MP, Dick Douglas, defected to the SNP over the poll tax issue. The last year in which Militant and its sympathizers were able to make an impact on a Labour annual conference was in 1988. A Glasgow councillor, James McVicar, was cheered as he told the delegates, in a speech which certainly was not weakened by being understated, that: 'The poll tax represents the most regressive and vicious anti-working-class law that any government in this country has ever attempted to introduce . . . Are we going to provide the leadership that our class demands? Are we going to provide a serious campaign of non-payment of the Tory poll tax, embracing the power of this mighty Labour movement, the Labour Party and the trade unions, with all the force and bludgeon that can stop Thatcher's poll tax?'[41] But Blunkett had been around this course before during the rate-capping saga and had no intention of revisiting it. Against the background of continuous heckling, he replied: 'What we are sick of in this party is sectarianism that turns in on ourselves and campaigns against the party and not for it . . . If we advocate something that we know will fail, the people will not turn on the government, they will turn on us for misleading them.'[42]

Jack Cunningham, as the long-serving Shadow Secretary of State for the Environment, had borne much of the flak during the rate-capping episode and was now also at the centre of the poll tax controversy. The son of Andy Cunningham and a former parliamentary private secretary to Jim Callaghan, Cunningham was sometimes seen as a product of the old right; but he was quick to decide that he preferred to have Blunkett on his team than loose in the back row, and pushed for his appointment against opposition from Roy Hattersley. Blunkett was the first of the new intake, along with Marjorie Mowlam, to be promoted to the frontbench.

Blunkett was not, officially, the spokesman on local government finance, which is usually regarded as one of the three or four most senior jobs outside the Shadow Cabinet, too senior for someone who had been in parliament less than two years, but he was the man with the contacts. During the rate-capping dispute, a number of Labour councils had combined to create the Local Government Information Unit in London, with

Blunkett as its founder chairman. This meant that he had a direct line to researchers who could follow the poll tax legislation in detail. As it progressed through parliament, it became possible to calculate its impact precisely and compare the results with the forecasts of government ministers. The government, for instance, claimed that its transitional relief scheme would ensure that no one would be more than £3 a week worse off when the poll tax replaced the rates in England and Wales. In November 1989, Blunkett published detailed figures demonstrating that this was a fiction, based on the meaningless assumption that all councils would keep their budgets within government guidelines, when 90 per cent of them would go above the guidelines. Similarly, he demonstrated that the Environment Secretary Chris Patten's forecast that the average poll tax would be £278 was grossly optimistic. All Blunkett's claims were true. The fault in them, events proved, was that he underestimated the scale of the débâcle ahead.

At the same time, Labour needed to have its own means of financing local government worked out, if the promise to abolish the poll tax was to have any meaning. Again, it was Blunkett who had access to the sources of research enabling him to take control of this project. Whether the Blunkett scheme would have succeeded in practice or not is conjecture, since the poll tax was abolished by John Major's government. What can be said with certainty is that in its short-term political impact, it was a disaster.

Blunkett agreed that the old rates system had been unfair, particularly on people with low incomes living alone in properties with a high rateable value. On the other hand, he knew that taxing property is an efficient way of raising revenue and difficult to evade. As early as December 1987, he was consequently advocating a hybrid solution, involving 'a property tax that is supplemented by a fair tax on incomes: that means a local income tax'.[43] A great deal of detailed work went into devising how such a complex scheme could be introduced. The drawback was that it was offering 'two taxes for one', and therefore promised to be a propaganda gift to the Conservatives. Also, because of its complexity, it denied the Labour Party the opportunity to promise to abolish the poll tax immediately on taking office. That could be done simply by promising to restore the rates, with an improved rebate system for those hardest hit. The Shadow Chancellor, John Smith, was particularly keen on simplicity, having become convinced that the poll tax was so unpopular that the public had almost forgotten how they disliked the rates. The general feeling among Labour MPs was that Smith was right, and the Blunkett scheme was too complex and risky by half.

This argument became so intense that someone, inevitably, was going to pay a price for being on the losing side. Unfairly, it was not Blunkett but his boss, John Cunningham, who came eighteenth in the Shadow Cabinet elections, in the contest for eighteen places, before Neil Kinnock moved him to the post of Campaigns Coordinator. His successor, Bryan Gould, was apprehensive about having to work with Blunkett at all, but quickly decided to trust him and back him.[44] Gould was consequently sucked deeper into a conflict with John Smith which had originated in a disagreement over the European Monetary System and which eventually destroyed Gould's career. Again, Blunkett escaped the political consequences. This Houdini-like quality in him may be in part down to his blindness, which gives other politicians scruples about manoeuvring against him too blatantly; but it is also because even those who disagreed with him accepted that he had put in the hours to master his subject and devise a credible scheme.

One of the people whose respect Blunkett earned was the last minister in charge of poll tax, Michael Portillo, who also supervised the tax's abolition. On the day when votes were counted in the 1992 general election, Blunkett was surprised to receive a telephone call from Portillo to commiserate with him over the fact that he would be back on the opposition benches, and to pay his respects.

After the general election, Blunkett once again displayed his capacity for joining a losing cause without personally emerging as a loser, when he agreed to be campaign manager for Bryan Gould in the leadership and deputy leadership elections, which ended with Gould being soundly beaten in both contests and relegated to the post of Shadow Secretary of State for Heritage. Most members of the frontbench who had been unwise enough to support him paid the penalty when John Smith distributed frontbench responsibilities. Michael Meacher, for example, was relegated to the post of Spokesman on Overseas Aid, which was scarcely an important enough job for any Shadow Cabinet member.

Blunkett, by contrast, was one of only two members of the 1987 intake to be elected to the Shadow Cabinet, the other being Marjorie Mowlam.

Only Gordon Brown had made a quicker rise to the top in the entire period in which Labour had been in opposition, having reached the Shadow Cabinet in just four years. Whereas Mowlam was given a relatively junior posting, Blunkett was propelled into the prestigious post of Shadow Health Secretary. This gave him two years in a job which attracted endless publicity without dragging him very often into internal party politics.

When John Smith died, Blunkett was halfway through his year as party chairman, a task still handed out, in best old Labour style, to the longest serving NEC member who has not already performed it. He consequently resisted the temptation to come out on the losing side, maintaining a neutrality throughout, until the time came to cast his vote for Tony Blair. In Blair's Shadow Cabinet, he was moved into the politically more sensitive role of Shadow Education Secretary. Blair told him that he wanted education 'on the front page' and in no time, Blunkett obliged, by giving an interview to the *Sunday Times* in which he repeated what he thought was still party policy: that a Labour government would consider making private school fees subject to VAT. He was wrong on two counts. First, VAT is a 'tax' not an 'education' issue, and consequently it should have been left to Gordon Brown, as Shadow Chancellor, to deliver a judgement. Second, Blunkett's remarks ran counter to what Blair and Brown wanted to achieve, by giving the impression that Labour would penalize the upwardly mobile who were trying the best for their children. A decision had been taken the previous November to rule out VAT on school fees, but no one had told Blunkett. Hours after his words had reached the news stands, Blunkett was eating them. He announced on radio: 'The Shadow Chancellor and the Leader think it is helpful to rule out that possibility in order to avoid confusion.'[45] The wording is significant in that all he was doing was acknowledging the higher authority of Blair and Brown; he was not saying what he personally thought. 'I never retracted because I never pronounced on policy. I just kept quiet and let other people make a mess of it,' he later said.[46]

Despite that bad beginning, it turned out to be an inspired appointment by Tony Blair, because Blunkett's former Bennite radicalism only covered the fields of economics and defence policy. On state education and other aspects of social policy Blunkett was an old and unreconstructed modernizer who had been pushing the themes of social discipline and high quality service delivery since his days as a Sheffield councillor. Within days, Blunkett firmly promised that league tables comparing the performances of individual schools would continue to be published under a Labour government, because 'without such comparisons it is difficult to judge objectively the progress of one's child and the school's success rate'.[47] Soon, he was talking about closing state schools which failed to meet government standards, a sentiment previously associated with Conservative education ministers. He told a conference of the Association of Teachers and Lecturers in Harrogate: 'A school identified as failing would be closed and a new school opened on the same site for a new school year. The new school, with a new governing body teachers and headteachers would be able to offer pupils a fresh chance.'[48] This sort of talk was not welcomed by the teachers' unions, who saw it as another example of a politician blaming educational failure on teachers rather than on underfunding and endemic social problems. A few days later, Blunkett made an appearance at the annual conference of the National Union of Teachers, where he was mobbed by a small group of angry demonstrators and trapped in a small side room for thirty minutes while stewards restored calm. The television coverage of militant teachers shouting at a blind man was hugely embarrassing to the NUT leadership, whose president, John Bills, declared that the perpetrators should be sacked. Three were in fact called before their headteachers, but were not disciplined.

There was a more emotive question even than the threatened closure of bad schools. This was the future of the small number of comprehensive schools which had opted for 'grant-maintained status', and the related issue of whether schools were to be allowed any freedom to pick and choose which pupils they accepted. It ran contrary to the grain of New Labour to impose a rigid rule about catchment areas, not because anyone of any consequence in the party proposed to reinvent the old 11-plus exam and consign failures to somewhere equivalent to the old secondary modern schools, but because the party was striving not to be 'paternalistic', to offer free choice wherever possible rather than appear to be telling the public what was good for them. The Blairs, famously, showed the way by sending their son to the Oratory, a grant-maintained Catholic school eight miles from their Islington home. The school had been the first in the country to withdraw recognition from the NUT. The oldest child of the Shadow Employment Secretary, Harriet Harman, was also a pupil there.

This turned into the most emotive issue of the year within the Labour Party, generating more passion even than the rewriting of Clause Four. The scale of the reaction took Blair by surprise. He wrongly suspected it was being whipped up the Conservatives; in fact, it was coming from loyalists in the Labour heartlands. Blair had simply not appreciated the extent to which the Labour Party had become the political wing of the teaching profession. An astonishing 60 per cent of delegates to the 1995 annual party conference were teachers or school governors. According to Blunkett: 'The seam runs very very deep in terms of the struggle for comprehensive education in the 1960s. People who are now in senior positions in the party, and their friends and relatives, grew up with it. It became an article of faith, linked with all the other issues relating to equality of opportunity. Also, there are more teachers in the Labour Party per square inch than there are bristles on a hedgehog.'[49]

The prime example is Roy Hattersley who, having been the candidate of the right in the 1983 leadership election, appeared to undergo a reincarnation as Red Roy, the hero of the left. Actually, Hattersley's views on education in 1995 were no more 'left' than when he was opposition spokesman on education in 1972–74. Then he told the private schools that a Labour government would abolish them, for which Harold Wilson denied him a seat in the 1974 Cabinet. No party leader had risked putting him in charge of education since.

In summer 1995, Blunkett had issued a document called *Diversity and Excellence*, which promised to create a new entity called Foundation Schools, which would employ their own staff and would be broadly similar to grant-maintained schools but with the legal status of charities.[50] Hattersley went directly into the attack, complaining that it did nothing to tackle the 'social selection' by which middle-class parents talked their children into the 'best schools', which he saw as a device by which a small number of state schools could become centres of privilege for the children of parents with sufficient motivation and social skills to obtain a place for them. He wanted an end to the practice in certain schools of calling parents in to be interviewed before their children were admitted. When he addressed the annual party conference, Hattersley was cheered to the rafters by sections of the audience who might previously have been expected to heckle him. It was very different from the opening of a party conference nine years earlier, when Blunkett had warned the leadership generally and Shadow Chancellor, Roy Hattersley, in particular against going 'mad over moderation' by protecting people on middle-class incomes below £28,000 a year from tax increases, criticism which Hattersley's economics adviser, Doug Jones, dismissed as 'ridiculous'.[51]

In this tense situation, Blunkett's long-standing reputation as a member of the 'soft left' with a mind of his own, only recently reinforced by his refusal to support the barring of Liz Davies as a parliamentary candidate, came to the rescue. At the end of his conciliatory speech, a visibly relieved Tony Blair came over to shake him publicly by the hand. On that day at least, Blunkett was once again the man the party leader could not manage without.

Soon afterwards, when the government merged the departments of education and employment, Blair repaid his debt by giving Blunkett the enhanced job of Chief Education and Employment Spokesman in preference to Harriet Harman, the former Shadow Employment Minister. That may well go down as the single best or luckiest act of personnel management during Blair's entire term as opposition leader, in view of the reaction when it was learned the following January that Harman's second child had been placed in a selective, grant-maintained school in Bromley, one of the few remaining parts of the country where the education authority was Conservative controlled.

Blunkett proved reliable in this and other difficult situations, including the instance when Gordon Brown set off a reaction inside the Shadow Cabinet by giving an interview for the *Daily Telegraph* in which he said that claimants who repeatedly refused the offer of training places would have their benefits docked. He appeared to be calling for a British version of the American 'workfare' system, which requires claimants to work for their benefits. The accompanying document, which did not mention any such penalties or the word 'workfare', was jointly launched by Brown and Blunkett. Although Blunkett was not happy about the way Brown had floated an idea which was bound to be sensitive within the party, he basically agreed. 'I was brought up in a council house, and I know that the only way the Labour Party can really help the disadvantaged is not to appear to condone the downright idle.'[52]

This only reinforces the point that there is nothing 'trendy' about Blunkett. Neither, for that matter, does he make any attempt to follow the fashion for smart suits which distinguishes New Labour from the condescending attempts of radicalized middle-class activists to dress like workers. Trivial though it may be, his absence of dress sense – like the way his eyes move about nervously under television lights – may have caused some people to think of him as one of the also-runners in the Shadow Cabinet. This is to underestimate him. Blunkett has reached his position without being indebted to Tony Blair or anyone else by shrewdly retaining a political base in the party outside, while being one of the fast-rising parliamentary performers of the early 1990s. In the event of the Shadow Cabinet becoming the Blair government, he will be the only member with relatively recent experience of running a huge organization employing thousands of people and disbursing a vast budget. In government, the ability to run a department is more likely to matter than a sharp eye for a good suit. The public may then discover that there is much more to David Blunkett than a blind man who relegated his disability to a mere inconvenience.

CHAPTER FIVE

CLARE SHORT

Less than three months after the general election of 1983, the Commons was treated to an extraordinary spectacle when one of the brand new MPs accused a Minister of the Crown of being drunk at the despatch box. To catch its full flavour, we must remember how much the House of Commons is ruled by tradition, particularly as regards the use of language. In this world in which MPs never speak to one another directly, always referring to one another in the third person singular, never mentioning other MPs' names, referring to them only by their constituencies, in which all MPs are 'honourable', and no one may be accused of lying or behaving disreputably, there have been occasions when members have rolled into the Chamber so drunk that they can barely stand up and have then tried to make a speech, safe in the knowledge that their slurred meanderings will be tidied up and made coherent in the official record of proceedings. No MP accuses another of being under the influence of alcohol.

On this occasion, the minister in question was sufficiently in control of his facilities to retain a clear memory of the experience, which is fortunate, because he was the now-celebrated diarist Alan Clark, who was then Under Secretary of State for Employment. It was his task to present to the Commons, at 10.30 on a Wednesday evening, some new European regulations on equal pay for women. Given Clark's unremitting male chauvinism and his hostility to the European Commission, he was not the best person to be presenting a statement such as this, drunk or sober; and earlier in the evening he had been at a wine-tasting ceremony at which he had compared the merits of '61 Palmer, and '75 Palmer, switching back to '61 Palmer and rounding off with a 'really delicious' Pichon Longueville. As he returned to the Commons in a chauffeur-driven Princess, sucking on a large Havana cigar, he tried to get to grips with the 'fucking text' handed to him by his civil servants, but it was in language alien to him. The 'sheer odiousness' of it impressed itself upon him with full force as he began reading it out in front of an unexpectedly large turn-out of MPs. Before he had completed three paragraphs, he was compelled to admit out loud that he was losing the attention of his audience. MPs on both sides were shouting at him to hurry up. One Tory MP, Elaine Kellet-Bowman, sarcastically suggested that he take lessons in how to read more quickly. He insisted that he would continue at his own pace, whereupon he was challenged by 'a new Labour member whom I had never seen before, called Clare Short, dark-haired and serious with a lovely Brummie accent', who accused him of not believing a word of the statement he was reading out. She was right, and what followed might have been avoided if he had made a more gracious attempt to conceal it. Instead, he replied condescendingly: 'When you have been here longer, you will appreciate that a certain separation between expressed and implied beliefs is endemic among those who hold office.'

Clark now decided that his best chance of survival was to complete the wretched statement as fast as possible, and words tumbled out in an incomprehensible stream until another Labour MP, Greville Janner, intervened to ask him to slow down, turn back and explain what the paragraph he had just read out actually meant. It was an awful question to put to the swaying minister. 'How the hell did I know what it meant?' he confided in his diary. He promised to 'settle for a median delivery' in the hope of placating those who were clamouring for him to hurry up and those who protested at not being about to follow him. One more slurred paragraph and Clare Short could brook no more. 'On a point of order,' she exclaimed, 'I have read in the newspapers that in the House one is not allowed to accuse another Honourable Member of not being sober. However, I seriously put it to you that the Minister is incapable.' For minutes, business was brought to a halt by 'screams, yells, shouts of "withdraw" and counter shouts'. The chamber began to fill with MPs, and the press gallery with journalists, as word rapidly spread around the Palace of Westminster that there was good entertainment to be had. The awful vista opened before the trapped minister that the business might be aborted and rescheduled for another evening, but he soldiered on until the statement which he could not understand and did not believe in duly passed into law.[1]

The incident made everyone want to know who this person was, this

Clare Short, recently arrived from Birmingham, who had blurted out what everyone else had been too polite to mention. There were more than 120 new MPs in the House, including Tony Blair and Gordon Brown, to name but two on the Labour side; ahead of all of them, Short had established herself as a personality who was not going to be easily silenced. But she had left herself in an exposed position, as the venerated traditions of public hypocrisy enclosed the minister in its protective embrace. Although everyone in the Chamber could see that she was telling the truth, the Deputy Speaker, a Labour MP named Ernie Armstrong, compelled her to withdraw. Some of the resulting coverage suggested that she had admitted making a false accusation, but what she actually said was: 'If I am allowed to withdraw when the House understands that I meant what I said, I withdraw.' Until the publication of Clark's diaries ten years later, no journalist would have dared remark that this convoluted retraction was only a formality required by House of Commons tradition, which should not be taken to imply that the minister was sober.

It was all very much in character. Clare Short was angry because, unlike Clark, she understood the draft Equal Pay (Amendment) Regulations 1983 and thought they were important. She thought he was taking the piss. As the truth dawned, typically it was Clare Short who created a sensation in which the original point of the argument was lost and she was left exposed in open terrain. Anyone who publicly condemns a minister for drinking too much ought really to be either teetotal or very abstemious, to avoid the charge of preaching one thing and practising another, but during her time on the backbenches, Short was almost masculine in her barroom sociability.

Throughout her turbulent career she has taken extraordinary risks, with consequences which would easily have destroyed a weaker character. On several occasions, she has deliberately gone into action against powerful vested interests, knowing that they were in a position to hit back, including the Murdoch empire, several times over, the West Midlands police, W.H. Smith, the Labour-controlled Birmingham city council and the region's right-wing trade unions. Also on the list of interest groups with a grievance against Clare Short are Zionists, Trotskyists, Ulster Unionists, the Catholic Church and Peter Mandelson – all causes sacred to those who believe.

Clare Short has not made her way to the top by consistently courting powerful patrons either. She is also almost the only exception to the rule that anyone who was sacked or resigned on political grounds from Labour's frontbench during the opposition years stayed out for good. Uniquely, she resigned twice, came back both times and fought her way on to the Shadow Cabinet. Another unique fact about her, which has so far passed unnoticed, is that she is the only member of the Shadow Cabinet who has never voted for the winning candidate in any election for a party leader or deputy leader since 1983, not even when Tony Benn challenged Neil Kinnock in 1988. Yet, far from being a heroine of the outside left, she is uniquely unpopular among the dissident elements grouped around *Left Labour Briefing* in particular, who regard her as an authoritarian careerist.

The emergence of Clare Short as a scourge of Trotskyism in the 1990s is not wholly inconsistent with the Bennite radicalism she was expounding a decade earlier. The Bennite left was not a monolith. Even before it divided into what is now called its 'hard' and 'soft' components, it was already a teaming mass of grouplets and movements between whom there was the ever-present risk of conflict. One way of trying to inject intellectual order into this jumble would be to draw a dividing line with 'workerists' on one side, who thought of the working class broadly as Karl Marx did, as one homogeneous entity capable of acting in its own collective interest; and on the other, the libertarians, feminists and others whose political ideas were constructed upon the observation that the working class was fragmented and that the majority of working-class people were suffering at the hands of other working-class people while hardly ever coming into direct contact with the boss class. On the 'workerist' side were to be found most of the Campaign Group of MPs, Arthur Scargill, the 'confrontationist' councillors in Liverpool, Lambeth and Southwark, the newspaper *Labour Herald*, most Trotskyite groups including Militant, and the pro-Soviet wing of the Communist Party and its fellow travellers; and on the other side, the women's movement, the gay rights movement, the Black sections, CND, the GLC and other left-wing London councils, *Tribune*, *Marxism Today*, the Eurocommunists, etc., and Clare Short.

These profound differences were partially concealed while Tony Benn's political skills enabled him to draw support from the whole gamut of the left. They were much more obvious when Arthur Scargill finally broke away to form the Socialist Labour Party in 1996. Although he attracted a huge amount of publicity and some influential support within a few industrial unions, his organization had no more attraction for the majority of disillusioned Labour Party members or ex-members than its rival Militant Labour because, since the mid-1970s, anyone who watched the left closely could observe that overall the 'workerists' were in decline while the 'libertarians' were on the increase, notwithstanding the warning issued in 1985 by the venerated academic Ralph Miliband that 'to make gender or race or whatever else *the* defining criterion of "social being", and to ignore or belittle the fact of class, is to help deepen the divisions that are present within the working class'.[2]

Though Clare Short's speeches and occasional writings are scattered with references to working people, it usually emerges that she is referring to the oppressed within the working class: Asians, West Indians, Irish Catholics, the young unemployed, the low paid, part-time workers, women workers and, most often and most generally, women. For a Birmingham MP, she has shown less interest than she might in promoting the interests of skilled and highly paid car workers. After the demise of the GLC, she became arguably the single most prominent and effective exponent of the idea that socialism was about raising the social status of people who were individually isolated and powerless. To Clare Short:

> Socialism is an ethical and not an economic system. We start from the premise that each and every human being in the world is of equal value and is equally entitled to take control of their life and develop it as they see fit.[3]

She has been known to quote J.S. Mill's *On Liberty*: 'We will truly know that we live in a free society when there are plenty of eccentrics living in it'. She is not, however, a liberal. She is of the view that to create a society which accommodates eccentrics, there must be regulation, imposed if necessary by the centralized state. She was a keen exponent of minimum wage legislation in the years when some of the larger trade unions were sceptical or hostile to it. She believes in censorship, where it is deployed in favour of the powerless. She was pilloried as 'Killjoy Clare' in the tabloid newspapers owned by Rupert Murdoch because she campaigned for legislation to curb pin-up photographs. She was also one of the most energetic exponents of positive action and, in particular, the introduction of all-women shortlists in winnable parliamentary seats, which parts of the Labour Party thought of as oppressive, and which was eventually adjudged to be discriminatory. Moreover, her tolerance of eccentrics does not extend to Trotskyites, as she demonstrated by her very public role in the proscription of Liz Davies, a would-be Labour parliamentary candidate who had been chosen in a constituency party ballot from an all-women shortlist.

The Clare Short campaign against pin-up girlie photographs began in circumstances similar to the verbal assault on Alan Clark, with a remark made on the spur of the moment during a debate to which she had not intended to contribute at all. This is not as unusual as it may seem, at least not in her case, because in the 1980s she was an assiduous attender of Commons debates, particularly those which affected the status of women, and would frequently leap to her feet when something she heard provoked her, or would shout out from a sitting position, often making unguarded comments which were pounced on by alert Tory MPs.

There was, for example, the farcical occasion when the Tory MP Jerry Hayes accused her of accusing him of being the father of illegitimate children. When issues like abortion or the care of unwanted children were under debate, Short frequently came close to telling male MPs that they had no business to speak because they had never given birth, unless of course they wanted to acknowledge their part in causing unintended pregnancies. During the passage of a Private Member's Bill to restrict abortion, introduced by the Catholic MP David Alton, she declared that:

> Every man in this House who has ever used a woman's body and walked away and did not know the consequences has no right to vote on the Bill . . . If men in the House were honest, most would have to walk away.'[4]

There is no disputing that the Commons has its notorious womanizers, but to put 'most' in that category is at best unprovable.

On another occasion, when Michael Meacher, as Shadow Social Security Secretary, was criticizing the proposal to establish a Child Support Agency, fearing that the new legislation would compel unmarried mothers to disclose to the agency the names of violent fathers, or lose their benefit, Short was irritated by hearing a Tory MP shout, 'Why shouldn't they?' and called out: 'Some of the children are yours!' Up jumped Jerry Hayes, claiming that the accusation had been levelled at him. She explained that she had been 'pointing out to Conservative Members that some of them may have fathered children that they do not know about'. Instantly, Short was into a pointless confrontation. Conservative MPs were demanding that the Speaker, Bernard Weatherill, discipline her, while he politely but firmly told her that she was out of order. Pride would not allow her to back down, and she was warned no less than ten times in quick succession by the ever-patient Weatherill that if she did not withdraw the allegation, worse would follow. Still she refused, saying, 'One of the reasons I came into politics was that I did not like bullying.' To defuse the situation, the Speaker sent for *Hansard* so that he could check exactly what she had said, but even when it arrived, she was determined to have the last word. She said: 'I dispute the words that you read out from *Hansard*, Mr Speaker . . . Therefore, as I did not utter the words, I am happy to withdraw them.'[5] It was just enough to save her from a period of expulsion from the Palace of Westminster.

Afterwards Jerry Hayes approached Short privately, hoping she could be persuaded to laugh it all off as a joke – to no avail. She quite failed to see what was funny about Tory MPs scoffing at unmarried mothers and ganging up on a woman who spoke up for them.

Short had to be more careful when what she regarded as unacceptable male behaviour was coming from the Labour side rather than the Tories, though there were occasions when she forgot the normal restraints of party politics, most notably in the Cleveland case of alleged child abuse. In the mid-1980s, dozens of Cleveland children were removed from their parents' care by social workers who believed they had uncovered evidence of sexual abuse. The case provoked a national outcry, not against child abuse but against the social workers who had broken up families on the strength of specious evidence. Stuart Bell, Labour MP for Middlesbrough, ran an energetic campaign on behalf of the aggrieved parents, attacking without inhibition Cleveland's Labour-led county council and forcing a judicial enquiry. His role attracted a great deal of criticism from within the Labour Party, especially from women, including his parliamentary neighbour, Marjorie Mowlam. One of those who attacked him loudest was Clare Short, who had already clashed with him when Bell was Northern Ireland spokesman. As far as she was concerned, incest and paedophilia were the real evils, not the officiousness of social workers. She told delegates to the 1987 party conference: 'The tragedy of Cleveland, whether mistakes were made or not, is that where social workers and doctors were attempting to tackle the problem, suddenly this great attack was unleashed on them. The message to other social workers and doctors . . . is "don't get into this, the popular press will go for you and, sadly, a Labour MP will . . . attack you".[6] Later, after she had resumed the attack, Bell threatened to sue her. However, the incident had no long-term consequences, unlike the occasion when she took on the tabloids.

This time, it was on a Friday morning, the period normally set aside for debates on Bills presented by backbench MPs, most of which disappear, forgotten, into the parliamentary memory hole. The only reason Short had stayed in London at all was to take part in a manoeuvre to block Enoch Powell's Protection of Unborn Children Bill, which would have banned embryo research, denying infertile couples the hope of having children. This was second in the list of bills to be debated on 24 January 1986. The most obvious way to block it, therefore, was to have a long argument about the one which preceded it, a Bill presented by the Tory MP, Winston Churchill, on obscene publications. She consequently spent five minutes on her feet, explaining why she thought the Bill was 'defective' because it did not address some of the most dangerous forms of obscenity, like the depiction of sadistic violence. In passing, she commented: 'I may bring forward a ten-minute Bill to outlaw showing pictures of partially naked or naked women in mass circulation newspapers.'[7] The whole speech was unscripted. As in the Clark case, Short was provoked by the suspicion that men on the Tory side were taking the mickey out of an issue she took seriously. In brief, she was 'carried away'. At first, her remarks made almost no impact, because the press gallery was virtually empty, but during the following week, Short was surprised by the number of letters she received from women, who had presumably read her remarks in their local newspapers, urging her to go ahead. From that unplanned beginning, she walked into a conflict which would make her a celebrity and cause her untold personal stress.[8]

Having begun on impulse, Short proceeded with determination, with a Bill which would have banned the 'display of pictures of naked or partially naked women in sexually provocative poses in newspapers'. She turned out at 6 am, outside the appropriate room in a corridor high above the Commons debating chamber, to be first in the queue to present it, but found someone there ahead of her. She therefore tried again another day, at

4 am, but was still too late. At the third attempt, she camped out all night in the corridor. The resulting debate, on 12 March 1986, was certain to bring out the worst in certain Tory MPs. Actually, it was the harmless Robert Adley, best remembered in the Commons as a railway buff, who complained that the Bill might deprive him one of the 'few pleasures left to us today'.[9] One right-wing Tory, Tony Marlow, objected to Adley's flippancy. A few others, including Teddy Taylor on the right and Sir Peter Tapsell on the Tory left, backed Short. Tony Blair was among about ninety Labour MPs who voted for the measure. Three Labour MPs, Andrew Faulds, Austin Mitchell and the former Chief Whip, Michael Cocks, voted against.

What happened in the Commons chamber, however, was not vastly important. Short's bill was principally aimed at the *Sun*, the treasure house of the country's biggest media empire and the Conservative Party's most valuable supporter within the fourth estate. To a lesser extent, she was also taking on the *Daily Mirror*, the Labour Party's most valuable supporter, and the *Daily Star*. Against interests such as those, she could only shake her fist at the castle wall and wait to see what the defenders on the parapets poured on her head. The ingenuity of some of the nation's highest paid journalists was deployed in belittling and ridiculing her. *Sun* readers were offered free car stickers and a freepost address to which they could write to express their objections to the Bill, plus:

20 THINGS YOU NEVER KNEW ABOUT CRAZY CLARE!
Lefty who likes to travel first-class

Crackpot MP Clare Short is trying to outlaw the *Sun's* gorgeous Page Three girls . . . Here are 20 fascinating things you did not know about kill-joy Clare.

The piece, which consisted mostly of well-known facts, was written by John Kay who – fascinatingly – had himself been subjected to a thorough and professional psychiatric examination after he killed his wife. Fortunately, he was found to have been genuinely crazy, and consequently escaped a life sentence and was able after suitable treatment to return to work.[10]

Undeterred, Short went back into the attack in March 1988, with another identically worded Bill, which attracted more opposition and more support than its predecessor. Among 165 MPs who backed it were Gillian

Shephard, Ann Widdecombe and the future Tory defector, Emma Nicholson. One of Short's pet hates on the Tory benches seems to have been the 'wet' MP Robert Hughes, who frequently received the sharp end of her tongue, including an occasion when she accused him of making an 'ignorant, stupid and ill-informed speech' about dole claimants,[11] or another time when she stopped herself in mid-sentence to exclaim: 'Who is that silly little man?'[12] Yet, to do him justice, the 'silly little man' defied majority opinion in the Tory party to vote for her Bill. This time, no Labour MP voted against.[13]

Later, Short widened her target to take in magazines which featured pin-up pictures and the shops which stocked them. In November 1989, she led a squad of thirty women who made a well-publicized raid on a branch of W.H. Smith to sweep the offending publications off the top shelf.

At the same time, Short fearlessly invited the hostility of the police, particularly in her home region of the West Midlands. In this field, she was all the more dangerous an opponent because she had some inside knowledge of the subject. Her first job after university, in 1970–75, had been as a civil servant with the Home Office, where she was private secretary to a Tory Minister of State, Mark Carlisle, and then to his Labour successor, Alex Lyon. After she left, she worked for three years as Director of All Faiths for One Race in Birmingham, which brought her into daily contact with young Blacks who relayed stories of police harassment and corruption. The first publication to bear her name was *Talking Blues: A Study of Young West Indians' Views of Policing*, in 1978, followed in the same year by the *Handbook of Immigration Law*. In one of her first Commons speeches, she singled out the years 1977–78 in particular as a period when 'utterly innocent, law-abiding, hard-working young Black people lived in constant fear of being stopped by the police . . . [who] searched young West Indians, making them turn out their pockets and bend over cars, and using abusive and racist language'.[14] A few months later, she led a backbench attempt to amend the 1984 Police and Criminal Evidence bill to make racial discrimination by the police a specific disciplinary offence, telling the Commons: 'I have many Black friends, and I have known over many years that the police . . . are not little angels who always obey every rule.'[15] The move was blocked by an unusually large turn-out of Tory MPs. Her statements on race brought in sporadic piles of hate mail, which may have been organized by right-wing groups.

Short did not believe that Blacks were the only minority at the receiving end of oppressive police operations. She campaigned for years for the release of the Birmingham Six, long before more senior figures in the party like Roy Hattersley or Jack Straw were prepared to believe in their inno-cence. By chance, she was in Birmingham on the night when twenty-one people were killed by IRA bombs. One of her brothers was a regular at one of the pubs targeted by the IRA and, in the immediate aftermath, the fam-ily feared he was dead. Given the number of her constituents who had lost friends or relatives in the Birmingham pub bombings, to appear as a plat-form speaker at the first rally in Birmingham in defence of the Six, as Short did in November 1986, required some courage.

On another occasion, when Short was moving an amendment to the government's Police and Criminal Evidence Bill, she complained that:

> serving police officers throughout the country get dressed up in ways that they think will make them attractive to gay men, go to places where gay men are known to meet and put themselves around so that they are approached, and then arrest people. We are talking about policemen deliberately going not just to public lava-tories, but to pubs and clubs where gay men are known to meet.[16]

At the time she said this, a scandal appeared to be breaking over the head of a Tory MP who was accused of making advances to a male police officer in a bar. The case was later dropped. The man was a happily married het-erosexual, who appeared to have wandered absent-mindedly into an embarrassing predicament. Where other Labour MPs were looking forward to a by-election, Short only saw that the law applied unequally to homo-sexuals and heterosexuals, and ought to be changed.

She became involved in almost direct engagement with the police later, when one of her constituents, Paul Dandy, was arrested and held for ten months as a category A prisoner, until his solicitor was able to prove that the only evidence against him, his alleged confession, had been forged. Having been approached by Dandy's solicitor, Short took the case to the Police Complaints Authority and raised it in the Commons, wringing an admission from the Home Office minister, Douglas Hogg, that the officers who forged Dandy's confession were not disciplined for that, but for destroying the original piece of paper on which the forgery was based. She was also taken to meet other solicitors practising in Birmingham and Wolverhampton, who all related stories of faked confessions and other malpractices. One case involved one of the police officers who had handled the case of the Birmingham Six. 'I have heard before of allegations of mal-practice in the police force and did not think that I would be easily shocked, but the degree and breadth of the allegations of malpractice which have come to me from solicitors in Birmingham has shocked me,' she told the Commons.[17]

Having made enemies in the tabloid press and among the less scrupulous members of the police force, Short was now open to the risk that they would combine to take revenge. Act One came in 1990, after a woman was arrested during a police raid in which pornographic videos were seized, and police officers discovered that she had worked in the Commons seven years earlier for several MPs including, briefly, the newly elected Clare Short. The upshot was a headline in the *News of the World*, on 28 October 1990, 'Anti-Porn MP's ex-aide quizzed over Porn!' She complained to the police and received a warm letter of apology from Commander Richard Monk, head of the Obscene Publications Squad at New Scotland Yard, and a brief apology from the newspaper.

The next attack was more serious, and probably hurt her personally more than anything else that has happened in her public life. At the age of eighteen, Short had rushed into marriage with a fellow student at Leeds University, which broke up within a few years. Early in 1991, a mutual friend from Leeds rang her to say that her former husband had been visited by John Chapman, a well known dirt-digger from the *News of the World*, who had asked questions with 'horrendous, deeply hurtful, unbelievable and completely false implications'.[18] As she understood it, the newspaper had offered sums ranging from £5,000 upwards for photographs of the teenage Clare Short in a nightdress.

One thing which her former husband was able to warn her about was that the newspaper had information which could only have come from the West Midlands police, about a man who had lived in the same house as she had in Birmingham in the 1970s. It was a large house in which, at various times, two of her sisters, her brother, a refugee couple from Chile, an American writer and architecture students had lived. John Daniel, who lived there for several years, had several criminal convictions dating from the 1960s about which she says she knew nothing until her solicitor heard it from the *News of the World*. In the late 1970s he went back to Barbados, but returned in 1979 and was gunned down in Birmingham in what appears to have been an unsolved gangland killing.

By now, Short had already taken the sort of punishment which destroyed Deirdre Wood and has driven others into terrified obscurity. The prospect of all this appearing in print, possibly accompanied by a lurid photograph, distressed her so much that she must have wondered whether she could survive, politically or emotionally. After some days' hesitation, she decided to tackle it head on. She secured an opportunity to attack the *News of the World*, before they attacked her, by revealing in the Commons what they were proposing to print, and accusing the West Midlands police of cooperating with the Murdoch paper in a smear campaign. That weekend, the full details appeared over two pages of the *News of the World*, along with an editorial explaining that 'Despite Ms Short's attacks on US, we ADMIRE her reputation as a hard-working Labour MP and her campaigning against pornography (although we don't share her opinion that Page 3 girls fall into that category)'.[19]

From there, Short carried on belligerently determined to fight anyone on any grounds until the crisis was over. In this period, she had a direct confrontation with Neil Kinnock over the quite separate question of the Gulf War, and quit the front bench. She took the *News of the World* to the Press Complaints Commission, putting its editor, Patsy Chapman, on the defensive, as a newly co-opted member of that body. The newspaper adamantly denied attempting to buy compromising photographs of her, but could not dissuade the Commission from reaching the 'inescapable conclusion' that it had been conducting a vendetta against her. Most of the country's newspapers took her part. In the *Evening Standard*, the right-wing writer, A.N. Wilson, was given space to explain 'Why I love Clare Short'. Much more significantly, the Police Complaints Authority ruled during the summer that police officers had misused their position to pass information about her to the *News of the World*, confirming that the information in the article was identical to what was in confidential police files.[20]

Short also, rather rashly, rang the *Sun*, complaining about the library photograph of her which they had used repeatedly, in which the camera had caught her with dishevelled hair and a harridan-like expression. She had had abusive letters from *Sun* readers which referred to the way she looked in the photograph and she asked if anything could be done about it. She was advised to send them a better likeness. Appealing to reason from that quarter was like cuddling a monkey in a dustbin. The newspaper published both photographs on its front page, with a mocking article by John Kay, and offered readers three phone numbers to ring, one for either picture and the third if they preferred never to see a photograph of Clare Short again.[21] Predictably, the readers voted for no pictures of her, though many months later the *Sun* broke its self-imposed ban by illustrating a story that Labour image advisers had urged Labour frontbenchers to shave off their beards with a picture of what Crazy Clare might look like with a beard.

This ordeal was made worse by domestic unhappiness. Years earlier, when she was a twenty-eight-year-old Home Office secretary, she had embarked on an affair with the Minister of State, Alex Lyon, during a working visit to India. He was married, with children, and her senior by fifteen years. Their working relationship ended soon afterwards, and then Lyon was sacked when James Callaghan became Prime Minister in 1976. Why he was sacked is open to speculation. Probably the reason was political, because Lyon was one of the ministers who, less publicly than Benn, was undergoing a left-wing conversion in office. His reputation was as a social democrat and protégé of Roy Jenkins. He was one of the sixty-nine MPs who had rebelled in 1972, in order to take Britain into the Common Market. That in itself would not necessarily have commended him to Callaghan, who was less pro-European and substantially less liberal on immigration policy than Roy Jenkins and other social democrats. Anyway, Lyon's relationship with Jenkins had deteriorated and he no longer had powerful protectors. He subsequently renounced the social democrats and identified with the Bennites, saying that much of what he and other social democrats had done in the early 1970s 'has been proved palpably wrong by experience in the years since, and if the party has been listened to, perhaps we might not have made some of the mistakes'.[22]

During the last years of his working life, as Chairman of the UK Immigrants Advisory Bureau, Lyon became increasingly critical of Labour's immigration policy. At the 1981 party conference, the high watermark for the left, he backed a resolution calling for greater political control of chief constables through elected police authorities, complaining that 'one of the reasons why we are in the mess we are in with the police' was their chief officers' freedom to exercise power without democratic control. These sentiments are too alarming to be heard from anyone on Labour's frontbench as it is constituted fifteen years on, but had fairly wide support within the party as it was then. Among the other backers of the same call for 'effective democratic control' of the police was the recently elected MP for Blackburn, Jack Straw, who said: 'There has always been political control of the police . . . the issue is one of handing back to our great cities and our towns like Birmingham, Manchester, Blackburn and Liverpool the power which they once had to run their own police force in their own way and not be dictated to by the Home Secretary or by police chiefs.'[23]

To someone of Short's strict Catholic upbringing, the rest of the story of her relationship with Alex Lyon must have had ghastly echoes of divine retribution, given that she never felt easy about her part in the break-up of his first marriage. In 1979, when she was appointed Director of Youth Aid in London, she moved in with him, into a large house in Clapham. They married in 1981. On the day she was elected to parliament, Lyon lost his seat, and consequently he now became her secretary, a reversal which he took a lot better than many men would have done. However, his health began to deteriorate, and in 1984, at the age of fifty-two, he was forced to give up work. At first, he was diagnosed as having spinal muscular atrophy, but his behaviour became progressively stranger in inexplicable and distressing ways. For instance, he started moving furniture about in the house they shared in Clapham, rearranging it in a way which seemed pointlessly annoying. By the time the *News of the World* were after Short, she was convinced that he had been wrongly diagnosed, and that she was watching his brain and personality crumble. Lyon told her a confused story about being visited by a stranger, whom she suspected was a journalist, although the newspaper denied sending anyone. Eventually, Lyon was diagnosed as suffering from Alzheimer's disease from which he died not long afterwards.

The explanation of why Short ventured into such dangerous political waters, and where she found the fortitude to survive, must lie partly in her childhood. Some years ago, researchers for a television programme approached a number of MPs to ask them to which social class they believed they belonged and how that affected their politics. One of the sample, predictably, was Dennis Skinner, who is everyone's idea of a working-class MP, having experienced everything in his early life which qualifies him for that description: his father was a miner, unemployed through most of the 1930s after being blacklisted for union activities; his brother was one of the celebrated Clay Cross councillors, surcharged and disqualified by the Conservatives in the early 1970s; and he was himself a coalface miner for twenty-six years, who owed his further education to the union, which arranged for him to go to Ruskin College. Yet Skinner did not claim to be working class; he said: 'I come from the working class, and I've tried to hang on to my roots as best I can, which isn't easy in the House of Commons.'

When Clare Short was asked, she replied that people no longer thought of themselves as working class or middle class but as ordinary working people. Asked to define her own social position, she said: 'I am just an ordinary working person.'[24] A grammar school and university education, a high-flying job in the civil service, marriage to a former government minister and election to parliament are not everyone's idea of the outline of an ordinary working life. However, there is a sense in which she is more 'ordinary' than most of the well-known exponents of what is sometimes called race-and-gender politics.

Libertarian, anti-discriminatory politics became devalued in the 1980s by some of the eccentric obsessions which took hold in parts of the London Labour Party. Although many of the stories about London's 'loony left' were either invented or exaggerated, it is a fact, for instance, that after the Fulham by-election in 1986, Labour's Walworth Road headquarters received a formal protest from a party branch in Haringey about an election address containing a photograph of the candidate and his family, because such images are 'heterosexist'. As a result, causes like gay rights became associated with the 'bedsit left', the socially mobile, wandering activists who turned up in a community and because of their experience at participating in meetings, instantly claimed the authority to speak on behalf of others. This was principally, though not exclusively, a London phenomenon.

Though Short is often fighting the same causes as these people, she is not a wandering activist who turned up in Birmingham Ladywood in pursuit of a busy political career. She was brought up there and has a large extended family there. Her father, Frank Short, who died in 1986 aged eighty-three, was an Irish Catholic from Crossmaglen who moved to Birmingham and found a job as a schoolteacher. As an unwavering republican, he resigned from the Labour Party in the late 1940s in opposition to the Attlee government's Irish policy, resuming his membership many years later. Her mother was born in Birmingham, with the surname O'Loughlin, but she had a great-grandfather who fled Ireland to Birmingham to escape the potato famine. Short's parents arranged for her to have a Catholic education, to which her reaction was evidently mixed. The experience of being beaten on the hand by a nun at the age of six, and the observation that the tough kids in the class gloried in being beaten, instilled a lifelong view that heavy-handed punishments produce the opposite effect from the one intended. Later, she went on to St Paul's grammar school, sister of the slightly better-known St Philip's school for boys, where her brother and numerous uncles and cousins were educated. Like many others raised as Catholics, Short had an uneasy relationship with the church in adult life. Her greatest quarrel with Catholics was over feminism and, in particular, over abortion and the related issue of embryology, and women priests. She once complained:

> When one looks at the writings from the days of the early fathers of the Church . . . some of them are horrendous in its [sic] hatred of women, and rejection of their sexuality and any rights. That is all pre-reformation and forms part of the origins of . . . the Catholic Church.[25]

Holding these views was not made any easier by her close emotional ties with her immediate family, many of whom were devout Catholics, though that did not include any of her four sisters. When she was opposing Enoch Powell's Protection of Unborn Children Bill, Short had a large number of letters from Catholics, including one from the priest who had baptized her and who, at that time, in 1985, was regularly visiting her parents' home to give communion to her elderly father. After his death, Short's mother moved into her home in Clapham and continued to attend mass every morning.

But Short did not deny that the selective Catholic schools gave their pupils a first rate education. Indeed, she vigorously protested when the Oratory Fathers decided years later to close St Philip's because it had too many non-Catholic pupils. As the second of seven children – born on 15 February 1946 – and the second of five girls, she inevitably had to learn to look after herself more than most children of her age, and act as occasional mother to younger siblings. This may explain why one of her contemporaries at St Paul's remembers her as the most self-confident girl in the class. Like Neil Kinnock, her generation was the first in the family to go to university. Coincidentally, she was interviewed for a university place soon after Hugh Gaitskell's supporters had lost the battle to remove Clause Four from the party constitution. The seventeen-year-old Clare Short was asked whether Labour could ever form a government again while the Clause remained. She answered confidently that it could, the essence of socialism being common ownership. A little over thirty years later, having lost her faith in 'common ownership', Short reluctantly supported Tony Blair's decision to abolish the Clause.

Poverty was something she witnessed in her fellow pupils at school, rather than experiencing it directly herself. Years later, she recalled 'the white, grey faces of poverty, thin clothes and poor shoes [whose] skin showed that they were not living in decent conditions [or] obtaining good food'[26] among her classmates – a spectacle which disappeared in the 1960s and 1970s, to return after the recession of early 1980s, at about the time when she was elected MP for the area. Even the fact of being Irish by descent did not prevent her being positively vetted to work in sensitive positions in the civil service; nor did the radical views she held as a student prevent her working with a Tory minister – a job which one day involved her in taking a long telephone message from Mary Whitehouse, who was ringing in with explicit details from a new film which she wanted banned.[27]

Moreover, the working class with which Short identified was not the army of unionized industrial workers who had formed the original base of the Labour Party. Her work in Birmingham, and subsequently as Director of Youth Aid and the Unemployment Unit in 1979–83, brought her into contact with people for whom the wages of a West Midlands car worker would have seemed like riches indeed. Similarly, as an MP, she was representing the seat with all the problems of a rundown inner city. In 1983, the newly created Ladywood seat had 50 per cent male unemployment, the sixteenth worst level in Britain. Out of 1,389 school leavers in the area served by the Handsworth career service in 1983, only 101 found jobs before the end of the calendar year; whereas when she left school in 1962, everyone in the class found work of some kind.[28] Half of her constituents were Black or Asian, and even the white half was made up largely of first- or second-generation immigrants from Ireland or elsewhere.

Consequently, the people for whom Short spoke were the underclass – the unemployed, the badly paid, the ethnic minorities and women – rather than the organized working class. She spoke eloquently in defence of the principle of a national minimum wage before it was Labour party policy and despite the line taken by the AUEW, which had its main stronghold in Birmingham. She claimed that if Britain continued to tolerate the phenomenom of the 'working poor', whose number she put at seven million, then 'we are showing a preparedness to live in a disgusting society in which people are so crudely unequal'.[29] She was, however, expounding the policy of NUPE, the union which sponsored her. A few months after a national minimum wage became party policy, Short was elevated to her first post on Labour's front bench, as a Shadow Employment Minister, in a team headed by John Prescott.

In some respects, it was bad luck that the turmoil in the Labour Party happened to coincide with a cultural change in Britain's ethnic communities, so that in the same period in which it was coping with the political ramifications of the miners' strike, with rate-capping and with the confrontation with Militant, the party was coincidentally plunged into a public and damaging controversy over Black sections. This was one problem which could not be blamed on bad party management or the failings of the previous Labour government. Its origin lay within the Black communities, where there was a visible generation gap between older community leaders who were almost all first-generation immigrants, conscious of their separateness from the white majority and with strong ties to their Asian or Caribbean homelands, and younger activists who had either been born in Britain or who had arrived when very young and consequently knew no other home. In 1974, to pick a year at random, it was almost unknown for anyone of Asian or West Indian descent to be a councillor, or an officer of the local party, or even to take part in party meetings. They had their own clubs, societies and social networks, with recognized leaders who dealt directly with the appropriate white representatives, such as the local councillors or race relations officers. By 1984, a number of younger and more adventurous Blacks, such as Paul Boateng, Diane Abbott, Sharon Atkin, Ben Bousquet and Bernie Grant, all of whom were London councillors, had pushed their way into 'white' politics. They were floating the idea that the Labour Party should encourage the formation of exclusive Black sections, which would be formally recognized as affiliated organizations entitled to representation on constituency general committees, and so on, in exactly the same way as women's sections. These sections would be closed to white party members whose presence might inhibit disaffected young Blacks whom the organizers hoped to draw into political activity.

This issue arose when the Bennite left was undergoing an Indian summer. Already beaten in the battle for control of the Labour Party, it was still strong enough to defeat the party leadership on single issues. But it was also in the process of breaking up. It is not surprising, therefore, that Black sections should have been seized upon as an issue by libertarians in the Bennite left. It really took hold only in a few urban centres: London, Nottingham and Leicester, and to a much lesser extent in Bristol and Birmingham. Principally, it was the London left which took up the cause and – to the irritation of many young Black males – bracketed it alongside feminism and gay rights under the general heading of positive discrimination.

Since, as a general rule, the libertarian wing of the Bennite left was more amenable than the 'workerist' left to accommodation with Neil Kinnock, it did not automatically follow that the Black sections' cause would turn into an open challenge to the leader's authority. Rather the opposite: one of the first whites to put the case for Black sections was Patricia Hewitt, when she was General Secretary of the National Council for Civil Liberties, shortly before she moved into Neil Kinnock's office. She arranged a meeting between Sharon Atkin and the party leader, which went off better than either probably expected. On the first occasion when the issue was raised at a meeting of the NEC, the chairman, Eric Heffer, intervened before anyone could speak to object to what he regarded as an unwarranted division of the working class along racial lines; the first reply came from Neil Kinnock, who insisted that they keep an open mind because 'some very serious people' were promoting the idea of separate Black sections.[30]

Heffer was by no means the only voice on the so-called 'hard left' to oppose Black sections. When the issue was eventually put to the vote at a deeply divided NEC, there were two demonstrations on the pavement outside, one by the Black sections, the other a counter demonstration organized by Militant. Those who attempted to set up a Black section in Liverpool found the Militant-dominated city Labour Party every bit as hostile as in right-wing strongholds like Birmingham. The incident shows up the limitations of dividing the Labour left simply between the 'hard' and the 'soft', unless we take it that, on this issue, Eric Heffer and Militant were being 'soft'.

There was a genuine problem confronting even those who wished the Black sections well, which was how to define a 'Black' person. The organizers proposed to use 'self-definition', on the grounds that Black people knew they were Black, having learned from the prejudice they encountered from whites. However, if Black sections were to be allowed delegates on constituency general committees, a situation could arise in which a sitting Labour MP was deselected by a narrow vote in which Black representatives took part. Given the increasing number of internal party disputes which were being settled in court, that could have led to Black-section delegates having to prove in law that they were in fact Black, which would have been unpleasantly reminiscent of apartheid. Even this need not have been an insuperable problem, given the number of barristers involved in the Black sections. Poale Zion, long recognized as a Jewish section of the Labour party, provided a working model. Sharon Atkin and Diane Abbott in fact arranged to meet Kinnock in June 1985 with what they believed was a legally acceptable solution. But on the morning of the planned meeting, they were startled to read in *The Times* an uncompromising attack on Black sections by the Labour leader. The meeting lapsed into confrontation and mutual incomprehension. Afterwards, the two women gave a press conference attacking Neil Kinnock and, from there on, there could be no reconciliation.

The Black sections movement was itself deeply divided and close to splitting, because fundamentally they had not agreed on their long-term objective. Founders of the movement, like Paul Boateng, saw it as a temporary expedient to lever a few Blacks into prominent positions within the established political structure. Young Blacks leaving school in 1985 had almost no role models to emulate, unless they wanted to be athletes or popular musicians; the election of a few Black MPs and council and trade union leaders would be visible evidence that white society was not entirely closed off. Others, like the London television journalist, Marc Wadsworth, and Linda Bellos, who succeeded Ted Knight as leader of Lambeth council, were less interested in creating 'role models' and more concerned with forcing the issues in which Blacks had a special interest, like racism and inner-city decay, to the front of the political agenda. They wanted Black sections as a permanent power base. Narenda Makenji, a Haringey councillor and secretary of the Black Sections national Committee, explained: 'We're about power. It's absolutely blunt: we want power and we will go wherever power is.'[31]

These differences of emphasis were not mutually contradictory and, until October 1985, both parts of the Black sections could unite around the single demand for formal recognition from the party; but after they had been heavily defeated at that autumn's conference, they were in a real dilemma as to where to go next. A number of leading Black section activists had a real chance of being adopted for winnable or even safe parliamentary seats; but in general it was these very constituencies in which local activists were defying the party rules by extending formal recognition to the Black sections. If Black section delegates attended selection conferences and voted, the NEC automatically refused to accept the legitimacy of the meeting or endorse the chosen candidate. For example, Stuart Holland, the sitting MP for Vauxhall, in Lambeth, was still not formally endorsed as a prospective Labour candidate when the 1987 general election began. The NEC circumvented that difficulty by imposing him as the candidate, doing away with the necessity of holding a valid selection conference. Russell Proffitt, a prominent Black sections activist, was selected for the winnable seat of Lewisham East, but was denied formal endorsement for months until the constituency party backed down and held a second selection conference from which Black section representatives were excluded. An even more extraordinary event took place on the night Paul Boateng was selected by Brent South as the first Black candidate in a safe Labour seat, ensuring there would be at least one Black MP in the next parliament. He had to walk in past a hostile demonstration organized by Marc Wadsworth and Sharon Atkin, who objected that the meeting was being held in accordance with the rule book, with no Black section delegates taking part. Their behaviour convinced Boateng that the movement was being 'hijacked' and hastened his eventual break with them. Ben Bousquet also broke with them, before his selection as candidate in Kensington for the 1987 election. Others including Diane Abbott, Bernie Grant, Russell Proffitt and Keith Vaz, were obliged to stop acting as Black sections activists as they too were adopted for safe or winnable seats, and the field was increasingly left to the most disaffected Black activists to make the running.

Even if they agreed among themselves, the Black sections would not by any means have been speaking for all Afro–Asian members of the Labour Party. Their supporters tended to be the young and socially mobile, who had lost the tight religious, linguistic and clan loyalties imported from the old country, without feeling integrated into white society. Sharon Atkin, for example, was born in Ealing, of an Irish mother and West Indian father. Linda Bellos, who rocketed to fame in 1986, was half Jewish and a lesbian, who had been deeply involved in Poale Zion before discovering the Black sections. They and other uncompromising radicals like Marc Wadsworth, were as much a threat to established leaders of the large Moslem, Sikh or Hindu communities as to white politicians. The party's main spokesman on immigration issues, Alf Dubs, began the year 1985 by supporting the principle of Black sections, but having canvassed the opinions of Black and Asian party members, he came out against them. Roy Hattersley's Sparkbrook constituency party instructed its delegate to the 1985 annual conference, Arif Mohammed, to oppose the Black sections. Hattersley was thus enlisted as the Black sections' most important opponent. The deputy leader's nickname, Hatterjee, dates from the occasion when he announced that 'my Asians' – i.e. those in Sparkbrook – did not require a Black section, a remark which Sharon Atkin, for instance, interpreted as evidence of a 'patronizing, condescending attitude'. He defended his choice of pronoun by saying that: 'I refer to my party . . . my constituency . . . my football team . . . my mother; I refer to all those people whom I regard as being my family as mine. They are mine and I am theirs.'[32]

Against that sort of opposition, there was no realistic prospect of the Black sections forcing the party to recognize them. Yet, while the wise and the cautious took care to avoid being associated with a losing cause, one of the few white politicians to stand by the Black sections throughout was Clare Short.

A few weeks before the 1987 general election, when it appeared that the simmering mistrust between the Black sections and the party leadership had settled down for the time, it suddenly exploded again. The figure at the centre was Sharon Atkin, a woman who roused strong feelings and who used strong language. She had been one of the thirty-one Lambeth surcharged Labour councillors in 1986, a double catastrophe in her life because one of the first acts of the new Labour administration which took over as she, Ted Knight and the others were disqualified was to remove her husband, Ed Atkin, from his post as Lambeth's Director of Housing. The people she despised most, therefore, were Lambeth Labour councillors like Linda Bellos, who in national politics appeared to compete for the title of the most provocative of the Black sections' ideologues, while introducing an element of pragmatism into Lambeth politics, to the extent that Ted Knight and Sharon Atkin accused her in *Labour Herald* of selling out to the 'white right'. Sell out or not, Bellos was subsequently expelled for bringing the Labour Party into disrepute, as a yet more mainstream Labour administration moved into Lambeth's troubled town hall. One of its members was Cathy Ashley, a head office researcher who, upon complaining in 1991 that her car tyres had been slashed in what she suspected was a piece of political vindictiveness, was reportedly told by Atkin: 'Violence is part of the rough and tumble of British political life: if you can't take it, you shouldn't be a councillor.'[33]

Early in April, Black activists in the Birmingham Labour Party, principally from Clare Short's Ladywood constituency, organized a public meeting which was supposed to persuade disaffected young Black radicals that it was worthwhile involving themselves in the Labour Party, entering it via the unauthorized Black sections. Other Birmingham Labour MPs, led by Roy Hattersley, expressed their disapproval in a letter to the national press. Sharon Atkin, who had been in two minds about accepting an invitation to the meeting, read their letter and resolved to go. In a heated session, during which she was barracked for being a parliamentary candidate, she declared in the presence of television cameras: 'I was told not to come to this meeting if I wanted my parliamentary seat. I wouldn't want my parliamentary seat if I can't represent Black people . . . I don't give a damn about Neil Kinnock and the racist Labour Party.'

Retribution came at the next meeting of the NEC, just over a fortnight later, when Sharon Atkin was barred from being a parliamentary candidate, and a new candidate, Mohammad Aslam, was imposed in Nottingham East. Atkin missed the hearing which ended her political ambitions because of illness. She perhaps was not cheered very much by the fact that the person who came out loudest in her defence was the despised Linda Bellos, who deliberately went on television to repeat the allegation that the Labour Party was racist. Ted Knight, Diane Abbott, Russell Profitt and the executive of Nottingham East Labour Party also defended her, but the only support she got which really counted for anything came from Birmingham, where she benefited from being associated with a West Indian councillor, Phil Murphy, who was suspended from the Labour group for participating in the same meeting. About seventy party members turned out to a special meeting in their defence, chaired by Clare Short. While there was not the slightest possibility of having Atkin reinstated as a candidate, it was possible to protect her and Linda Bellos from further reprisals; and the fact that neither was expelled from the Labour Party in 1987 was attributable in part to Clare Short's intervention.

By defending Sharon Atkin, Clare Short was inviting the disapproval of powerful elements in the Birmingham Labour Party. Her adoption as a candidate prior to the 1983 general election had been greeted with relief, because although she was a known Bennite, she was less unacceptable to the right-wing leaders of the city Labour Party than her main rival for the nomination, Albert Bore, who was prospective candidate for the old Birmingham Ladywood constituency, as it existed prior to the 1983 boundary changes. The new Ladywood seat took in part of Birmingham Handsworth, which had been represented since 1979 by Sheila Wright, who decided to retire only three years after her election. Clare Short's adoption as her successor was therefore uncontentious. Bore, on the other hand, became a parliamentary candidate when the Ladywood party abruptly deselected its sitting MP, John Sever, who had won Ladywood in 1977, at a time when Labour was grateful to win any by-election, even in a seat which they had held since 1945. When he was deselected, Sever was less than forty years old, the only victim of deselection in the 1979–83 parliament who was either aged under fifty, or had been an MP for less than a decade. In the game of musical chairs between incumbent MPs and prospective candidates which followed the boundary, Bore was punished for his role in the Sever affair by being left without a seat.

Very soon after her election, Short came into direct conflict with the city council and its new leader Dick Knowles – now Sir Richard Knowles – who had worked for thirty-three years as a full-time party organizer and was therefore formidably well-connected on the traditional, union-based Labour right. He and other senior councillors were sold on the idea of boosting Birmingham's tourist industry and the prestige of the city, first by building the prestigious National Exhibition Centre and then by holding a formula one car race through its streets, as Britain's version of the Monaco Grand Prix. From the start, Clare Short opposed the race as an expensive waste of precious municipal funds. She believed these would have been better invested in renovating tower blocks in her constituency – overlooking the circuit – which were deteriorating into litter-strewn slums, without caretakers and with lifts which stank of urine.

In her opposition to the race, Short was not alone. Large numbers of council tenants in her constituency, whose homes were alongside the track, complained about the unbearable noise and were issued with free earplugs. Worshippers in nearby churches claimed they could not hear themselves pray while the race was on. Three other Birmingham Labour MPs, Roy Hattersley, Jeff Rooker and Terry Davis, also opposed the race, but the doyen of them, Denis Howell, former Minister for Sport, was enthusiastically in favour, as were the remaining Labour MP, Robin Corbett, and all the Tory MPs. The opinions of MPs counted, because the race required a special act of parliament. Its fiercest opponent in the Commons was Clare Short. On the first occasion when parliament debated the Birmingham Super Prix, one of its supporters, the Labour MP, Peter Snape, accused her of shouting into his right ear. Never one to let an argument drop, she rose on a point of order, that she was in fact shouting down his left ear.[34]

The first two races, in 1986 and 1987, made a combined loss of £1 million, but the third showed a profit of £536,000 in the accounts drawn up by the city council. It emerged, though, that this had been achieved by making an estimate that the race had generated free publicity worth £600,000, and transferring that amount from the council's advertising budget to cover what would otherwise have been a loss. This was more than an interesting piece of bookkeeping. When the bill was passing through parliament, Short had succeeded in having a clause inserted, stipulating that the race must be self-financing and the accountants were looking for a way to save it. She told the Commons: 'I am upset and surprised that the city council of Birmingham, with the full agreement of all parties and its senior officers, is willing to behave so dishonourably.'[35] After the race had been scrapped for failing to break even, Short claimed later that it was 'unprofitable and enormously . . . unpopular with my constituents who lived in houses that were being whizzed around'.[36]

An issue which probably mattered far less to Birmingham's citizens, but caused far more lasting ill-feeling within the Labour Party, was who would succeed Denis Howell when, in February 1989, he announced his intended retirement as MP for Birmingham Small Heath, which he had represented since 1961. It was a case similar to that which arose in Knowsley North five years earlier, in which the complexity of the party rule book all but guaranteed a result which many would regard as grossly unfair. One difference was that the Small Heath selection battle was fought under rules which applied only between the 1987 and 1992 general elections, after Neil Kinnock had successfully put through a reform giving every individual party member a vote in the selection contest, but allowing trade unions and other affiliated organizations to retain up to 40 per cent of the total vote in the electoral college. Another difference was that, in Small Heath, the dominating issue was race.

The selection battle was fought out between Muhammad Afzal, chairman of Birmingham city council's Urban Renewal Committee and the owner of an Asian restaurant on Lozells Road, and Roger Godsiff, a full-time union organizer from Catford, in south London. Politically, there was little to choose between them. Afzal was in the centre of the party while Godsiff was on the right, but that does not appear to have materially affected the outcome. They even belonged to the same union, Apex, of which Denis Howell was national president for twelve years. In other respects, the political advantages seemed to lie with Afzal, who was the hard-working son of an army officer, born in a village on the Pakistan side of the Kashmir border, and a Moslem who disapproved of the death threat against the author Salman Rushdie while maintaining that the book's publication had been offensive. Had Afzal been selected, he would have been Birmingham's first Black MP and the first Moslem ever elected to the British parliament – an appropriate choice, on the face of it, in a constituency in which Blacks and Asians had made up 43 per cent of the population at the time of the 1981 census and by now were thought to outnumber whites, with the largest single racial group being the Kashmiris. It appears that if the selection had been conducted under a simple one-member, one-vote system, Afzal would have won, although like many other constituency parties in safe Labour seats, membership had been allowed to decline drastically, so that only 221 individual party members cast their votes. The result was 102 for Afzal, 100 for Godsiff and 15 for two other candidates: Najma Hafeez, the wife of Albert Bore, and Stewart Stacey, a Birmingham councillor. Afzal's supporters believed that had the contest gone to a second round he would have won 116–101.[37]

However, Afzal was up against an experienced union fixer. Godsiff had been one of the small circle of union officials who, when everyone else in the Labour Party appeared to retreat before the advancing Bennites, set about counting where the block votes lay and brokering secret deals to turn them over. Most of the key members of the circle had connections with the West Midlands. The ringleader, John Golding, was MP for Newcastle Under Lyme. John Spellar, political officer of the EEPTU, was a Birmingham MP in 1982–83. Other important figures in the right-wing caucus on the NEC included Denis Howell, who cut an incongruous figure as Chairman of the Youth Committee in 1982–83, and Ken Cure, from the West Midlands region of the AUEW, who chaired the NEC Appeals Committee. Within this group, Godsiff, as political officer of Apex, was the man with the pocket calculator, who worked out exactly how many block votes were pledged to each candidate in the annual NEC elections.

In Small Heath, Godsiff applied these talents to ensuring that the votes of trade unions and the Co-op party piled up for him. This had to be done before Denis Howell formally announced his retirement in February 1989, because from that point no new union delegates could join the general committee to participate in the selection conference. Almost at once, complaints came in alleging that GMB delegates had only recently joined the committee, who were not members of the GMB. Three GMB branches had five delegates, implying that they must each have had at least 401 levy-paying members living in the constituency. The number of EEPTU delegates had suddenly jumped just before Howell's retirement, and it was alleged that four of their delegates were not EEPTU members. Protestors hired a Birmingham solicitor to represent them, and with his help were able to have the total GMB delegation cut to three. A dispute within the Co-op party about how its delegates should vote led to an expensive court case, won by Godsiff's supporters. The dispute over the EEPTU's representation proved unresolvable. In addition to the allegations of vote-rigging, there were stories of threats of violence against Afzal and Hafeez. The Asian vote was not by any means one united entity. Some of the bitterest opposition to Afzal came from fellow Asians, including Kashmiris. When the votes were finally cast on 11 November 1990, party officials refused to count them, anticipating that they would produce a victory for Godsiff. The ballot papers were locked in a safe in a local solicitor's office for nearly twelve weeks while the NEC debated what to do.

Clare Short was by now a member of the NEC and determined to find a way, if possible, to prevent the selection from being won by the time-honoured union habit of vote-fixing. This made her, by default, an Afzal supporter. After the party's Director of Organization, Joyce Gould, had come forward with a proposal that the votes should be counted twice, once with the disputed EEPTU votes included and once without, Short demanded and got an inquiry into the whole selection procedure. Unfortunately, it produced nothing more than a month's delay, after which she proposed that the EEPTU votes should be disqualified. She lost, despite the support of the only other Birmingham MP present, Roy Hattersley. The votes were counted in the two separate ways proposed by Joyce Gould. With or without the EEPTU, it was clear that Godsiff had won. Nonetheless, at the following NEC meeting at the end of February, Short led a rearguard action to block him, but was outvoted sixteen to five.

As in other campaigns she had run, Short was running the risk that those she was pitted against might take revenge. Like every other Labour MP, her survival depended on her being readopted as a parliamentary candidate by her constituency party. During 1990–91, the number of EETPU delegates accredited to the general management committee of the Ladywood constituency party suddenly rose from four to seventeen. Sardul Marwa, an EETPU member and the manager of a training centre for the unemployed in Handsworth, was elected constituency party secretary. In the complex rivalries within the Birmingham Labour Party, Marwa was one of those who did not appreciate Clare Short's support for Black sections or for Muhammad Afzal, and maintained that Asians could resolve their own problems without her assistance. He put himself forward as an alternative candidate. He may or may not have been put up to it by John Spellar, who by now had been selected for the nearby safe seat of Warley West: it is not a subject which Spellar will discuss; but the union backed Marwa. Since half the union delegates on Ladywood's general committee were now either from the EETPU or AEU, Marwa began with two-fifths of the total vote he needed to win. Like Small Heath, Ladywood's total individual membership was pitifully small, totalling only 375, of whom an estimated 70 per cent were Black or Asian. In fact, the threat came to nothing. Even among the right-wing members of the NEC, there was no real wish to see someone as prominent as Clare Short deselected with help from some old-fashioned union-fixing, and if she had been in real danger, the selection contest would probably have been cancelled and she would have been imposed. In fact, she won anyway, early in 1992, but Birmingham Ladywood was the last winnable Labour seat to choose its general election candidate.

The legacy of the Small Heath and Ladywood manoeuvrings lingered long after the 1992 election, when both Short and Godsiff were returned with increased majorities. It left Godsiff an isolated figure. When the Tribune group of Labour MPs, for instance, planned its first meeting in the new parliament, invitations were sent to every new MP, including Peter Mandelson, with the exceptions only of John Spellar and Roger Godsiff. In Birmingham, Godsiff was in no doubt that there would be an attempt to deselect him at the first opportunity, which may help explain his robust opposition to John Smith's reforms, which removed the union vote from selection contests. The bulk of his parliamentary activity seemed to consist either of taking up causes of special concern to inner-city Birmingham, or of campaigning for the liberation of Kashmir from Indian rule.

Meanwhile Birmingham Small Heath Labour Party went from having one of the smallest memberships to one of the largest. By 30 April 1993, membership had leaped in three years from less than 300 to 1,428, making it the third largest constituency Labour Party in Britain. Even Tony Blair's Sedgefield Labour Party, which became celebrated for the efficiency of its recruitment drive, was then lagging behind with 1,200 members. Individual membership in Roy Hattersley's Sparkbrook seat next door had also shot up. Party organizers suspected that the explanation was the impending changes in the Birmingham constituency boundaries, which would reduce the number of Labour seats by one, meaning that at least one of the quartet of sitting MPs – Hattersley, Godsiff, Clare Short and Jeff Rooker – was going to be without a seat in the next parliament. Even when Hattersley announced that he would be retiring, the problem was not solved, because Birmingham's increasingly active Asian groups were in no mood to accept the allocation of three inner-city seats to three white MPs.

The recruitment was bought to a sudden halt in 1994, when the *Observer* revealed that one of Godsiff's recruitment techniques was to advise individual voters, principally Asians, on how to put themselves at the front of the queue for scarce housing-improvement grants. What he was doing was legal but it did not impress the National Executive Committee, who immediately suspended all four constituency parties. They were still suspended when the *Birmingham Post* produced a damaging revelation that Godsiff had removed both his children from the state school system in London and transferred them to fee-paying private schools.

There were other complaints from different cities about large numbers of members being suspiciously signed up as Labour Party members, purely in order that they could influence the outcome of selection contests. The reason that it might be worth somebody's while to try to fix a selection by enlisting a large paper membership is the very generous rule which says that any paid-up party member is entitled to a postal vote in any selection contest. In official elections, to parliament or to a council, applications for postal votes have to be accompanied by a reason for not being able to go to a polling-booth in person. When constituency Labour parties hold selection contests, there is one hustings meetings open to all party members, but it is not necessary to attend. There were bitter complaints about some selections, notably in Swindon and in Glasgow Govan, where the problem was disputed postal votes.

Where suspicious mass recruitment was taking place, more often that not it involved Asians, because the Asian community was still coming out of isolation to participate in political activity. Consequently, the NEC put together a Membership Abuse Committee, headed by Clare Short, which in spring 1995 produced a three-page document urging that every person who applied to join the party should be personally visited by a team of volunteers. The document stressed that, particularly where the applicants were from ethnic minorities, the visiting team must be 'woman-friendly' and 'non-intimidating'.

Partly because of the Black sections, Clare Short's break with the Bennite left and her *rapprochment* with Neil Kinnock came some years later than David Blunkett's or Tom Sawyer's. In summer 1985, when 'realignment' was in the air, she accused the party leaders of being under the 'illusion' that 'keeping the left under control, compromising a bit, offering an attractive image (and) winning an election' would be sufficient to cope with problems ahead, like the resistance within the finance and banking world to any large-scale plan for job creation and the international repercussions of a non-nuclear defence policy. Far from wanting an accommodation with the leadership, Short wanted the Campaign and Tribune groups to cooperate in drawing up a slate of candidates in Shadow Cabinet elections to break the 'disproportionate' influence of the right by removing some of those who were 'half-hearted' in their commitment to policies laid down by the annual party conference.[38] She named no names, but she clearly meant the nine out of fifteen Shadow Cabinet members who had been elected on the Manifesto group slate, and not necessarily its more obscure or less talented members. In September 1986, she called on Denis Healey to resign when, under pressure from a *Panorama* interviewer, he said that a Labour government might renounce its non-nuclear defence policy if pressed by its NATO allies.[39] By contrast, when Eric Heffer stormed off the conference platform the previous year in protest at Neil Kinnock's attack on the Liverpool left, Short defended his action on national television on the basis that Liverpool was 'his city.'

Until March 1988, Short's complaints about the failure to agree a joint-left slate were an implicit criticism of members of the Tribune group like Jack Straw, Gordon Brown and Tony Blair, who refused to vote for Tony Benn or other Campaign nominees. However, the intransigence of the Bennite rump on the NEC, and Benn's own implacable refusal to make any accommodation with Kinnock's leadership eventually convinced her that they were the problem. The final act in her five-year membership of the Campaign Group was a heated argument over Benn's intention to run for the leadership against Neil Kinnock, during which she was shouted at by some of the male members present. On the day when the group decided that the challenge should go ahead, she, Margaret Beckett, Jo Richardson and Joan Ruddock resigned.

That did not by any means make her a fully signed-up supporter of the Kinnock–Hattersley ticket. First, she was bound by political loyalty to John Prescott and had no hesitation about supporting him against Roy Hattersley, but she was in a real dilemma over the Kinnock–Benn contest. Out of 221 MPs who turned out at Brighton to vote, she was the only one to abstain in the leadership election. Others who had been much closer to Benn in the recent past, including Michael Meacher and Chris Mullin, voted for Kinnock.

The political issue which finally provoked Short's resignation from the frontbench was Northern Ireland. More specifically, it was the Prevention of Terrorism Act, since that was the issue on which there was a contentious vote in the Commons, though it could have been Labour's Irish policy generally. The Labour Party line was to seek the reunification of the island of Ireland by consent, which meant 'no change in the constitutional position of Northern Ireland without the consent of the majority of people who live there'.[40] With her republican background, Short was convinced that consent would never come, because the Unionists would always use gerrymandering and discrimination to retain their majority position in the Six Counties. Consequently, 'Britain should, must and one day will reunify Ireland by seeking the consent of the people of Ireland and not looking only to the Loyalist community in the North for their consent.'[41] However, having once accepted a frontbench position, Short was constrained to keep quiet on this, and on the related topic of the PTA.

In December 1988, when morale and discipline in the parliamentary Labour Party hit its low point, the Shadow Cabinet decided to abstain in the annual vote on whether the powers conferred on the government by this piece of legislation should be renewed for another twelve months. Since Short was below Shadow Cabinet rank and not part of the Northern Ireland team, she was naturally not consulted, although it was a subject on which she had a measure of specialist knowledge. When the Labour Home Secretary, Roy Jenkins, introduced the Prevention of Terrorism Bill to the Commons in 1974, against clamour from the opposition benches for the reintroduction of hanging, one of the advisers on the bench reserved for senior civil servants, close to the Speaker's chair, was Clare Short. She was next to the man who actually drafted the Bill. As she listened, she leaned over to whisper to him that it would do nothing to prevent an outrage like the Birmingham bombings. According to her recollection, he whispered back: 'You know very well that is not what it is about. We have to appease them. They are after capital punishment. They have to be given some-thing.'[42] Short's objection to the Bill was that it had created a type of 'little Siberia' or administrative exile to one part of the United Kingdom for one part of the community only, the Irish Catholics. She also objected to a mea-sure enabling the authorities to seize the property of convicted paramilitaries, because it was drafted to put the onus on the individuals to prove that their belongings had been obtained legitimately. Generally, she feared that repressive legislation like this and the introduction of intern-ment and the abolition of trial by jury in the province simply tied whole families into the terrorist network. A visit to Northern Ireland in the autumn had also convinced her that Catholic support for the IRA was start-ing to crack and that part of the Sinn Fein leadership was looking for a pretext to initiate a ceasefire. Consequently, she maintained that Labour's line was 'muddled' and 'extremely foolish', and while she was about it, she pointedly veered from the line Neil Kinnock had been expounding since the mid-1980s, that the IRA was fundamentally a criminal gang. She said its activities were 'wrong' and 'absolutely counter-productive', but added:

> I understand why mostly young men – and some young women – in Northern Ireland are willing to join paramilitaries. Their sense of grievance and injustice and their belief that Britain will not listen, so there is no political route to justice, makes them willing to engage in paramilitary violence.[43]

Having thus purchased, at a price, the freedom to speak her mind on the backbenches, Short made surprisingly little public use of it. She returned to the subject of the PTA in a Commons speech eight weeks later, but only to deliver a passionate condemnation of strip-searching, which may have irri-tated the authorities but was uncontroversial in party terms. So were the other subjects she chose to speak on: social security, low pay, and corruption in the West Midlands Serious Crime Squad.

In the background, Short was involved in a serious attempt to reorganize the 'soft left' within the parliamentary Labour Party, as one of those who now regarded the Campaign Group as hopelessly ghettoized, and the Tribune Group as too all-inclusive to be an effective pressure group. She and Allan Roberts, the MP for Bootle who died early in 1990, were the main organizers of an informal group who, mimicking the dining clubs which are a feature of the Conservative Party, jokily called themselves the 'Supper Club'. Supper was, in fact, a buffet of sandwiches, crisps and other cheap delicacies in a room above a Westminster pub, usually on Monday night. The group had no leader, though the most forceful personality to be invited was John Prescott. Margaret Beckett, Ann Clwyd, Michael Meacher and Jo Richardson were the other Shadow Cabinet members who took part, Beckett less often than the others. Robin Cook was not invited, in case the meetings became an arena in which powerful personalities could compete for the leadership of the left. Neither was Bryan Gould. The group's existence became public knowledge in February 1991, because Mark Fisher, who had chaired a meeting in Short's absence, drew up a note about it which was slipped to journalists. It was at a time when the Gulf War was threatening to pull the Labour Party apart and the Supper Club was seen as the centre of covert opposition to the Kinnock–Kaufman line. Nothing tangible came of these meetings, but it is not entirely coincidental that Prescott and Beckett, the two people who were able to round up enough nominations to compete for the deputy leadership in 1992 and for the leadership in 1994, had both tasted the fare at Clare Short's Supper Club.

Short also reportedly used this quiet period to read up on the subject of defence policy, on which she admitted that her knowledge was limited. During the horse-trading which accompanied the NEC's adoption of the document *A Power for Good*, prior to its passage at the 1989 party conference, Short successfully argued for the inclusion of a reference to the general uselessness of Trident, or any other 'independent' British nuclear deterrent, which the Shadow Foreign Secretary, Gerald Kaufman, accepted without demur.

During 1989, Short returned to the frontbench, as a Shadow Minister for Social Security. Her new team leader was Michael Meacher, another old Bennite who had gone a long way towards making common cause with the leadership, but not quite far enough. He had been demoted from his old job as Shadow Secretary of State for Employment, where he had been too accommodating to trade union demands for the repeal of Conservative industrial relations laws, and replaced there by Tony Blair. In party terms, social security was then regarded as a zone free of political danger, where dissidents like Meacher, Short, Robin Cook and Margaret Beckett could be safely employed. That attitude was revised after the 1992 general election. In the meantime, Short was occupied staying up late in the evening to argue over complicated matters like the rules requiring dole claimants to prove they were actively seeking work, or the proposal to create a Child Support Agency – which Short feared would be used to recoup benefits on the government's behalf, rather than for its stated purpose of helping women who were bringing up children on their own.

Short's concession to the leadership over unilateral nuclear disarmament was perhaps not as personally difficult for her as it was, for example, for Robin Cook or even Neil Kinnock, who had been more publicly associated with CND. There is no evidence that she had ever been strongly concerned with nuclear weapons as such. But, more generally, she had an abiding dislike of violence, and of macho behaviour, in fiction as in real life, which made her, by instinct, profoundly anti-war, almost to the point of being pacifist. It was therefore probable that at some point she was going to break and oppose Britain's involvement in the Gulf War. It was over this that Short resigned from the frontbench for the second time, but in circumstances so ambiguous that there has to be some doubt about what political point she was making.

On the one hand, Short was in no doubt that Iraq's Saddam Hussein was a 'monstrous tyrant' who had launched an unprovoked attack on Kuwait, and that removing his army from that country was a 'just cause'. On the other hand, she was a long-standing opponent of the Israeli occupation of Palestine, which she had twice visited as a guest of the Arab League. She believed that the US and Britain had a great deal to answer for in the region, having supplied Saddam's war machine during the Iran–Iraq war, and ignored the gassing of Kurdish villagers. She believed that sanctions against Iraq would be sufficient to free Kuwait without military action and, once the conflict began, she believed it should have the limited objective of removing the Iraqis from Kuwait.

Included at the last minute in the NUPE delegation to the 1990 party conference, in place of Alice Mahon, who opposed the war, Short was part of the majority of one who added the union's block vote behind the NEC's position on the Gulf War, which was carried comfortably.[44] Within the NEC, she consistently supported the majority against the Bennite rump who opposed the war outright, but when the Commons voted on 15 January 1991, she was one of the fifty-nine who abstained while the majority of Labour MPs backed the government. The following day, she and Dawn Primarolo submitted a resolution calling for sanctions to be given 'maximum time' to work, which was passed overwhelmingly but too late. The bombing began that night.

On 13 February 1991, a bomb dropped on Baghdad landed inside a bunker and killed hundreds of people sheltering from the air raid. The allies at once put it down to error, but the incident severely strained the loyalty of some members of Labour's frontbench, not least Joan Ruddock, the former CND leader, whose comments on the war earned her an appointment in Neil Kinnock's office, where she was told that she must either stick exclusively to her brief, discussing London's transport problems, or resign from the frontbench. Ruddock chose to stay, explaining: 'I believe my voice was less likely to be heard as a voice criticizing the war than as a voice criticizing the Labour Party leadership. I wasn't prepared to be used as a catalyst for helping a media scenario of a divided Labour Party.'[45] The next person into Kinnock's office was Clare Short, who was delivered a similar warning. She decided to resign rather than be silenced.

But, having again chosen the freedom of the backbenches, Short was very circumspect in how she used it. When the Commons debated the Gulf in the week after her resignation, she declared that 'once we were at war and had given up sanctions, it was not right for me simply to rail against the war. As a politician, I thought that it was our job to ensure that the war was cut short, to minimize casualties and to achieve a just settlement'.[46] Apart from her earnest wish for a 'just settlement', and a suspicion that the Labour leader was not as concerned as she was to minimize casualties, nor as anxious to be even-handed in condemning Israel's flouting of international law in the same breath as Iraq's, nothing else emerged to indicate why Short needed to resign. Her decision was taken at a time when she was under intense strain because of a combination of the Gulf War, her husband's illness and the *News of the World* foraging in her life. She remarked soon afterwards that 'being a second-rank frontbencher doesn't give you much glamour or status, especially on social security where it is a lot of hard work'.[47] Furthermore, one of the few people outside her immediate circle whom she wholly trusted, her researcher Virginia Heywood, who had worked with her since 1985, was heavily pregnant and could not defer her maternity leave any longer. When to that was added what seemed to her like an order from Neil Kinnock to shut up, she decided not to take it. She says: 'The point was that I was deeply concerned about the war. I still believe we were lucky that it was not much worse. Neil said I must agree to say nothing on the war in or outside the Chamber. I wouldn't agree to this. It was my duty to use my voice in whatever way I could. I still don't think I could agree to his conditions with any honour.'[48]

Whatever the reason, Short brought more animosity and aggravation on her head than her previous resignation, because it was a second offence and close to a general election. If she was in any doubt about that, it was brought home by the sarcasm and hostility she encountered a month later, when she decided to speak on a Bill which would enable the courts to try some very elderly east European refugees living in Britain, who were suspected of having committed war crimes almost half a century earlier. She opposed the Bill, on the grounds that identification would be impossible after such a delay and that it would be a matter of chance who was tried and who escaped. These reasoned observations produced a sarcastic observation from Roy Hattersley that he personally would vote for the Bill whatever she said, because in a free vote 'I am no more bound by the rules of collective responsibility than she is.' Worse, when Short stated that she had voted for the Bill on its first appearance in the House, Llin Golding – a party whip and a member of the right-wing union network in the West Midlands which held Clare Short in contempt – flatly contradicted her. Points of order bounced back and forth between the two women for some minutes, with Short producing the appropriate page of *Hansard* to prove that she was right and Golding wrong. It culminated in an exchange which begs for the description 'pointless':

Ms Short: Point of order! As I was accused, in effect of being a liar. . . .
Mrs Golding: Point of order! Was it in order for my Honourable Friend to call me a liar?
Ms Short: I did not. I said you called me a liar.
Mrs Golding: I was quoting from *Hansard*, which cannot lie, as we all know.
Madam Deputy Speaker (Betty Boothroyd): Order. I have had enough points of order.[49]

After that, Short went uncharacteristically quiet. Having been a persistent and energetic Commons performer for eight years, she allowed more than two years to slip by, during which, although she intervened numerous times to ask questions, to interject on other MPs' speeches, she herself made only one speech, a long and carefully thought out exposition on the Maastricht Treaty. It is likely that part of the reason was that her long relationship with Alex Lyon was in its final tragic stage. As he had become progressively less responsible for his own actions, she had had to take a succession of painful decisions, like stopping him from driving. In 1991, he was admitted into a home and in September 1993, ten years after the onset of his illness, he died. His first wife was one of the mourners at his funeral.

When Short made her next Commons speech, only her second in more than two years, it was another international conflict which brought her to her feet, as if she had lost interest in anything other than direct issues of life and death. She wanted the UN to create and police safe havens for Bosnian Moslems or, failing that, to lift the arms embargo on the former Yugoslavia to enable the Bosnians to arm themselves against the Serbs. That put her in direct conflict with Labour Party policy, but she was still a backbench Labour MP and consequently there was nothing to stop her saying what she thought. Soon afterwards, in July 1993, John Smith brought her back as junior Shadow Minister for Environmental Protection and she was caught in the old dilemma that, to retain her place on the frontbench, she had to stay silent about the big issues while she devilled away preparing speeches on such matters as the preservation of towpaths. Short delivered one on energy conservation at 2.15 in the morning. Though it could not have been much less of a grind than studying the social security system, this time she stuck it out and was rewarded in the autumn with promotion to the more rewarding post of Shadow Minister for Women.

As an annual competitor in elections to the Shadow Cabinet and National Executive Committee, Short had been rather lax about canvassing support, which for some participants becomes something of an obsession. With the guaranteed support of NUPE's huge block vote, and a political base in the 'Supper Club' left, she was never going to be humiliated in either contest. For several years, she was among the first half dozen runners-up for a place on the Shadow Cabinet, and believed that because women candidates were so thin on the ground, she was bound to succeed eventually. At the 1988 annual party conference, with Joan Maynard having retired, the TGWU switched its block vote of 1.333 million to Clare Short, and she was propelled on to the National Executive Committee.

As an employer now of the party's head office staff, Short had very definite reservations about the prestigiously successful campaigns and communications operation. Not trusting the official spin doctors, she went through a phase of being an exceptionally active briefer of journalists on her own account. When Peter Mandelson stepped down in 1990, Short was one of the most enthusiastic backers of his ill-fated successor, John Underwood. When Underwood resigned, she accused Neil Kinnock of having behaved in a 'very Thatcherite and undemocratic way' in letting him go.[50] After the 1992 defeat, therefore, it is no surprise to find her leading the charge against the threatened 'Clintonisation' of the Labour Party and 'the secret, infiltrating so-called modernisers . . . [who] have been creating myths about why Clinton won, in order to try and reshape the Labour Party . . . [and] have very little understanding of Labour's traditions'[51] and their strategy of creating 'an image of supposed competence expressed in sound bites and led by pollsters', which had now, in her view, lost the party two elections. She added:

> The modernisers claim that the problem is that Labour is seen as backward-looking and standing for things that people do not find attractive, such as the poor and the unions. Others of us think that Labour is not worth having without these values.[52]

During the two leadership election contests of 1992 and 1994 Short put herself unerringly on the losing side, backing Bryan Gould for leader and for deputy in 1992, and Margaret Beckett in 1994. In 1992, when Neil Kinnock was urging that the issue of the future of the union block vote must be settled, she was one of the NEC members who overruled him, deferring the decision until 1993. She was scathing about Tony Blair's contribution within the review group on trade union links, especially his 'downright silly' proposal that the party should use one-member, one-vote referendums to try out policies on party members.[53] In May 1993, when it appeared that Smith's proposals to curb the block vote were heading for defeat, she gave an interview to BBC Radio 4's *The World This Weekend* programme, blaming a 'poisonous whispering campaign' which had put it around that the real intention was to end the link between the unions and the party.[54] Subsequently, when Tony Blair launched the campaign to rewrite Clause Four, Short was not the first to leap to his support. She complained that the calling of a special conference had been 'indecently hasty' although she conceded that the old clause would have to go because it said too little about equality and democracy and because 'the old idea of public ownership of all our major industries is not our inspiration'.[55] All of this caused her to be cast as a leading 'traditionalist'.

However, if a 'traditionalist' is one who wishes the old ways to continue unchanged, Short was no such thing. The crunch question in 1993 was whether the unions would hold on to their block votes in leadership elections, the selection of parliamentary candidates, and at annual party conferences. On each she came out straightaway in favour of reducing or abolishing the block vote. With her recent experiences in Birmingham, she was hardly going to defend the role of unions in selection conferences. As she put it:

> the link (between party and unions) has been misused by fixers and twisters who have helped to create a 'fixing' culture . . . which the public find deeply distasteful. The abuse of the power of local unions to affiliate in the case of Small Heath, and the attempted corruption in Ladywood, are examples of gross misuse of the link. Modernising the link means that the opportunity for such misbehaviour must be ended.[56]

There Short was referring to right-wing vote-fixers. She was even more vehement when dealing with their far-left equivalent, the hard-line Trotskyites from Militant. Like others on the 'soft left', she began by saying in the early 1980s that the Militant Tendency should be defeated in rational argument, not by administrative means. More recently, she has come to see the expulsion of Trotskyites as almost a moral duty, and certainly an elementary protection for any democratically run organization, and indeed for the Labour Party left, which evidently needs to be protected from its own foolish enthusiasm by an administrative wall blocking it off from entryist groups:

> My own conclusion, after very many years of activism in the left spaces of the party, is that Trotskyist entryism has been massively destructive for the left . . . The left has had enormous difficulty in understanding the entryist movements. This is because the left has always been libertarian and has needed the freedom of democratic

debate. It is also because the Trotskyist tradition is deeply dishonourable. It is a movement born out of a tradition that organised for revolution in a repressive and authoritarian state and therefore believed it to be completely honourable to lie about one's political analysis. Thus we have members whose first loyalty is or was to Militant, Socialist Organiser or the International Marxist Group or its successors, who have an organised political project but will not tell the rest of us . . .

The problem . . . is that the left always wants to support the most radical demands. And thus the left, well beyond the Trotskyist entryists, keeps lining up behind impossible demands that cannot be delivered in practice. The consequence is that the whole left becomes mired in dishonest politics.[57]

When decision time came, as the NEC went into the attack after the Walton by-election, Short had made up her mind. She was going to support the impending expulsions not only of those who had been involved in Lesley Mahmood's campaign, but of the MPs Terry Fields and Dave Nellist too. The fact that Nellist was a popular figure in the parliamentary party, whom she herself liked, she dealt with in a blunt public statement on 24 July, the day the NEC suspended eighty-five party members and decided that the cases of Fields and Nellist would be handled in September: 'Whether they are nice or nasty, hardworking or lazy, if they are Militant they are not entitled to stay in the Labour Party.' At that meeting, Short helpfully found a way out of what might have been an awkward impasse. Terry Fields was at the time in prison for non-payment of his poll tax. A draft motion from Neil Kinnock proposed to investigate the circumstances of his imprisonment, among other possible disciplinary charges. Roy Hattersley balked at the idea, whereupon it was Short who proposed an amendment merely specifying that Fields' activities generally should be investigated. When Dave Nellist appeared before the NEC in September, it was Short who persistently demanded from him a 'yes or no' answer on whether he was still linked to Militant. When Militant held a rally at the opening of the party conference a few days later, Dennis Skinner accused her of having 'harassed' Nellist. Unrepentant, Short waited patiently in a nearby hotel as Nellist went before a special meeting of the National Constitutional Committee in West Bromwich, in order to go on television afterwards and applaud the final decision to expel him from the Labour Party.

Having thus learned the habit of dealing mercilessly with Trotskyites, Short applied it again in the one-off case of Liz Davies. It was one-off in the sense that it is difficult to see what precedent it sets – how or whether some other parliamentary candidate can be disqualified under the 'Liz Davies rule', or what such a rule might be. One of the ironies is that before Clare Short took the lead in destroying Davies' chances of becoming a Labour MP, she unintentionally and indirectly helped her. She had been one of the most vigorous supporters of all-women shortlists as a means of doubling the number of women Labour MPs in one general election. In 1990, while she was chairing the NEC women's committee, Short co-wrote a Fabian pamphlet claiming that women's 'precarious hold on public office' had barely improved over the years and was unlikely to unless the party took drastic measures to force the adoption of women candidates in safe or winnable Labour seats.

In 1993, the party's annual conference agreed that the constituency Labour parties in half the marginal seats and half the Labour seats where the sitting MP was retiring would choose their candidates from all-women shortlists. In most regions, a sufficient number of local parties were persuaded to accept this voluntarily, though the Slough Labour Party had one imposed on it, in what some suspected was a manoeuvre to prevent the party's full-time agent for Slough and Reading, Eddie Lopez, from being adopted again to fight the seat which he narrowly lost in 1992. However, it was not Lopez but an eccentric named Peter Jepson who brought the process to a halt by complaining to an industrial tribunal that he had suffered discrimination by being prevented from joining the shortlist of candidates in Westminster North. Jepson was not from that constituency. He was a member of Feltham and Heston Labour Party, where he had been decisively beaten when he attempted to win the nomination prior to the 1992 election. He also had a long history of being at the centre of arguments of one kind or another, and there is no convincing evidence that any constituency Labour Party would have wanted him for a candidate. However, he had a law degree and, with one other aggrieved male, successfully argued that you never can tell in politics. The policy of all-women shortlists was abandoned, probably for good – saving the party from the interesting situation developing in places like Jarrow, on Tyneside, where deeply traditional parties were gearing themselves to repel all-women shortlists.

While it was still in force, the policy led to the adoption of about three dozen women candidates. Leeds North East was one of the constituencies which had volunteered to take part. On 1 July 1995, Davies emerged as the unexpected winner in a properly conducted ballot – helped, possibly, by the decision of some party members to boycott the contest. She did nothing after her selection which justified the action taken against her; but within days, it was evident that there was trouble ahead. The result ran counter to what was expected of one-member, one-vote ballots, in that the party had opted for a declared supporter of the Campaign Group, and a supporter of political baggage like Clause Four, unilateral nuclear disarmament and the repeal of Conservative trade union legislation, which the modernizers had thrown overboard. In a letter to party members, Davies also revealed that she had refused to pay her poll tax, a point quickly picked by the *Daily Mail* as evidence that the 'loony left' was at large again. The story then ran for two weeks in the Yorkshire press, which played up the revelations that she had campaigned for gay and lesbian rights and in support of Winston Silcott, who had been cleared of murdering PC Keith Blakelock during the 1985 Broadwater Farm riots.

Although the public at large – and, probably, most party members in Leeds – had never heard of her before, Davies was well-known among activists in London, especially in Tony Blair's home borough of Islington, where she was a councillor. There she had the reputation for being 'oppositionist'. She had twice broken the whip on Islington council to vote against cuts in nursery and adventure playground provision. When the council and its former leader, Margaret Hodge, were under fire over a report by two outside social services managers, alleging that the 'political correctness' of councillors, in discriminating in favour of Black and gay employees, had allowed child abuse to take place in council homes, Davies wrote an article asserting the opposite: that 'far from being a soft touch, Labour councillors seemed to harden themselves against members of staff, especially anyone claiming discrimination, and when there was any doubt they always preferred the word of management over staff'.[58]

Davies also had a well-known connection with the magazine *Labour Left Briefing*, having contributed to it, chaired its editorial board and lived with its editor, Mike Marqusee. It is a scabrous left-wing publication, whose personal attacks on individual opponents have drawn the expressed disapproval of Tony Benn. In March 1992, it featured Clare Short in what was then a regular Class Traitor of the Month slot, calling her 'a useful idiot' who was 'easily manipulated by the leadership'. (If that were not bad enough, the same magazine once described me as 'one of the most gullible journalists in Westminster'. That field is so crowded that I would not presume to compete in it.) Short could not believe that anyone associated with it would want to stand for parliament as a Labour candidate.

The trouble with being in Islington, rather than a town in the provinces, was that Davies was well-known to people who were close to Tony Blair. The Hodges, for example, live in the same street as the Blairs. One Islington councillor, James Purnell, had been attached to Blair's private office; another, Tal Michael, worked for his father, the MP Alun Michael, who had been Blair's deputy and interim successor as Shadow Home Secretary. A third, James Kelly, was well-connected as a former Editor of *Tribune*. All three wrote to the NEC urging that Davies should not be selected. They were supported by Margaret Hodge, who spoke of Liz Davies with curious respect as a competent, pleasant and determined character whose strong points did not include a great loyalty to the Labour Party.

In July, the NEC voted by seventeen to six not to endorse her candidature. The case then went to a disputes committee, and back to the NEC in September, where the vote again went against her, this time by seventeen to five, despite the fact that three Shadow Cabinet members on the NEC – Margaret Beckett, David Blunkett and Joan Lestor – either abstained or, in Blunkett's case, voted with the minority. A resolution in Davies' support was easily defeated at the party conference a few days later, with Clare Short leading the attack as the representative of the NEC:

> The most difficult task I have ever undertaken as a member of the NEC was the action we took to declare Dave Nellist and Terry Fields unsuitable as Labour MPs . . . The decision was difficult and painful – not least as the two did not admit they were members of Militant. But it was right and all reasonable people agreed with it . . .
>
> Liz Davies has declared . . . that she is not a Trotskyist. So be it. But. . . .

But, what? The nub of Short's argument was that the accused behaved like a Trotskyite with her long record of causing 'trouble and conflict', and her association with a publication 'more vicious and destructive than any Tory tabloid'. Until this point, every individual who had been disciplined for being a covert Trotskyite had been told what organization they were suspected of belonging to, which in every case had meant either Militant or Socialist Organiser, and had been expelled with little prospect of readmission. The sentence was mandatory. Davies, however, was not expelled, or even barred from sitting as a Labour councillor in Islington. Whatever else could be said about someone who criticized Islington councillors for not being correct enough in their application of positive discrimination for gays, she plainly was not an orthodox disciple of Leon Trotsky. It was rumoured that she was a former member of the International Marxist Group, which she denied, and since she was born in 1964 and the IMG was disbanded in the late 1970s, she could not have been in it for long. It was as if she had opened up a new category of offender: an entryist who belonged to no identifiable entryist organization, who was sufficiently Trotskyist to be barred from standing for parliament, but not Trotskyist enough to prevent her being an otherwise active party member.

Private conversations with some of the main protagonists in this story suggest that Davies' association with *Labour Briefing* was a side issue to the Islington modernizers who began the action against her. Their real objection was a hard-headed calculation that the first Blair government might have a very slender parliamentary majority, already dependent on the support of a hard core of Campaign Group MPs so alienated from the leadership that they are well capable of sticking to their principles even if it means allowing the government to be defeated, and that endorsing Liz Davies' candidature could have added one more to their number.

The political reality was that Davies was doomed from the minute her case was raised as test of the mettle of the new party leader. After the battles which Neil Kinnock had been through to expunge genuine entryist groups, there was not the slightest possibility of Blair, so early in his tenure as party manager, overruling his own 'modernizer' allies to secure the election to parliament of a member of the Socialist Campaign Group Supporters' Network. In an interview with the *Guardian*, Blair suggested Davies was 'piggy-backing', remarking, 'If they stood on a *Labour Briefing* platform, they'd get 500 votes'. This is true, but it could be applied to Diane Abbott, Tony Benn, Jeremy Corbyn, Ken Livingstone, Alan Simpson, Dennis Skinner and many more.

It has been many years since any Labour Party member has been barred from standing at a general election for purely political reasons, as Konni Zilliacus was in the 1940s. During Harold Wilson's leadership, an informal truce operated between the two sides on the National Executive, which meant that the NEC never used its power to block a candidate for overtly political reasons, but only where there had been an alleged breach of rules. There were complaints that the rules were selectively enforced for political ends and they were rewritten for the special circumstances of by-elections; but, imperfect or not, the truce operated whichever side controlled the NEC. When a candidate who had been selected in a properly run one-member, one-vote ballot was barred solely because the leadership in London found her politically objectionable, an ominous precedent was set. That was why David Blunkett, for example, opposed it. Either it was an isolated event attributable to certain special factors like the Islington connection, or it is a harbinger of a split in the party, which may not be many years away.

Days after leading the attack on Liz Davies, Clare Short was belatedly elected to the Shadow Cabinet. Her political base had shifted: she was excluded from the secret slate operated by the Campaign Group, although others who had long since broken with the Group, like Margaret Beckett, or who had never associated with the left at all, like Tom Clarke, enjoyed its backing, on the general principle that they were people Tony Blair might not want on his team. However, Short picked up support from others who had not voted for her before, but liked the way she faced down Liz Davies' supporters at the party conference.

Once Short was elected, Tony Blair showed surprising trust in her, given her own 'oppositionist' record, by making her Shadow Secretary of State for Transport. This put her in the epicentre of the complex and drawn-out argument over whether Labour should undertake to renationalize Railtrack and other parts of the railway network which the government was selling off. Her predecessor, Michael Meacher, was moved because he was thought to be unreliable on this issue: he was too willing to treat Labour's commitment to a 'publicly owned, publicly accountable' railway system as a pledge to renationalize.

Apart from finding herself in the middle of a complicated, technical and emotive political tug of war, Short's new position required her to be an instant expert on a subject in which she had never taken any interest, unless her campaign against the Birmingham Super Prix is classified as a 'transport' issue. She also found herself placed between the party's deputy leader, who had made transport his specialist subject for the previous twenty-five years, and a deputy, Brian Wilson, who had also become formidably well-informed and had contacts inside British Rail feeding him leaked information. Short therefore faced the real danger of being squeezed out of the complicated decisions. One interview she gave to the *Today* programme about reducing pollution from car exhaust must stand as a classic example of a politician trying to soldier through an interview with nothing much to say – not least when she told the nation's radio listeners that 'all you need is the air that you breathe'. The only solution was to immerse herself in hours of research and background reading, which had the temporary effect of making her less visible than she had been.

Short was also now subject to the rules of collective discipline. At one of her first Shadow Cabinet meetings, she watched Robin Cook lead an attack on the Shadow Chancellor, Gordon Brown, for remarks he had made introducing 'workfare'. As a Shadow Social Security Minister six-and-a-half years earlier, Short had denounced government plans to compel the unemployed to participate in training schemes as 'dishonest'.[59] Now she kept her counsel. In March 1996, the Shadow Cabinet agreed that Labour MPs should abstain on the renewal of the Prevention of Terrorism Act rather than vote against, the very question on which Short resigned from the frontbench in 1988. She kept quiet.

However, she could not avoid the unexpected question during a television interview, and twice ran into trouble. The second time was a pure accident. Asked about Harriet Harman's decision to send her younger child to St Olave's, a grant-maintained grammar school, Short replied that it was something for which Harman would have to answer to her constituents, a throwaway line which the BBC interpreted as a coded attack which she did not intend. Her own brother, Michael Short, had two children at St Olave's.

The earlier occasion was more serious and substantial. Towards the end of a long early morning television interview, Sir David Frost cunningly asked her whether she had changed a view she had held for her whole political life, that cannabis should be legalized. Not sensing a trap, she replied: 'Lots of people in the police have said we should look at that and I think we should look at it, and I think we should not be cowards.'[60] It was only three months since the Littleborough and Saddleworth by-election, in which Labour had pilloried the successful Liberal Democrat candidate, Chris Davies, for holding the same view. The airwaves were soon humming with the sound of official representatives of the Labour Party explaining that Short had been expressing a personal opinion, which was not the official party line. She had no choice but to present herself in Tony Blair's office to apologize and promise to be more circumspect in future.

Generally, Sunday morning television programmes seemed to be a rich source of indiscretions from Clare Short. On 14 April, on GMTV, she made a throwaway remark that 'in a fair tax system, people like me would pay a little more'. Long before most correspondents were into work, Labour's press advisers were busy trying to blunt the impact of words which they feared might frighten off middle-income voters. Booked to give TV and radio interviews on the railtrack privatization, she was pulled off and replaced by Brian Wilson. On Monday morning, she retaliated by going on BBC Radio 4's *Today* programme to attack the anonymous party sources who had been attacking her, and to proclaim, 'I will not be silenced'.

Meanwhile, her transport team was wracked by a fierce dispute over whether it should be Labour policy to renationalize Railtrack. Short agreed with Gordon Brown that it would be an expensive folly, and produced a detailed policy document whose main emphasis was on increasing the power of the regulator. Relations with her deputy, Brian Wilson, became so bad that he was moved to another job.

She had delivered for Tony Blair on this, on Clause Four and on the Liz Davies affair, but when staff on the London Underground called a legitimate series of one-day strikes, she chose not to join the Blair-inspired call for the action to be called off and the dispute referred to binding arbitration. On 24 July, she walked out of a television interview to avoid being questioned about the strike. That evening, having taken third place in the last Shadow Cabinet election, she was told by Tony Blair that she was to be moved. She took it as a betrayal and contemplated resignation, but was persuaded to accept the post of Shadow Minister for Overseas Aid. Writing in the *Daily Express* on 26 July, she complained: 'I have not until recently faced up to the full nastiness that is in politics, the vanity and ego, the manoeuvres and dishonesty . . . I must admit that, if I had a daughter, I would advise her not to go into politics.' In all, she had discovered that the Shadow Cabinet was not the sort of free society envisaged by J.S. Mill, in which eccentrics could be tolerated.

CHAPTER SIX

THE MYTH OF PETER MANDELSON

Anyone who follows modern politics closely knows that there lurks an 'evil genius' in the Labour Party called Peter Mandelson, whose name is often invoked even by so highly placed a person as the Prime Minister, usually without any explanation as to what it is that makes him so significant or so sinister. A great many people have heard a version of a story about Mandelson, mushy peas and avocado. What he actually does is wrapped in mystery. He is a star, in the old Hollywood sense of someone famous for being famous.

The mushy peas story goes like this: in Hartlepool, the town he represents in parliament, or some other out of the way place inhabited by working-class people, Peter Mandelson ventures into a chip shop to place an order; there he sees a bowl of mushy peas on display and innocently asks for a portion of the 'avocado dip'.

This myth seems to have a cyclical life. It goes through a phase of being retold in the gossip columns, as if it revealed something significant about the contemporary Labour Party. There is then a counter-attack by political analysts and profile writers, who are likely to be getting their information from Mandelson himself, who make a stab at telling the true story of the middle-class socialist who mistook avocado for mushy peas, and try to analyse what compels journalists to pin it on Peter Mandelson.

Actually, something of the sort did happen during a by-election in the mid-1980s, but Peter Mandelson was nowhere near the scene at the time. The setting was Knowsley North, near Liverpool, in November 1986. A team of professionals were there from London to run the campaign, which was being boycotted by most of the leading members of the Knowsley

North Labour Party, in protest at having a candidate imposed on them. The *Daily Telegraph* described them as 'the bright new young men and women from party headquarters, who jog each morning around the streets of Knowsley and who, with red roses in their lapels, are competing for the title of the best-dressed by-election worker.' The winner of that title was the future Labour MP for Liverpool Walton, Peter Kilfoyle. Working from a disused office in what had been the industrial quarter of Kirkby before recession had reduced it to a brick-strewn wasteland, their only source of quick food was a chippie nearby in a small row of shops where the shutters stayed up all day long as a precaution against vandals and iron cages separated counter staff from customers. Sometimes, the chippie would run out of potatoes, and there would be no food for sale at all. It was the land which capitalism forgot, and so very different from the home life of Shelley Keeling, daughter of a wealthy East Coast American businessman, who was completing her studies by spending a year working as a volunteer in the parliamentary office of Jack Straw, who was in Knowsley North as the candidate's political adviser. Another member of the team, a party researcher named Julian Eccles, one day treated himself to takeaway chips and mushy peas. When she saw this fare, Shelley's eyes lit up and she exclaimed: 'That looks delicious – it must be avocado!'

Two or three days later, Shelley was alarmed to receive a transatlantic phone call from her father. Fortunately, nothing was wrong. He was one of the few thousand Americans who regularly read the *Financial Times* and had been amused to find a story there about his own daughter. It was also spotted by Peter Taaffe, editor of *Militant*, who related it to a crowd of 5,000 people who packed the Royal Albert Hall for a Militant rally on 15 November 1986, two days after Knowsley North had returned a Labour MP. Thus the story of the yuppie who could not tell mushy peas from avocado was born. How or when this metamorphosed into a myth about Peter Mandelson, who never set foot in Knowsley, no one knows for certain. His admirers blame Mandelson's enemies inside the Labour Party, or journalists, or both. Bryan Appleyard of the *Sunday Times* reckoned: 'It is a tale that tells people what they want to hear about Mandelson: that he is a cold-eyed, rootless operator, a scheming corridor cowboy who has sold the soul of the Labour Party to get what he wants.'[1]

Yes, but at Blackpool in October 1990, Neil Kinnock gave a short speech at a social gathering to mark Mandelson's departure from his post as the party's Director of Communication. He told this very story as if he had witnessed it personally, claiming that it had taken place in a by-election in Brecon in summer 1985. But what could have prompted Neil Kinnock to misremember an anecdote which had been circulating for four years, and to connect it with Peter Mandelson? Had he perhaps read it in *The People* four weeks earlier? *The People's* political columnist was playing a game beloved of journalists, of repeating a story which had appeared in another newspaper, in this case the *Hartlepool Mail*, knowing it was untrue and, by denying it, giving it new life. All the standard details were there – Mandelson going into a Hartlepool fish and chip shop and mistaking the mushy peas for avocado mousse, plus a joke to the effect that you can tell that politicians eat mushy peas because they are so full of wind. And who was *The People* columnist spreading this story? None other than the self-same Peter Mandelson.[2] One of the unsolvable mysteries about this complex character is whether he attracts myths by accident, or creates them deliberately to encourage people to talk about him.

The Labour Party is dominated by yuppies in the original sense of 'young, upwardly mobile professionals' who were saved by the state education system from ever having to work with their hands, as their parents or grandparents had had to. Not Peter Mandelson. When, inevitably, he was featured in *London Labour Briefing* as their 'Class Traitor of the Month', it was his formidable mother, whom he calls the 'Duchess' who asked the pertinent question – which class did they suppose he was a traitor to?

Mandelson's mother was the only child of the formidable Herbert Morrison, the pre-war leader of the London County Council, wartime Home Secretary, and post-war deputy to Clement Attlee. At the age of eleven, Mandelson learnt from an ITN newsflash that his grandfather was dead. His mother never forgave the fact that a television company was tipped off before she knew. She and Mandelson's father, Tony, an executive on the *Jewish Chronicle*, were both members of the Labour Party in Hampstead Garden Suburb, and friends and near neighbours of Harold and Mary Wilson. In a party full of people who fear that the increasingly specialized nature of political activism is making them lose touch with their social roots, the mushy peas story is a nice vignette about someone who benefits from never having had any working-class roots to lose.

The myth of Mandelson as the Labour Party's evil genius has had a more complicated evolution. No one else in the Labour Party has attracted anything like the extravagant praise or the venomous hostility that he has. In the mid-1980s, he appeared to be so dazzlingly gifted that the mainstream of the party was ready to forgive his excessive self-confidence. Only the Bennite left was overtly hostile to him. But over the years, the number and variety of his enemies increased, taking in important members of the Shadow Cabinet, including some who had been his friends and mentors. John Prescott, who was Mandelson's referee for the Labour Party job, became so contemptuous of him that he refused to pronounce his name properly, calling him 'Mendelson'.

It ought not to have been a difficult name to pronounce, because Mandelson was the first Labour politician since Tony Benn to become an eponym, but with one significant distinction: the words to which Benn gave his name – Bennism, Bennite, Bennery – were nouns, while Mandelson is more commonly heard as an adjective. There are no Mandelsonites, but things are done in a Mandelsonian way, just as things were done in the 1950s in a Morrisonian way. Where he achieves the status of a noun, it is by way of a verb, as in this extract from a speech at the Westminster Club Lunch by the Conservative Cabinet Minister, John MacGregor, Leader of the House of Commons: 'I find myself most unusually in agreement with Mr Ken Livingstone who said in a newspaper article recently, referring to the Labour Party's former Director of Communications, "The result of the 'Mandelsonisation' of Labour is that we seem to stand for nothing positive and clear whatsoever"'.[3]

That was dated 1991. The accusation it contains – that Mandelson was single-handedly depoliticizing the Labour Party – was mild compared with what was levelled at him after the election of Tony Blair to the party leadership, and not necessarily from the old Bennite left. Against this, there is the opinion of Colin Byrne, who was Mandelson's deputy at Walworth Road in 1988–90, that everything Mandelson has done in the last decade has been for one purpose only: to secure the election of a Labour government; or of Gavyn Davies, one of Britain's foremost economists, one of the 'seven wise men' called upon to provide the Treasury with their personal economic forecasts, who warned the Conservatives to beware that Mandelson was back, having been underused during John

Smith's 'complacent' leadership (although that provoked a rejoinder from Mike Gapes, a Labour MP who had worked at Labour Party headquarters with Mandelson, who icily pointed out that Labour had done better at the 1992 general election, without Mandelson, than in 1987); and, most significantly, there is Tony Blair's opinion. For good measure, there is Mandelson's own assessment of himself, as expressed on television: 'I am the nicest person I know and what I say is the truth as I see it'.[4] Clearly, these opinions cannot all be right.

The origin of the myth can perhaps be traced to a remarkable *Panorama* documentary by Michael Cockerell in 1979, which revealed the role of image-makers like the Saatchi & Saatchi advertising agency in securing the general election for Margaret Thatcher. That working-class electors could vote for a right-wing ideologue was a difficult phenomenon for liberal intellectuals to explain. Therefore, there was a willing audience for the idea that parties rose or fell on the strength of their presentation rather than their ideology. In 1983, Labour conducted what Ken Livingstone justifiably described as 'the worst campaign of any major political party in a western democracy in the post war world,'[5] culminating in the worst result for either of the main parties for over half a century. Afterwards, one thing which a deeply divided party could agree on was that they must improve their presentation. It was something to which they had given almost no thought at all. In an internal paper written soon after the 1983 defeat, the head of the Walworth Road research department, Geoff Bish, admitted that party policies were written without the least thought about their impact on party opinion. 'We work out what we think needs to be done, given the basic attitudes of the party conference, and then plonk it before the electorate . . . to take it or leave it as they wish,' he said, urging that in future there be fewer policies and that their 'essential backcloth' should be 'an understanding of public opinion rather than only party conference policy'.[6] The party press office, as its name implied, was no more than an information service which answered enquiries from journalists and issued politicians' speeches on request, without ever being seriously involved in the formulation of political strategy.

As the party's electoral fortunes were beginning the slow climb upwards from the trough of 1983, the head office was sensibly restructured to cut the number of department heads by half, creating a new position of

Director of Campaigns and Communications. Peter Mandelson, who was then working as a producer for London Weekend Television, won the job by a narrow majority after Neil Kinnock had been persuaded at almost the last minute that he would be more committed to it than the *Guardian* journalist, David Gow. He took up office on 21 October 1985, which was coincidentally his thirty-second birthday.

He did not disappoint. Within an organization long accustomed to the idea that second-best will do, he displayed an exacting professional standard and demanded it from others. He was routinely the first at work and the last to leave, and thought nothing of a thirteen- or fourteen-hour day, endlessly listening, explaining, exhorting, planning and plotting. Within eighteen months, a department which had been regarded throughout the Westminster village as a joke took on the reputation of a ruthlessly efficient propaganda machine. 'Mention of Mandelson', by one later account, 'appears to cast a respectful terror in the hearts of Tory strategists, much as the name Rommel gained a mythical status among Allied generals.'

Labour had a great untapped asset which, before Mandelson's arrival, was lying just out of sight like an unexploited oil field, in the large number of highly qualified professionals prepared to work for the party for love instead of money, if only the party machine were in a fit state to make use of them. In the early 1980s, potential sympathizers not already repelled by the spectacle of rival party leaders feuding in public found it impossible to make contact with anyone inside the apparatus competent to make decisions. This problem was on the way to being resolved by the time Mandelson arrived. In 1983 a 'breakfast group' was set up by Neil Kinnock's press secretary Patricia Hewitt, the head of the MORI polling agency, Bob Worcester, and Chris Powell, head of the advertising agency Boase Massimi Pollitt. They transformed Labour's party political broadcasts by hiring a BBC current affairs producer, John Gau, to refashion them in the style of the BBC 'Nationwide' programme. For better or worse, they also gave Neil Kinnock's Labour Party a theme tune, a snatch of Brahms which would blast out over the loudspeakers at the beginning of the leader's public appearances.

However, the use of outside expertise vastly increased after the party's head office had acquired a competent manager who was trusted by the party leader and could therefore deliver prompt and firm decisions. This led to the creation of the 'Shadow Communications Agency', a conduit through which a small army of advertising copy writers, psephologists, market researchers, graphic artists and others contributed unpaid labour which would have cost millions of pounds at the market rate. The most immediate and visible effect was that the design of backdrops at party press conferences and the lay-out and design of press releases and other documents suddenly improved. Symbolically, the red flag, which had decorated party publications for as long as anyone could remember, was replaced with a red rose logo, the trademark of several European social democratic parties.

The first meeting of the agency was chaired by Chris Powell, but its central figure was Philip Gould, an advertising executive who had done well in his profession, is married to one of the leading figures in the publishing world, and who, in his late thirties, was looking for a new outlet. He and another advertising executive, Deborah Mattinson, formed Gould, Mattinson Associates, the only consultants' firm contracted to work for the party. Instead of relying exclusively on one polling organization, MORI, and one maker of political broadcasts, John Gau, the party spread the tasks around. During the 1987 campaign, Labour released a political broadcast by Hugh Hudson, director of the award winning *Chariots of Fire*. It is still regarded in the industry as an epoch-maker, and is the first and only political broadcast to be repeated by public request. It was a video portrait of Neil Kinnock which began with a shot of gulls flying over a clifftop, featured the leader's attack on the Liverpool Militants, and concluded with the speech in which he asked, rhetorically, why he was the first Kinnock in a thousand generations to go to university. In its immediate aftermath, Neil Kinnock's popularity rating in opinion polls showed an extraordinary increase which, unfortunately, was not durable enough to influence the election result a fortnight later.

For several years, the shadow communications agency stayed in the shadows. All journalists' enquiries to Gould, Mattinson were invariably referred to the Walworth Road press office, and only insiders were aware of the extent of their contribution to the party's revival. The names of numerous voluntary helpers are not publicly known even now. Every alteration or improvement therefore tended to be attributed to Peter Mandelson, who acquired the reputation of an 'image-maker', concerned with superficial appearances and able to disguise unpalatable policies beneath soft pastel shades. The Prince of Wales greeted Mandelson at a Kensington Palace reception with the words: 'Ah, the Red Rose man!'[8] – though it was ultimately Neil Kinnock's decision to introduce the rose, while Mandelson was the aide who knew someone in television who introduced him to someone in advertising who knew a designer who commissioned the artist who designed the rose.

Not all encounters with high-flying professions were so happy and productive. One of the first decisions Mandelson was prevailed upon to take was to hire Lynne Franks, who headed her own highly successful public relations organization, to be the party's consultant on youth. There were some rave notices about how 'The Labour Party this week launched its new yuppie image . . . aided by Buddhist mother of two, high priestess of fashion, Lynne Franks.' According to the *Daily Express*, 'she has a Buddhist altar in the front room and prays there twice a day. This former kosher cutie is now a member of the Nichiren Shoshu sect . . . Buddha however had nothing to do with persuading the Labour Party leader to attend the *Absolute Beginners* opening night showbiz razzle, where he stood out like a Savile Row suit in an Arab bazaar.' This free publicity helped Lynne Franks on her way to becoming so well-known that she is reputed to have been the model for the character played by Jennifer Saunders in the television series *Absolutely Fabulous*. For Mandelson, it was a huge embarrassment. Her contract with the party having come to an ill-tempered end, Lynne Franks later said that the red rose logo reminded her of lavatory paper.

This was an exception. Most of the working relationships formed while Mandelson was based at Walworth Road survived his departure. The party continued to produce high quality political broadcasts and to mount well-staged press conferences without him, thereby demonstrating that this was not the most important of the various functions which Mandelson had carried out on Neil Kinnock's behalf.

In between the daily grind of staging press conferences and organizing long-running campaigns around themes like Freedom and Fairness, Mandelson also planned the 1987 election effort, which surprised everyone by the meticulous detail with which it had been prepared. There were charts drawn up well in advance detailing where leading members of the Shadow Cabinet would be and what they would be doing on predetermined days.

Mandelson had even decided, for instance, that precisely one week before polling day there would be a horror story about the National Health Service running on the news. This happened on schedule, producing scenes akin to panic in Conservative Central Office, where the party's Deputy Chairman, Lord Young, seized the chairman, Norman Tebbit, by the labels to tell him in barrack room language that they were in danger of losing. It would make sense if every political party prepared every general election in that sort of detail but, in practice, they seldom do. The party of government is hampered by the fact that the people who matter are cabinet ministers and therefore too busy, day-by-day, to concentrate their minds on the task. Opposition parties are seldom that well-led.

Mandelson's reputation was consolidated by the campaign which Labour conducted during the 1987 general election, which was, it must be said, like one of those high quality advertising campaigns which win awards within the industry but fail to sell their product. Afterwards, Neil Kinnock spoke of the unusual experience of travelling the country and hearing party members praise head office. At the national executive committee that followed, Tony Benn also praised the quality of the material put out during the campaign. That period probably marked the peak of Mandelson's prestige within the party. Afterwards, his reputation as a formidable operator continued to spread, as he used his position to have a more overt influence over the formulation of party policy and to intervene in internal power battles; but this was a more controversial role in which he rapidly accumulated enemies. But even before he became a target of suspicion, there seems to have been confusion about precisely what Mandelson did to create his extraordinary reputation.

There had been one previous occasion when Labour had taken observers by surprise by the professional excellence of its campaign. That was in 1959, after eight years in opposition. The heroes of that campaign were two young Labour MPs, Woodrow Wyatt and Tony Benn, who later went their separate ways, having helped to demonstrate, as Mandelson did in 1987, that well-run campaigns do not necessarily win elections. It is not that which has given him political weight in Labour Party circles. His reputation rests principally on his skill as a 'spin doctor'.

When Mandelson first started exercising this political black art, there was no phrase in common usage by which to describe it and consequently, though almost every political journalist of any importance knew he was doing it, none of them wrote about it. When the expression 'spin doctor' finally drifted across the Atlantic and into British political slang after the 1988 US presidential election, it was instantly attached to Peter Mandelson. Spin doctors are a product of the age of instant communication, operating in the tiny space between when a political event takes place and when it is first reported to the wide public. It is now an axiom of political journalism that the public must be given more than the bald facts. Every event must be placed in a context. It must be a victory for someone in the public eye, or a setback for someone else. If it is an internal development within a political party, it must either be good news or bad news for the party leader. Spin doctors try to be the first to put their interpretation, or 'spin' on events, preferably by having a quiet word with correspondents on the spot, before they have even reported back to their newsdesks. To take one example, Tony Blair did not – as is widely supposed – announce in his speech to the Brighton party conference in 1994 that he wanted to delete Clause Four of the party constitution. He made some pointed remarks about 'saying what we mean and meaning what we say', without being specific about what *he* meant; but within minutes, journalists knew. At the edge of the hall, Arthur Scargill was encircled by journalists clamouring for an instant reaction. The ever suspicious miners' leader said that reading between the lines of the Blair speech, he had a very strong suspicion that a plot was afoot to abolish Clause Four. This made the surrounding journalists impatient: they all knew that was exactly what Blair meant. It had already been broadcast on television. The word had been spread in hurried private conversations behind the speaker's platform, between knots of political journalists and two or three spin doctors, one of whom was Peter Mandelson.

Accidents can happen when there are no spin doctors in the house, because correspondents have no choice but to arrive at their own interpretation of what they have been told. To take a real example from Mandelson's period as communications director, a press release was issued by Neil Kinnock's office one lunchtime in 1989, which said:

> Austin Mitchell MP is being released from today from his frontbench responsibilities in Bryan Gould's Trade and Industry team.

It was not obvious to those who put out the release that disaster lay ahead, because Mitchell was – to quote his own words – 'a nobody in a job that most people didn't realise he had in the first place'.[8] He had been sacked because his lucrative sideline as a broadcaster had repeatedly conflicted with the general obligation on all MPs with front positions to be careful what they say on the air. For instance, during a radio panel game, Mitchell described 1988 as the year when 'Owen flipped, Thatcher flapped and Kinnock flopped', producing a day of newspaper stories about the Labour frontbencher who thought his leader was a flop. Now he had accepted a post as co-presenter, with Norman Tebbit, of a current affairs programme on Sky TV. Its format presented all manner of problems. It was possible, for example, that Bryan Gould might appear as a guest, being cross-examined simultaneously by Tebbit and by a member of his own team. Any Labour Party leader would have been acting reasonably by insisting that Mitchell either turn down the offer from Sky or go on to the backbenches.

However, there was no one on hand to explain these simple points to correspondents puzzled and bemused by the leader's terse announcement. By chance, Peter Mandelson was away and Patricia Hewitt was out of the office. Any journalist who enquired was informed that Kinnock had nothing to add to what was on the press release. The field was therefore left open to Norman Tebbit, who made himself available for every news bulletin to spread a rumour that Mitchell had been sacked as an act of spite against Sky TV, which belonged to Rupert Murdoch, whose newspapers had been boycotted by Labour during the industrial dispute at his Wapping plant two years earlier. This seemed to be unjust, since Tony Blair and Michael Meacher had been able to contribute to *The Times* without being removed from the Shadow Cabinet, just as Conservative ministers had occasionally written for the *Daily Mirror*. By six o'clock, Tebbit was on national television denouncing 'one of the most appalling acts of bigotry and arrogance that I have ever encountered'. The only person who felt able to come forward and put the Labour Party's side of the story was Austin Mitchell, who tried to turn it all into a joke. By the time the leader's office was offering a rational explanation, the story had run away. The next day, it was the main front page story in *The Times*.

There was, by contrast, an occasion when the party was hit by an almost wholly unexpected public relations disaster and Mandelson happened to be on hand to cope with it. On 25 May 1989, soon after eleven staff at the

Soviet embassy had been expelled from Britain as KGB operatives on information supplied by the high-ranking defector, Oleg Gordievsky, BBC's *Nine o'Clock News* led with the startling claim that their activities had included blackmailing certain unnamed Labour MPs. Allegations that some Labour MPs are KGB 'agents of influence' have bumped around in the murkier areas of British public life for a long time, but when the telephone calls began coming through from journalists demanding an instant reaction to the BBC story, Mandelson was in no position to know the truth about KGB activities. He was probably into the thirteenth hour of his working day; he had been caught completely by surprise and, as luck would have it, he was in no position to check the facts. The only person who could tell him was Neil Kinnock, who would have been informed privately if evidence of that kind had come into the hands of British intelligence. But Kinnock was on a train, in Wales, out of telephone contact. ITN's *News at Ten* and numerous newspaper editions would have passed long before he could be reached. Denying the story might force an embarrassing retraction later, if it turned out to be true; but to concede that it might be true would add to the damage already done. The easiest answer would be to say nothing at all, but that would simply allow the story to run on unchallenged. 'I had to say something to play it down,' Mandelson said later. 'The report was very damaging for the Labour Party. My task was to do everything I could to stop others reporting it, so I set about carefully rubbishing it. But at the back of my mind I knew the formulation of words had to be such that if I subsequently discovered it was true, I had kept a chink open.'[9] His tactic was to take the fight to the enemy by demanding that the BBC produce the evidence for its accusation, without dwelling on whether it was true or false. The story unravelled within a few days. Unusually, it was denied by the Foreign Secretary, Sir Geoffrey Howe. The BBC then gave its source as the Foreign Minister, William Waldegrave, in a private conversation over lunch with the BBC's Chief Reporter, John Sargeant. Mr Waldegrave denied saying any such thing. What might have been an embarrassment for the Labour Party became a public row between the BBC and the government from which only Labour emerged well. Not everyone could have turned such an unwelcome surprise to their advantage.

In the long run almost no one remembers the circumstances under which Austin Mitchell left the opposition frontbench or what the BBC said about the expulsion of Soviet diplomats; but these incidents have a cumulative effect. If they are badly handled, one after another, they add to the impression that the party concerned is unable to handle its own affairs competently. Conversely, if they are repeatedly handled well, they instil self-confidence and improve party discipline. Hence the value of good spin doctors. It cannot be seriously disputed that Peter Mandelson is one of the best there is.

Very soon after taking office he had assembled an idiosyncratic web of contacts in newspapers and broadcasting through which he channelled a flow of selected information by which he set out to alter the way political journalists perceived the party and its leader. There are senior political journalists who by 1995 had relied on him for the best part of ten years as their best source of information about internal party affairs. He not only briefed efficiently, with a good grasp of how to present information in a way that conforms to contemporary views about what is or is not news; he provided a sort of after-briefing service. It was common, for example, for broadcasters to receive a morning telephone call to tell them that a report written by A in newspaper X was interesting, accurate and worth following up, unlike the shoddily researched piece by B in a rival newspaper. What this implied, though the broadcaster might not know it, was that A had faithfully reproduced the content of a Mandelson briefing. Thus his clients would not only be given a well-sourced story to write, but would have their reputations upheld among their peers.

Mandelson's years as a producer had also provided him with an understanding of the complicated management structure of television companies, which he put to good use. Peter Allen, then a political correspondent for ITN, was once broadcasting live for the lunchtime news outside Labour's Walworth Road headquarters and said something about the proceedings inside which evidently displeased Mandelson. By the time he had finished his piece to camera and rung into the office to ensure that there had been no technical problems, he learned that there had already been a complaint which his editor considered to be valid. The political correspondent, Nicholas Jones, has also recorded bruising episodes of being reported to his superiors by Mandelson. Jones also recorded the comment made in 1990 by Ian Hargreaves, then the corporation's director of news and current affairs, à propos Peter Mandelson, that: 'You learn to ignore the dog who barks too often,'[10] but even that disclaimer implicitly acknowledged that, provided the dog only barked often enough, it was effective.

Shortly before Mandelson's arrival, the Labour Party had seemed to be thrashing about helplessly, riven by internal dissent over the miners' strike and militancy in the town halls, and unable to win elections when it mattered. Activists on the spot believed Labour would win the Brecon by-election in summer 1985, only to have the show stolen at the last minute by the Liberals. Soon afterwards, Neil Kinnock appeared to be getting a grip on the Militant problem, Labour pulled off a sensational by-election victory in Fulham, the Conservative administration was torn apart by the Westland débâcle which forced two Cabinet resignations, Labour took an impressive lead in opinion polls and the party was at last learning how to use the media to its own advantage. All of these, except the last, would have happened without Peter Mandelson; but it was the dramatic improvement in media presentation which impressed most forcibly on journalists and therefore on everyone else in the Westminster village.

In no time, the Conservatives were saying that they too needed a media wizard like Peter Mandelson. They did, in fact, appoint a thirty-two-year-old television producer to head the press and publicity department at Conservative Central Office. Only after Mandelson had been in the job about four years did it become apparent that he had no exceptional insight into the techniques of marketing and public relations. By vocation, he was neither a television executive, nor a public relations specialist like Lynne Franks, but a political operator. He was already a political activist between leaving school and entering university, though not in the Labour Party but in a pro-Soviet branch of the Young Communist League, for whom he sold newspapers outside Kilburn tube station and acted as a steward at their Scarborough conference.[11] From when he left St Catherine's College, Oxford, until he joined LWT in his late twenties, Mandelson's career was that of an aspiring professional mainstream Labour politician, including two years as Chairman of the British Youth Council and two years as political assistant to Albert Booth, opposition spokesman on transport. Mandelson had also served as a Labour councillor in Lambeth. It hardly need be said that he and that council's ultra-left leader, Ted Knight, had their disagreements. For example, when Councillor Knight complained after the Brixton riots that 'Lambeth is now under an army of occupation',

Councillor Mandelson retorted that the council leader was not helping a difficult situation by 'screaming and raging and saying the most bizarre things'. However, he added emolliently: 'Basically, I'm a supporter of much that Ted stands for – after all he's given me an important position within the council. [He was vice-chairman of the planning committee.] He has devoted great energy to get the Lambeth response right to the Brixton problems but on the other side he speaks to fringe left groups and goes over the top.'[12]

During 1981, Mandelson was suspected by left-wing party members in the borough of being tempted to defect to the SDP. There is no evidence to support this other than his friendship with Roger Liddell, a councillor who took on leadership of the small SDP group on Lambeth council. Mandelson himself has flatly denied that he ever contemplated the idea. The link to Booth suggests that, like Neil Kinnock, he thought the future lay with the 'soft left'. It was through Albert Booth that he knew John Prescott. He was also involved in 1981 in Jon Silkin's ill-fated attempt on the deputy leadership.

A year later, Mandelson apparently decided there was no future in the Labour Party at all, or at least not in the short term. It was then that he left to acquire three years' valuable experience in a specialized corner of television, where the Brian Walden Sunday morning political interviews were prepared. Even there, according to Peter Lennon, who was around at the time, 'Colleagues were astonished that such a brilliant mind should show not the slightest interest in film-making. His reasons for enjoying the work on *Weekend World* are transparently those of a trainee politician.'[13] He gave up his three week summer holiday in 1985 to go to Brecon and help out in the by-election, and to make discreet enquiries about the new job at party headquarters.

Mandelson's television experience had given him an advantage over other 'trainee politicians'; nonetheless his real value was his instinctive understanding of the political machine within which he was operating and of the mind of its leader. Spin doctoring was a knack which he picked up as he went along – unless he learned something about it from his grandfather who was, in his day, a spin doctor of some distinction, as is attested in this entry in the *Crossman Diaries* for the day when Morrison resigned the post of deputy leader, having lost to Gaitskell in the 1955 leadership election:

> From 6.30 until 7.45 I sat with Morrison discussing publicity and throughout this time he was being telephoned . . . by most of the press correspondents . . . It must have been very trying for him to have me there throughout and certainly from that hour and a half [*sic*] I learnt how carefully and systematically he has cultivated the press.[14]

Incidentally, my own relations with the grandson were similar to Crossman's encounter with Herbert Morrison, except that I was around, getting on Mandelson's nerves, for almost three years until summer 1988. Latterly I was his deputy. In July 1995, when he was questioned by Sir David Frost about something I had written about him in the *Observer*, Mandelson archly replied: 'Andy McSmith may be a friend of the Labour Party but he is no friend of mine.'

It was after the 1987 general election that the suspicion increasingly took hold in Labour Party circles that Mandelson was not a neutral servant of the party, but a player in the political game. There was a certain inevitability about this, because the political emphasis shifted from the improvement of presentation to the policy review. Unless Mandelson was going to allow his influence to wane he was going to have to be involved in defending party policy as Neil Kinnock wished it to be rather than as what it actually was. He could at least see the humour of the situation. Once, at a staff social in the midst of the 1988 controversy about unilateral nuclear disarmament, Mandelson was told that Anna Healy, a party press officer, had had a heated argument with Joe Haines of the *Daily Mirror* on the subject. He mused: 'Anna has rather extreme views on defence: she *agrees* with Labour party policy.'

Mandelson was also suspected of using his position to promote some Labour politicians, himself included, at the expense of others. The breach with John Prescott came in January 1988, when Prescott's office heard from journalists how David Hill, Hilary Coffman and Peter Mandelson had toured the parliamentary press gallery rubbishing Prescott over his threat to challenge Roy Hattersley for the deputy leadership. This was made public by Prescott's aide, Mike Craven, in the newsletter of the Labour Co-ordinating Committee.[15]

Whatever the politics of this incident, the propriety was that Hill and Coffman, who worked in Roy Hattersley's and Neil Kinnock's private offices respectively, were entitled to put their employers' point of view, as

Craven was entitled to defend Prescott's. But Peter Mandelson was a party official, employed technically by the National Executive Committee, and would therefore have been expected to observe a semblance of neutrality. This was, however, only one of several instances which support the assessment made by Patrick Wintour of the *Guardian* that 'he did not simply see his role as a neutral party official providing a platform for policy initiatives . . . he saw his role to act very much on behalf of the leader's office, rather than solely as a servant of the party.'[16] One of the most remarkable examples of this was the collapse of the working relationship he had had with Bryan Gould.

In 1986, Gould had the good fortune to be elected to the Shadow Cabinet at the same time that Robin Cook temporarily lost his place on it, creating a vacancy for a new Campaign Co-ordinator. During the general election campaign, the job involved being on television practically every day as the front man available to speak on any new development or defend any aspect of party policy while other leaders were out on the road. Gould handled this tricky task with consummate skill and for several months afterwards enjoyed an immense political authority. He topped the elections to the Shadow Cabinet by a huge margin and was elected to the National Executive – a double triumph for which there had been no precedent for a decade. His relations with Mandelson were also, then, very good. Like Mandelson, he had television experience, having worked as a journalist between losing his seat in 1979 and regaining another in 1983. He had given Mandelson a reference when he was seeking a job with LWT. Gould was also politically identified with the old 'soft left' rather than the right-wing faction to which Roy Hattersley and John Smith belonged. In 1987–88, it was the received wisdom that the next party leadership election would be a contest between Smith and Gould. It was not then obvious who would win. In his memoirs, written from his native New Zealand, Gould surveyed the ruins of a brilliant career, and attributed no small part of the blame to his former protégé:

> It was becoming increasingly clear to me over this period that Peter Mandelson was working to his own agenda – on what I and others began to call the 'Mandelson Project'. The 'project' was to ensure that Peter's protégés – Gordon Brown as the prime contender, but with Tony Blair as a fall-back – should succeed to the leadership. Peter was undoubtedly loyal to Neil but I do not think Neil realised that he was merely a player in the Mandelson strategy . . .

A good deal of the Mandelson strategy therefore concentrated on clearing the way for the eventual succession by undermining as much as possible the credibility of other possible contenders. If this activity were ever challenged, it could always be justified to the leader in terms of loyalty to his cause. As a member of the Shadow Cabinet I realised this 'playing of favourites' by the party's communications director caused a great deal of unhappiness . . . It probably did more to undermine Shadow Cabinet unity . . . than any other factor.[17]

There is one part of this account which cannot be denied. Mandelson and his allies within the party apparatus, like Julie Hall and Colin Byrne, were closely linked to the political group associated with Gordon Brown and Tony Blair, which was coming to be known as the 'modernizers'. Party officials are required at least to give an appearance of neutrality in internal party politics, and by tying himself in so closely with the two youngest members of the Shadow Cabinet, Mandelson was taking a risk, which paid off well.

In other respects, the Mandelson version of where his relationship with Gould started to go wrong is predictably different from Gould's. Early in 1988, Gould was considering challenging Roy Hattersley for the deputy leadership. He sounded out Mandelson, who refused to support him. He believes that Gould's political judgement became increasingly erratic thereafter. The other weakness in Gould's story is that he himself dates his decline from autumn 1989, when remarks he made during a television interview about the future of the water industry brought down a torrent of bad publicity on his head, with the suspected connivance of Walworth Road. Gould had a similar experience after being shifted sideways to the post of Shadow Environment spokesman over David Blunkett's proposed alternative to the poll tax. The blows which finished his career fell in 1992, after Neil Kinnock's resignation. He was evidently unaware that Mandelson's political position was very much weaker after the summer of 1989 than it had been in the previous four years, and he was in no position to conduct a private vendetta against a Shadow Cabinet member. What is interesting about Gould's version of events is not its accuracy, but the fact that a former contender for the party leadership should believe that Mandelson wielded such formidable influence. It is an indication of the uncomprehending pain which politicians who have been favourites of the media feel when good publicity turns to bad. It was the belief that

Mandelson understood and could control the mysteries of the media which accounted for his fabulous reputation, rather as the Pharoahs derived their power from their servants' ability to predict the tide.

The crisis in Peter Mandelson's political career came about through his own decision to look for a seat in the House of Commons. In one respect, this was the saving of him. If he had remained where he was, an outpost of Neil Kinnock's private office in Walworth Road, he would presumably have sunk with the rest of Kinnock's office after steering the party through a second general election defeat. On the other hand, by entering the political game in his own right, he almost ruptured his relationship with Kinnock and left himself vulnerable to his growing number of enemies.

During the early part of 1989, friends and contacts of Mandelson's in the East Midlands area were pleasantly surprised to hear from him out of the blue. One, who was cheered by an unexpected phone call, was surprised when the conversation turned to Labour Party affairs of Stoke-on-Trent. When the recipient of the call admitted to knowing nothing whatever about the town, the conversation was rapidly concluded. Jack Ashley, Labour MP for Stoke-on-Trent South, had announced that he would retire at the next general election.

Then Mandelson was spotted one weekend in Hartlepool, in the north-east of England, at a football match. His journalist friend, Alastair Campbell, may have been the person who first explained to him the intricacies of the game: that the ball is spherical, that it is kicked, that there are goal posts at each end of the playing field and so on. Ted Leadbitter, the long-serving MP for Hartlepool, was retiring. The finest moment of Leadbitter's long career was when he threatened to resign the Labour whip and to refuse to vote in the Commons again, at a time when the Wilson government was struggling by on a majority of only three, because the Post Office had erected a telegraph pole outside the home of one of his constituents. Mandelson's presence in the town could mean only one thing.

This was four years before the Labour leader, John Smith, risked his political life to introduce changes which took away from the trade unions the very considerable influence they wielded in selection conferences. Prior to the 1992 election, big unions retained squads of delegates on the party committees in safe Labour seats, who voted for the candidate approved by their regional secretary. Consequently, the way for an outsider like

Mandelson to become Labour MP in a town like Hartlepool was to obtain union backing. Fortunately, he knew Tom Burlison, regional secretary from the North East's biggest union, the GMB, who had spent the 1987 general election accompanying Neil Kinnock everywhere he went. Burlison was at first in doubt about introducing a Londoner to a northern seat. He could still remember the difficulties the northern region of the GMB had in the early 1970s trying to get the Durham town of Chester-le-Street to accept Giles Radice, who also came from London. Fortunately, Mandelson's charm and his celebrity status worked in his favour.

Even with that impressive backing, Mandelson faced a hard-fought contest against Stephen Jones, son of Barry Jones, who was then a member of the Shadow Cabinet. Kay Jones, Stephen's wife, and a TGWU branch secretary, wrote a long letter to Walworth Road in November, accusing Mandelson of breaking party rules by using his press contacts to canvass support, which candidates in a selection conference are barred from doing. Her view of Peter Mandelson was that he was 'rather a shark in a pool, quite cold-blooded if not downright bloodless. I just got the feeling he was assessing the electoral worth of everyone.'[18] Nonetheless, he easily won the selection contest. His impending career change was judged to be such a significant event that an ITN camera crew was waiting outside to record the result for the *News at Ten*.

It was not so well-received either in Neil Kinnock's office nor by members of the National Executive Committee, who were still nominally Mandelson's employers. There was an obvious problem if the party official whose job it was to play a pivotal role in the next general election campaign was going to be away fighting a constituency 300 miles to the north. A similar difficulty had arisen in the North West, where the regional organizer, Peter Kilfoyle, was a parliamentary candidate. Two head-office researchers, Mike Gapes and Gordon Prentice, had also found seats. All Mandelson's fellow directors at party headquarters and John Evans, who chaired the relevant NEC committee, took the hard-line view that staff members who became parliamentary candidates would have to offer their resignations. On the other hand, John Cunningham who, as campaign co-ordinator, would be fronting the next election, as Bryan Gould had in 1987, and Roy Hattersley, who thought Cunningham could not be trusted to do it properly, were both adamant that Mandelson should stay at his post. However, because he was a party employee, the decision rested with NEC members. At the NEC meeting in January 1990, Mandelson and other staff had to leave the room while the issue was being discussed. There could be no doubt that, if it went to a vote, there was a majority ready to force Mandelson and Kilfoyle to leave.

Until now, as Bryan Gould remarked, 'one of the main reasons for Peter's influence was that it was widely believed that he acted with Neil's authority'.[19] He was part of that invisible inner circle of people whom Kinnock genuinely trusted, an achievement all the more remarkable in that the party leader was generally suspicious of paid staff whose names were frequently in the newspapers. There had been at least one case of an individual being refused a temporary post in Kinnock's office because her name had appeared in print too often. But Peter Mandelson had read the leader's mind so skilfully that there had not been a known occasion in four turbulent years when he had said anything to journalists which had had to be retracted or clarified later because it did not reflect the official line.

However, the trust that Kinnock invested in members of the inner loop could be very abruptly withdrawn if they stepped outside it, as his former researcher, John Reid, had discovered when he was adopted as Labour candidate for Motherwell North before the 1987 election. Kinnock did not want to lose the best media spokesman he was ever likely to find to gain another Labour MP and he was not prepared to fight this battle and risk defeat within the NEC on Mandelson's behalf. When the NEC's Organisation Committee met in February 1990, Kinnock made an angry comment about staff who used their positions to get into the Commons which shocked and secretly rather delighted most of those who heard him. After the NEC meeting a fortnight later, Kinnock was getting back into his car in the courtyard at Walworth Road when Mandelson approached him to speak. Whatever he said went down badly, because Kinnock began loudly berating him. The courtyard is overlooked on three sides by office windows. Party staff three storeys up could hear what the party leader was saying and were taking gleeful pleasure in watching their legendary Director of Communications grappling with a severe communication problem.

Charles Clarke, Kinnock's chief of staff, also believed that Mandelson would have to go, and told him so. It was suggested in private negotiations that his successor should be appointed in June or July and he should leave after the party conference in October. The idea of a long handover period did not appeal to Mandelson, who proposed that if he had to go, he should leave as soon as possible. He agreed to stay for the extra months only after Neil Kinnock had asked him to.

It says a great deal for Mandelson's skill that all this was kept almost secret. *Tribune* carried several items on it, fed to them by left-wing members of the NEC. There was also one short piece in the *Daily Mirror* which said that the party was introducing a general rule for all employees who obtained parliamentary seats, and that Mandelson in particular had been 'ordered' to step down from his post. The *Mirror* is widely read in Hartlepool and the piece had an immediate impact on Mandelson's standing with the constituency Labour Party. A day or two later, the newspaper printed a correction, saying that its earlier report had been authoritatively denied. The original piece was under my name; the retraction was written by the *Daily Mirror's* Political Editor, Alastair Campbell. Generally, it is notoriously difficult to induce a tabloid newspaper to retract anything, particularly a story that would obviously stand up in court. Mandelson achieved it only by being able, once again, to call upon his relationship with Neil Kinnock.

Having fought with such skill to keep his temporary rift with Kinnock secret, Mandelson himself casually made it public years later, when interviewed by Tony Blair's biographer, Jon Sopel.[20] In contrast to Kinnock, Blair had been delighted at the idea that Mandelson should become his parliamentary next-door neighbour and an ally in the internal feuds within the northern group of Labour MPs, and had loaned Mandelson his spare bedroom in Sedgefield as a base from which to conduct his selection campaign. By 1994, political circumstances had changed. It was to Mandelson's advantage that he should be seen as having been exceptionally close to Blair while slightly distanced from the former leader. Truth has been a good friend of Peter Mandelson, always adapting to his needs.

The mutinous mood within the NEC was demonstrated when it came to choosing Mandelson's successor. His own preferred choice was his deputy, Colin Byrne. Neil Kinnock voted for Byrne but, by a heavy majority, the NEC selected a TV journalist named John Underwood, whose experience was entirely in broadcasting and who turned out to be an innocent in the world of politics. This was the last occasion until after the 1992 general election that Kinnock was defeated within the NEC on any matter of consequence and it turned into a story with an unhappy ending.

After several months working for SRU, a firm of management consultants whose founders included Peter Yorke, joint author of *The Sloane Ranger's Handbook*, and in a clutch of other part-time occupations, Mandelson was recalled in April 1991 to participate in a by-election in Monmouth, where Labour had a chance of taking a seat from the Conservatives. Neil Kinnock had an uneasy relationship with the party organizer in Wales, Anita Gale, and wanted Mandelson there as his eyes and ears. By now, there was a changed political landscape. John Major had replaced Margaret Thatcher, the Gulf War had been fought, and the opinion polls were giving no clear picture of which party was ahead. The decision to call for Mandelson was seized upon by the Conservative Party's Chris Patten as evidence that Labour was staking everything on winning Monmouth. Patten had a grudging respect for Mandelson and embarked on a round of unattributable briefings about the importance of his return.

It was unlikely that the Tories would ever hold on to Monmouth, despite their 9,000 majority, because if they had, it would have been their first by-election success for more than two years and their last for at least another five years. Their candidate, Roger Evans, who eventually took the seat in 1992, had some eccentric right-wing opinions, while the Labour candidate, Huw Edwards, could be relied on to say nothing out of place. He was backed by a team of about seventy professionals, some of them veterans of twenty or more by-elections. Labour had a solid base in Monmouth, having held the seat under different boundaries in the 1960s, and pulled off a creditable win, although the swing was far less than had been achieved in Mid-Staffs the previous year when public opposition to the poll tax had been at its height. However, some newspapers went into overdrive with their accounts of how this victory had been snatched by the unique political talents of Peter Mandelson who had single-handedly pulled off victory. A profile in the *Sunday Times* three days after the by-election reported that Mandelson's technique had been to 'nail down Monmouth and its 100 villages so that nothing could move without (his) knowledge and consent', before soaring to rhetorical heights about his past and future contribution to Labour's fortunes and, indeed, to British democracy:

You could argue that he's done a lot for British democracy. He stopped the Labour Party shooting itself in the foot and made it electable or, at least, marketable. He created a viable opposition by turning a crazed gang of fissiparous ideologues into a solemn army marching behind a designer rose . . . He is an operator of genius . . . He is fun, edgy and excitable. He is impossible to dislike and he will put Kinnock in Downing Street.[21]

This sort of hyperbole was being actively encouraged by the Conservatives. The Cabinet met in political session on the day Monmouth's voters went to the polls, and decided on a common approach to turn the bad publicity of a defeat to good account. For more than two years, Conservative support had suffered from a highly effective campaign orchestrated by Robin Cook, around the theme that the hospitals which were being converted to self-governing trusts were being removed from the NHS. A hospital in Abergavenny, at the extreme western tip of Monmouth constituency, was about to take on NHS Trust status, arousing local fears that it might cease to treat NHS patients. Whether it influenced voters in other parts of the strewn-out rural constituency such as Chepstow, forty miles away, is debatable. When the *Daily Mirror* descended on the seat looking for former Tory voters who were switching to Labour, they easily located six in one day, none of whom mentioned Abergavenny Hospital, but it certainly undermined support for the Conservatives in the Abergavenny area. The line worked out by Chris Patten and agreed by the Cabinet was to attribute both the by-election defeat and the government's unpopularity to a black propaganda campaign about the health service. To make this story credible, it required someone versed in the black arts to have been present in Monmouth – and Mandelson fitted the part very nicely. In a press conference they gave in Monmouth the next morning, Chris Patten and the defeated Tory candidate invoked the name of Mandelson three times, attributing defeat entirely to a misleading campaign about the health service. On Saturday, John Major was out on a visit and told a television crew who followed him down the street that 'Labour's campaign is based on a central lie – that NHS Trust hospitals are "opting out" of the NHS. That was the big lie Labour pedalled to voters in Monmouth.'

This all helped to enhance Mandelson's reputation, even in the highest quarters. Not long afterwards, a Labour Party press officer, Lesley Smith, was introduced at a polo match to the Prince of Wales, who immediately asked whether it was true that Mandelson was making a comeback. The reaction it provoked inside the Labour Party was a lot less helpful to him. It was nonsense to suggest that nothing moved in Monmouth without Mandelson knowing about it. It was only the second time in his life that he had been involved in a parliamentary by-election. The constituency had been flooded with another seventy or so paid party workers, some of whom had been at twenty or thirty previous campaigns, and certainly could have worked out for themselves that the future of Abergavenny Hospital was a good issue to run.

What made the situation worse was the general suspicion that it was not only Chris Patten who had been pedalling the story that Mandelson had won the campaign single-handed. He believes in the maxim laid down in Gerald Kaufman's handbook, *How to be a Minister*: 'If you turn out to be a good minister, make sure everyone knows about it. Only the press, tele-vision, and radio can tell them.'[22] However, just as it is bad for the electoral system if civil servants become overtly involved in party politics, it can damage a party organization if the paid officials working in backrooms advertise their achievements and compete for attention with elected politi-cians. Officials compete for approval within their own peer group, while politicians compete for public attention. Since the early 1990s, other senior Labour Party officials whose names have started to crop up in newspapers have been quietly warned against becoming 'another Mandelson'.

Mandelson's defence was that he could not stop journalists from writ-ing about him. That did not stop a stream of internal complaints that he was a credit-stealer, using the efforts of others to private advantage at the party's expense. When the Monmouth result was discussed by the NEC, Dennis Skinner made a mischievous tribute to the collective effort behind it and said how disappointed he was to read that it was all the work of one 'John Wayne' figure. He claimed later that nothing he had said at an NEC meeting for many years past had been so well-received and that no one in the room looked more pleased than Mandelson's successor, John Underwood.

Underwood had won the job against competition from two experienced political operators: his deputy, Colin Byrne, who had Kinnock's and Mandelson's backing, and Roy Hattersley's aide, David Hill. He had a good reputation as a television journalist, but arrived in a difficult political situation like a babe in the woods. He aspired to be a neutral party servant, whose expertise was on offer both to the party leader and to potential rivals like John Prescott, Robin Cook and the rest. But he made the painful discovery that officials who tried to be impartial when Kinnock expected loyalty and commitment, only got on his nerves and were shut out of the circle of people whom the leader trusted. Without privileged access to the leader, Underwood was of little use to political correspondents who wanted briefings from an insider. To add to Underwood's distress, his deputy, Colin Byrne, was a Kinnock trustee, with the added advantage of being engaged to be married to Julie Hall, who had succeed Patricia Hewitt as the leader's press and broadcasting secretary. Moreover, Byrne, Hall and Mandelson all lived under one roof, in a mews house in Bloomsbury. They were, said one wag, 'living in spin', with one home telephone number at which journalists who rang out of office hours had not one but three chances of an accurate background briefing. During the Gulf War, politicians like John Prescott and Robin Cook suspected that much of the bad press they attracted for their unwillingness to see Britain drawn into the conflict emanated from that home in Bloomsbury. Its address and a picture of its ivy-clad frontage were published in the *Daily Mail.*

The spectre of Mandelson making a highly publicized return to some quasi-official role was too much for Underwood. During the Monmouth by-election, he decided to force matters to a head by sacking Colin Byrne. He was persuaded not to, but refused to be reconciled to having Byrne for a deputy. If he had taken the matter to the NEC for a decision he could easily have won, given the build-up of hostility to Mandelson there, but he decided that he needed the personal endorsement of Neil Kinnock if he was to carry on. Kinnock was the wrong person to approach with what amounted to an ultimatum which was bound to cause pain to one of his personal staff. Underwood resigned. To outward appearances, Mandelson had won another victory. Contemporary press accounts, which treated the whole story like a soap opera, certainly believed he had proved that his power in the party was undiminished. In reality, it only compounded the difficulties caused by all the complaints about him emanating from Monmouth.

The truth is revealed in a letter in Mandelson's hand, written to Charles

Clarke in the same week that the *Sunday Times* was hailing him as an 'operator of genius.' The letter has never been made public, but is preserved in the Kinnock Archive in Churchill College, Cambridge. There had evidently been a confrontation during the week, in which Clarke had told Mandelson that it would be impossible for him to work for the party again until after the general election. Mandelson wrote to thank Clarke for his help in 'what I had not realized before was such a difficult situation', adding 'I am presently trying to put my bruised feelings aside.' He gave thanks for being allowed to participate in the Monmouth campaign at all and pleaded: 'I think I can contribute more in the same way, in a quiet, tactful, reasonable way . . . [although] I know you don't share this view.'

The tone of this letter is testimony to the fact that during the Kinnock years when Mandelson was written up as if he, rather than Neil Kinnock, were the real Labour Party leader, he was not even the most important of its paid officials. Charles Clarke, as Kinnock's chief of staff, carried more weight throughout, not least because he systematically discouraged any publicity about himself to avoid any suspicion that he spoke for anyone but the leader. However, one of the perks of being a good spin doctor is that where you desperately need to please someone, you arrange a little flattering publicity in a friendly outlet. Five days after the letter was written, a rare acknowledgement of Clarke's importance surfaced in the *Guardian*, written by Patrick Wintour – who is sometimes berated for being too 'old Labour' and not fully signed up to the Blair–Mandelson revolution, and at other times for taking too many Mandelson briefings.[23] Wintour wrote that Mandelson 'worked very closely with Charles Clarke, Mr Kinnock's personal assistant and most trusted aide. The relationship between Mr Clarke and Mr Mandelson was the central girder around which the reformed party was built.'[24]

Mandelson was, in fact, allowed to participate in one more by-election, when Labour took a seat from the Tories in Langbaugh in November 1991. This was in its way a remarkable victory, because in a predominantly white area, the Labour candidate, Ashok Kumar, became the first Black or Asian to win a parliamentary by-election in Britain. In view of what had been happening behind the scenes, it would have been awkward for Peter Mandelson if this had been written up as his personal achievement. Fortunately, it was not.

The Tory obsession with Mandelson the vote winner had a spin-off benefit in that Central Office funds were diverted into running a serious campaign in Hartlepool, which they knew they had no hope of winning, in order to tie him down there. He was not, however, involved in the 1992 general election campaign in any central role. In some respects this was to his advantage, because, in the bitterness of unexpected defeat, much of the Labour Party turned on the spin doctors and image-advisers. There had been trouble brewing for months before the campaign opened in March 1992 because there was no official at the centre of the entire operation in the way that Mandelson had been in 1987, but rather a jumble of official or unofficial advisers including David Hill, who had succeeded John Underwood, as well as Julie Hall, Patricia Hewitt, back in an advisory capacity, and Philip Gould, who were not all pulling in the same direction at all times.

In addition, the politicians themselves were falling out. The worst problem was the growing estrangement between Neil Kinnock and John Smith, compared with which the fact that Roy Hattersley was barely on speaking terms with John Cunningham, who was coordinating the campaign, was but a minor problem. The friction between Kinnock and Smith, which focused around tax issues, has been well documented, though, as often happens in politics, there was a personal element aggravating a technical difference of opinion. This concerned Julie Hall, the leader's trusted press secretary, about whom Smith had a blind spot, though he never allowed his objection to her to be made public. It dated back to when Smith was lying in an intensive care ward in October 1988, having almost died of a heart attack. One and only one journalist managed to get close enough to have a note passed to him asking to interview him. It was Julie Hall, then an ITN correspondent. Smith never forgave her.

Hattersley's complaints about John Cunningham have also never been made public. They were expressed in handwritten notes from the deputy leader to the leader which, by accident, were gathered in cardboard boxes when Kinnock's office was cleared out after his resignation and preserved in the Kinnock Archive in Cambridge. As early as November 1990, Hattersley was having to communicate in writing because he had been eased out of the inner circle of those who knew what was going on. At that time, Kinnock was trying to steer the party towards supporting a single European currency.

'As I understand it,' wrote the deputy leader, 'the line which appeared in *The Times* and the *Independent* is the one which you believe the party should follow on monetary union. I am in total agreement . . . The problem is not disagreement but the possibility of complaining that no proper discussion had been held,'

The following September, Hattersley became exasperated by the contrast between the Conservative campaign operation, coordinated by Patten and involving regular meetings of an inner group of Cabinet ministers, and Labour's haphazard effort, which had resulted, he said, in John Major appearing on two bulletins out of three during August, Paddy Ashdown on two out of seven, while Kinnock was virtually off the air. Hattersley warned: 'It is impossible to maintain the popularity you deserve unless you compete against those figures . . . We have had a very bad summer – we have done little or nothing to keep domestic politics on the agenda. So far as I can see, we had no strategy for doing so . . . Whilst half a dozen Cabinet ministers meet regularly to determine the direction of the Tory Party, our progress is determined by David Hill and whoever is on duty in your office. One of the problems is a Campaigns Coordinator who does not seem to believe in campaigning of the sort we need. But . . . I suspect we shall continue to disagree on that subject.'

In January 1992, Labour's tax plans came under concerted attack, aided by an ill-concealed disagreement between Kinnock and Smith over a proposal to change the rules governing National Insurance in a way which would have affected everyone on a salary of £21,060 a year or more. This inspired a private memo from Michael Meacher, who offered detailed figures to show how the plans could be amended so that every taxpayer whose salary was below that figure enjoyed a tax cut, while no one on less than £23,060 paid more, and separately another *cri de coeur* from Hattersley, who had computed the figures and worked out that the amount that Smith proposed to raise in extra tax was more than was actually necessary to cover the party's spending plans. 'The risk that you imagine I am panicking after one weekend of moderate opinion polls is one that I will have to take. No one who has attempted to obtain clarification on our tax and spending proposal can doubt that ambiguity exists . . . Ergo, do we know what we are doing?'

Had he still been Director of Communications, Mandelson might have been able to enforce order on the gathering chaos. If not, the ceremonial head on a platter might have been his. As it was, he did not merely escape the flak, he contributed to it. Specifically, he claimed that by opening up talk of a Lib–Lab pact as the campaign entered its final weekend, Labour had wasted two precious days which could have been devoted to more important issues like the recession and the implications of another Tory term in office, and had frightened wavering Tory voters into thinking that a vote for the Liberal Democrats was tantamount to voting Labour. He was, by implication, criticizing Neil Kinnock and those who advised him into this course, principally Patricia Hewitt.

Mandelson was not, however, claiming that one bad tactical decision had thrown away an election victory. In view of what Mandelson had to say about John Smith's Shadow Budget after Smith's death, it is worth noting that at the time when Smith was on the point of being elected party leader, Mandelson loyally praised his 'neat and clear-cut Shadow Budget', implicitly absolving his decision to abolish the ceiling on National Insurance contributions, thereby increasing the tax liability of anyone on an annual income of £21,000 or more, from having contributed to the defeat:

> The argument that Labour would have been elected had the tax proposals 'hit' fewer people is shallow and false. Wherever taxes 'hit', they would have been the subject of scaremongering and distortion.[25]

This time, according to Mandelson, the Labour Party had made no serious mistakes in drawing up the policies in the manifesto, but what the party lacked was sufficient 'credibility' to calm fears about what a Labour government's programme would cost the average taxpayer, which tabloids like the *Sun* had so expertly played up. 'It was a credibility gap, not a policy chasm, that Labour had to bridge in 1992.'

A few months later, Mandelson returned to Westminster as the new MP for Hartlepool, under a new Labour Party leader. John Smith took an old-fashioned view that new MPs must serve their apprenticeship on the backbenches. He never appointed any member of the 1992 intake to an official position on the party's frontbench. He would perhaps have broken that rule eventually had he lived longer, but it is by no means certain that the first to benefit would have been Peter Mandelson. After the 1992 election, a reaction had set in against spin doctors and image-advisers. Smith to some extent shared the general prejudice against them, particularly in regard to Julie Hall and Colin Byrne. Byrne, for instance, was the author of what was probably the most damaging public attack ever made on Smith by any Labour Party member. In a letter to the *Guardian* a few days after the 1992 general election, Byrne accused Smith of having avoided committing himself over the years on all the most sensitive issues, from the expulsion of Militant to the Gulf War.[26] Mandelson had not been involved in the election campaign. Neither was he responsible for the subsequent attack on Smith by Colin Byrne. He had in fact tried to dissuade Byrne from writing it and would not speak to him for several months afterwards; but the incident drew attention to the fact that relations between Smith and some of those who made up Mandelson's circle of intimates were not good.

Soon after his entry into the Commons, Mandelson hired a researcher named Derek Draper, who was in many ways an image of his new employer: a precociously talented operator zealously identified with the 'modernizers'. He was first spotted when, as a student at Manchester University, he participated on Roy Hattersley's side in the 1988 deputy leadership election. Thereafter, he was to be found passionately involved in this or that campaign or pressure group. There was also a touch of glamour in his life: his former girlfriend was the journalist, Charlotte Raven, who, since the break-up of their relationship, has written rather eloquently about professionals who view politics as if it were a service industry without ideology or underlying purpose.[27] For some reason, which is not entirely clear, Smith took against him and was overheard on at least one occasion exclaiming: 'What has that little bastard Draper been up to now?'

Mandelson's talents were too valuable to be entirely wasted. He was called upon to give the leader's wife, Elizabeth Smith, some advice on handling the media, and he was sent to Newbury to be the candidate's minder in the first by-election of the new parliament. It was at Newbury that Labour scored its lowest percentage of the poll in any parliamentary by-election since the war. Fortunately, no one attached much significance to Mandelson's presence there.

Otherwise, Mandelson was free to do what other ambitious backbench MPs do: ask questions, take up causes, join committees and look after constituents. Around this time, he was privately complaining that he was tired of being typecast as a spin doctor. A criticism levelled at him even by his admirers was that he was interested only in the political process, nothing more. Now he had an opportunity to expand his repertoire.

He certainly tried to take good care of Hartlepool. On one occasion, he spoke up for the town with such panache that he won one of the coveted *Spectator* annual awards for outstanding parliamentarians, as 1994's 'member to watch'. He intervened after a Tory MP had raised a question about the future of the royal yacht *Britannia*, to urge the Defence Minister, Jeremy Hanley, that the vessel 'should receive a comfortable and dignified retirement as befits her age in the new maritime heritage centre at Hartlepool'. The rest of the exchange was knockabout comedy, enjoyed by everyone present except Mandelson and the Speaker, Betty Boothroyd, who by the end of it was quivering with rage:

Mr Mandelson:	Are you aware that I have discussed the matter personally with Her Majesty the Queen who has expressed her interest in that? Will the minister confirm . . .
Madam Speaker:	Order. I am sure the Hon. Gentleman is proud, but he should not be divulging conversations that he has had with Her Majesty.
Mr Mandelson:	Is the Minister aware that Her Majesty's private secretary has graciously given me permission to disclose that information? Will the Government, therefore, confirm that they will consider the option most positively?
Mr Hanley:	If such are Her Majesty's instructions, I could do no less.
Madam Speaker:	It is the Speaker of the House who rules here and not Her Majesty's private secretary.[28]

A long-standing local grievance in Hartlepool was that its old borough council had been abolished in the 1974 boundary review, when the town was incorporated in the new county of Cleveland. With another boundary review impending, Ted Leadbitter had vowed to support a local campaign for Hartlepool to become a 'unitary' authority outside any administrative county. In his maiden speech to parliament, Mandelson pledged that in this respect he would follow Leadbitter's lead. He was as good as his word, although it brought him into open conflict with the leaders of Cleveland county council.

Technically, for once, Mandelson was defending 'old' Labour Party policy, in that the 1992 election manifesto had promised to dispose of the county and district system, covering England with single-tier authorities which in most cases would be based on communities like Hartlepool. Otherwise, once the party's plans for regional government had been implemented, people in rural England could find themselves paying dues to no less than four councils: their parish, their district, their county and their regional authority, not to mention the government in Westminster. Jack Straw, for instance, wanted Blackburn out of the administrative county of Lancashire, even though it was Labour controlled.

However, the old policy was effectively forgotten as Labour county councils mounted highly effective campaigns to protect themselves from being abolished by the Conservative government, frequently with the support of their local Labour MPs. A notable example was Durham county council, next door to Cleveland, which rallied support from every MP in the county, including Tony Blair. Cleveland also enlisted support from two of its four Labour MPs, Frank Cook and Marjorie Mowlam. The other two, Mandelson and Stuart Bell dissented, and advocated the break-up of the county. This did not make them popular with sections of the Cleveland Labour Party. When Mandelson claimed on local radio that opinion surveys had shown that public opinion was against the retention of the county council, its leader, Paul Harford, publicly accused him of engaging in 'nonsensical fantasy'.[29] When a vote was taken in parliament, Labour MPs were instructed by the whips to support the county. Bell and Mandelson declined. Mandelson himself was, by then, a Labour whip. The result was a rare example of a whip voting against the line laid down by the whips' office without being required to resign. Not only that, but Mandelson tried ten times in four minutes to interrupt a speech by Marjorie Mowlam in defence of Cleveland county, persisting despite three warnings from the Deputy Speaker to sit down.[30] His stand has often been cited since as evidence that a favourite of Blair's is allowed to get away with indiscipline in a way that left-wing MPs are not. There is, however, an old tradition which allows MPs to dissent on issues that have particular relevance to their own constituency.

There were two other issues which threw up considerable emotion and on which an informal party line was enforced, but Mandelson exercised his right to differ. One was the vote on unrestricted Sunday trading, which most Labour MPs opposed. Although it was technically a free vote, a lot of informal arm-twisting was taking place, orchestrated by the veteran whip,

Ray Powell, to get Labour MPs to fall in line with the policy of the shop-workers' union, USDAW. Mandelson refused.

A well-organized group of Labour MPs also campaigned against the National Lottery, principally because of fears that it would put the pools companies out of business, with catastrophic effects on employment on Merseyside. Mandelson had been brought up in a puritan left-wing tradition which frowned on gambling and – in contrast to Robin Cook or the late Ian Mikardo – has probably never placed a bet in his life. He might therefore have been expected to join the opposition to the Lottery. On the contrary, he condemned that opposition as a 'colossal mistake', because it meant 'going against the tide of public opinion . . . as though we were, in an old-wordly way, against innovation', because 'it was unfortunate and highly undesirable for the Labour Party to appear to be under the sway of a vested interest', and because it might appear that the party was adopting 'a rather sniffy, moralistic and intolerant attitude to those who want to have a flutter'.[31]

In each of these three apparently unconnected issues it is possible to see a common thread. In every case, there was a 'producer' interest and a 'consumer' interest. The instinct of most Labour MPs was to defend the jobs of the employees of Hartlepool county council and Littlewoods Pools, and the working conditions of supermarket shop assistants. Each time Mandelson sided with the consumer. On a separate occasion, he told the Commons that 'unemployment is not just a social evil . . . it is an economic calamity'[32], but there were occasions when he demonstrated that minimizing unemployment was not his only priority.

During the stormy parliamentary passage of the Maastricht Treaty, when the Labour Party was broadly divided into those who opposed the Treaty, those who were for it and those who simply wanted to defeat the government one way or another, Mandelson emerged as one of the most committed pro-Europeans on the Labour side: an overt supporter of a single European currency for whom the prospect of handing economic power to the governors of a new Bank of Europe held no terrors, because 'A monetary policy implemented by a European central bank . . . has a far better chance of achieving rational coordination of policies . . . than the present arrangement, in which, like it or not, the Bundesbank determines its own priorities and others simply must respond.'[33] Later, he accepted a post as vice-chairman of the cross-party European Movement, putting him along-side Sir Edward Heath, its President, and Edwina Currie, another vice-chairman.

Indeed, Mandelson's main contributions to the long Maastricht debate were examples of those occasions when MPs from the opposite side sit back and watch as members of the same party tear into each other. Every few minutes, one of the critics of Maastricht on the Labour left – usually Bryan Gould, Peter Shore, Denzil Davies, Jeremy Corbyn, Roger Berry or Peter Hain – would interrupt to have an argument with him. At one point, Mandelson told them: 'It is not good enough for those who disagree to bawl and shout and attempt to prevent [me] from speaking. That is an unattractive characteristic of this debate. It shows an obvious weakness of argument.'[34] But he gave as good as he got: minutes later, he interrupted one of Peter Hain's speeches to accuse him of making selective quotations from the Treaty, and carried on barracking him until the Deputy Speaker ordered him to be quiet.[35]

The nub of Mandelson's argument with the left was over Article 3A of the Treaty, which requires Member States to 'maintain price stability' and to pursue 'stable prices, sound public finances and monetary conditions and a sustainable balance of payments'. Some of the anti-Maastricht left con-strued 'price stability' to mean no inflation at all, rather than the more common interpretation of very low inflation; but even a commitment to low inflation would severely limit the investment which a Labour govern-ment could pump into the economically depressed regions, apparently clashing with the party's nominal commitment to eliminate unemploy-ment. Mandelson accused them of being obsessed with the words in the Treaty and of forgetting that elected politicians would retain some freedom of action. Besides, he argued, 'Why should we be in favour of unsound public finances and an unsustainable balance of payments?'[36] In this argu-ment about the relative importance of jobs or a stable currency, Mandelson can again be seen defending what can broadly be called the 'consumer' interest.

He was also an assiduous member of the Commons committee which scrutinized the autumn 1992 budget, line by line. He was elected secretary of the backbench treasury committee, on which he established himself as a reliable ally of Gordon Brown, who was now Shadow Chancellor, sending out warnings to other Labour MPs through the letters page of the *Guardian* that anything that could remotely be interpreted as a promise to spend money would be logged at Conservative Central Office and used. 'Let us remember that Smith Square snoopers and Tory antennae are active all the time,' he wrote on one occasion,[37] following that a few weeks later with a warning that 'those who want Labour to spell out a shopping list of commitments . . . and pledge a multi-billion pound increase in borrowing and taxes . . . are not doing the party any service'.[38]

The picture that was emerging was of a pro-European, a believer in sound money, whose views on local democracy were sufficiently ruthless to allow him to be an accessory to the dismantling of a large Labour-controlled authority and who was on good terms with the Queen. There we see the outlines of a populist social democrat.

In this period, Mandelson was less personally unpopular than he had been either before or since. The House of Commons is habitually unfriendly to new MPs who are famous before they arrive, because the attention they attract is an affront to those who have sat unnoticed on the green benches through successive parliaments. Of the three celebrities who arrived after the 1992 general election, he adapted to the place more quickly than either Glenda Jackson or, on the Tory side, Seb Coe. Early in 1994, the left tried to remove him from the secretaryship of the backbench treasury committee by running the Tribunite MP Roger Berry against him. On the same day, they also tried to remove the committee chairman, Alan Milburn. Milburn held on by forty-seven votes to twenty-two, Mandelson by thirty-nine votes to thirty, suggesting that there were only eight MPs who voted against Mandelson because they objected to him personally.

Suddenly, in May 1994, the interlude was over. John Smith was dead and, almost at once, Mandelson, the conscientious backbencher, resumed his old role as Labour's own Francis Urquhart of *The House of Cards*, wheeler-dealing in the corridors of the Commons and illicitly briefing journalists. It mystified many of those who thought they knew him why he should agree to go back into this line of activity, which in no time made him quite the most unpopular figure in the parliamentary Labour Party. On numerous occasions, he had confided that he was tired of being stereotyped as a spin doctor and wanted to be a rounded politician. Politics is peppered with stories of people who took the fast lane into a position of great influence, as an adviser of some kind, only to find that they were stuck because the luminophobic skills which made them useful to a powerful patron did not serve them well in wider democratic politics. But it is possible to make the switch. There was the example of Gerald Kaufman, who went straight from being a working journalist to having extraordinary access to the inner recesses, as Harold Wilson's press officer in 1965–70. There is a comment in Tony Benn's diaries about going to Chequers to participate in Harold Wilson's 'kitchen cabinet': 'At a meeting like this, with Gerald Kaufman who was just a press officer present, matters that were not even discussed at Cabinet were considered.'[39] In 1970, Kaufman was in a position analogous to Mandelson's in 1992. He had arrived in the Commons as a backbench MP, a position further away from the centre of the action, and he was made a tempting offer which would have saved him from the tedious round of committee work and speeches delivered to a half empty House late at night, when Wilson invited him to be his Parliamentary Private Secretary. Kaufman shrewdly turned him down. In time, he established himself as Kaufman the Labour politician who did not require the description 'ex-Downing Street spokesman' or 'ex-Wilson aide'.

While he was earning his keep on the backbenches and receiving no special favours from John Smith, it appeared that Mandelson too might eventually be better known for his views on fiscal policy and the single European currency than as a spin doctor. In his book, Mandelson praises Tony Blair for 'doing the unions a favour' by 'tackling unacceptable union practices' and thus enabling them 'to receive credit from the public for ending behaviour that was wrong in principle . . . and to increase their legitimacy'.[40] In a similar sort of way, John Smith had perhaps been doing Mandelson a favour by making him work hard on the committee scrutinizing the Finance Bill instead of playing big boys' games conspiring with and against members of the Shadow Cabinet.

However, between Smith and Mandelson there was a fifteen-year age difference, but Smith's death was going to propel into office a new leader who had been Mandelson's contemporary at Oxford University. They were separated in age by only six months, and in political experience the advantage was on Mandelson's side. He had been the Director of Communications, a trusted adviser with daily access to the party leader, when Blair and Gordon

Brown were beginning to make their ways as junior members of the front-bench. It was expected of Mandelson that he would become a big player in the events which were about to unfold. Gerald Kaufman, for instance, considered it important that there should be only one 'modernizer' candidate in the leadership election. He unloaded this opinion on Mandelson, on the assumption that he was in a position to induce Gordon Brown to pull out.[41]

The assumption was well-grounded. When Blair heard the news of Smith's death, the first person he called was his wife and, after that, Mandelson. Later in the same day, Mandelson was at Gordon Brown's London flat. He was the first, therefore, to be in a position to gauge the mood of the two leading modernizers and to discern that Brown was hesitant while Blair's mind was made up. He also knew, or was beginning to know, that the old guard party establishment – Neil Kinnock, Denis Healey, Kaufman and others – were heavily behind Blair rather than Brown. The obvious course, therefore, was to join the Blair camp and advise Brown as tactfully as possible that if he ran, he would be heading for defeat. Since the party was in a period of mourning, there was also an obvious case for keeping his head down.

Instead, Mandelson seemed to go out of his way to draw attention to himself. On Saturday evening, MPs turned on their television to see a relatively new MP who had never been close to John Smith being interviewed on Channel 4's *A Week in Politics* about what kind of person was needed as his successor. Mandelson did not ask for an invitation on to the programme, but neither did he turn it down. Without committing himself, he conveyed the impression that he intended to back Blair. It was taken as a signal that he now saw himself as back in the big league. The next morning, when the *Sunday Times* carried a rumour of a pact between Blair and Brown that they would not run against each other, the Brown camp suspected, without proof, that Mandelson had planted it to put pressure on their man to stand down.

If this was odd, Mandelson's role in the leadership election proper was even more peculiar. Officially, by agreement, no one declared their candidature until after the elections to the European parliament had been completed on 12 June. By then, however, a huge amount of spadework had been done on Blair's behalf, so that even as the votes in the Euro-elections were being counted, the list of Labour MPs who were backing Blair was being made public. There were 135, out of a total of 268, including thirteen out of eighteen members of the Shadow Cabinet. In the next three days, that number climbed to 154. The work had been done by Marjorie Mowlam, Peter Kilfoyle, who was then a party whip, and other members of the frontbench close to Blair. Both Mowlam and Kilfoyle warned Blair not to enlist Mandelson on his campaign team, because the only possible effect could be to erode support among other MPs. The warning was reinforced by Jack Straw, who was asked at a few days' notice to be Blair's campaign manager. Other Shadow Cabinet members also asserted that Mandelson's involvement would only blight what promised to be a spectacularly successful campaign. If they did not tell Blair that to his face, they were certainly saying it to one another.

Their motives were the usual mix of base jealousy and altruistic concern for the good of Tony Blair and the Labour Party. They feared that if Mandelson was seen to be part of the Blair team, the Monmouth by-election would be written again, on a larger scale, and when Blair came triumphantly home, Mandelson's circle of media contacts would not attribute this to Blair's popular appeal and the good sense of almost a million party members and supporters, but to the manipulative skills of one Svengali figure. Apart from being galling to everyone else who had contributed, it would not be good for Blair.

Blair himself was not impressed, attributing the objections to the cattish jealousy of politicians. He was undeviating in his opinion that the Labour Party was going to concentrate its every faculty on winning the next election, which would mean making use of Mandelson's exceptional skills. However, he evidently did not feel strong enough to tell this to the people who were running his election campaign, and he embarked on an extraordinary arrangement by which Mandelson was given back-door access to him, in order to advise him and brief broadcasting journalists on his behalf, without his official campaign managers knowing about it. The mystery is that either of them could have believed that such an arrangement would stay secret. It suggests that Mandelson's acute judgement of political realities sometimes deserts him when he tries to judge his own situation.

Here, with apologies, I have to lapse into the first person singular, because I wandered innocently into this strange situation. Having been told by the *Observer* to prepare a piece on the campaign teams for the three leadership candidates, I turned up in Blackpool on 13 June to hear Blair, John Prescott and Margaret Beckett address the annual conference of the GMB. I came upon television and radio journalists talking animatedly among themselves about the stream of telephone calls they had been receiving from Peter Mandelson, briefing them about the speech Blair would be giving. Two days later, I spoke to one of the official managers of the Blair campaign, who gave me a guide to who was doing what, without mentioning Mandelson. When I queried this, he laughed and happily assured me that he and others had successfully frozen Mandelson right out of the operation and that there was no way he was getting back in. Towards the end of the week, as a courtesy, I rang him back to say that although I believed he had been telling me the truth as he understood it, he was mistaken. Mandelson was, unbeknown to the official campaign team, very actively involved.

Within a very short time, the *Observer* had received a phone call from a furious Peter Mandelson, alleging that I was behaving unprofessionally by spreading stories about him which were untrue, and demanding that his name should not appear in the piece I was writing. However, by the time we spoke, it was a hurt and harassed Peter Mandelson, rather than an angry Mandelson, at the end of the telephone. He explained that because of his previous employment, hundreds of journalists had his telephone number and he was receiving unsolicited calls all the time. Obviously he could not conceal that he was a friend of Tony Blair's and he tried his best to be helpful, but it would cause him immense problems if it were suggested that he was actually involved in the Blair campaign. He was extraordinarily indiscreet, considering that he knew that I intended to write about him, and at no point did he suggest that the conversation was 'off the record'. He made one remark which, even now, kindness would not allow me to transcribe from the shorthand record.

Unfortunately, I knew that the story that he was telling me was untrue, because I had taken the precaution of checking. I knew that he had rung at least three broadcasting journalists to brief them on the speech which Blair made to the GMB. He had used identical words to each of them, implying that he was reading from a prepared brief and suggesting that he was acting in a recognized capacity. So I asked him whether he was quite certain that he had not rung any broadcasting journalists on Monday, without their having approached him first. There was a pause, a weary sigh, and back came the answer: 'Well, if I did, I can't remember.' It was Friday.

One thing which shone through all this deviousness was his unswerving loyalty to Tony Blair. By far the easiest line of defence he could have adopted was to say that Blair had gone behind the backs of Jack Straw, Marjorie Mowlam and others by conscripting him into the campaign and that it would create difficulties for Blair if the secret came out. But he did not. He took the whole responsibility upon himself and pleaded his cause on the grounds that he was the one who would be landed in trouble. He even suggested that if I wanted to damage him, I might prefer to write about how his relationship with Gordon Brown had broken down.

Even after the *Observer* piece appeared, I was accused by another of the organizers of the Blair campaign of having invented Mandelson's role. I was told in no uncertain terms that had Mandelson been anywhere near the campaign, it would have been impossible to round up the signatures of 154 MPs. There was general disbelief that Blair would want to risk the sort of reaction in the parliamentary party which Mandelson's involvement might trigger. *Tribune* had been intending to name Mandelson as a member of Blair's team, but received such an adamant denial from one of Blair's campaign managers that the Editor, Mark Seddon, decided not to. He subsequently received a genuine apology.

It was all still officially a secret on the day of Blair's election, when around 300 politicians, peers, celebrities, thinkers, organizers, officials, office-holders, friends, relatives and others who had participated in his campaign gathered for the victory celebration in the hall next to Westminster Abbey. Like an Oscar winner, Blair ran through a long list of people whom he wished to thank for their efforts over the previous few weeks, some of them famous, some close to him personally. In the middle of it all, without any explanation, he gave thanks to *Bobby, who worked so hard.* Later, when the speeches were over and there was time for small talk, this cryptic phrase lingered tantalizingly in the memory. No one outside the tiny circle of the new leader's advisers knew of any 'Bobby' who fitted such a billing. Those in the know refused to say.

When the following Sunday's *Observer* ran a photograph of 'Bobby', informing those who had not already read it tucked away in the

Peterborough column of the *Daily Telegraph* that he was Peter Mandelson, and that the nickname was derived from a joke within the Blair circle that he was like a younger brother to a reincarnated Jack Kennedy, it provoked mystified telephone calls from Labour MPs who still refused to believe that Mandelson was really that close to the new leader. All such doubts were laid to rest by the BBC's incorrigible Nicholas Jones, who wrote an account spread across two pages of the *Guardian* about Mandelson's part in the campaign. One detail he gave was that he had personally received five messages on his bleep in one day, telling him to ring Peter Mandelson.[42] This was not a record: there is another television journalist who had six bleeps in one day, all with the same message.

The effect of all this secretiveness and its inevitable exposure was to catapult Mandelson to a level of personal unpopularity exceeding anything that had come before. It is almost a truism to say he became like a lightning-rod for Tony Blair. Direct attacks on the leader himself from within the Labour Party were very rare, because of the scale of his victory in the leadership election and because the party so badly needed him to succeed; but to attack Mandelson as the favourite who has no friends became a popular sport. For instance, Clare Short, then Labour's Shadow Minister for Women, inserted a throwaway line in the midst of an essay on the meaning of 'socialism'.

> Our right are the pragmatists who seek power in any way that is available. As Herbert Morrison said – and no doubt his grandson agrees – Socialism is whatever the Labour Government does. Politics needs pragmatists – just as it needs creeps – but it also needs honest, creative thinking and pragmatists tend not to produce it.[43]

There was an occasion when Mandelson was sitting alone on parliament's green benches waiting for Prime Minister's Question Time to begin. As other MPs piled in, the spaces on other side of him remained unfilled. One MP sat down on the bench behind him and remarked, loudly enough for him to hear: 'I don't want to sit next to the most hated man in the Labour Party!'[44]

In 1995, after Mandelson had supported Smith's reforms, and Burlison had moved to London, there was a half-hearted attempt from within the regional GMB to take revenge on him by deselecting him. It came to nothing, not least because the unions had lost the power they once had to influence the choice of MPs.

There was some speculation in the tearoom as to what made Mandelson do it, because he had put himself in the difficult position where his entire political future, for as far ahead as anyone could see, would depend on his relationship with Tony Blair. It was mischievously suggested that he could not help himself: he enjoyed the secret power exercised by spin doctors so much that he was addicted to it. If so, presumably someone will spot a gap in the market and open a de-tox unit one day for compulsive spinners, in which patients will have to be deprived of newspapers, televisions, radios and telephones, and then carefully watched in case they take the ancillary staff to one side to tell them – on the strict understanding that this information must never be traced to its source – that close friends of the patient have been impressed by his progress.

Because Mandelson's position as a confidential adviser was unofficial and semi-secret, it invited exaggeration and each exaggeration added to his unpopularity. Rumour had it that he was the author of Blair's first leader's speech to the Labour Party, with its coded reference to the abolition of Clause Four. Mandelson had indeed been consulted, and was acting as an unofficial spin doctor at the party conference, but as Blair's new press secretary, Alastair Campbell, pointedly remarked in a newspaper article, 'I know from the days when Peter was a *People* columnist that writing was never his strong point, and that he had to look to his friends to help him out.'[47] Those who worked on the *Daily Mirror* political staff at the time were conscious of the weekly calls to Alastair Campbell as Mandelson agonized over his column.

Conversely, during the political struggle which preceded the abolition of Clause Four, a BBC correspondent reported an unnamed source close to Tony Blair who had described the TGWU leader Bill Morris as 'confused, muddled and pusillanimous'. On this occasion, Campbell used the columns of *Tribune* to exonerate himself, without denying that the quote was genuine, leaving no one in serious doubt as to who had made it.

In April 1995, news leaked out that Mandelson was on the point of being given his first formal position in the parliamentary party, as a junior whip, along with five other MPs from the 1992 intake. At once, the whips' office was inundated with complaints from MPs, creating such a furore that the announcement had to be held up for five days to overcome objections from the deputy chief whip, Don Dixon.

Later in the year, Mandelson was sent to be the candidate's minder in a by-election in Littleborough and Saddleworth, a rural, Tory-held seat in the Pennines, between Oldham and Rochdale. Times had changed since his last by-election in Newbury. First, Labour no longer allowed contests like these to go by default, knowing that if their vote fell it was only because their supporters were defecting to the Liberal Democrats, increasing the chance of a defeat for the Tories. After another bad by-election result for Labour, at Christchurch in July 1993, Mandelson had written a warning that if the Liberal Democrats were allowed to grow unchallenged, they could help the Conservatives to hold on to seats where the opposition was evenly divided, or even take votes off Labour.[46] The point had been taken. Since the Eastleigh by-election late in John Smith's tenure, the party had gone into these seemingly hopeless seats with the serious intention of at least coming second behind the Liberal Democrats, if they could not win.

The other difference was that Mandelson himself was no longer a junior trying to impress the leader, but the leader's trusted adviser. The strategy pursued in Littleborough and Saddleworth had to be cleared in every detail with a campaign committee which included John Prescott and Philip Gould, but it was without doubt Mandelson's campaign. He sat at the candidate's side at every press conference, personally fielding many of the trickier questions and giving private briefings afterwards to anyone thought worthy of them.

A memorable campaign it was too. Labour's candidate, Phil Woolas, was a successful student politician who had served time in television and was currently Director of Communications at the GMB. During the biggest political battle of John Smith's leadership, over the one-member, one-vote issue, the GMB had been his most important opponent, and Woolas personally was plainly not signed up to the 'modernizer' agenda. It might also be relevant to mention that as a student Woolas had been a fan of The Stranglers, whose greatest hit, *Golden Brown*, has been interpreted as a panegyric to cannabis. Come the by-election, he had been transformed into a family man, a regular churchgoer and an out-and-out modernizer with very stern views on drugs. Labour ran an aggressive campaign aimed directly at the Liberal Democrat candidate, Chris Davies, concentrating in particular on a speech he had made to a Liberal Democrat annual conference calling for a Royal Commission to look into the possibility of legalizing cannabis. Not only that, Davies was attacked for favouring tax increases. Notes supplied to Labour canvassers urged them to tell wavering Liberal Democrat voters that Davies had 'weird' ideas.

Running such a calculatedly right-wing campaign predictably did not please everyone. Most notably, the 'soft left' MP, Richard Burden, a former Liberal, complained afterwards: 'I, for one, was ashamed of some of the messages we were outing at Littleborough and Saddleworth and I think the time has come to say so.'[47] At the last meeting of the parliamentary Labour Party before the summer break, the veteran MP, David Winnick, loudly complained about a junior whip who appeared to have more power in the party than any member of the Shadow Cabinet. His remarks were greeted by loud cries of 'Name him!' But whether they liked it or not, the campaign ended successfully: Labour's vote increased by a third on its 1992 level, while the Conservative and Liberal Democrat votes fell. Moreover, the campaign seemed to repair Mandelson's relationship with John Prescott. In the next reshuffling of Labour's frontbench, the following October, Mandelson moved up to be a Shadow Minister in Prescott's team, responsible for civil service issues and for campaigning in marginal seats.

More importantly, Mandelson was soon back performing part of the function he had carried out so successfully at the 1987 general election eight years earlier, after yet another Director of Communications had resigned. Joy Johnson, former Westminster News Editor for the BBC, left after a difficult year in charge of planning the impending general election, another experienced journalist who had discovered that operating in the political jungle close to a beast as carniverous as Mandelson was more aggravation than it was worth. No one was formally appointed to fill her vacant post. Instead, Tony Blair informed the Shadow Cabinet during one of its weekend meetings that, from there on, Mandelson would be in charge of all the physical arrangements for the coming general election.

Despite all these commitments, Mandelson pushed ahead with an ambitious plan to re-establish himself as a politician rather than a mere spin doctor, by publishing a book of political philosophy. Daringly, he teamed up with Roger Liddle, a former special adviser to the last Labour Secretary of State for Transport, William Rodgers, one of the founders of the SDP. Liddle's last important foray into national politics, before teaming up with Mandelson, was as SDP candidate in the Fulham by-election. Fortunately for the party he subsequently rejoined, he was a poor candidate and was easily beaten by Labour's Nick Raynsford. His connection with Mandelson dated back to when they had both been Lambeth councillors.

The book appeared in February 1996 after a trickle of speculation which guaranteed enough sales to repay the publishers' investment. Helped by a generous advertising budget, it went almost immediately into the best-seller lists. This was remarkable for any book about politics, particularly one written so cautiously. Large parts of it are infested with sentences which express one opinion while simultaneously covering its opposite. To quote a real example, 'While giving people real hope of change, Labour must take care not to promise more than can realistically be delivered.'[48] This style of writing, common in political manifestos, is not so much a stimulus to thought as a series of instructions as to what you may not think. You are not to expect unrealistic promises, but neither must you think that the hope of change will be unreal.

There are other passages which are not written in the cautious language of politicians, but where assertions are made whose meaning is unmistak-able. For example, there is a condemnation of the British education system for having 'always given priority to the interests of an academic élite rather than to high general standards of education and the promotion of voca-tional qualifications for the broad majority of young people'; of the teachers' unions for having concentrated on 'pay and resources, rather than on the curriculum and pupil attainments'; and of 'education egalitarians' for showing 'a far greater concern for the social balance of a school's admissions than for the destination of a school's graduates'.[49]

When Roy Hattersley intervened in the debate on Labour's education policy, critics suggested that as the childless husband of a former head-mistress, he represented the 'producer' interest whereas Blair and Blunkett spoke for 'consumers' as the parents of children of school age. Blair and Harriet Harman have famously come under fire from other quarters for putting their children's interests before the party's. If or when Mandelson establishes his reputation as someone with stimulating views on educa-tion, someone will ask how he can be so certain that he knows what he is talking about, having no connection with the education system as either a producer or a consumer.

Part of the answer is that Mandelson has spent huge amounts of time in the past decade ingesting and distilling polling data. The Labour Party began the gathering of political intelligence by sounding out the opinions of small target groups, which is known as qualitative polling, only after Mandelson became Director of Communications. He has probably been involved in this activity more than any other practising politician. As a means of informing policy, it has obvious appeal to someone with a compulsive need to be in control, because it necessarily concentrates influence in a few hands. The people who make up the sample do not know they are giving valued advice to a political party, or the point of the exercise is lost; and only a limited number of people who do know can be allowed to listen while they are talking. This makes many politicians hostile to qualitative polling. According to Tony Benn, hearing the first presentation by the Shadow Communications Agency of the results of qualitative polling made him feel 'physically sick', the findings being full of 'what you can read every day in the *Sun*, the *Mail*, the *Daily Express*, the *Telegraph*, and so on'.[50] Some MPs prefer to rely for their information on the state of public opinion on the letters they receive, the people who visit their surgeries and the audiences in public meetings; but the discipline of having constantly to hear the sometimes unpalatable views of people who are not involved in politics must guard against over-optimistic assumptions about the state of public opinion.

At a later point in the book, the authors praise Margaret Thatcher's fortitude in forcing through the privatization of the British National Oil Corporation against the sullen resistance of the civil service and claim that with her resolve she had more in common with Tony Blair than John Major. It would seem an obvious point to make here that Thatcher was driven by ideology. There is an ambiguity at the centre of the book, in that the authors praise Tony Blair for being a strong leader capable of routing opponents in intellectual debate, but they themselves seem to make a virtue of having no philosophy, but only everyday virtues: 'There is no single big idea, no clever policy wheeze which is going to transform Britain's prospects overnight,' they say at one point; and at another 'the new politics is not – rather should not be – a question of high theory'.[51] Elsewhere in the book, the authors praise an audience of young party members who gave the former Prime Minister, Jim Callaghan, a hearty round of applause, in that it showed a new respect in New Labour for the party's leaders, but they themselves, in their first excursion into political philosophy, do not reveal much reverence or even curiosity about others who might have provided the Labour Party with intellectual inspiration in the past. Crosland is dealt with in two paragraphs for displaying his 'sadly misplaced' optimism about economic growth and for failing to appreciate the risks of an 'over-mighty and overly high spending state'. There is no reference to anything he got right, but at least his name is mentioned. The writers who influenced the young Tony Blair are also listed but, overall, the impression is that New Labour is a set of ideas with no intellectual antecedents, belonging to no intellectual tradition because it is rooted in reality in a way which no previous set of ideas has ever been.

They would have written a much more remarkable book if they had adhered to the original outline which was sent to at least one other publisher and probably more, before a contract was signed with Faber and Faber. What appears in it must represent what Mandelson really thinks, because it would have been less than honest to offer the synopsis to a publisher if he did not believe it and had no intention of writing it.

While the published book applauded the young activists who applauded Jim Callaghan, the unpublished synopsis – without directly mentioning the former Prime Minister – was merciless in its analysis of his leadership style and the old union-based right of which he was the most distinguished member. The late Harold Wilson was also implicated in a 'steadily corrupting relationship between Labour government and the trade unions':

> The price which Labour had to pay to the unions ossified industrial structures, damaged economic performance, inhibited the development of modern social policies and public service reform, affronted popular ideas of liberty and, worst of all, distorted Labour's sense of right and wrong. It is an experience Labour must never ever repeat.

It promised 'illustrative anecdote' – coming, probably, from Roger Liddle and other former SDP members who had been on the inside track in 1974 to 1979 – to demonstrate the 'undue influence of trade unions and the timidity of Labour ministers in standing up to bullying behaviour', plus examples of 'hard decisions which Labour dodged because it was in hock to producer interests'. Further into the synopsis, the authors asserted that 'Labour found it impossible to overcome interest group resistance to public service reform; on social security, the defenders of Beveridge refused to give an inch.' It also promised anecdotes to illustrate how the Callaghan government's limited initiatives on social policy 'further identified the party with the inner-city poor and one-parent families'.

Callaghan's brief stint as leader of the opposition was also going to be rigorously exposed, in a chapter in which the atmosphere within the party after 1979 was to be 'vividly' recalled, including 'the pusillanimity of the Shadow Cabinet at the time which through spinelessness and fear allowed the SDP split to happen'. It was also going to 'explain the motives of those who set up the SDP'. In a later chapter, the authors announced they would praise the SDP's 'bold and early advocacy of trade union reform'.

The outline also promised to knock some of the shine off the reputation of John Smith, by 'criticizing John Smith's obstinacy in sticking to an electorally doomed Shadow Budget despite Neil Kinnock's better judgement' – a somewhat different story to the one Mandelson wrote while Smith was still alive. It promised details of the 'clash between Brown and Smith after the 1992 election over full employment', from which it may be surmised that Brown would have emerged in a better light than Smith.

The most contentious chapters promised to be the ones covering constitutional reform and electoral tactics. The authors were evidently not impressed with the Plant Commission, set up under Neil Kinnock as a quasi-Royal Commission on electoral reform, and promised to kick its main conclusions 'into touch'. Beginning with a sensible warning that over-ambitious plans for constitutional reforms could turn into a legislative nightmare which consumed so much time that more important questions were neglected, they then moved into politically dangerous waters. Their one 'safe' conclusion, in party terms, was that the demand for devolution in Scotland and Wales was genuine and would have to be met, but it was followed by the assertion that 'regional government for England should be firmly rejected' which would have landed Mandelson in severe difficulties within the northern regional Labour Party had it ever found its way into print, although it was qualified by a call to introduce 'democratic accountability' into the layers of regional administration which already exist; followed by the yet more contentious acknowledgement that the over-representation of Scotland and Wales at Westminster must end – with 'major political consequences for the Labour Party'.

Finally, there was to be a chapter with the provocative heading 'Does Labour Need a Coalition to Succeed?', which hinted that it might, because a Labour government would need more than one parliamentary term to enact its programme, and might not be able to win an overall majority a second time:

> No doubt some in both parties would explode at the prospect of doing a deal. But the majority would prefer to see a longer term stable left of centre government than a risky short-term, go-it-alone attitude prevailing. The worst scenario would be to dismiss any idea of a pact, only to be forced to confront it later if the election goes less well than expected. Taking on the issue in advance is the better option.[52]

At least here they were offering ideas rooted in past experience, from the troubled history of the Labour Party in the 1970s and 1980s, and they were proposing to take sides in the bitter schism within the right wing of the Labour Party at that time, between Callaghan and the 'cloth cap' faction on the one hand and the social democrats on the other. By praising the Social Democrats for their political foresight, blaming the schism on Callaghan and those who remained in the party, and suggesting that Labour's future might lie in a coalition with the Liberal Democrats, they would have been clear about which tradition they were upholding and might have performed a valuable service to the Labour Party. After the 1981 schism, social democracy became the strand of thought which dare not speak its own name, because in the atmosphere of suspicion and betrayal of the time, to call a Labour Party member a Social Democrat was to accuse them of being a potential traitor. It would have been a bold move indeed if a political figure of Mandelson's prominence had declared that, despite the gross tactical blunder committed by Roy Jenkins, David Owen and the rest, social democracy has always been in the mainstream of Labour Party thought and has made no small contribution to the liberties and social benefits Britons enjoy.

Unfortunately, the political risk was too great. Had he written the book he originally offered, Mandelson would at the very least have been forced to leave the frontbench. Consequently, New Labour as expounded in *The Blair Revolution* is a creed which sprang into being in 1994, acknowledges no authority within the party other than that of Tony Blair, and looks outward for all other sources of inspiration and authority. One reviewer, Will

Hutton, compared it with a 'political patchwork quilt which can easily be unpicked'.[53] Roy Hattersley complained that 'its domestic policy prescription is feeble and its excursion into political philosophy is absurd'.[54] Another Labour MP, Peter Kilfoyle, castigated the book for being 'dangerous in its reduction of complex social issues to glib phrases'.[55] Both Tony Blair and John Prescott took care not to be too closely associated with it, by letting it be known that they had not read it prior to publication, although it had been read by Blair's staff. It did, however, have box office success.

It is proof, if needed, that Mandelson is hard-working and talented. But the legend that he is an evil genius[56] is out of synch with reality. First, it is wrong to use the word 'evil' about someone who has not done anyone any genuine harm. He has helped to damage the careers of a few ambitious people while never knowingly underselling his own merits, but that is not the same as being fundamentally malignant. An unexpected and little-known side to his character is the way he relates to young children. Generally, the falsified sincerity which has been the making of so many successful politicians does not work with children, who respond only to what they can detect is genuine; and yet, unexpectedly, the Labour MP whom other politicians see as the reincarnation of Machiavelli has a wonderful rapport with the very young. There are numerous parents who can attest to his ability to talk to children without a trace of condescension, entering into their mental world as if he were their own age.

It is as if Mandelson is trapped in his own reputation for political deviousness, based on his successful dealings with journalists. In an age when a public, fed on images like that of Francis Urquhart, will believe almost any story about the depths of deviousness indulged in by professional politicians, Mandelson has been cast in that stereotype. In reality, someone as unscrupulous as Urquhart could only travel a certain distance even in the Conservative Party before being found out. In the Labour Party, the best way to succeed is to manoeuvre ruthlessly without anyone noticing. The late John Smith is a good example. It was Smith who destroyed Bryan Gould's career, but he did it with such an absence of personal malice that, in his memoirs, Gould seems unable to attribute any of his misfortunes to the former leader, venting his frustration on Mandelson as the one identifiable source of negative press coverage. Recalling how *The Times* had praised 'Sensible Mr Smith' for winning an argument over Labour's alternative to the poll tax, Gould was driven to comment, 'I still have no idea where these reports came from.'[57] Perhaps the first question to ask is who gained from them; but sensible Mr Smith comported himself with such an air of honest geniality that to this day no one believes that he might on occasions have played dirty. Had his heart not given out, he would have become Prime Minister.

Mandelson, by contrast, can hardly walk down a corridor in the House of Commons without everyone he passes pausing to wonder where he is going and what he is up to. A compulsive politician, with no private life, no personal hinterland and no political base of his own to sustain him should he ever fall out with the party leader, he is certainly clever, but perhaps not as shrewd as others who are playing the same game.

CHAPTER SEVEN

CALLING TONY BLAIR

Who, or what, or why, or where is Tony Blair? He rose through parliament at immense speed, to become the youngest ever leader of the Labour Party at the age of forty-one, with a prospect of being the century's youngest Prime Minister by the age of forty-four. Yet he arrived with clean hands, having stitched up no dirty deals, nor tacked with the political wind, abandoning long-held beliefs to hold a political base together. He was not even helped by nepotism. There was no Tony Blair the Elder. Bob is not his uncle, although he has a useful friend called Bobby. British Prime Ministers have for centuries been selecting their colleagues, but if it were still the prerogative of Labour MPs to choose their own leader, it is by no means certain that in 1994 they would have elected Tony Blair. He is the first leader of a major political party chosen by plebiscite.

The crowd made a competent choice. Blair applies himself to every problem with a steady and determined intelligence, without the flashy and erratic brilliance often found in the precociously successful. All the tasks that a modern politician is required to do, Blair does well. He can write coherently, speak fluently, smile continually, look relaxed on television, handle parliamentary debates, grasp the essentials of complicated policies or legislation quickly, stake out a clear position, give orders and inspire trust. Good luck has been his faithful companion. Blessed with a sharp mind, imposing good looks and a happy and secure family life, he also had the good fortune to begin a political career at just the right time to allow him to rise and rise without ever meeting a serious obstacle or suffering a serious setback, as if everything had been done to clear the way for him.

In 1983, the year when Tony Blair entered parliament, a much depleted band of Labour MPs returned to the Commons after the party's worst election for over fifty years and collectively resolved to settle down under new leaders and stop fighting among themselves. The big battles within the Labour Party after that date were fought outside parliament. Most MPs who entered parliament from 1983 onwards were therefore spared the worst of internecine party warfare, as well as being denied the pressures of government office. Blair is the most eminent of those who have enjoyed the benefits of battles won by Neil Kinnock, John Smith and many others.

Somewhere in the future, luck, youth and good looks will desert him and the boyish zest with which he exploited his early good fortune will fade into the past. That is the moment at which Blair's enemies hope his fairy-tale success story will end. The most enduring taunt levelled at him is that he is Tony Blur, the shallow product of clever marketing, a man of no experience with no strongly held opinions. In moments of crisis, political leaders who lack deep conviction revert to type and career helplessly from one short-term solution to another, pushed this way and that by whoever shouts loudest. This is what the Conservative Party expects and hopes will happen to Tony Blair.

They may be disappointed. The fact that Blair is untested does not make him a weakling. In the year 1978, Margaret Thatcher was an unknown quantity who had been cushioned by her husband's money and by the dearth of women Tory MPs capable of holding their own at Cabinet level. She was projected into office by the obstinacy of Edward Heath and the indecision of his natural successor, William Whitelaw. She was not held in great public esteem and she won the election on the unpopularity of the Labour government rather than any qualities of her own. No one could have accurately forecast whether she would hold her nerve in crises like the 1981 recession or the invasion of the Falklands.

It is illustrative that Tony Blair appears to identify more with her than with Harold Wilson or other election-winning leaders of the Labour Party. He does not betray much respect, either, for John Major, who exhibits the same none-too-honourable skill as Wilson at manoeuvring and manipulating to hold together a weakened administration and a divided party. Survival for survival's sake is evidently not on Blair's list of aspirations. In one famous comment, he listed Margaret Thatcher, Neil Kinnock and John Smith as leaders he admired. He has good reason to be grateful to

Kinnock and to Smith, who cleared the way for his meteoric rise. The mention of Thatcher was what caused comment at the time. It was assumed to be a shrewd pitch to win back the skilled working-class vote which Thatcher stole from the Labour Party, but it also appears to have been his way of indicating that his intention is to be as true to himself under pressure as she was to herself. 'The great thing is to stick by what we think and believe,' he said; though he added, by way of a qualification, that 'then she came to confuse the notion of knowing your own mind with refusing to listen to anyone else. I do not admire that.'[1] Lady Thatcher returned the compliment, by saying of Blair: 'He says he believes in the things he is advocating and I believe he does.'[2]

Since a Prime Minister in waiting is necessarily unknown and untested, one way to try to define Tony Blair is to use Spinoza's maxim that finite things are defined by what they are not, and run though some of the things which cannot be said of Tony Blair.

He is not an obsessive who is unaware that there is life outside politics. He became a political activist surprisingly late, after leaving university, at the same time as he was establishing an alternative career for himself, and he has gone to great pains to protect his family life. He is not a wheeler-dealer, or a vote-fixer, or a front man for entrenched interests. Between 1980 and 1993, the rules of the Labour Party compelled any credible leadership candidate to build a political base among the big affiliated trade unions. Neil Kinnock and John Smith were selected first and foremost by the union block vote, but it is highly improbable that any convocation of general secretaries would have chosen Tony Blair. Nor did he win the 1994 leadership contest by being a compromise candidate tolerable to both wings of a divided party, like Michael Foot or Neil Kinnock. On the contrary, in the struggle between 'modernizers' and 'traditionalists', Blair's emergence was an outright win for the modernizers, which a large majority within the Labour Party saw as a disturbing and ominous development.

Blair is not a fanatic, and with due respect to the authors of a book called *The Blair Revolution*, he is not a revolutionary. Although he is a radical Christian, he does not promise a future in which the first shall be last and the last shall be first. In Blair's Britain, the first shall face fair, non-punitive rates of taxation and the last shall have enhanced opportunities for reskilling and self-improvement. 'A hand up, not a hand out,' is one of Blair's aphorisms.

Although he is in the Labour Party, he is not really *of* the Labour Party. The cultural icons which hold the party together – the *Red Flag*, the Tolpuddle Martyrs, *The Ragged Trousered Philanthropists*, banners emblazoned with the names of defunct miners' lodges, composite resolutions to party conference – these foolish things do not mean very much to Tony Blair. There are people for whom the Labour Party, in or out of government office, is a way of life worth preserving for its own sake. Not Tony Blair. For him, the purpose of democratic political activity is to be in government. During one of his speeches to a trade union audience, which was going badly and threatened to be greeted with polite applause at best, he suddenly livened up by giving vent to his frustration at being out of power:

> I sit there in the House of Commons, I have ever since 1983, sitting there opposite me are people doing things – the poll tax, the benefit cuts, the privatization of decent public health services, what has happened in the Health Service, in our education service – I have sat there and I have watched those people ruin our country, ruin it . . .
>
> In my own mind, I have complete confidence in the beliefs I hold dear. I know why I am in the Labour Party. I know why I have joined this Party and worked for it for the last twenty years. It is because when you look around your society you see the injustice, you see the opportunity denied, you see the unfairness, you see all that élitism at the top, you see that establishment still there . . . and you look around even beyond our country and you see a world which has plenty and yet is torn by starvation and war.
>
> There are still great causes to unite decent people. There are still great fights and struggles to be won out there. But what has come home to me more than anything else is the utter futility of Opposition. I did not join the Labour Party to join a party of protest. I joined it as a party of government and I will make sure that it is a party of government.[3]

As it happens, Labour was the party of government when he joined, because he was already out of his teens when he decided to become politically active. But why, given his firm views on the futility of opposition, he should decide to become a Labour MP in the early 1980s is not instantly obvious. There was a history of political ambition in the Blair family, but it was not directed towards the left. His father, Leo Blair, was chairman of the Durham Conservative Association with a good chance of becoming a Conservative MP had he not been struck down by a stroke in 1963. No other family member, nor any of Blair's friends from childhood or adolescence, took up politics, with the striking exception of his office manager, Anji Hunter, whom he has known since the age of sixteen.

Blair himself does not encourage the idea that there is an early formative experience which made him a man of the left, which can be uncovered by rooting around in his early life. His father's illness caused a sharp drop in his social status and in the family income, but this seems to have had less effect on Blair than a similar blip in the family fortune had on an adolescent John Major. Blair emerged from his childhood with the easy confidence of someone raised in a middle-class milieu, within which ambition, competitiveness and success were the norm. Like a member of the old British ruling class, Blair had no particular geographical roots. When he was five, his parents settled in Durham, but he was not a Durham boy in the way that John Smith, for example, was from west Scotland, or Neil Kinnock from south Wales. He hardly had time to acquaint himself with Durham Cathedral before he was off, spending more time in boarding schools than at home. Until he was ten, there was a powerful if distant figure of authority dominating the home, then, suddenly, that man was transformed into someone frail and dependent on a self-effacing mother who never competed in the outside world, believing that a woman's role was to hold a family together.

However, since much has been made of Blair's middle-class background, it is perhaps worth pointing out that, like Vladimir Lenin, he was only a generation away from humble beginnings. His mother, Hazel Corscadden, came from Donegal, but moved to Glasgow after her father's death. Her stepfather was a butcher. The person Tony Blair knew as his paternal grandfather was a former Glasgow shipyard rigger named James Blair. Leo Blair's first political experience was as a member of the Young Communist League, an unremarkable beginning for a working-class boy from Clydeside. He moved up socially and changed his politics before he had returned from military service, married, taken a job with the Inland Revenue and begun his law studies.

There was a secret in the Blair family, which emerged only when the *Daily Mail* researched the family tree of the prospective new Labour Party leader in 1994. Leo Blair was not the natural son of James Blair, but the product of a liaison between a married woman named Celia Ridgeway and an actor named Charles Parson, who used the stage name Jimmy

Lynton.[4] Seemingly, even Leo Blair's three children – two sons and a daughter – did not know of this, although their natural grandfather was commemorated in the middle names given to the second son, Anthony Charles Lynton Blair, born in Edinburgh on 6 May 1953.

Soon after Tony's birth, the family moved to Adelaide, where Leo had obtained his first lectureship. They settled in Durham in 1958 and there Leo Blair enjoyed a glittering career as a self-made Tory and regional television celebrity. Tony Blair later recognized in both Thatcher and Norman Tebbit the sort of Conservative his father might have been.[5] However, in 1963 Leo Blair was struck down by a massive stroke which killed his political and professional ambitions and caused an acute drop in the family's living standards – although happily he survived and joined the Shrewsbury Labour Party during a recruitment drive inspired by his son in September 1995. Previously, there had been no problem about paying for the two boys to be privately educated. Subsequently, if Tony had been less bright, he would have had to go to a state school, but in fact he won a scholarship to Fettes, one of Scotland's top public schools.

It might be possible to construct an explanation of Blair's politics out of this childhood disaster, which brought home to him the limits of self-sufficiency. He was to have another early and grim reminder of the value of the National Health Service when his younger sister, Sarah, fell seriously ill from rheumatoid arthritis just as her father was beginning to mend. She was confined to hospital for two years. 'My early years seem to have been spent in and out of hospital in Durham,' he later remarked.[6] Tragedy struck the family for the third time almost immediately after Blair graduated from Oxford University, when his mother died. And, just in case he had forgotten, he was given another sharp reminder of human vulnerability very soon after his election to parliament. At a public meeting in Blair's Sedgefield constituency, in November 1983, a local man named Arthur Whiteley rose and spoke with some passion about the NHS, having recently been told that he would have to wait to twelve to eighteen months for the open heart surgery he needed. Soon after he had sat down, he had a fatal heart attack.[7]

It would have been understandable if the disruption and instability which illness introduced to his family life had turned the young Blair into an adolescent rebel – which, after a fashion, it did. As a teenager, he was difficult to control and enjoyed showing off. At school, he showed promise as an actor. He was chosen to play Mark Antony in *Julius Caesar* at the age of fifteen, and followed that in his final year by playing the star role in R.C. Sherriff's *Captain Stanhope*. At university he was, famously, the lead singer in a band called *Ugly Rumours*. His first choice of profession, as a barrister, has obvious attractions for a natural exhibitionist. Young, tall, good-looking, clever and self-confident, he was a nightmare for some of the teachers who had to exert authority over him. 'He was the most difficult boy I ever had to deal with,' one former master at Fettes was reported as saying.[8]

Yet Blair was deeply serious, hard-working, religious and single-minded. Even as a long-haired rock singer at university in the early 1970s, he never so much as smoked one cannabis joint, although in a sideswipe at US President, Bill Clinton, he later claimed that if he had, he would have inhaled.[9] Instead, time which could have been spent stoned and listening to Pink Floyd was given over to an intense discussion group centred around a mature student from Australia called Peter Thomson, who was one of the first to discover that Blair's anarchic exterior was no more than a façade. When he encountered people in authority who made sense to him, Blair could be respectful and loyal, as he was with Thomson.

Having decided there was more to life than running his father's estate agency, Thomson was partway through a spiritual journey which would include being removed from one curacy in Melbourne as a suspected communist, and from another for establishing a scrap-metal business to create jobs in his parish, before he made a well-publicized return to Britain in 1996 to become, at Blair's suggestion, Vicar of St Luke's, Holloway, and a spiritual confidant of the Labour leader. He was blending his own mix of liberation theology based partly on the writings of a 1930s philosopher named John Macmurray, to whom the Labour Party leader acknowledges an intellectual debt,[10] whose most famous quote is that 'All meaningful knowledge is for the sake of action, all meaningful action is for the sake of friendship.' The idea of defining your own being through relationships with others, in a voyage of discovery which was allowed to be great fun as well as deeply serious, had instant appeal for Blair. 'I remember the first time I met him in that Afghan coat,' Thomson recalled later. 'He wasn't particularly religious, but he was just alive. Tony had never heard theology spoken of in this way and he devoured the stuff quickly, but I had no idea just how deeply it had got to him.'[11]

The circle around Peter Thomson was not really one for future politicians, although one or two of its members took up activism in an amateurish way. Blair had not yet made any of the political contacts which would be useful to him later, and came out of Oxford University still apparently untouched by political ambition. His first recorded political act was to cast his vote in the 1975 referendum in favour of Britain's continued membership of the Common Market. Then, very soon after leaving university, he leased a basement flat in Chelsea and joined the Labour Party. As sometimes happens to those who show a beginner's enthusiasm, he was made branch secretary, and therefore *ex-officio* a member of the constituency general committee at his first meeting.

This was the activist's route into politics, but not the one for Tony Blair. He made a much more important decision, in retrospect, when he accepted an invitation to a friend's birthday party at a golf club in Beaconsfield, one of the most middle-class and Tory-voting towns in southern England. There he become involved in a conversation with Colin Fawcett, a QC who lived in Beaconsfield, from whom he sought advice on his own professional future. Possibly because of Blair's political sympathies, which were unusual in that setting, Fawcett agreed to mention his name to a fellow barrister, Alexander Irvine, who was also a Labour Party member. Irvine had been a contemporary and friend of John Smith's at Glasgow University and would rise to be made a life peer in 1987 and Shadow Lord Chancellor in 1992. There was no vacancy in Irvine's chambers for a new pupil, because he already had one in Cherie Booth, whose academic qualifications were more impressive than Blair's, since she had obtained the top law degree of her year at the London School of Economics. Nonetheless, Irvine was persuaded by Blair's infectious enthusiasm to take on a second. His two pupils began as rivals and colleagues, and became husband and wife.

While Blair's commitment to the Labour Party was something he reached relatively late, Cherie Booth's background was steeped both in Labour politics and in social insecurity and hard times. Her mother came from a working-class, Labour-voting Roman Catholic family in Liverpool and had been, in effect, a single parent, moving from job to job, including work in a fish and chip shop while raising her two daughters. Their actor father, Tony Booth, enjoyed a life of heavy drinking and celebrity status as the fictional scouse son-in-law of Alf Garnett in the hugely popular television series *Till Death Us Do Part*. In the late 1970s, Booth curbed his drinking, achieved a reconciliation with his daughters and formed a stable relationship with the *Coronation Street* actress, Pat Phoenix. Both became well-known as active Labour Party supporters. The older Booth, in particular, was a committed Bennite. Visiting Chesterfield in March 1984 to campaign for Tony Benn, he took exception to hearing Pat Phoenix being asked by a BBC radio reporter, John Harrison, whether she was putting her career at risk by associating with a politician as controversial as Benn, and shouted at him to direct similar questions to stars who had declared their support for the Conservative Party. The exchange was recorded, and may even now be awaiting rediscovery somewhere in the BBC's vaults.[12]

Cherie Booth consequently moved into political activism earlier than Blair. She was a party member from 1972, sharing a house with a fellow lawyer, Maggie Rae. Maggie was then in the Communist Party but later switched to the Labour Party and married Alan Howarth, who worked for the party in the House of Commons. By night Howarth was active in the Newham North East Labour Party, which became infamous for deselecting its sitting Labour MP, the former Education Secretary, Reg Prentice.

In the early 1980s, Cherie was adopted as Labour candidate for Thanet North. It was a safe Conservative seat which she had no chance of winning, but having fought one hopeless seat could only improve her chances of a winnable seat at the following election. The high point of the 1983 election campaign in Thanet North was a public meeting during which she shared a platform with 'the two Tonys who have inspired her in her quest for socialism'. Blair was not one of the Tonys. They were her father, Tony Booth, and Tony Benn. The photograph of the three was dug out of the archives and used by the *Daily Express* during a brief attempt in 1996 to expose Cherie as Britain's version of Hillary Clinton, a political wife with a potentially sinister influence over her husband. Cherie Blair's activism continued after the general election, when she was elected to the executive of the Labour Co-ordinating Committee, before she pulled out and transferred her ambitions to her career as a barrister.

Tony and Cherie married in 1980, and shortly afterwards moved into their first house, in Mapledene Road, Hackney, transferring their party membership to the Queensbridge ward. Their circle of acquaintances widened. The house which backed on to the Blairs' was occupied by Charles Clarke, who was employed as researcher to the Shadow Education Secretary, Neil Kinnock. The next-door house in Mapledene Road was bought by Barry Cox, who rose to be head of corporate affairs at London Weekend Television, and one of a clutch of LWT executives who became millionaires as a result of the merger with Granada. Cox is one of many people who met Blair by accident early on, and became a lifelong admirer. In summer 1994, he was the main source of cash for the Blair leadership campaign, and took time off to be its office organizer. One of Cox's journalist friends, who then lived in Hackney and came to know the Blairs well, was the *Financial Times* journalist, John Lloyd, a future editor of the *New Statesman*. At a dinner party at the Irvines', the Blairs met Henry Hodge, another barrister on his way to becoming an important figure in the Law Society, and his wife, Margaret, the long-serving leader of Islington council.

Politically, the Blairs were located in what would now be called the 'soft left'. To some of those on the right, like Reg Prentice, who watched in horror as the Labour Party metamorphozed before their eyes, the distinction between 'soft' and 'hard' left was academic. They were all threatening the traditional relationship of docile respect which Labour MPs enjoyed with their constituency parties. Even then, however, there were significant differences of opinion over how activists were to exercise the increased power they were claiming. At their first meeting of Queensbridge ward party, the Blairs were part of the minority who agreed in principle to widening the franchise for electing the party leader, but wanted it done on a basis of one-member, one-vote rather than an electoral college.[13]

Their friend, Alan Haworth, was one of the 'Newham Seven' who came close to being jailed for their part in the plot against Reg Prentice, in which the Militant Tendency was also implicated, yet Haworth was able to continue working as a trusted official, privy to Shadow Cabinet meetings. He became a friend of John Smith, who elevated him to the position of Secretary of the Parliamentary Labour Party in 1992. In 1981, Haworth became membership secretary of the Labour Co-ordinating Committee, one of the most influential and enduring of the party's left-wing pressure groups, and persuaded Blair to join. The LCC was also identified as part of the Bennite coalition, but by 1981 those who saw it close-up could already see it as a potential nucleus for a breakaway 'soft left', distrustful of Benn, hostile to Trotskyism and willing to cooperate with Michael Foot. Like other future 'modernizers', Blair's sympathies in the 1981 deputy leadership election were with the compromise candidate, Jon Silkin. He had no vote, but when asked how he would have voted in the second round, after Silkin's elimination, Blair pronounced that he would not have voted for Benn.

The feud between the rising Bennite left and the traditional right was fought more bitterly and destructively in the capital than anywhere else in the country, not least in Hackney, where the sitting MP was Ron Brown, brother of the former Deputy Prime Minister, who had to fight off a spirited attempt to deselect him in 1981 for his suspected SDP sympathies. No sooner had he been saved by the efforts of Tony Blair and others than he let them down by jumping ship anyway. Only after Blair had become leader of the Labour Party did Brown commit himself to voting Labour again.

The single most memorable piece of legal advice Blair ever gave was to the General Secretary of the Labour Party, Jim Mortimer, who was engaged in the first moves to expel Militant's leaders from the party, and proposed for this purpose to define 'members' of the Tendency as those who could be shown to hold a leading position in it. John Smith doubted whether the definition would hold up if it was challenged in court, and urged Mortimer to consult Irvine's Chambers. The advice received from barristers Alexander Irvine and Anthony Blair was that constitutionally the National Executive would be 'obliged to expel all Militant Tendency members once the Militant Tendency had been declared ineligible to affiliate to the Party'.[14]

So, from the moment he entered Irvine's Chambers, Blair had access to people whom he could never have reached through doggedly attending branch party meetings. He and Cherie both specialized in employment law, which allowed him to develop useful contacts in the trade unions and get his name into print for the first time, writing for the *New Statesman*. Blair moved easily in the company of professionals who were ambitious and on their way to becoming eminent in their fields. Maggie Rae, who knew him professionally as well as socially, said: 'If you have given him a tricky job to do and he has put his mind to it, you'll see that he will do it brilliantly. He does not do it effortlessly, but he does it brilliantly. When people say he is shallow, they haven't understood him at all. He has worked hard at ideas, just as he worked hard mastering complicated briefs.'[15]

However, in the London Labour Party of the time, Blair was not so obviously on the road to success. Brian Sedgemore, a fellow barrister and former parliamentary aide to Tony Benn, who fitted more comfortably into the London left at the time, is not so flattering about Blair, the young party activist, whom he remembers as a figure on the edge, who amazed everyone when he revealed his parliamentary ambitions. Soon after Blair's accession to the leadership, Sedgemore said:

> I have been quite surprised at how he has coped with questions and interviews since he was standing. He is quite stoically bland. The sheer blandness of it is difficult to penetrate, if he can hold it and not be embarrassed. The blandness is so totally inherent that it is quite difficult to embarrass him. He will cope with the party because I don't think anyone will launch an attack on him, at least until he is Prime Minister. After he is Prime Minister, I think the whole thing will change. Then he will have a lot of problems in the Labour Party.[16]

When both the Blairs set out looking for a seat in 1980, Cherie at least had the advantage of being a woman at a time when positive discrimination was coming into fashion; but neither Tony Blair's politics nor his personal background worked in his favour. There were not many former public school boys chosen to fight safe Labour seats in 1983; but there was a glut of lawyers on the candidates' circuit. The story is told that when Blair was introduced by Barry Cox to the future television mogul, Greg Dyke, and admitted he wanted to be a Labour MP, Dyke exclaimed: 'Not another fucking London barrister!' On the other hand, when he went seat-hunting in the north-east of England, hoping to capitalize on his Durham childhood and union contacts, he looked suspiciously left wing for the old heartland where the right never lost control. He received one nomination when he put in for Middlesborough, and failed to make the shortlist. The seat went to Stuart Bell, a Newcastle-based barrister whose credentials were better established on the right of the party.

Blair then had a lucky break in April 1982 when he was selected to fight a by-election in Beaconsfield, caused by the death of the ultra-right-wing Tory, Ronald Bell. He benefited from his young, clean-cut appearance which was likely to appeal to Labour voters tempted to switch to the feared SDP–Liberal alliance. As it happened, it made no difference whom Labour selected. On 3 April, Argentina invaded the Falklands, and the whole campaign was fought against the background of the 'Falklands Factor', making it the only parliamentary by-election in the entire period of Conservative rule from 1979 to produce a swing in favour of the government. The campaign introduced Blair to the rigours of press conferences attended by aggressive journalists from unfriendly national newspapers, and introduced him to visiting Labour MPs and to the party's Walworth Road headquarters. He called there to ask for literature to read so that he could familiarize himself with party policy. Years later, he recalled the astonished expressions of the researchers who had to deal with him. In that period of the Labour Party's history, candidates rarely seemed to care what the official line was, particularly if they were standing in the Tories' rural heartland, yet here was one, turning up on their doorstep, demanding to be told what he was supposed to say. One face was familiar: Adam Sharples, a researcher and the main author of the party's highly ambitious Alternative Economic Strategy, was the self-same Adam Sharples whom Blair remembered well as one of the musicians from *Ugly Rumours.*

Blair's courtesy made a lasting impression on Roy Hattersley, who turned out to campaign in Beaconsfield. He was touched afterwards to receive a hand-written letter from Blair, thanking him. From all the dozens of by-elections in which Hattersley had taken part, Blair was the only candidate other than Tony Benn to take the trouble to write. Meanwhile, it was his loyalty which commended him to Michael Foot. The old rebel had had so much trouble by now from the right and the left that it was a relief to turn up in Beaconsfield to meet a bright young candidate who was anxious to give him all the support he could. He was so delighted, in fact, that he singled Blair out for praise on *Newsnight*, forecasting that he had 'a very big future in British politics'. This future was not in evidence on the night when the votes were counted, as Labour's share of the vote dropped from 20 per cent to 10 per cent, and Blair forfeited his deposit.

After that, there was no obvious next move. Every safe Labour seat already had a candidate in place. The only mention of Tony Blair in the guide to general election candidates published by the Labour Party when the campaign began is, by implication, as the husband of Cherie Booth. Then came a glorious muddle, of the type which could only have occurred in the Labour Party as it was then. There had been a redrawing of constituency boundaries, which the Labour Party unsuccessfully contested in the High Court, in the hope of increasing the number of seats in urban

Tyneside. To avoiding weakening their case, the party had selected candidates only on the old constituency boundaries. So when the election began,
there were technically no Labour candidates at all in the North East.
However, the regional office had a cunning plan to fill every seat with no
fuss or time lost, by allotting one to each MP or prospective candidate
without allowing anyone else having a look-in. It only required everyone
concerned to cooperate and take the seat allotted to him, taking advantage
of a rule which said that no outsiders could enter a contest against sitting
MPs or endorsed candidates for old seats whose boundaries overlapped with
the new ones. Under this plan, the new Sedgefield constituency was to go
to the Deputy Speaker, Ernie Armstrong, who had represented a corner of
it for many years as MP for North-West Durham. Unfortunately,
Sedgefield did not include the little mining village where Armstrong had
lived all his life, and he refused to cooperate, insisting on having a selection
contest in the revised North-West Durham constituency. There he beat
David Watkins, the incumbent MP for neighbouring Consett. The unfortunate Watkins was therefore seatless, and since his former constituency did
not overlap with Sedgefield, he had no more claim on it than any other
party member who fancied a go at it.

They came from all over: ex-MPs who had lost out from boundary
changes somewhere else, footloose union officials, and local activists. The
front-runner was thought to be the Bennite, Les Huckfield, who had made
the mistake of abandoning his old seat in Nuneaton in the hope of a safer
berth in Wigan, only to be ousted from there in what proved to be the end
of a parliamentary career which had begun brilliantly when he had won a
by-election at the age of twenty-four. Other contenders included Joel
Barnett, who had been Denis Healey's deputy in the Treasury, and the left-
wing MP Reg Race – both of whom had lost out in the boundary changes
in other parts of the country – the railwaymen's leader, Sid Weighell, the
leader of Sedgefield district council, Warren McCourt, Ernie Armstrong's
ambitious daughter Hilary (who now occupies her father's former seat),
poor David Watkins and sundry others. There were rumours, which may
have been apocryphal, that the competition became so intense that members of one ward turned out to their monthly meeting to discover a crate of
champagne waiting at the back, a gift from one of the hopefuls.

Something made Tony Blair decide that he should join in. Apart from his boyhood link to the north east, he had revisited the region for a TGWU weekend school and had picked up rumours that Ernie Armstrong's obstinacy might throw the Sedgefield seat open to a contest. Perhaps it was a rush of hyped-up optimism of the kind that afflicts candidates who think they have done well in a parliamentary by-election. It cannot have been that Sedgefield was familiar political territory. As Blair himself admitted in his maiden speech in the Commons: 'Travelling north to Sedgefield, one enters a different world altogether. One can tell that it is different because it is the place where the SDP ceases telling people that it represents the Labour Party of Attlee and Gaitskell and begins saying that it represents the Tory party of Butler and Macmillan.'[17]

Whatever the reason, instead of staying home to give Cherie moral backing in the Thanet North campaign, Blair set off north and was not seen again until he returned as Britain's youngest Labour MP. His first task was to find a trade union or party ward which had not yet nominated a candidate, because without a nomination, he could get no further. His first attempt was Thornley ward, which was about to hold a meeting for potential nominees. Unfortunately, he arrived late and they would not let him in. There are Thornley party members still trying to live down having slammed the door on their future leader.

Blair's second approach was to ring John Burton, secretary of Trimdon Village ward, which had also not yet nominated. The telephone call was made on 11 May 1983. As it happened, Burton had a group of friends meeting at his house that night to celebrate their success in the recent council election. Even when he turned up at Burton's door at 9 pm, Blair was made to wait until the end of the European Cup Winners' Cup Final before they gave him a hearing. One of the five people at the house found Blair's views too right-wing to be worth supporting; the other four became the backbone of his future political base in Sedgefield. Burton hurriedly convened a ward party meeting three days later, which duly nominated Blair. Subsequently, Blair also picked up a nomination from a TGWU branch. On 18 May, the constituency's executive committee met and drew up a shortlist of six from the sixteen nominated candidates. It was made up of four local people and the sitting MPs Huckfield and Race. Blair, being neither local nor a nationally known figure, was not on it.

However, the party rules gave the larger general committee the power to amend the shortlist. Generally, such things happened only when a small group of entrenched leaders was being challenged by a new wave of activists, which in those days usually meant that traditionally right-wing leaders were being supplanted by Bennites. In Sedgefield, the left had control of the executive, but not of the general committee, which met on the day after the shortlist had been drawn up. The meeting was taken up with a series of wrangles about the shortlist. Rather misleadingly, John Burton produced the endorsement which Blair had received from Michael Foot after the Beaconsfield by-election, conveying the impression that this young unknown from London was a personal protégé of the much-loved leader, and by a margin of one vote out of more than eighty, Blair's name – and his alone – was added.[18]

That, as it turned out, was the vital vote. This was a new constituency, in which only the Bennites appear to have organized themselves properly around a favoured candidate, but County Durham was not natural Bennite territory. In many ways, it was an ideal constituency for a future party leader. An archipelago of villages including Sedgefield itself, Huworth, Middleton St George, Whessoe, etc., strung across the beautiful Durham countryside, it was a world away from the deteriorating inner-city Labour strongholds where society itself was on the brink of disintegration. All the pits were already closed, and it was said that the only enterprise in the area which was growing was the unemployment office. In the Wingate area, joblessness among men exceeded 40 per cent and would rise to 57 per cent with the anticipated closure of the Fishburn coke works; but the old working-class communities still held together, giving the new MP a reference point from which he could stay in touch with settled communities, immune from the restless radicalism of the cities. Trimdon Labour Club, where Blair made the announcement eleven years after his election to Parliament that he was a candidate in the party leadership election, is where he goes to keep himself in touch with what the average Labour voter is saying and thinking.

As Blair said at the time: 'The local party grows out of – and is part of – local life. That is its strength. That is why my constituents are singularly unimpressed when told that the Labour Party is extreme. They see extremism more as an import from outside that is destroying their livelihoods.'[19] Or as John Burton expressed it, years later: 'They are not the intellectual side of the Labour Party that like to spout on about their socialism but are not really in touch with the reality of what people want. These are ordinary people who know what they want.'[20] There was a natural anti-Huckfield majority, which only required a credible candidate around whom to coalesce, and the argument over shortlisting established Blair as their man. At the subsequent selection conference, he was ahead from the first round of voting onwards. On 9 June 1983, just four crowded weeks after his fateful telephone call to John Burton, Blair entered Parliament.

In parliament, he was quick to add to his list of political contacts, feeling his way carefully through the minefield of alliances and factions of the parliamentary Labour Party. It was open to him to rush in and become an important figure within the Solidarity group, on the right, given that Roy Hattersley and John Smith had already spotted him as a man with a future and that the group also included John Cunningham and Giles Radice, who were then the two most senior Labour MPs in the northern group. But Solidarity already had the look of a society for former government ministers bewildered by the changes overtaking the party in opposition. Blair was too cautious to throw in his lot with them.

As the contest for a new party leader opened, Blair turned up at an early, ill-attended supporters' meeting for Peter Shore, who differed from most Solidarity members in that he actually supported the party's policy of withdrawal from Europe and was close to Michael Foot. Bryan Gould, who was managing Shore's lacklustre campaign, was understandably pleased to see the young newcomer – until 'I realised he had gone to every candidate's campaign meeting, rather as an Oxford fresher might join each political club.'[21]

In the end, Blair voted as most Labour MPs did, for the winning ticket of Neil Kinnock, with Roy Hattersley for deputy, and joined the left-of-centre Tribune group, which had been Kinnock's political base. In this way Blair placed himself vaguely on the left, without being overly identified with it. He was never attracted by the chimera of reuniting the Bennites and the Tribunites. The main effect of his selection for Sedgefield had been to prevent Les Huckfield's return to parliament, for which reason he was already marked down by members of the Campaign Group as not one of them. He had quite an unpleasant encounter with Dennis Skinner at his first public meeting in the north east soon after the election. Nor did he ever attempt to identify himself with Robin Cook or others on the 'soft left' who aspired to be Neil Kinnock's loyal critics, holding him to the left-of-centre position on which he was elected. Nor was he among those who privately sniped at Kinnock from the left, holding him in secret contempt for changing colours half-way through his career. He had no personal recollection of Kinnock as a left-wing backbencher and respected and defended him as a dynamic party leader. Presumably, even in 1983, voices in the Trimdon Labour club were telling him that some parts of the Labour Party's political programme could usefully be forgotten, like the commitment to withdraw from the EC; but as he demonstrated in the Beaconsfield by-election, the young Blair held a rather strict view that anyone who stood as a candidate for a party embraced all its policies, without picking and choosing. It appears that he revealed his pro-Europeanism in the privacy of his selection conference, but publicly he did not depart from party policy.

One of the most important political decisions Blair made in the early days concerned the seemingly mundane business of finding an office. The Palace of Westminster was even more overcrowded then than it is now and new MPs were required to work in disgracefully cramped conditions, two to a room at best. When he first arrived, Blair was assigned to share an office with, of all people, Dave Nellist, the Militant MP for Coventry.[22] That relationship was doomed to end in divorce. Very soon, he was able to arrange to pick a new roommate. This was Gordon Brown, recently arrived as MP for Dunfermline East, who even then was being tipped as a future leader of the Labour Party.

Brown was the object of bewildered admiration among his contemporaries. While other new MPs struggled to learn the basics of their trade and were proud of themselves when their names appeared in their local papers, Brown appeared to have a string of contacts inside the civil service who leaked him sensitive documents which he used to full effect, getting his name on the front pages of national newspapers. His other advantage was that he never stopped. While Blair maintained a routine of slipping off home to see his children to bed whenever he was able, Brown carried on working. At weekends, he returned to his Edinburgh flat to do more work. On holiday, he would take a pile of books. He was always the senior member of the Brown and Blair partnership, slightly older, more experienced, better known and with the larger personal following. At an age when Blair was showing off by singing for the *Ugly Rumours*, Brown was already emerging as a precocious force in Scottish politics. The second son of a Church of Scotland minister in Kirkcaldy, Brown took his O levels at the age of fourteen, obtained a place to read history in Edinburgh University at sixteen, gained a First and was elected Rector of the university in his last year there, at the age of only twenty-one. He also sprinted for his county in the national athletics championship and was a promising football and rugby player until a kick in the head during a school rugby game put him in hospital for months and permanently blinded his left eye. Between university and his arrival at the Commons, Brown had been a lecturer and television journalist, including a period as current affairs editor of Scottish TV, the co-author or editor of three books on Scottish politics and devolution, and a youthful chairman of the Scottish Labour Party. The room he shared with Blair reminded those who visited it of a student's room, piled high with documents, with items of sportswear untidily stored in every available corner.

Fortunately, Blair was too level-headed and secure to waste energy being jealous of his friend. He was not looking for success as an opposition politician. Unusually for a Labour MP, Blair did not even list the positions he held on Labour's frontbench in his *Who's Who?* entry, because he did not consider being Shadow Minister for this or that as a real job. Since he had the good sense not to let Brown's success worry him, he benefited from it. Those who admired Brown also respected Blair as the great man's closest confidant. Conversely, because Brown was the one being tipped as a future party leader, he was the one who accumulated enemies. One of the first was Dick Douglas, who had been MP for Dunfermline until the 1983 boundary changes, when he had to settle for the more marginal Dunfermline West, having been beaten by Brown in the Dunfermline East selection conference. Douglas never recovered from the humiliation of losing to someone twenty years younger. His resentment was one of the factors which drove him to defect from Labour and join the Scottish Nationalist Party, soon after Brown topped the poll in a Shadow Cabinet election. Brown was to Blair as Chataway was to Roger Bannister: setting the pace until the distance had almost been run.

There was one surprising exception early on to the general rule that

Brown led and Blair followed. It was Blair who was the first of the 1983 intake of new MPs to be appointed to a place on the frontbench, despite being the youngest Labour MP in the House. Even though he had avoided signing up to the traditional right, the right worked for him. He was helped to make his mark in the Commons by being chosen by John Smith, who was employment spokesman in 1983–84, to help out with trade union legislation. In November 1984, the Shadow Chancellor, Roy Hattersley, appointed Blair to the treasury team. His stretch as a backbench MP had lasted only eighteen months. (By contrast, members of the 1992 intake had to wait almost three years before any of their number were appointed shadow ministers by either John Smith or Tony Blair.) Brown was also offered a position at the same time, but it was as a junior member of the Scottish team, which would have ended the relations he was beginning to cultivate with journalists from national newspapers. A year later, Brown joined the Trade and Industry team, headed by John Smith, as spokesman on regional affairs.

One effect of his promotion was that, by convention, Blair was prevented from expressing opinions on any subject thereafter, except the one for which he was official spokesman. Even as a backbencher, he had confined himself mainly to economic affairs, particularly industrial relations law, in the brief period where he was able to pick and choose. For the next eight years, Blair held nothing but economic briefs. He was a treasury spokesman in 1984–87, still picking over the small print of Chancellor Nigel Lawson's latest budget after the general election had been lost. He was then made spokesman on the city, in the Trade and Industry team headed by Bryan Gould. Informally, that had now become the most senior position outside the Shadow Cabinet, having been held previously by Gould and then by Robin Cook. His first Shadow Cabinet post was as Shadow Secretary of State for Energy in 1988–89.

This concentration on economic issues helps explain how Blair left so few hostages to fortune during his early days in parliament. One fact dug up by Conservative Central Office after his accession to the party leadership was his brief membership of parliamentary CND. Like every other Labour parliamentary candidate in 1983 and 1987, Blair was required to give at least formal support to the policy of unilateral nuclear disarmament, but joining CND was a voluntary act, presumably motivated by conviction. At some point in the late 1980s, Blair ceased to be a unilateralist, but there is no empirical evidence to say when. Frustratingly for the Conservative Party, he never spoke on the subject of defence. Similarly, there are no early Blair speeches on education, devolution or the welfare state. Even his views on law and order hardly had an airing until he became Shadow Home Secretary in 1992.

There was one issue, however, on which he clearly staked out a personal position radically different from the one he held by the time he had become party leader. This was trade union reform, which he chose as his specialist subject in his first months in parliament. The first time he ventured into something bigger than the parochial concerns of Sedgefield constituency in a Commons speech was when he attacked the 1983 Trade Union Bill, under which it became obligatory for a trade union to hold a ballot before a strike. This was the law under which the assets of the National Union of Mineworkers were sequestered in 1985. On the subject of the strike itself, Blair was discreet. Although all the pits in his Sedgefield constituency had closed by 1983, it was an old mining area nonetheless, where feeling ran deep against the destruction of the industry. In later years, the NUM leadership invariably featured high on Blair's list of those who almost drove the Labour Party out of business during the first half of the 1980s, but he did not attack them while the strike was in progress. He confined himself to supporting the economic case on which the strike was based, as opposed to the tactics which the union pursued under Arthur Scargill's presidency, asserting that: 'there is no inevitable or inexorable fate that dictates that mines must close. It is a matter of political choice and judgement . . . There is nothing odd about subsidising an industry. To proceed in such a way is sensible.'[23]

By contrast, Blair was quite clear in his objections to intervention by the state in trade unions, even after the sporadic scenes of violence when massed pickets collided with the police. 'The purpose of the bill is to render the trade union movement ineffective and inefficient,' he claimed. 'It is a shabby, partisan stratagem designed to assist the Conservative Party and employers.' He complained about the 'overt and blatent political bias' under which there was to be one set of laws for unions and quite another for employers, and about the way the Bill appeared to have been drafted to make it as difficult as possible for unions to comply with the law, even if they wanted to. Moreover, the statutory wording of strike ballots, which had to ask union members whether they were prepared to strike 'in breach of their contract', Blair regarded as 'rigged'.

He also had other detailed objections but, in a sense, they were beside the point. 'The issue,' he said, 'is not whether elections are good or bad, but whether it is right for the state to intervene and to dictate to trade unions how they should conduct their affairs.' He considered it an 'extraordinary proposition . . . that it is the proper role of government to interfere in the due process of a voluntary organisation'. The Bill as a whole was a 'scandalous and undemocratic measure'.[24] Across the floor, Michael Howard had just arrived as a new Tory MP in a hurry, hoping to win promotion by being the hammer of the unions. This last phrase of Blair's stuck in his memory, and he repeatedly threw it back at him eight years later, when Howard was Secretary of State for Employment and Blair was his shadow.

When the Bill came back to the Commons for a third reading, Blair went further, objecting to the legislation from what a Militant supporter might have called the 'class perspective', that in the struggle between workers and employers, the government was deliberately framing laws to assist the boss class:

> Most people would accept that an employer gains if a trade union is weakened. The proposed form of electoral procedure imposed and enforced upon every trade union will enmesh trade unions in legal battles and cause them administrative obstacles. That will weaken their ability to pursue the industrial interest of their members.[25]

That then was the position held by the young Tony Blair. It seemed to imply that the succession of laws which Conservatives imposed on the trade union movement, at a steady rate of one act of parliament per year, were all objectionable. It made little difference that some items of legislation, like mandatory strike ballots, had more public support than others: unions had a right to defend their members, they were voluntary societies and it was illiberal for the state to be legislating on how their rule books should be written.

Compare this with what Blair told the TUC more than a decade later, when he addressed them as leader of the Labour Party:

> We are not going back to the old battles. You have heard me say this many times: I will say it again. There is not going to be a repeal of all Tory trade union laws. It is

not what the members want; it is not what the country wants. Ballots before strikes are here to stay. No mass or flying pickets. All those ghosts of times past . . . it is time to leave them where they lie. The only people who are really interested in them are a few people on our side but mainly Tory Central Office, and I do not intend to give them any more weapons.[26]

As Blair himself acknowledged, he had changed his mind. He moved with the flow of public opinion. Over the years, even trade union leaders doubted if it was to their advantage to have their old privileges back, giving free rein to rank-and-file militancy, which often embarrassed full-time union officials as much as it inconvenienced employers. The section of Blair's speech quoted above was actually interrupted by applause, to his own obvious surprise. Had he delivered it in the same hall ten years earlier, he would certainly have been booed off the stage.

Blair was a good frontbench performer, with a barrister's capacity to absorb and understand the complexities of a difficult government Bill. Even in the bear garden of the House of Commons, beneath the ritual insults which fly between opposing parties, genuine ability is usually given its due. From the start, Tory MPs spotted that Blair was cleverer than the average Labour MP, and they were prepared to say so. There were exceptions, of course. Lord Young, the Trade and Industry Secretary, thought he 'reacted hysterically' to one of the big takeovers of the late 1980s, when Rowntree was bought by Nestlé;[27] Tim Smith, Tory MP for Beaconsfield, thought him 'thoroughly dull, unimaginative [and] negative',[28] but Smith perhaps did not hold very fond memories of his opponent in the Beaconsfield by-election. Generally, from the right-wing of the Tory Party to the Labour left, it was recognized that Blair was special. When the Thatcherite, Alan Clark, was appointed an Employment Minister in December 1984, and had to steer his first parliamentary bill through its committee stages, he noted nervously in his diary that 'Labour has a very tough team. Little John Smith, rotund, bespectacled, Edinburgh lawyer. Been around for ages . . . and two very bright boys called Brown and Blair.'[29] Later, when Blair moved to the treasury team, Nicholas Soames – then a backbench Tory MP with no visible prospect of being anything else while Margaret Thatcher was in Downing Street – forecast that 'he will bring an economic literacy, ability and good humour that has been sadly lacking from the opposition frontbench'.[30] Later still, when Blair was a contender for the party leadership, he received unexpected support from Chris Mullin, a left-wing MP still unrepentant about being Tony Benn's campaign manager in 1981, whose argument was that although Blair was of the right, 'he has a track record of success on difficult issues'.[31]

That said, Blair's parliamentary speeches from those days are not compelling reading. They will have been examined in great detail by researchers from Conservative Central Office hunting for anything the future party leader may have said which can be used to embarrass him, but there is not much to find. He was a solid performer who could say things like 'one of the matters that concerned people was whether the 5 per cent excess of assets over the liabilities took sufficient account of the difficulty of assessing precisely what the value of the assets and liabilities may be, given the number of variables involved'[32] and know what he was talking about.

However, the underlying beliefs which governed his attitude then to interrelated questions such as inflation, government borrowing, and the European Monetary System were undoubtedly more 'Keynesian' than the economic policies assembled later under the stewardship of party leader Tony Blair and Shadow Chancellor Gordon Brown. This could be explained by the fact that he had to defer to two senior members of the Shadow Cabinet, John Smith and Roy Hattersley, who had less compunction than Blair and Brown about increasing taxes and public spending to create jobs and fund the welfare state, but there is no record of any conflict at the time between Blair and his team leaders. He was assumed to be slightly to the left of Smith and Hattersley, given his membership of the Tribune Group. It is likely that Blair believed what he said when he said it, but amended his opinions in the light of the 1992 general election defeat.

Just as Sir Edward Heath is commemorated as the Prime Minister who took Britain into the Common Market, it is possible that Sir Anthony Blair will eventually occupy a similar status for subsuming sterling into a single European currency. It is interesting, therefore, to discover him laying into Roy Jenkins, then leader of the Social Democratic Party, for his and the Liberals' eagerness to enlist Britain in the Exchange Rate Mechanism, the precursor to a single currency which Britain eventually joined in 1990, only to leave in spectacular style on Black Wednesday two years later. The SDP–Liberal alliance had been arguing the case for British membership years before it happened, and to that end arranged a Commons debate in

January 1986. Blair intervened to warn that that membership would be tantamount to putting the governor of the *Bundesbank*, Karl Otto Pohl, into 11 Downing Street. Blair's main point was that if Britain had joined only two or three months earlier, when the pound was strong, it would have entered at a rate of 3.6 DM, or at best 3.5 DM, to the pound; but over the Christmas period, a fall in world oil prices had weakened the pound and strengthened the Deutschmark, so that parity was down to 3.33 DM. Had this happened with Britain inside the ERM, the Chancellor would have been compelled to hike up interest rates, as Norman Lamont did in September 1992 in a last desperate attempt to keep sterling within the ERM. It is, warned Blair, 'important that our choice is informed and not a careless embrace of anything with the word "European" in it', adding that 'The only compelling argument in favour of the European Monetary System is that it provides a hedge or some certainty against short-term instability in the currency.' His opinion, echoed since by uncounted Conservative ministers, is that Germany's fiscal policy was 'too tight', implying that he, Blair, would tolerate a little bit of inflation if it helped reduce unemployment.

However, before we run away with the idea that in 1986 Blair had an objection in principle to a unified European currency, it is important to put his remarks in their contemporary context. At that time, Britain was a substantial oil exporter, Germany an importer of oil. Any change in the world price of oil therefore had the opposite effect on the British and German economies, and a wedding to the stronger Deutschmark would force Britain to do the opposite of what came naturally, forcing the value of the pound up when oil prices dipped, and down again when prices rose. It is, Blair stressed, 'not an ideological argument but a practical one', with the 'balance of advantage' then weighing against British membership.[33]

Given the avowed intention of a Blair government to reduce income tax for the lowest paid, the young Tony Blair on the folly of reducing income tax is also an interesting read. It is easy to imagine Shadow Chancellor Roy Hattersley nodding in agreement as his deputy declared:

> Income tax cuts are the worst thing that can be done for the economy and the least effective way to provide jobs.[34]

Out of their context, these words look like powerful evidence to support the Conservative claim that all Labour politicians, even Tony Blair, are compulsive tax-raisers. Actually, the background was a serious argument about how to cope with the particular problems of a consumer boom which began just before the 1987 general election, fuelled by rising house prices and easy credit which were encouraging consumers to borrow recklessly. In these circumstances, Nigel Lawson proposed to cut income tax, increasing the volume of disposable wealth in the pockets of private consumers. The consequences are well known: the Conservatives won a second massive election victory, which was followed by a recession, a collapse in house prices, increased unemployment, increased government borrowing and, eventually, tax increases. So when Blair warned that 'the worst thing we can have is income tax cuts which will fuel the consumer boom even more'[35] he was right, although these were not vote-winning words.

Blair's reaction to Robert Maxwell's purchase of the Mirror Group Newspapers in 1984 also provides a contrast with his later attitude to media moguls. With masterly understatement, Blair warned then that 'one must be concerned when newspapers are to be owned by an individual who gives unenforceable guarantees of independence'.[36] Ten years later, as leader of his party, he dined privately with Rupert Murdoch in December 1994, then travelled across the world the following July to talk to News International executives, then had another private dinner with the media mogul in September 1995. Any concern about whether Murdoch's newspapers had any guarantees of independence at all, enforceable or unenforceable, had to be put to one side because of the alluring prospect that the media mogul might order his newspapers not to repeat their customary role of working for a Conservative victory at the next election. Murdoch reputedly described Blair as one of the world's great statesmen.

The good manners which so impressed Roy Hattersley after the Beaconsfield by-election were also on parade. Speaking soon after the 1987 general election, Blair remembered to heap praise on all the new Labour MPs who had just made maiden speeches, most of whom were older than he was. Neil Kinnock's former researcher, John Reid, had made a 'witty, brilliant speech', the one from Blair's future parliamentary private secretary, Bruce Grocott, was 'excellent', Keith Bradley and Martyn Jones were both so good that it was easy to see how they had overturned Conservative majorities in their respective seats, Rhodri Morgan was 'absolutely superb',

Calum MacDonald 'fascinating', and even the Glaswegian, James Hood, a long-serving NUM official who embodied much of what Blair would later call Old Labour, merited praise for his 'passionate, good defence of the basic principles of trade unionism'.[37]

None of these comments will have done Blair any harm when in summer 1987, for the first time, he stood for election to the Shadow Cabinet and only narrowly missed. He collected seventy-one votes, putting him seventeenth in the contest for fifteen places. He would have needed fourteen more votes to win a place. It was impressive for someone who had only been in the Commons for four years, but he was still a fair distance behind Gordon Brown, whose eighty-eight votes made him the youngest member of the Shadow Cabinet that season. A little over a year later, in November 1988, Blair arrived in style, in ninth place with 111 votes. The only thing which would have caused him a twinge of jealousy was that Gordon Brown was still way ahead, having amazingly topped the poll with 155 votes. Not only was Blair the youngest Shadow Cabinet member then. Seven annual elections later, when he was into his third year as party leader, he was still the youngest member of the Shadow Cabinet which he dominated, partly because so many of those who had arrived ahead of him – Brown, John Prescott, Robin Cook, David Clark, Donald Dewar, Frank Dobson, Michael Meacher and Jack Straw – were still there.

Blair's first Shadow Cabinet post, as Shadow Energy Secretary, was demanding in that it required him to lead Labour's opposition to electricity privatization, but it was not controversial in party terms, since the entire Labour Party basically supported the leadership's position. Blair's achievement was that he handled a complex issue very skilfully, concentrating on the weak points in the government's case. 'He thinks strategically,' said Chris Mullin, who served on the committee handling the Bill. 'Instead of wasting hundreds of hours on irrelevant trench warfare, he identified the half dozen or so key issues and arranged for them to be debated at a time when the outside world was still awake.'[38]

The one internal ripple his appointment caused was that he was put there in place of John Prescott, who had held the job for only a year. Prescott believed he was being sidelined as a punishment for challenging Roy Hattersley for the deputy leadership. What increased Prescott's irritation was that he learned about his impending move and Blair's appointment by reading about it in the *Sunday Mirror* before the Shadow Cabinet elections had been held. Fortunately, he did not blame Blair for that, but Neil Kinnock and his press aide, Peter Mandelson, whom he suspected of tipping off the Political Editor of the *Sunday Mirror*, Alastair Campbell.

What is perhaps most illuminating about Blair's handling of electricity privatization was not what he said about the details, but how he did not take the opportunity to make a general statement of economic philosophy. He was apparently sincere when he claimed that electricity would be cheaper for the consumer when provided by a state-owned industry. He certainly intended his warnings about 'the impossibility of running an energy policy simply at the behest of the market'[39] to be taken seriously, but he chose not to take this opportunity to make any general statement on the desirability of the public ownership of a strategically important means of production. When John Smith was opposing the privatization of British Airways some years earlier, he had been categorical: 'The Labour Party intends to reacquire those assets, because it believes in the public ownership of a national airline'[40] but Blair was already opening the way for the eventual formula of tougher regulation of the industry rather than a return to state ownership:

> We are proud that we took the industry into public ownership. When we come to power, it will be reinstated as a public service for the people of this country, and will not be run for private profit.[41]

The idea of renationalizing electricity was effectively dropped while Blair was still in his post as Shadow Energy Secretary. In its report to the 1989 party conference, the Policy Review Group on the economy emphasized that 'the water industry, in particular, must be an early candidate for a return to some form of public ownership', but pointedly did not say the same of electricity.[42]

The most notable loser from electricity privatization was the poor, battered National Union of Mineworkers, which had still not recovered from the traumas of 1984–85, and was now faced with losing the biggest customer for British coal as privatized power stations switched to gas or bought abroad. Blair saw this coming, although his forecast of fifteen pit closures and 15,000 more miners out of work,[43] which sounded a little wild at the time, turned out to be a gross underestimate. Given the explosive emotions which pit closures provoked, especially within the Labour Party in places like County Durham, Blair might have been more lyrical about the potential destruction of mining communities and the end of Britain's centuries old self-sufficiency in coal, which had been the economic foundation of an empire. Instead, he was as measured and factual as ever, provoking a prescient taunt from the energy minister, Michael Spicer:

> On the one hand, he and his new-style socialists see the coal industry as baggage that they would like to discard. It reminds them of Mr Arthur Scargill . . . On the other hand, they have to contend with [Dennis Skinner] and other opposition members . . . telling them that coal lies at the very foundation of the Labour movement and that for Labour to turn its back on it is to turn its back on years of struggle.[44]

A year later, Blair was moved to the job of Shadow Employment Secretary, in place of Michael Meacher, who had fallen foul of Neil Kinnock during a bitter and extended argument over which bits of trade union legislation imposed since 1979 would be repealed by a Labour government. Michael Meacher proposed to give the unions more even than the most powerful general secretaries were asking, including a statutory right to union recognition, the legalization of some forms of secondary picketing and restoration of union immunities. The argument became impossible to resolve. After Meacher had given a television interview on a Sunday, party press officers rang round journalists disassociating the party from what he had said. The policy was finally taken over and rewritten by Charles Clarke, aided by Lord Irvine.[45]

Blair was never going to get into that kind of conflict. He had decided by now that certain time-honoured trade union practices, like the closed shop and the block vote, were not only bad for the image of the Labour Party, but were in some circumstances wrong in principle. He had once thought it an 'extraordinary proposition' that the state should interfere in union affairs; now he accepted without demur what was already the firm view of the party leader. In fact, he went further. He was the one who accepted, on behalf of the Labour Party, that trade union closed shops should be illegal.

It began with a confrontation in the House of Commons, on the seemingly innocuous subject of the European Social Charter. This proposal, emanating from EC Commissioner Papandreou, of Greece, was anathema to the Conservatives, because it proposed to introduce certain minimum Europe-wide standards of employee rights, relating mainly to hours worked and the treatment of part-time employees. Blair was at the Despatch Box, declaring that 'the government's refusal to countenance the basic social rights in the Charter severely undermines the interests of British employees and the irrational conduct and bad faith that characterize our isolation in Europe profoundly damage Britain's interests abroad', when he allowed himself to be interrupted by Tory MP Timothy Raison, whose question was short and lethal. He pointed out that the draft Charter would also guarantee an individual's right not to join a trade union, which clearly cut across the closed-shop arrangements which were still woven into much of British industry, and which the trade unions were determined to preserve. Raison asked whether Blair would support that bit of the Charter.

Whichever way he answered, Blair was going to land in difficulties. The best he could do was to reply weakly: 'If it has that meaning, it also has the meaning that one has a right to be a member of a trade union.'[46] The Tories were not taking that for an answer and barracked him continually as he struggled through the rest of his speech.

The worst of it was that Raison was quite right about the wording of the Charter, which stated unambiguously that 'every employee and every worker shall have the freedom to join or not join such organizations [as trade unions] without any personal or occupational damage'. Blair knew perfectly well that it meant what the Tories claimed it meant: that no one could be compelled to join a trade union and that the closed shop was consequently obsolete. He also knew that another Employment Bill was about to go before the Commons and that it would be used without mercy to taunt him over the ambiguity of the Labour Party line. He decided that there was only one way out: he would have to present the union leaders with an accomplished fact – that he intended to accept the end of the closed shop and defy them to do anything about it.

Having made up his mind, Blair acted with remarkable speed. Within days he had spoken to Ron Todd, John Edmonds, Brenda Dean of the print union Sogat and others and had them all either on his side or neutralized. As early as 6 December, 1989, one week after his embarrassing Commons appearance, he was able to hint that change was on the way. He announced it by the ruse of issuing a statement to the Sedgefield constituency Labour

Party on 17 December, which was dressed up as the first of a series of 'policy clarifications' in which he confirmed that the Social Charter would 'prevent the refusal of a job or dismissal of an individual solely on the grounds that he or she is not a trade unionist', and that Labour would support it because of the other rights which the Charter guaranteed for workers.

It was not a 'clarification' but an entirely new policy, as most alert party and union members well knew. Yet the reaction to it from the Labour side was surprisingly muted. Brenda Dean set the tone by saying: 'We'd prefer not to see the closed shop go, but the Social Charter has caught the imagination of everyone and the whole movement has latched on to it. The end of the closed shop is part of that.'[47]

The debate on the Employment Bill duly came round and Tory backbenchers, seemingly primed by out-of-date information from the whips, duly did their bit, interrupting Blair to demand a clear answer on the future of the closed shop. He told them to wake up. The minister, Tim Eggar, was better informed. He asked whether Blair had consulted the union before his abrupt change of policy. Blair replied: 'There they were, all togged up in their party best and they put their hands into the magician's hat, hoping to pull out a nice, bright, sprightly, lively rabbit, but instead find they are holding a very dead fox.'[48] He was right. One fast move by Blair was sufficient to take out the power of the trade unions as an issue of contention in the 1992 general election.

However, the Employment Secretary, Michael Howard, was far too clever to chase a dead fox when there was a plump rabbit in sight – as there was, in Labour's proposal to introduce a national minimum wage, which in 1992 was set at £3.40 an hour. Years earlier, this had been a hotly contested issue inside the labour movement, with Neil Kinnock, the respected backbench MP Frank Field, the TGWU and the AUEW in the 'anti'-camp. By the time Blair took on responsibility for the policy, the last important opponents remaining within the Labour movement were the engineers' leaders, who feared that the deferentials painstakingly achieved for their skilled members would be eroded by state-imposed pay increases for the lowest paid. The most vehement opposition was from the proprietors of small businesses who claimed they would have to shed labour to avoid bankruptcy.

This was enough material for Michael Howard to launch an aggressive campaign, cleverly capitalizing on the public perception of the Labour Party as well-meaning but incapable of running an economy efficiently. His argument was that the minimum wage would have the opposite effect from what was intended: instead of helping the low paid, it would drive them on to the dole. Using assumptions which had been deliberately skewed to produce the worst possible outcome, Howard estimated that the policy would put two million jobs at risk. His figure was easy to refute, except that whenever Blair did so, Howard came straight back and challenged him to say what the correct figure was, if not two million. Here Blair was up a blind alley. He did not want to concede that any jobs were under threat, but he could not plausibly argue that no employer was going to sack anyone rather than raise their employees' wages. Even those who supported the national minimum wage conceded that it must cost some jobs. In 1991, a Fabian pamphlet by Fred Bayliss, Professor of Employment Studies at Nottingham University, put the cost at a maximum of 800,000 jobs. This was an attempt to be helpful and informative about a policy which Professor Bayliss actually supported, but it only added to the pressure on Blair to be specific. More tellingly, John Prescott bluntly conceded in an interview on Sky TV that there would be 'some shake-up in some of the jobs in certain areas . . . any damn fool knows that'.

The best Blair could do was to concede that a Labour government would need to be careful not to set too high a figure, and argue that evidence based on academic calculations was not proof, while his own case rested on 'empirical evidence of the impact of what has happened elsewhere, the balance of which is overwhelmingly positive'.[49] This unsatisfactory line caused him to take refuge occasionally in outright obfuscation. In one article, published in the *Independent* in 1991, Blair used a sentence for which he was remorselessly mocked by the Tories, when he asserted: 'I have not accepted that the minimum wage would cost jobs . . . I have simply accepted that econometric models indicate a potential jobs impact.'

In the longer term, Blair decided that Labour's mistake was that the policy had been too specific. By giving a figure for the national minimum wage, the party had provided the fact on which guesses about potential job losses could be built. In 1995, when Blair was party leader, and Harriet Harman was Shadow Employment Secretary, they decided that calculating the figure for the national minimum wage would be delegated to a commission established by the incoming Labour government, so that the party could fight an election still promising to end 'poverty pay' without saying what precisely they meant.

In general, Blair emerged from the election and pre-election period with his credit rating inside the Labour Party improved. He was seen to have stood his ground under formidable pressure on an issue of social justice. He was also benefiting from the advice which Philip Gould and other specialist advisers had given, basing on polling evidence: that instead of trying to promote Neil Kinnock as an individual, Labour should fight the 1992 campaign on the strength of the team who surrounded him. The advice was not entirely welcome in the leader's office, because of the implied observation that Kinnock himself was not a strong selling point. But he generously accepted it and, through 1991, there was a sequence of stylish party political broadcasts introducing the team. The personnel varied only a little from broadcast to broadcast. Four members of the Shadow Cabinet, jealously known to their rivals as the 'favoured four', appeared each time: John Smith, Margaret Beckett, Tony Blair and Gordon Brown. Already, Blair appeared to be part of an inner Shadow Cabinet.

After the election, and the resignations of Neil Kinnock, Roy Hattersley and Gerald Kaufman, three of the four most senior Shadow Cabinet members, it was never in doubt that both Brown and Blair would move up to become Shadow Spokesmen for the so-called great offices of state. Brown, in fact, became Shadow Chancellor and Blair Shadow Home Secretary. The only surprise was that neither aimed any higher, but left Margaret Beckett, Bryan Gould and John Prescott to fight it out for the deputy leadership.

With Kinnock's departure, the burden of pushing forward the modernization of the Labour Party was expected to fall to Brown and Blair, since neither Smith nor any of the three candidates for deputy were wholly trusted by the modernizers. Brown's abstention from the race was explained by the general prejudice that the party could not have a Scottish leader and a Scottish deputy, therefore Brown could not deputize for John Smith. But there was no argument to stop Blair entering the contest, in which he probably would have performed credibly even if he lacked the trade union support to win. He thought about it, hesitated, and in the end did not run, giving the disingenuous excuse that he was concerned about the effect on his family.

The true reason was that he was put off by John Smith. The two men had got on well for years, but Smith not only failed to encourage Blair to run, he clearly indicated that he wanted Beckett for his deputy. Where Blair saw an opportunity to put the case for modernizing the party, Smith only saw potential problems. The Blair candidature would create waves, polarizing opinion for and against the modernizer project. John Cunningham, who was close to Smith, still saw himself as the senior Northern English MP and might have entered the contest if Blair had. And if Blair won, his victory would have settled the question of who was next in line in the event of Smith's departure, but there was no great advantage from Smith's point of view to having his successor irremovably installed in the office downstairs.

Besides, of the two rival modernizers, Smith on the whole preferred Gordon Brown, whose politics were closer to Smith's. Although Smith's life had been spent on the right of the party, he was less iconoclastic about the traditional Labour movement than Blair. Viewed from his Scottish home-land, the Labour Party worked: it was in power, it had never fundamentally changed – it was only in England that it had been wracked by internecine warfare and deserted by the voters. To Smith, the young London-based modernizers who were demanding that the party be turned upside down quickly were in danger of causing unnecessary trouble within the Labour Party before a general election which Smith was convinced they were going to win anyway. He preferred to trust his fellow Scots, Robin Cook, Donald Dewar and Gordon Brown.

In the new leadership structure, therefore, while Margaret Beckett was Smith's deputy in all party matters, Brown was effectively in command in parliament. He was made chairman of the newly created Economic Policy Commission, a joint committee of Shadow Cabinet and National Executive Committee members, which Smith intended to be the final arbitrator of economic policy. Outwardly, therefore, he was still the senior half of the Brown and Blair partnership. Brown and Blair both announced on the same day in July 1992 that they intended to run for election to the National Executive Committee, taking advantage of the new one-member, one-vote system. Brown came in third, behind Neil Kinnock and David Blunkett, Blair two places behind. In the 1992 Shadow Cabinet elections,

Brown topped the poll for the third time in four years, with Blair in second place. Implicitly, Brown's political base was stronger than his friend's both among Labour MPs and party members, but this hardly mattered because they were politically so close that senior party staff referred to them in private conversation as 'Pushmepullyou', a name borrowed from the two-headed llama from the Dr Doolittle stories.

Yet it was around the year 1992 that things seemed to go wrong for Brown. The first signs of trouble, which predated the general election, were almost imperceptible except to those absorbed in the Westminster gossip mill, where one of the distractions was the growing tension between Kinnock and John Smith. With one side putting it about that if Kinnock did not follow Margaret Thatcher into premature retirement he would cost Labour the election, and the other side whispering that Smith was not quite so clever as he thought he was and altogether too pleased with himself, the idea arose that perhaps the succession should skip Smith and pass directly to the young and talented Gordon Brown. Speculation of this sort did not help Brown at all. Some of Neil Kinnock's devotees, who were becoming more edgy and suspicious by the day, suspected Brown of disloyalty and began discreetly briefing against him. Some of the 'modernizers' who had seen Brown close-up and might have been expected to be his natural supporters, like Marjorie Mowlam, who was Shadow Minister for the City when Brown led the Trade and Industry team, and the Kirkcaldy MP, Lewis Moonie, let it be known that privately they did not think he was up to being party leader. Alastair Campbell, who was closer to Labour's inner circles than any other political journalist, issued a warning in the *Daily Mirror* that the rubbishing of Brown could only harm the Labour Party.

Added to this was the little noticed fact that Blair himself had never promised to stand aside for his friend in the event of a leadership election. Like others, I assumed he would, until one day shortly before the 1992 election when I was talking to Blair with another journalist, who jokily forecast that Blair would one day be Brown's campaign manager. To my surprise, Blair reacted sharply, was clearly on the point of correcting him, then changed his mind and said nothing. It was the first indication I ever had that Blair's ambitions ran to something greater than being Gordon Brown's second-in-command.

On the weekend after the general election, a letter appeared in the

Guardian, written by the Labour Party's former chief press officer, Colin Byrne, who was privy to the inner circle around Neil Kinnock. It aired all the complaints which the Kinnock camp had against John Smith and asked rhetorically what the old right had done during the bitter years of Militant's ascendancy or when Labour was at war with itself over Europe, or relations with the trade unions. 'The answer, as I saw myself,' Byrne wrote, 'was usually to sit on their hands and let the Kinnocks and the Blairs take the flak.'[50] There was no mention of Brown, an indication that the Kinnocracy already viewed Blair, not Brown, as the best candidate to carry on the Kinnock reforms.

That same view was enthusiastically taken up by Andrew Neil, then Editor of the *Sunday Times,* who was not bashful about using his position to intervene in Labour Party matters. Neil was perhaps the most important of a number of leading opinion-formers who began to promote the idea that the Labour Party had missed a chance once again, because Smith was the right leader for the last election, but the wrong one for the next. In Neil's case, he made the point by having the *Sunday Times* colour magazine run a five-page profile of the 'leader in waiting' in the very weekend of Smith's election as party leader. Written by Barbara Amiel, wife of Conrad Black, owner of the *Daily Telegraph* and *Sunday Telegraph,* it included the portentous observation that 'Yesterday Labour elected a new leader. Some feel the party should have skipped a generation and gone for Tony Blair.'

By 1992, therefore, Blair was already the preferred choice of the Kinnock circle and of smart establishment opinion. One of his biographers, John Rentoul, infers that if Smith had died suddenly at the end of 1992, Blair might even then have beaten Brown in a leadership election 'even under the old block vote system'.[51] That has to be treated with caution. The block vote system put the leadership largely in the gift of trade union leaders like John Edmonds and Rodney Bickerstaffe whose first choice was not Blair. His lack of a strong trade union base would have made Labour MPs think twice about declaring their support for him. In such circumstances, the backing of the Tory press and the Kinnock circle, whose influence dropped sharply as soon as the general election was over, could have done Blair more harm than good, making him another figure like Roy Jenkins, whose standing in the Labour Party fell in proportion to the support he gathered outside.

However, Blair had other factors working for him. First, there was his own solid good sense. He did not allow a laudatory profile in the *Sunday Times* to go to his head. Instead of behaving as if he, too, thought he was the 'leader in waiting', he settled down to concentrate on the job he had been given, without complaining that it was less important than Gordon Brown's. Soon, the very fact that Smith had put him slightly at arm's length worked spectacularly to his advantage.

During the Smith interregnum, very little happened in the way of developing party policies. This was a deliberate tactic on Smith's part. Supremely confident of winning, he decided to proceed by setting up a network of commissions and committees to work on ideas, leaving the decisions until later. Very few had been made by the time he died. But on the larger canvas of national politics there was one huge event in the latter part of 1992, which dwarfed all others and fatally undermined John Major's government. This was the United Kingdom's forced exit from Europe's Exchange Rate Mechanism in September 1992. Although it was an unmitigated disaster for the Conservatives, the one plausible line of defence which ministers could offer was that, on the available evidence, Labour would have handled the crisis as badly as they did. Their best alibi was Gordon Brown, an avowed believer in controlled exchange rates, who defended the ERM in principle up until the day the pound collapsed. That unpopular judgement, coupled with the appearance of nothing much going on, lowered Brown's stock. In autumn 1993, he failed for the first time in five years to take first or even second place in the Shadow Cabinet election, falling behind Robin Cook and John Prescott – though still ahead of Blair. But in the meantime, from being a competent spokesman on economic affairs, Tony Blair had reinvented himself.

In January 1993, Blair and Brown paid a joint pilgrimage to Washington to meet some of the advisers who had organized Bill Clinton's election campaign and were now helping to prepare for the Clinton presidency. There was already a link between the Clinton team and the Labour Party, in the person of Philip Gould, who had been an adviser to both. The trip itself was arranged by Jonathan Powell, Political Secretary at the Washington Embassy, and younger brother of Chris Powell, founder of Labour's Shadow Communications Agency. It was made against the background noise of a lively but essentially meaningless argument about whether or not the

Labour Party was to be 'Clintonized', with John Prescott leading the charge against the Clintonizers. Huge parts of the American experience were untranslatable into British politics, but Blair returned having made two significant observations: that in order to emphasize his status as an outsider free of the glitter and corruption of Washington, Clinton had styled himself leader of the 'New Democrats', and that he had been very tough on crime.

Days after their return, Blair gave a radio interview in which he launched the slogan 'Tough on Crime, Tough on the Causes of Crime'. It was probably the cleverest political slogan any Labour politician had hit upon in fourteen years of opposition. It is neatly phrased so that it sticks easily in the mind – and it is open to all manner of mimicry and parody. All the countless jokes about Blair being 'tough on socialism and tough on the causes of socialism', etc. only reinforce the impact of the original message. More significantly, it went straight to the heart of one of Labour's greatest political problems: that working-class voters, who are the most frequent victims of crime and anti-social behaviour, suspected that the Labour Party was a political home for liberals whose theories did not deter offenders and did not work. The punitive language used by Conservative ministers had manifestly failed, too, since crime figures and the fear of crime had continued rising almost without interruption. Blair had found an idiom through which he could talk of applying social remedies without giving the impression that he was going to let the offender get away with it. He made the same point time and again, in different words:

> Of course there is never any excuse for crime and those who commit crimes must face justice, but if children grow up in a world without hope or opportunity, with poor education or housing, with no prospect of work or training, with no stake in society that demands respect from them, is it not common sense that crime is more likely to breed in such conditions?[52]

It was, actually, Gordon Brown's slogan – yet another debt which Blair owes to the friend he overtook. However, political leadership does not necessarily entail being the first to come up with a good idea. Blair's achievement was to make the idea credible. He could moralize, without grating on the ear. Although privately he had deeply held religious convictions, he had never referred to them in his public life. But now he began to do so, following the example of John Smith. (Later, as party leader, Blair roused a strong reaction when he was misquoted as suggesting that it was impossible to be a Christian and a Conservative. What he actually said was less controversial: 'My view of Christian values led me to oppose what I perceived to be a narrow view of self-interest that Conservatism – particularly its modern, more right-wing form – represents. Every human being is self-interested. But Tories, I think, have too selfish a definition of that self-interest. They fail to look beyond to the community.'[53])

The month after Blair first used his 'tough on' slogan, public opinion was horrified by the murder of two-year-old James Bulger by two ten-year-old boys. In a speech delivered in Wellingborough, Blair warned: 'We cannot exist in a moral vacuum. If we do not learn and then teach the value of what is right and wrong, then the result is simply moral chaos which engulfs us all.'[54] Other politicians warning against 'moral chaos' would sound shallow and opportunist. From Blair, the words came over as if he really meant them. His speech inspired approximately a thousand members of the public to write to him and, conversely, inspired sixty Tory MPs to sign a Commons Early Day Motion whose sole purpose was to try to discredit Blair's record on law and order. 'The succession is decided. The heir is chosen,' one Tory Sunday newspaper reported at the end of February. 'Step forward Tony Blair. Give way Gordon Brown.'[55]

Blair's skill at giving voice to public anxieties became an increasing problem for the Tory government. The Home Secretary at the time was Kenneth Clarke, one of the Cabinet's most experienced bruisers who had made fools out of a long line of opposition MPs – but Clarke simply could not get the better of Blair. Clarke was struggling to change the pay and working conditions of the police in a way which they did not welcome. In May 1993, he was heckled by the annual conference of the Police Federation, where one speaker called him 'an arrogant, rude social snob', whereas Blair was heartily cheered when he appeared at a rally of 21,000 police officers at Wembley Stadium in July.

Even in the annual ritual of the renewing the Prevention of Terrorism Act – which every year, Labour opposed, giving the Home Secretary of the day an opportunity to accuse the opposition of being soft on terrorism – Clarke could not bring himself to be personally offensive about Tony Blair, even conceding: 'He is as opposed to terrorism as I am, and does not intend to give help or encouragement to terrorists in this country, but he is in danger of doing so by accident' – which did not deter Blair from accusing him of 'playing politics' with the issue.[56]

The problems Clarke experienced in landing a punch on Blair were exacerbated by the struggle to have the Treaty of Maastricht ratified by the Commons against highly organized opposition from the Conservative right, sometimes in cahoots with the Labour left. Clarke was more committed to Maastricht than any other Cabinet minister – so committed that he took it on trust and never read it – and became embroiled in several parliamentary confrontations in which he was frankly glad to have Blair on the same side.

For example, when Blair was speaking on how the Treaty would affect British immigration law, he was interrupted by Jeremy Corbyn, Harry Cohen, Peter Shore, Ted Grant, Ken Livingstone, Nigel Spearing and Max Madden from the left, who feared that standardized immigration laws would mean that 'the lowest common denominator' would apply everywhere, and by the right-wing Tories Tony Marlow and Teddy Taylor, who were convinced that, on the contrary, they would open the United Kingdom to floods of non-Commonwealth immigrants, until Clarke intervened to praise Blair for having presented the case 'impeccably and correctly'. Blair replied that a vigorous attack from the Home Secretary might have been more help.[57] The next day, on cue, Blair was subjected to a sarcastic tribute to his 'brilliant' speech from Ken Livingstone:

> I do not think that he could see the approval, the absolutely elated look, on the faces of Home Office civil servants in the Box behind the [Speaker's] Chair. They were nodding enthusiastically as my Honourable Friend [Blair] gave the most clear exposition of government policy that we could have heard. The Home Secretary was nodding. He was clearly delighted because, as he told us, he has not read the Treaty and could not have done anything like as good a job. One almost had the feeling of watching an American gangster movie in which Mr Big sits and beams with delight as his bright young protégé announces some new way of ripping off society and making them rich. It was like coalition government.[58]

The following week, Blair was back in action, soaking up so many objections and interruptions that he was driven to remark that 'It is an extraordinary feature of these debates that saying something that one thinks is entirely uncontroversial provokes a storm of outrage.' Among that day's 'uncontroversial' observations from Blair was the assertion that the concept of being a citizen of the European Union, first introduced in the Maastricht Treaty, did not imply a loss of British national identity. Once again, Clarke had nothing but praise for his young shadow 'whose views on the European Community are indistinguishable from my own'[59] – a remark which haunted Clarke long afterwards.

The other factor which vitally affected Blair's future was that party reform was back on the agenda and the future of the trade union block vote was back under discussion. It was Neil Kinnock, once again, who kick-started matters by trying to rush through reforms before his retirement from the leadership, to eliminate the block vote from the selection of MPs and the election of the leader and deputy leader. Kinnock's haste irritated influential trade unionists like John Edmonds; and John Smith put the issue on hold for 1992. The following year, a decision had to be made, one way or another, so that constituency parties could begin the process of selecting candidates.

By now Blair was an elected member of the NEC, able therefore to be directly involved for the first time in an internal party issue. He was co-opted on to the Union Links Review Group, alongside John Prescott, Margaret Beckett, Robin Cook and Clare Short, four senior union officials and the academic, Lewis Minkin. By the time Blair arrived, the cause of one-member, one-vote was almost dead. The committee was on the point of agreeing a compromise which would allow levy-paying union members to vote as individuals in selection contests, rather than having votes cast on their behalf by the union delegates to constituency general committees. In other respects, the committee was proposing no significant changes.

At first, Blair appeared to be in a minority of two, his one ally being Nigel Harris of the AEEU, as he stuck out obstinately for a straight-forward one-member, one-vote system. However, unexpectedly, John Smith went on breakfast television on 10 January 1993 and emphatically restated that the block vote would have to go, putting a majority of the review committee in the uncomfortable position of having to back down or defy the party leader. John Prescott and Tom Sawyer now came to the rescue with a scheme which allowed the trade unionists to retreat with dignity, by proposing a levy-plus system under which levy-paying trade union members could qualify as full party members by paying a sum £12 below the annual subscription rate.

Smith, who throughout had blissfully underestimated how difficult it would be to induce the unions to surrender their own power, imagined this was the answer and set off for a round of annual union conferences, hoping to sell it. Most of the assembled union delegates heard him out politely and voted to retain their powers intact. By July, it appeared that Smith was heading for certain defeat. The unions controlled 70 per cent of the votes at annual conference and were showing no inclination to use their block votes to divest themselves of the block vote. Then in a bold move, Smith unexpectedly turned up in person to the last meeting of the Union Links Review Group to use his own authority to get his way, refusing to allow the meeting to adjourn until, after an intensive meeting lasting six hours, they capitulated.

Even that was insufficient to guarantee victory. The intensive wheeler-dealing carried on even after delegates had assembled for the Brighton conference. It reached such a pitch that when Roger Lyons, of the Manufacturing Science and Finance Union, visited Smith to report that he had failed to win his delegation over, the leader uncharacteristically swore at him, telling him to go back and 'fucking well try again'. Lyons did, and the MSF delegation finally voted nineteen to seventeen to abstain. Had they voted against the package of reforms, Smith would have lost.

The leader's last act was to throw John Prescott into the fray, to deliver the speech of a lifetime, so full of emotion that its syntax collapsed. At the Conservative conference a year later, they mockingly played part of it backwards, prompting Prescott's wife, Pauline, to remark that it was easier to understand that way. Though it was difficult to follow exactly what he was saying, everyone understood what Prescott meant: that the party had reached an emotional watershed at which union delegates were being asked to do something which they found painful, but they were all members of one movement for all that. That speech, and the shared experience of working on the party reforms, transformed Blair's and Prescott's personal relationship. Where previously they had eyed each other with mistrust, they learned mutual respect.

Everything in Tony Blair's life was turned upside down on 12 May 1994, when John Smith suddenly died of a massive heart attack which hit him during an early morning bath at his flat in the Barbican, in central London. His death was a turning point in British politics. On that morning, public opinion not only knew that they had lost a decent man who could have given politics a better name, but a potential Prime Minister. Even the results of the local council elections a week earlier, in which Labour scored 42 per cent in a nationwide poll compared with 27 per cent each for the Conservatives and Liberal Democrats, had been received with the inbuilt scepticism of commentators who had been watching the Labour Party ride the crest of successive waves for fifteen years only to be in the trough whenever it really mattered. But the obituary of John Smith in the *Sun* began with the stark, simple statement 'Britain's next Prime Minister died yesterday.' It was as if, when tragedy turned everyone's attention to the Labour Party, observers suddenly recognized it as a potential party of government. Whereas in 1992 the party had chosen a new leader of the opposition, this time it could be electing a Prime Minister.

Even on the day Smith died, minds were beginning to concentrate on who that new leader might be and it did not take very long for the name of Tony Blair to emerge. There was some grumbling later that he was pushed forward as the choice of media commentators. This is partly true and I was myself partly responsible. In the middle of that afternoon, I was asked to record a tribute to Smith for a BBC television crew. I was taken by surprise when the interviewer asked me to name the next leader. I replied that it would be Tony Blair, for no other reason than that I did not want to be proved wrong. The reply was broadcast on the *Six o'Clock News*. A little over an hour later I was asked the same question live on Sky News, but was now fortified by the fact that Denis Healey had gone before the cameras calling for Blair's election, and by an article in that day's *Evening Standard*, by the former Political Editor of the *New Statesman*, Sarah Baxter, headed 'Why I think Tony Blair should be the next leader'. The same evening, Alastair Campbell, then of *Today*, was on *Newsnight*, and also forecast a Blair victory. If that was a media conspiracy, I can say in mitigation that the journalists involved did not know they were conspiring.

It was, of course, open to Blair not to run, or even to do something so foolish that he threw the contest away; but if he kept his nerve, he was sure to win. The reasons are twofold: first that the ideological tug of war between the modernizers and 'old Labour' had already been won, and because, by some barely visible osmosis, Blair was established as the leader of the 'modernizers'. The victory of the modernizers was not only foresee-able, but foretold in a passage which I wrote in 1993, which caused a reaction in the left press at the time:

> There is no doubt about how the contest between the modernizers and the rest will work out. One side is well-organized, with strong professional back-up. They have not one but two credible leaders in Gordon Brown and Tony Blair, Neil Kinnock in support, and a clear idea of what they want. Their Labour Party would be more European than the Tories, very strong on law and order, with a promise of electoral reform, and social welfare without excessive tax increases. Its internal democracy would be based on one-member, one-vote, minus the union block vote, and it would rely heavily on professional advisers and image-makers to dispose of the Party's traditional association with dying industries and decaying inner cities. It would be a Party where the upwardly mobile could feel at home, not unlike the one which David Owen tried to create a decade ago. On the other side there is not a dis-ciplined army, but a jumble of right- and left-wing factions opposed to one part or another of the Kinnockite project . . . the traditionalists, if they can be so called, are not a cohesive group with a common set of ideas, they have only a shared sense that the Labour Party has been through too much internal upheaval already.[60]

After Smith's death, there was an agreed period of mourning to allow his funeral to take place and for the Labour Party to concentrate its energies on the elections to the European Parliament on 9 June. Until then, no candi-date entered the contest and no Labour MP formally declared their allegiance to any potential candidate, although these ordinances were well-breached behind the scenes. By the time the contest began the modernizers had already demonstrated their mastery of the situation. The potential rivalry between Blair and Brown had been settled in Blair's favour. Media comment and opinion polls were already running for Blair. More impor-tantly, he had the overwhelming support of the parliamentary Labour Party. On the day he formally declared he was a candidate, his impromptu team were in a position to release a list of names of the MPs backing him, which included thirteen members of the Shadow Cabinet and 122 other MPs, more than half the total. Another nineteen names were added by the close of nominations on 16 June, giving him 154 votes compared with ninety-five for all other candidates.

John Prescott, by contrast, could muster the backing of only four of the less influential Shadow Cabinet members – Ron Davies, Doug Hoyle, Joan

Lestor and Michael Meacher, while Margaret Beckett entered the fray with no Shadow Cabinet backing at all. Inevitably, Prescott and Beckett competed with each other for the 'Old Labour' vote. Prescott proved himself the more expert fighter. Instead of trying to outflank Beckett on the left, he played up the close relationship he had come to enjoy with John Smith and, by appearing more of a 'modernizer' than Beckett, secured himself the deputy leadership.

The political issue on which John Prescott chose to challenge Blair, and came closest to forcing a concession from him, was on jobs. If there was a single theme to the Prescott campaign, it was 'full employment'. This was a politically loaded phrase within the Labour Party, especially when Tony Blair was involved. Full employment had been the objective of every postwar government until the early 1980s. Even when Margaret Thatcher's Cabinet acted as if permanently high unemployment was an instrument of government policy, ministers proclaimed themselves committed to bringing it down. Within the Labour Party, it usually took first place in the list of priorities. Labour fought the 1987 general election on a promise to reduce unemployment by one million within its first two years of taking office. The report of the Policy Review Group on People at Work in 1989 had a whole section headed 'Full Employment'.[61] The eloquence of the young Tony Blair on the damaging impact of widespread unemployment suggests that he, too, was in pursuit of this goal. In his maiden speech, he had declared that 'A government who are complacent or uncaring about . . . unemployment . . . are a government who have abdicated their responsibility to govern.'[62]

Yet for a brief period while Blair was employment spokesman, full employment disappeared from the litany of Labour's objectives. The phrase was not used in *Looking to the Future*, the first relevant policy document produced during Tony Blair's tenure as employment spokesman, because Neil Kinnock considered it an empty promise, with echoes of the rash commitments which had jeopardized two general elections. Blair seemingly agreed. The 1992 general election was fought on the modest pledge to 'make a swift reduction in unemployment'.[63] However, no sooner had John Smith succeeded Neil Kinnock, and Tony Blair's place as employment spokesman been taken over by Frank Dobson, whose beard is sufficient proof that he is 'Old Labour', than full employment was back on the agenda. Dobson told a party meeting in his Camden constituency in July 1992 that 'we need to put full employment back at the heart of economic policy. It can't be achieved immediately and it can't be achieved just in Britain. But full employment never will be achieved unless it is restored to its proper place in the political and economic ambitions of our country and the rest of the European Community.'[64]

By picking up this issue, Prescott therefore was consciously defending an item of agreed party policy with which Blair appeared to disagree. In his first speeches of the leadership campaign, to the GMB on 13 June and the TGWU three days later, Blair avoided the phrase, stressing only the importance of getting the unemployed back to work. While his long statement of aims was being drawn up, however, soundings were taken from a wide cross-section of MPs, while two researchers in the Blair office, Liz Lloyd and James Purnell, rang round sympathetic journalists and think-tanks. One result of this swift consultation was that Blair's statement of aims included the sentence:

> The 1944 White Paper on Employment said that it should be one of the primary aims and responsibilities of government to maintain 'high and stable levels of employment'. That goal – the goal of full employment – I reaffirm as the objective of any decent society.[65]

Once he had been elected, Blair dropped the loaded term 'full employment', but the expression 'high and stable levels of employment' remained. It was used twice in the document which the Economic Policy Commission drew up for the 1995 annual conference. The same document, *A New Economic Future for Britain*, also had a section headed 'Employment opportunities for all', and referred to putting an end to unemployment among sixteen- and seventeen-year-olds, and 'long-term employment', which was defined as being out of work for two years or more. But the implication was that some level of short-term unemployment among the over-seventeens would always be a feature of economic life.

During the campaign, the three candidates – Blair, Prescott and Beckett – appeared at several trade union conferences or congresses together, and several trade union general secretaries made their preferences known, but the impact was minimal. Union levy-payers, like the ordinary party members, voted on the strength of what they saw on television and read in newspapers, not in accordance with recommendations from their union leaders.

In a contest that stretched a little over a month, 952,109 votes were cast, of which 57 per cent, 508,149 votes in all, went to Tony Blair, 24 per cent to John Prescott and 19 per cent to Margaret Beckett. Each figure was a genuine total of individual votes cast, not an aggregate of nominal block votes. On 21 July 1994, at a brief ceremony in central London, Tony Blair became the first leader of the Labour Party to be elected without the help of power-brokers from the trade unions.

The new electoral system had allowed Blair to arrive without making bargains or being beholden to sectional interests inside the party. There were no union bosses or self-styled Blairites who would, within months, feel that their creature was betraying them, as the left had felt betrayed by Neil Kinnock. The twenty-page statement of principles accompanying his campaign, which was issued twelve days after the campaign began, offered no hostages to fortune. The section on economics promised to 'combine the innovating strength of a dynamic market economy with a fairer set of rewards'; while under the heading 'Partnership at work' was the statement that 'individuals should be entitled to join a trade union, just as they should be entitled not to do so'; and the section on party organization included a call to recruit thousands of new members.[66]

On his first full day in his new office, Blair told the trade unions to expect 'fairness, not favours' from a Blair government, explaining that: 'They will have the same access as the other side of industry. In other words, they will be listened to . . . We are not running the next Labour government for anything other than the people of this country.'[67]

Two days later, interviewed on ITV's *Walden* programme, the nation was reminded of Blair the moralizer, as he turned his disapproval towards single parents who chose to bring up children on their own, pronouncing that it was 'crazy' to suggest that it was best for children to be brought up in anything but a two-parent household. He warned that some of the views on family stability associated with the left were 'a million miles away' from those of ordinary people. He added: 'It is a matter of absolute common sense that it is best for children, if you can achieve it, that they end up in a stable family relationship with their parents.'

Next it was teachers. Labour's Shadow Education Secretary, Ann Taylor, was launching a new education document which promised, among other things, to abolish school league tables and return grant-maintained schools to local authority control. Blair turned out to the press conference in person, to present the policy in a different light. When asked about grant-maintained schools, he deliberately avoided verbs synonymous with 'abolish', stressing the importance of giving more autonomy to all schools. His message for teachers was 'those that prove unfit to do the job of good teaching should be removed', and for wayward parents: 'Parents have a right to a decent school for their children, but that right must be matched by responsibilities. Parents will be responsible for coming into school if their child is disruptive, cooperating with teachers to make homework an important part of their school day and making sure children turn up at school.'[68]

In the autumn, there followed a glitzy press launch of a new consultation on economic policy. Paid for by sympathetic businessmen and women from the Labour Finance and Industry Group, the event in the National Film Theatre included satellite links, enabling it to be addressed by two of President Clinton's advisers, the Labour Secretary, Robert Reich, and Professor Richard Freeman of Harvard University. Determined to give the event intellectual weight, Gordon Brown, the master of the soundbite, delivered a serious-minded address containing a sentence for which he was much mocked afterwards by the Conservatives: 'Our new economic approach is rooted in ideas which stress the importance of macro-economics, neo-classical endogenous growth theory and the symbiotic relationships between growth and investment in people and infrastructure.' Its author was a very bright young economist who had just joined Brown's staff, named Ed Balls. The following month, Michael Heseltine brought the house down at the Conservative annual conference by requoting the passage and proclaiming: 'It's not Brown's, it's Balls!'

Blair's remarks were easier to follow and more immediate in their political impact. He said: 'The old Labour language – tax, spend and borrow, nationalization, state planning, isolationism, full-time jobs for life for men while women stay at home – is inappropriate to the future.'

These were just openers for a much bigger drama on which Blair embarked in the autumn, as delegates gathered for the annual party conference, when he resolved to abolish the seventy-six-year-old Clause Four, Part IV, of the Labour Party constitution, with its reference to common ownership of the means of production. He opened his campaign like a tactical first strike against an unsuspecting enemy. Many of the assembled delegates heard his conference speech on 4 October right through and joined in the applause, discovering what he actually meant only when they heard the media commentaries that followed. The words that heralded the end of Clause Four were:

> Let us say what we mean and mean what we say. Not just what we are against, but what we are for . . . Stop saying what we don't mean and start saying what we do mean, what we stand by, what we stand for. It is time we had a clear, up-to-date statement of the objects and objectives of our party. John Prescott and I will propose such a statement to the NEC. Let it then be open to debate in the coming months.

In exhorting others to say what they meant, Blair had himself taken the precaution of not saying what he meant. That was done by the spin doctors, who fanned out as the hall rang with applause to explain their leader's precise meaning to knots of journalists.

As he had hinted in his speech, Blair had won over John Prescott, without whose support the operation might have been impossible. With the leader and deputy leader united, the Shadow Cabinet and most of the national executive rapidly fell into line, including Robin Cook, whose first instinct was to oppose the exercise. It then went out to be voted on in party branches and trade unions, for a vote at a special conference the following April.

There was at first no reason to doubt that Blair would win, until the entire campaign was suddenly overshadowed by an issue with no obvious logical connection to the common ownership of the means of production, and which blew up into a crisis no one could have foreseen. In December, while the Labour leader was in the West Midlands campaigning in the Dudley West by-election, the *Daily Mail* devoted its front page to the Blairs' decision to send the oldest of their three children to the London Oratory, a Roman Catholic school for boys about eight miles from the borough of Islington where they lived. The London Oratory had been one of the first schools in the country to become grant-maintained, a status which the Labour Party was nominally committed to abolishing. The school conducted an informal 'selection by interview' process – parents came in to meet the staff before their children were accepted – but, as Blair would point out countless times in the months that followed, it was a state-run comprehensive school, with no entrance exams. This story was not new. When Harriet Harman and her husband, Jack Dromey, decided in 1993 to send their son to the London Oratory, it was known then that the Blairs were interested in the same school. The story was resurrected by the *Daily Express* during the leadership campaign, without having any impact.[69] The third time round, it detonated a reaction inside the Labour Party which caused the first political crisis of Blair's leadership and threatened the success of his Clause Four campaign.

One way to understand the ripples of resentment this sent around the party is to look at some figures. Every comprehensive school had been compelled by legislation to make a decision that year on whether to apply for grant-maintained status. Consequently, the teachers and governors of 23,475 schools had been personally involved to some degree. More than 99 per cent decided not even to hold a ballot. In 210 schools, parents were balloted, and in 99 cases they voted against a change in the status of the school. In almost every ballot, Labour Party members helped organize the 'no' campaign. Thousands more party members successfully argued against holding a ballot at all. All were now presented with a reason to question whether their leader was fully on their side.

Another issue was the social world in which Tony Blair moved. His elevation to the leadership had set off an orgy of press comments about the smart people who lived in left-wing Islington: the well-to-do socialists like Lord Hollick, Margaret and Henry Hodge, media executives like Barry Cox, left-wing journalists like Martin Jacques and many more. Islington chic was definitely in fashion in 1994. Furthermore, Blair was staffing his private office with advisers whose unquestioned ability was not matched by any deep roots in the traditional Labour movement. They were mostly young and had proved themselves in careers in the outside world before stepping into Labour politics through the leader's office door. The best-known was Alastair Campbell, former Political Editor of the *Daily Mirror* and Associate Editor of *Today*. Blair's new chief-of-staff, Jonathan Powell, came from the British Embassy in Washington. His principal researcher, David Miliband, son of the venerated Ralph Miliband, came from the semi-independent think-tank, the IPPR. Tim Allen, his press officer, came from television. Anji Hunter, who organized the office, was a childhood friend who had worked as Blair's researcher before his elevation. The only member of John Smith's personal staff to continue working for the new leader was Hilary Coffman, who had also been the only member of Kinnock's staff to survive the changeover in 1992 – and even she believed she was out of a job until Campbell insisted on taking her back. Peter Mandelson and Philip Gould, who were in and out of his office, though not formally part of it, had been equally influential members of the Kinnock circle.

All this contributed to what one MP, as he came away from a bruising encounter with his constituency party, described as 'dangerous dislocation' between the leader and the rank and file, creating a more receptive atmosphere for the complaints of left-wing dissidents like the Islington MP, Jeremy Corbyn, who claimed that within the New Labour Party 'there is a veneer of openness, but behind the scenes the leadership is working ruthlessly to destroy any opposition. The danger is that it will destroy the morale of constituency activists'.[70]

Two incidents early in 1995 confronted Blair with the unpalatable possibility that he could actually lose the plebiscite on Clause Four, a defeat which would have inflicted untold damage to his personal authority. One was a survey by the newspaper *Tribune*. It reported that among the constituency Labour parties which had so far discussed the matter, 90 per cent were also opposed to changing it. The other was a newspaper advertisement paid for by a group of Labour MEPs which called for the retention of the old clause. The best-known of the MEPs involved was the veteran socialist, Ken Coates, whose views on Blair were succinct:

> He is, quite simply, a Liberal. He is sufficiently open and pleasant to give the impression that it would be quite easy to work with him on a variety of civil problems although he would not be very radical about most of them. But the frustration which is rising on the Left arises from the fact that this young man has not the faintest idea of how socialists think and does not begin to understand the mentality of the party which he has been elected to lead. It is certainly aggravated by the ruthless news management by the star cynics who filter his views across to the media.[71]

A third ill omen was in the offing: it was anticipated that the Scottish Labour Party conference in January would also vote to keep the old clause. None of these was as serious as it appeared. The *Tribune* survey was an

accurate snapshot of votes taken during normal monthly meetings of constituency general committees up to that point. It was never likely that a
majority of the activists who routinely turned out to GC meetings, nor
those who were elected as delegates to the Scottish conference, would support the abolition of the clause, particularly at this early stage when no
alternative was being offered. As to Labour MEPs, they had ample funds at
their disposal to place newspaper advertisements, but were not generally
well-known or influential people in the Labour Party. To borrow a word
used by one of Blair's by now notorious spin doctors, they were 'nonentities'.

But meanwhile, there were no 'good news' stories coming from the
ground, nothing concrete to answer allegations from the left that the old
Clause was in effect being bludgeoned out of existence without the consent
of the party membership. Without an alternative to Clause Four on offer,
there was nothing positive that the leader's supporters could do. This hiatus did not mean that the Clause itself would be saved, because voting at
the special conference was under the usual rules in which union block
votes predominated. At this stage, Blair could count on two of the four
biggest unions, the GMB and the AEEU, which commanded respectively
12 per cent and 9 per cent of the total voting strength, and probably
enough middle-sized unions to see him through, despite the opposition of
the TGWU, which had 14 per cent of the vote, and the uncertain position
of Unison, with nearly 12 per cent. But it would have been ridiculous for
Blair, the modernizer, in making the first big decision since his accession to
the leadership, to deploy the union block vote to overrule the mass of
party members. For the sake of his own standing in the party and the
country, he had to win the plebiscite.

Blair met this crisis with a shrewd mix of tactical retreat, ruthlessness and
persuasion. He travelled to Brussels to berate the errant MEPs for their
'infantile incompetence', but in a gesture to placate those who complained
about the élite social circles in which he mixed, he also authorized a similar operation against the millionaire thriller writer Ken Follett and his
celebrated wife, Barbara, Labour candidate for Stevenage. The Folletts were
well-known Labour supporters with a useful gift for raising money and
attracting star names to the cause. Barbara Follett was the driving force
behind Emily's List, which was devoted to getting more women adopted as
Labour parliamentary candidates. Early in 1995, the Blairs were invited to

dinner at their Chelsea home to meet a small group of select guests including the publicist Lynne Franks. As they arrived for what they thought was a private engagement, they were irritated to find a photographer waiting outside. The following day, the spin doctors went out to spread the news of Blair's displeasure with the Folletts, an act calculated to please those who had been complaining that the leader spent too much of his time in the company of rich socialists, but expensive for the Labour Party. Follett had recently taken two of the party's unofficial advisers, Patricia Hewitt and John Carr, to Washington to see how the Democrats had created a Rapid Response Unit to counter press attacks on Bill Clinton. The dinner had been arranged with a view to touching the wealthy guests for £250,000 to create a similar unit at Labour headquarters. Once attacked, Follett pulled out of fund-raising. The creation of the Rapid Response Unit was delayed for a year.

More importantly, Blair decided to take his case to the people. A sequence of public meetings were hastily organized, each open to an audience of several hundred paid up party members, starting in Gateshead on 26 January, and ending in Lewisham, in south London, on 19 April. What was most striking about the Gateshead meeting, the first in which the new leader had faced a large party audience other than in the more controlled circumstances of a party conference, was his easy self-confidence. After a few introductory words, he took off his jacket, hung it over the back of a chair, and proceeded to chat with the assembled activists as if they were all members of an extended family; he delivered direct and intelligible answers to two dozen questions in about an hour-and-a-half. That averages at three minutes per answer, compared with the twenty or thirty minutes it took Neil Kinnock to address each question when he tried to meet the party.

Endearingly, the only question Blair seemed to have difficulty answering, was number twenty-one out of twenty-four, from a middle-aged woman from North Yorkshire, who began with the declaration, 'Tony, you have given people hope.' At this early stage after his elevation, Blair appeared to have more trouble coping with extravagant praise than with opposition. He was more adept when answering the two self-styled 'hostile questions' from Louis Levi of Hexham, one of which, as Blair himself pointed out 'wasn't hostile at all', while the other was fairly tame. It was never likely that he was going to get a hostile reception, especially not in the north east of England, a region which traditionally treats the leader of the Labour Party with respect. Moreover, even in this traditional heartland, there were already hundreds of new party members for whom Blair's party is the only Labour Party they know. The Tyneside constituency of Blaydon, for example, had 400 members, a quarter of whom have joined since Blair has been leader.

Nevertheless, the accusation that his Islington lifestyle made him remote from the people was worrying him, as became apparent during a conversation I had with Blair earlier in the same day, an account of which appeared in that week's *Observer*.

On the train north that afternoon, a look of tired irritation had swept across Blair's face. Minutes earlier, when talking about Clause Four, he was sitting forward, looking directly at me, his face alive with conviction and enthusiasm. He is sure he is right, and determined to have his way. But when those wearisome words 'grant-maintained school' were introduced, his fists clenched on the table, and he sat right back, gazing out at the snow-clad fields flashing by. The pauses between his answer lengthened, as if he would rather not talk at all.

For the first time during our interview, his press secretary, Alastair Campbell, prompted him, to guide him back to the prearranged line of defence: the Conservatives are keeping this issue in the political domain.

Once reminded, Blair reeled off his well-rehearsed lines. 'The Conservatives now spend more time talking about the education of my child than they do about their own policies. The school we chose is a state comprehensive. The fact it is grant maintained has nothing to do with the choice that we made. So let's not fight the war that the Tories want us to fight.'

But what about those hundreds of party members who put so much effort into preventing their local schools from going grant maintained? Were they doing the right thing? 'That is a matter for them. They have got to decide, and of course I understand the reason why they have done that.'

And what is that reason? 'Because they preferred the school to remain under local authority control.' Close of subject, back to the snow-clad fields.

In the partial privacy of a railway carriage, Blair also reveals how Corbyn is right, in his way, to fear the ruthlessness of the new leader. There is an element in the Labour Party to whom Blair offers no quarter, and when he speaks about them he does not sound in the least bit like a cuddly character from a Disney cartoon.

There is, for instance, this observation: 'What you have to remember is that those who are running the Save Clause Four campaign – the Campaign Group and the NUM – those are the people who were in charge of the Labour Party in the early 1980s, when it nearly went out of existence.'

Or this: 'There are those who are content for the Labour Party to be a party of permanent opposition.'

Or this: 'I particularly resent the assumption that if you find these Neanderthal elements in the Labour Party, you have found the real party.'

What he resents, if the truth be told, is any implication that he and his modernizing allies are anything other than the life and soul of the party.

The meeting happened to be within the catchment of Whickham comprehensive in Gateshead, where there had been an attempt by the head and senior staff three years earlier to have the school converted to grant-maintained status. They were defeated by an energetic campaign which persuaded local parents to keep the school under the control of Gateshead's Labour council. Bob Davis, a former Gateshead councillor whose daughter was then at the school, said: 'After all those years of being in opposition, we found a battle we could win – and it felt wonderful. Now we are plunged into months of internal argument and, frankly, who gives a toss about the Clause Four debate?'[72] But sentiments like that were expressed outside the hall, rather than being thrown in the party leader's face. One of the main organizers of the Whickham campaign was Paul Tinnion, a fairly well-known mainstream member of the Labour Party establishment in the North East. He, too, said that the Blairs' choice of school stretched his loyalty, but he was not going to turn private disquiet into an overt challenge in a public meeting, because 'he's the Leader for all that'.

There was the risk of a more hostile reception at Blair's final rally, in Lewisham's Rivoli ballroom because, as the day approached, the organizers feared there might be an embarrassingly small turn-out. They abandoned any attempt to filter out potential troublemakers, throwing the meeting open to activists from anywhere in London. In fact, the audience was in a sense self-selected. Those who took the trouble to go out and listen to Tony Blair were predominantly those who wanted to hear him and were predisposed to support him. They were so much on his side that he was able to make a joke at the expense of one questioner from a previous meeting, who had told him: 'Tony, I have to be honest, I'm suspicious: I mean, I know Tories who are voting for you.' This audience laughed with Blair at the folly of the party member who could not see that the Labour Party must take Tory votes to win.[73]

By now, an alternative to the old Clause Four was on offer which expressed the belief that 'by the strength of our common endeavour, we achieve more than we achieve alone' and committed the Labour Party to working for 'a dynamic economy, serving the public interest, in which the enterprise of the market and the rigour of competition are joined with the forces of partnership and cooperation to produce the wealth the nation needs and the opportunity for all to work and prosper'. Solid evidence from early ballots showed that Blair would win overwhelmingly. The Communication Workers Union, whose 270,000 levy-paying members made it the party's sixth largest affiliate, voted nine to one in favour of the new Clause. Among constituency parties which balloted their members, the overall figure was 84 per cent in favour. The first and almost the only constituency party to produce a majority against the change was Jarrow, in South Tyneside.

By the time a special conference convened in Westminster on 29 April to ratify the new constitution, opinion was running so heavily in Blair's favour that the conference chairman had to call delegates to order when Arthur Scargill's speech was drowned out by slow hand-clapping. It was a cruel contrast to the way in which Scargill's conference speeches had electrified delegates a decade earlier. The abolition of Clause Four finally motivated Scargill to leave the Labour Party early in 1996 and to found the Socialist Labour Party.

Blair's confident speech included a renunciation of Labour's old bad habits: 'We confused means with ends, allowing one economic prescription to eclipse the aims it was supposed to serve; we permitted the party's structure and organization to fall into disrepair, prey to the politics of the vanguard, not the people; the idea of social action became dominated by the notion of a central state, and the party that came into being to change the world became frightened of changing itself.' There was also a tease. He said he had an announcement to make about the party's name, paused as delegates absorbed the implication that another huge symbolic upheaval was on the way, and then told them the name was staying as it was. The real joke was that Blair was changing the party's name by stealth, repeating the expression 'New Labour' so often that the words were being welded together.

In terms of what he wanted to achieve, Blair's tactics were immensely successful. This time, the general public appeared to accept that something truly significant had taken place within the Labour Party. The usual pattern with new leaders of the opposition is that their popularity is at its highest in the month they are elected, after which they enjoy a 'honeymoon' of a few months before they sink in public esteem. The Conservatives felt entitled to see Blair's poll rating fall around the end of 1994. In that respect, the furore around the choice of school for his oldest child began right on cue. Yet, curiously, public opinion refused to follow its charted course. In June 1995, almost a year after Blair's election, Gallup reported that he was the most popular opposition leader since records began. No less than 68 per cent of respondents stated that they thought he was doing a good job, surpassing even the figure attained by Harold Wilson in November 1963. Neil Kinnock had started at 58 per cent and never rose above it; poor Michael Foot never surpassed his starting figure of 38 per cent; and John Smith had peaked at 53 per cent.[74] Blair's personal popularity also rubbed off on the Labour Party, which repeatedly broke each polling data record with the size and durability of its lead over the government.

The best answer the Conservatives could produce to explain this popularity was that the voters had not embraced New Labour: they had been put off by the recession and the visible splits in the ruling party, but would return to it when the economy recovered. No one knew what Blair stood for, the argument went, but whatever it was, it was hugely different from the 'real' Labour Party which was entwined with the trade unions or busy running big-spending councils. Party chairman, Brian Mawhinney, claimed:

> What is clear is the growing gap between 'new' Labour's rhetoric and the actions of real Labour. Yes, Tony Blair has a way with words. Any Irishman can recognize the Blarney stone. But people search for real Labour. You'll find them in the Shadow Cabinet room doing secret deals with union bosses while telling the world that unions will get no special favour from 'new' Labour. You'll find them setting up Socialist Republics, as in Preston and Walsall. They run up debt burdens bigger than some sovereign nations, allow more empty council houses, have more uncollected council tax, and they are oh so politically correct . . . This is real Labour, bowing the knee to the unions, keen to nationalize, behaving as it has always behaved.[75]

Two separate charges are being laid here. One – to which we will return – concerns the nature of the 'real' Labour Party. The other is that Blair himself has the gift of the gab and nothing more. The basis for this is that Blair relies heavily on spin doctors and image-advisers – the assumption being that any politician who cares so much about the way he is presented must have very little to present. That is not necessarily true. A careful look at Blair's speeches and writings show he has a clear underlying philosophy and a set of ideas which appear to be workable. If they seem unexciting, that is because Blair is conservative on many social issues and extremely cautious in economic policy.

He is radical only in matters of constitutional reform. He inherited a package of policies on constitutional matters, including proposed assemblies for Scotland and Wales, regional government for England, and abolition of the voting rights of hereditary peers, all of which he retained as party policy. These measures will dominate the early years of a Blair administration.

His handling of internal party issues has also been radical in its way, but it is a radicalism borne of extreme caution. His tenure as leader of the opposition is haunted by the fear that the Labour Party might throw away yet another general election. His every move as a party manager is aimed at placating and reassuring middle-class voters and isolating those whom he held responsible for previous humiliations. In this, he is as remorseless as Neil Kinnock.

For over twenty years, there had been an agreement between left and right on the national executive that no parliamentary candidate was refused endorsement on purely political grounds. Anyone selected by a constituency party in accordance with the rules, who did not commit an offence against party discipline after being selected, was permitted to be a Labour candidate regardless of how objectionable their opinions were to the leader. Casualties like Sharon Atkin were disbarred for their behaviour after being selected. Under Blair's leadership, this convention went out of the window. First, Liz Davies was denied endorsement. Subsequently John Lloyd, who had been chosen in a properly conducted membership ballot in Exeter, was debarred because of the embarrassment caused by revelations from his distant past, when he was an ANC terrorist turned state's witness in South Africa.

When the citizens of Walsall elected a Labour council in May 1995 whose complexion was displeasing both to New Labour and to the white collar employees of Walsall council, the response was immediate. The Walsall District Labour Party was suspended on the morning after the first hostile report on the new council had appeared in the *Sunday Times*, in what proved to be the opening of a confrontation which ended in the expulsion of the council leader, Dave Church, and other councillors, who followed Scargill's example by setting up their own party. This, for the record, was not directly attributable to Blair. He was on holiday abroad when the first action was taken by the party's General Secretary, Tom Sawyer, backed by the Shadow Environment Secretary, Frank Dobson, despite the misgivings of John Prescott. Nonetheless, it reflected a leadership style which was Blair's own.

Blair was able to do all this without whipping up the kind of hostility within the Labour Party which Neil Kinnock encountered. Partly this was a tribute to his ability to shrug off internal opposition with the occasional joke. For instance, arriving for the Scottish Labour Party conference, Blair was informed that the veteran left-wing MP, Denis Canavan, had called him authoritarian. Blair feigned surprise, saying: 'I thought I told him not to say that.' Unlike Kinnock, he did not arouse contempt for being a turncoat, and could retain the personal respect of people like Dennis Skinner, who disagreed fundamentally with him but acknowledged that he could defend his beliefs with conviction. But the biggest single reason that he did not encounter the opposition which Kinnock faced was that the left had been so beaten down by more than a decade of defeats that there was little fight left in it.

While he was unforgiving to the left, Blair had no hesitation about welcoming back those who had left to establish the SDP with the intention of finishing Labour off as a party of government. Derek Scott, who had fought Swindon for the SDP in 1983, splitting the vote and letting in a Tory, was admitted to the inner circle as Blair's principle economic adviser. Roger Liddle, SDP candidate in the Fulham by-election of 1986, made a highly publicized return to the Labour Party shortly before featuring as Peter Mandelson's co-author. Several other former SDP MPs either rejoined the party or announced their intention to vote Labour. Roy Jenkins, the former SDP leader, received Tony Blair as a lunch guest at his country home in Oxfordshire and subsequently arranged a dinner at an exclusive London club for Blair to meet the Cabinet Secretary, Sir Robin Butler, and Jenkins' former Principal Private Secretary, Hayden Phillips, now Permanent Secretary at the Department of National Heritage.[76] In Kinnock's time, these overtures from old enemies were not offered and, if they had been, Kinnock might have judged that the reaction they would have caused was not worth the gain, as he did when privately approached by David Owen. Blair treated the split with the SDP like an old misunderstanding between friends which was best forgotten. 'In other European countries the Labour Party would be called the Social Democratic Party, in some countries the Democratic Socialist Party – the values are the same,' he once remarked.[77]

The crucial difference between Tony Blair and the Croslandite Social Democrats – perhaps the only important difference – is in his attitude to what economists call demand management. Crudely, this means the creation of jobs through public spending. In a long lecture on economics which he delivered in May 1995, written principally by Derek Scott, Blair proclaimed: 'Conservative and Labour governments in the 1950s and 1960s . . . had an exaggerated belief in demand management, and showed too little concern for the gradual build-up in inflationary pressure which took place from one cycle to the next.' Inflation, he asserted, was 'an evil which must be controlled', and he promised that a Labour government would have 'an explicit target for low and stable inflation'.[78] He blamed both unions and management for the 'polarized hostility' of industrial relations. Although he tempered his remarks with praise for the achievements of the post-war governments in providing a long period of economic growth and creating one of the world's finest welfare states out of a war-damaged economy, Blair was asserting that the Thatcherites had been right to put an end to the post-war consensus. He faulted them not for exaggerating the threat of inflation, but for having only one method of combating it: through interest rates.

Two pillars of Blair's economic policy were now out in the open, both of which could be expressed as negatives: neither taxes nor inflation were going to be allowed to return to anywhere like their 1970s levels. These were reassuring negatives: wage and salary earners did not want to be excessively taxed and people on fixed incomes did not want their savings to be eaten away by inflation. But it left observers wondering where the difference in economic policy was between New Labour and the Conservatives.

New Labour would offer certain limited rights of recognition for trade unions and worker representatives that they did not have under Conservatives, because of Britain's opt-out from the Social Chapter of the Treaty of Maastricht. It attached more importance to the availability of training than the Conservatives. Gordon Brown also fronted a highly effective campaign against the cornucopia of rewards enjoyed by directors of privatized utilities, vowing to impose a one-off tax on the past profits enjoyed by the utilities, most of which would be used to pay for the improved training programme. It was sensible, it did not frighten the voters, but it was hardly going to set them alight either. Where was the 'big idea' to match Harold Wilson's 1963 promise of a white hot technological revolution?

Wilson, incidentally, chose an annual party conference to unveil his big idea. Tony Blair, by contrast, went to Singapore on 8 January 1996 to share his thoughts with an audience of business leaders. The choice of venue was to emphasize the Labour leader's belief in a 'dynamic' economy, though there were other aspects of life in the Asian city state, including the very low level of state expenditure, which he did not propose to bring back to Britain. His big idea was the 'stakeholder society'.

A Stakeholder Economy meant 'a commitment by government to tackle long-term and structural unemployment' and a change in the 'corporate ethos – from the company being a mere vehicle for the capital market, to be traded, bought and sold as a commodity, towards a vision of the company as a community or partnership in which each employee has a stake'. A Stakeholder Welfare system was one which promoted 'security and opportunity across the lifecycle . . . of the whole population, rich and poor' through a combination of services as well as cash, childcare as well as child benefit, training as well as unemployment benefit.[79]

This same phrase is used in the highly influential book *The State We're In*, by the then Economics Editor of the *Guardian*, Will Hutton, to encompass 'a written constitution, the democratization of civil society, the republicanization of finance, the recognition that the market economy has to be managed and regulated, both at home and abroad; [and] the upholding of a welfare state that incorporates social citizenship'.[80] Hutton, however, was addressing a picture of society from which everyone but the privileged few was already excluded and 'the sense of belonging to a successful national project has all but disappeared'. The analysis of contemporary Britain implied in Blair's Singapore speech was not so pessimistic, although it still had alarming implications. He suggested that there was 'a better-off 30 or 40 or 50 per cent' whose talents were properly used and who could afford to provide for themselves. It was the rest, especially the unemployed and those living off social security, who needed to become 'stakeholders'.

This speech produced an extraordinarily strong reaction from the Conservative high command, who evidently suspected that Blair might be on to an idea with popular resonance and decided to present it in the worst possible light before it caught on. The aspect they attacked was the suggestion that private firms were to be made publicly accountable. Although Blair had said that firms could not be forced by legislation to behave responsibly, his words were interpreted by Cabinet Ministers as meaning nothing but a return to pre-1983 corporatist ideas about the state direction of private firms. A week later Blair was allowed space in the *Sun* to reply. He said, probably truthfully, that 'I could scarcely believe our luck when the Prime Minister attacked my vision of a Stakeholder Economy.' He went on to specify that a Stakeholder Economy 'means a new partnership at work – not turning the clock back on the trade union reforms but realizing, like our most successful companies do, that a well-treated workforce is a more effective workforce.'[81]

By chance, the arrival of 'stakeholding' coincided with another crisis inside the Labour Party, as big as the one set off by the Blairs' decision to send their eldest child to the London Oratory, and on an almost identical issue. Harriet Harman and Jack Dromey had chosen a school for their second child, only this time they had picked a school in Bromley, one of only five education authorities in Britain controlled by the Tories, which was not only grant-maintained, but put its prospective pupils through an entrance exam. The chairman of Labour's backbench education committee, Gerry Steinberg, was so outraged at this breach in Labour's long-standing opposition to grammar schools that he resigned. Another immediate consequence was that it put paid to a plan to call off the 1996 Shadow Cabinet elections. Peter Hain, one of the more influential left-wingers, had gone on record as saying that there was no real point in another election, and suggesting that the incumbent should carry on until the general election. John Reid, on the right, had gone a step further, giving notice of his intention to put this idea to the vote by Labour MPs in the very week in which the Harman controversy blew up. The idea had to be dropped because it would have denied Labour MPs their only chance to exact revenge on Harman by voting her off the Shadow Cabinet. The best that could be done to protect her was to ensure that the elections were not held until October. At an emotion-charged meeting of the parliamentary Labour Party, several MPs, including Clive Soley, who considered himself a friend of Harman's, told her to her face that she should resign. She replied with an unqualified apology for having given succour to the Conservatives, before Blair threw the full weight of his personal authority behind her, promising MPs that Labour's opposition to selection remained, but that 'The Tories want a scalp as their prize. If they get it, don't think they will stop there. I'm not going to yield on this. I'm not going to allow the Tories the pleasure of crucifying any member of the Shadow Cabinet.'[82]

In retrospect, it seems extraordinary how this relatively small matter could have seemed so serious. The reaction this time was so emotive that both Labour and Conservative MPs wondered – the one gloomily, the other optimistically – whether this was the turning point from which Labour would descend rapidly towards a fifth consecutive general election defeat. Blair described it as 'the toughest week I have had since becoming leader of the party'.[83] What it demonstrated was how Labour's confidence had been weakened and the Conservatives' fortified by the previous four election results. Periodically, a straw blowing in the wind would be taken as a sign of a lasting change in the political weather. Like so many others, this straw blew away. The next time the electors were able to cast their votes, at a parliamentary by-election in Staffordshire in April and in the council elections in May, they displayed no inclination at all to return to the Conservative Party.

One reason why disputes within the Labour Party in the first year-and-a-half of Blair's leadership were principally about symbolic issues, like the wording of the party constitution or the choice of schools for the children of Shadow Ministers, was the deliberate delay in arriving at detailed decisions over specifics like taxation and state benefits. As the election drew nearer, these questions had to be resolved. This put Labour's leaders under exceptional pressure, because the closer it comes to a general election, the more important it is that they not appear to be falling out with each other. And yet reasons for quarrelling are on the increase.

The single most important political relationship in Tony Blair's political life has been – and still is – with Gordon Brown. Brown was the one holding the line against 'tax and spend', and ingeniously devising ways to keep on attacking the government's economic record without revealing any of Labour's plans. He and Blair speak virtually every day, often several times in the same day. Much has been written about Brown's decision not to contest the party leadership in 1994, leaving the way clear for his friend. It was taken a week-and-a-half after Smith's death, when those closest to him, like the Newcastle MP, Nick Brown, and the Edinburgh MP, Nigel Griffiths, still believed he had a chance of winning, even against Tony Blair. It is open to question how big a sacrifice Brown actually made, because if he had gone into a contest against Blair, all the signs are that he would have lost. Since Blair would not back down, it was sensible for Brown to give way. Even so, it was a singularly difficult decision for someone whose life had been dedicated to politics and whose ultimate goal had always been to lead the Labour Party. Now he was required to settle for second place behind the friend who had once been his junior.

Brown had accumulated enemies as well as admirers. It was well-known that two of the Shadow Cabinet's Big Four – John Prescott and Robin Cook – could not abide him. Brown and Prescott fought one of their battles by proxy in Swindon, where there was a bitter contest over the choice of parliamentary candidate. The contestants were Michael Wills, a London television producer and former adviser of Brown's, and Jim D'Avila, a union convenor at the local Rover car factory. Wills narrowly won, but there were so many complaints that the matter was referred to the national executive, producing a rare instance of Blair and Prescott being on different sides of a public dispute. Prescott fought hard behind the scenes for D'Avila but, without Blair's backing, he was unsuccessful.

The shenanigans which followed John Smith's death had also ruptured Gordon Brown's relations with Peter Mandelson and put a temporary pall on his friendship with Blair himself. They disagreed over the question of who should be Blair's deputy. Nick Brown was canvassing for a Blair–Beckett ticket, which at one point in the campaign gave rise to a BBC report that Beckett was Blair's private preference, an idea swiftly contradicted on Blair's behalf by Peter Mandelson.[84] While Blair never publicly expressed a preference, it became quite clear that he was content with Prescott's victory. Then there was an unexpected twist in the 1995 Shadow Cabinet elections, when the Monklands West MP, Tom Clarke, recaptured the Shadow Cabinet place he had lost only a year earlier. His defeat was a spin-off from the controversy which engulfed Monklands district council, where Labour councillors had been accused of nepotism and of favouring Catholics over Protestants. None of this was ever proved, although enough dirt flew to threaten Labour with the loss of the Monklands East seat which became vacant when John Smith died. Clarke, a former Provost of Monklands, persisted in defending the Monklands councillors when the Shadow Scottish Secretary, George Robertson, and the by-election candidate in Monklands East, Helen Liddell, were disowning them. This cost him his Shadow Cabinet seat in 1994. His return a year later meant that John Cunningham, one of the few remaining members of Labour's frontbench who had had experience as a government minister, was removed, much to Blair's annoyance. Among the people who had been most assiduous in canvassing for Clarke were MPs like Nigel Griffiths, who were assumed to be doing so at Gordon Brown's behest. The Scottish MP, Henry McLeish, a former member of the circle of admirers who surrounded Brown, was so angry that he let fly at Brown in the crowded lobby of the House of Commons, accusing him of engineering Clarke's return.

This and other small twists in the Byzantine world of professional politicians produced rumours that Brown was working to some agenda all his own. More contributions to the rumour mill emanated from the engineering union, the AEEU, where there had been an upset when the right's candidate for the union presidency was defeated by Davy Hall, from the 'soft left'. One of the organizer's of Hall's campaign was Charlie Whelan, Gordon Brown's personal spin doctor.

In December, this blew up into a confrontation within the Shadow Cabinet. The immediate cause was an interview which Gordon Brown had given to the *Daily Telegraph*, in which he suggested that unemployed people who unreasonably refused places on training schemes created for them by a Blair government would have their benefits docked. In one sense, this represented nothing new: it had always been Labour policy, since the introduction of the modern welfare state, that people who refused to work would put their unemployment benefit in jeopardy. But the way Brown phrased his comments raised the spectre of American-style 'work-fare', under which the unemployed, crudely, had to work to earn their benefits. That was not party policy, as the chief policy coordinator, Robin Cook, pointed out when the Shadow Cabinet met. He was backed up by the PLP chairman, Doug Hoyle, and by Frank Dobson. Two others, Jack Straw and Mo Mowlam, also made passing criticisms about the way the idea had been presented, and Michael Meacher chipped in with his own outline proposals. John Prescott, David Blunkett and Chris Smith did not speak, but they had already complained privately to Blair that the Shadow Chancellor was out of line. Blair thought so too, but his more immediate concern was that no report should reach the public and he warned every-one present to keep their comments private.

This was all relatively good-tempered and lasted only a few minutes. Some of those who were present, including the then Campaigns Director, Joy Johnson, thought that Brown dealt with the criticisms adequately and came away having impressed everyone with the meticulous detail with which he had planned the following month's campaign against the Conservatives. However, in defiance of Blair's warning, full details of the row appeared in that week's *Observer*. (Since I was the author of the piece, I should say that having exploded on the night, Brown took it all with good humour afterwards.) Disturbed that someone privy to Shadow Cabinet deliberations would talk so freely, Blair issued a warning at the next week's meeting that anyone caught committing such a breach of secrecy would be denied a job in a Blair administration.

Four months later, Brown was the centre of controversy again. This time, it was not a personal clash or an argument about words, but a serious disagreement over important details. He was due to give the annual John Smith Memorial lecture, which he delivered at Edinburgh University on 19 April. The nub of the lecture was a serious argument about 'equality', a word which appeared to have passed out of fashion since Roy Hattersley's departure from the Shadow Cabinet, but which Brown insisted should be restored to its proper place in Labour's value system. However, he was not using the word in the sense in which it was deployed by Hattersley or by Anthony Crosland. He meant 'equality of opportunity', which implied that people should have recurrent opportunities throughout life to educate and better themselves. In particular, it implied that teenagers from working-class families should have the same access to higher education as the children of the well-off. To that end, he said, he had embarked with David Blunkett and the Shadow Social Secretary, Chris Smith, on a review of all public spending on further education, including grants and child benefit.[85]

It was not what he actually said which detonated a reaction in the party, but the interpretation put on it by spin doctors in advance of the speech. That morning's newspapers had been told that Gordon Brown would be announcing the abolition of child benefit for the over-sixteens, something to which neither Blunkett nor Smith had signed up. Smith's social security team had only just completed a draft policy document, which they had submitted for Blair's and Brown's approval, which included a closely argued defence of universal child benefit. For years, the Labour Party had defended child benefit against Margaret Thatcher's unfulfilled ambition to abolish it. The second largest item of expenditure in the shadow budget which John Smith presented during the 1992 general election was a proposed increase in child benefit, which had lost its value during the Thatcher years. Now, to the delight of Cabinet Ministers from John Major downwards, the roles were suddenly reversed and the Conservative Party could represent itself as the defender of child benefit.

At first, it appeared that the spin doctors may have overstepped their instructions. When Chris Smith raised an objection at the next Shadow Cabinet meeting, Alastair Campbell nobly took responsibility on behalf of himself and Charlie Whelan. But as the controversy dragged on, it became obvious that Brown really was intent on abolishing child benefit for the over-sixteens in full-time education, which he saw as an indiscriminate subsidy which went principally to middle-class families, when it could be better redistributed to students who needed it. Smith on the other hand, objected on principle to cutting off a source of income to mothers in order to redirect it to teenagers who might then still expect their mothers to feed and clothe them.

At the same time, Chris Smith had submitted another paper entitled *Welfare into Work*, on creating employment for the unemployed. It contained a number of proposals which had been worked out in detail, which would cost money in the short term but which the team claimed would pay for themselves as claimants came off state benefits. One proposal was to abolish the recently introduced Jobseekers' Allowance and return to the previous system, thereby increasing from six to twelve months the period during which a claimant was entitled to unemployment benefit before going on to means-tested income support. This was not being put forward as a simple act of compassion. The argument behind it was that many unemployed men had wives or partners in part-time work; once they went from the dole on to income support, their partner's earnings counted against them. In other words, extending the period of unemployment benefit was offered as a means of combating the notorious 'poverty trap' in which people on the fringes have no incentive to work rather than live off the state. But when it went before the Shadow Cabinet's Economic Policy Commission in early May, very soon after the child benefit issue had blown up, Smith was again overruled by Gordon Brown. This news seemed not to filter through to the employment spokesman, Michael Meacher, who put his name to an article for the radical magazine *Red Pepper* which flatly asserted that 'The Jobseekers' Allowance is unacceptable and Labour will abolish it.' Meacher was obliged to apologize. His cover story was that the piece had been written on his behalf by his researcher, Ian Willmore, who failed to show him the final draft. However, it is extremely unlikely that Willmore did anything other than faithfully represent what he knew his employer actually thought.

In each case, the left watched hopefully for evidence of a breach in the Blair–Brown relationship. It is frequently thought that the ambitious Brown will eventually come out in open conflict with his old friend and, if he does, he is likely to emerge on Blair's left rather than to the right; but in every instance Brown played the part of a Blairite modernizer to the full, and Blair gave him unqualified backing. The partnership of Blair and Brown was outwardly as secure as the old Brown and Blair duet. The economics of New Labour is at least as much the creation of Gordon Brown as it is of Tony Blair.

It is a very cautious economic programme, from which some socialist catchwords like 'common ownership' are banned outright and others, like 'equality' are deployed with the utmost care, hedged by narrow definitions. It is not 'socialism' in the dictionary sense of the word at all, because it is not a programme for transforming capitalism. It would place the free

market economy within a mild regulatory framework acceptable to enlight-
ened employers, to give it social cohesion and protect it from instability
caused by extreme poverty and helplessness. It is not revolution, but it is
achievable.

One of the more apposite remarks once made by Peter Mandelson, in
reference to Neil Kinnock, was that he intended to 'get his betrayal in
early'. Though it sounds cynical, that sentiment directly addresses the infamous 'crisis of expectations' which awaits each new Labour government,
like the equally predictable and catastrophic sterling crisis. If Labour voters
have been promised a white hot technological revolution, they expect to see
it happen and to feel the benefits. The Labour Party, more than thirty
years later, is still living with the consequences of Harold Wilson's inability
to match the expectations he aroused. Following Kinnock's example, Blair
has kept expectations so low that it is difficult to see how those who vote
him into power can be disappointed with the results. They may even get
more than they expect. All this accords with Blair's declared aim of preparing not for one term in office but for two.

He also put himself on a trajectory from which he will probably emerge
as a 'national' rather than a 'party' leader. It is unlikely that the Labour Party
will ever grant him the respect and affection accorded to party heroes like
Keir Hardie or Aneurin Bevan or Michael Foot. Generally, though, the
electorate appreciates political leaders who are seen to put the public interest above the interests of the party, which is what Blair appears to be intent
on doing. If the British monarchy finally implodes in the first quarter of the
twenty-first century and, in that moment of crisis, there is an urgent need
for a President of the Republic of Great Britain who will stand above the
sordid routine of party politics and speak for the nation, perhaps every section of the establishment except the residue of the Labour Party will be
calling for Anthony Charles Lynton Blair.

What the Conservatives hope, however, is that the tension between
Blair and the most active sections of the party he leads will become uncontrollable and the Labour Party will become as divided as it was in the early
1980s. However, Blair's not-so-secret weapon is that he can appeal over the
heads of activists to the membership at large, who in effect are just voters
with party cards. Each time he does so – in the leadership election, in the
campaign to abolish the old Clause Four of the party constitution or in

seeking endorsement for his general election manifesto – Blair scores huge majorities. This is the supreme achievement of the 'modernizers'. They have a leader who is elevated above the swirling morass of factions and interest groups which make up the party, who can exert his authority in his own way, free from the risk that he can be effectively challenged. For good or ill, that must permanently change the nature of the Labour Party.

NOTES

PREAMBLE

1. Leo McInstrey, *Fit to Govern?* (Bantam Press, London 1966) p. 1.
2. Ian McAllister and Richard Rose, *The Nationwide Competition for Votes – The 1983 British Election* (Frances Pinter, London 1984) p. 5.

1. NEIL KINNOCK AND THE RULE BOOK: A GUIDE

1. David Hare, *The Absence of War* (Faber and Faber, London 1993) p. 95.
2. *Daily Telegraph*, 8 June 1983.
3. *Daily Express*, 3 April 1991.
4. Interview with David Dimbleby, in 'Neil Kinnock – The Lost Leader' *BBC 2*, 5 December 1992.
5. Interview on *Channel Four News*, 11 June 1991.
6. *BBC 2*, 5 December 1992.
7. *Hansard*, 18 October 1990, col. 1375.
8. Eric Heffer, 'Keeping the Faith', *New Statesman & Society*, 29 March 1991, p. 19.
9. Alan Clark, *Diaries* (Weidenfeld & Nicolson, London 1993) p. 135.
10. *The Power to Defend Our Country* (Labour Party, 1986) pp. 7–9.
11. *Panorama*, 29 September 1986; Michael Leapman, *Kinnock* (Unwin Hyman, London 1987) pp. 149–54.
12. Denis Healey, letter to Neil Kinnock, Kinnock Archive, Churchill College, Cambridge.
13. Alastair Campbell, 'You Guys are the Pits', *New Statesman*, 3 April 1987.
14. *Guardian*, 20 June 1972.
15. *Hansard*, 26 February 1975, cols 610–11.
16. *Hansard*, 6 September 1990, col. 828.

17. Frank Allaun, *The Struggle for Peace* (A Labour Action for Peace Pamphlet, undated) p. 16.

18. Eric Heffer, *Labour's Future: Socialist or SDP Mark 2?* (Verso, London 1986) p. 17.

19. Michael Foot, *Aneurin Bevan*, Vol. 1 (MacGibbon & Kee, London 1962) p. 149.

20. David Owen, *Time to Declare* (Michael Joseph, London 1991) p. 477.

21. *Report of the Annual Conference of the Labour Party, 1979*, pp. 361–2.

22. Tony Benn, *Conflicts of Interest* (Arrow, London 1991) p. 515.

23. Private information.

24. Tony Benn, *Conflicts of Interest* (Arrow, London 1991) pp. 583–4.

25. *Ibid.*, p. 578.

26. David Owen, *Time to Declare* (Michael Joseph, London 1991) pp. 430–31.

27. *Hansard*, 3 April 1982, col. 661.

28. *Tribune*, 18 September 1981.

29. G.M.F. Drower, *Neil Kinnock – The Path to Leadership* (Weidenfeld & Nicolson, London 1984) pp. 90–91.

30. *Hansard*, 6 September 1990, col. 828.

31. *Observer*, 21 May 1995.

32. *BBC 2*, 5 December 1992.

33. G.M.F. Drower, *Neil Kinnock – The Path to Leadership* (Weidenfeld & Nicolson, London 1984) pp. 131–3.

34. Peter Jenkins, *The Battle for Downing Street* (Charles Knight, London 1970) p. 75.

35. Anthony Crosland, *The Future of Socialism* (Jonathan Cape, London 1956) p. 155.

36. *Ibid.*, p. 113.

37. Quoted in Radhika Desai, *Intellectuals and Socialism – 'Social Democrats' and the Labour Party* (Lawrence & Wishart, London 1994) p. 155.

38. Radhika Desai, *Intellectuals and Socialism* (Lawrence & Wishart, London 1994) p. 127.

39. Peter Mandelson and Roger Liddle, *The Blair Revolution – Can New Labour Deliver?* (Faber and Faber, London 1996) p. 124.

40. David Marquand, 'Inquest on a Movement: Labour's Defeat and its Consequences', *Encounter*, July 1979, quoted in Desai, *Intellectuals and Socialism* (Lawrence & Wishart, London 1994) p. 179.

41. Neil Kinnock 'My Socialism', *New Statesman*, 7 October 1983.

42. Roy Hattersley interview for *The Wilderness Years*, BBC 1.

43. *Sunday Times*, 16 October 1983.

44. Jon Silkin, *Changing Battlefields – The Challenge to the Labour Party* (Hamish Hamilton, London 1982).

45. Details of the make-up of Knowsley North Labour Party GC are taken from

an unpublished note prepared in 1986 by officers of the North West Regional Labour Party. Figures for membership of the three union branches in question are from the unpublished *Investigation into the Liverpool District Labour Party* (1985).

46. *Daily Mirror*, 23 July 1984.
47. Michael Cocks, *Labour and the Benn Factor* (Macdonald, London 1989).
48. *Report of the Annual Conference of the Labour Party, 1984*, p. 34.
49. Interview with David Dimbleby, in 'Neil Kinnock – The Lost Leader', *BBC 2*, 5 December 1992.
50. *Report of the Annual Conference of the Labour Party, 1985*, p. 154.
51. Patrick Seyd, 'Bennism without Benn – Realignment on the Labour Left', *New Socialist*, No. 17, May 1985.
52. From my own note of the meeting, which was unreported.
53. *Report of the Annual Conference of the Labour Party, 1985*, p. 128.
54. *Report of the Annual Conference of the Labour Party, 1987*, p. 61.
55. Private information.
56. For a view of the Greenwich by-election from the left, see in particular Richard Heffernan and Mike Marqusee, *Defeat from the Jaws of Victory – Inside Kinnock's Labour Party* (Verso, London 1992) pp. 71–4.
57. I can vouch for Mandelson's reaction because I was the one who told him about Deidre Wood's selection. This section is written with first-hand knowledge, because I was sent in by Walworth Road as the by-election press officer.
58. I was the other person in the room when this conversation took place, and made a note of it afterwards.
59. *Report of the Annual Conference of the Labour Party, 1987*, p. 9.
60. *Ibid.*, p. 47.
61. *Hansard*, 10 December 1971, col. 1745.
62. *Hansard*, 1 August 1972, col. 417.
63. *Hansard*, 16 January 1974, col. 690.
64. *Hansard*, 10 December 1976, cols 887–8.
65. *Hansard*, 12 December 1975, col. 828.
66. *Guardian*, 15 January 1988.
67. Peter Mandelson, 'People in Power', *The People*, 24 May 1992.
68. Tony Benn, Press Release, 30 January 1988.
69. *Morning Star*, 22 February 1988. The same manifesto was republished in Tony Benn, *Fighting Back – Speaking Out for Socialism in the Eighties* (Hutchinson, London 1988) pp. 299–300.
70. *Hansard*, 17 May 1998, col. 799.
71. *This Week Next Week*, BBC 1, 5 June 1988.
72. Neil Kinnock, Speech at the Northern Family Gala Day, Beamish, 11 June 1988.
73. *Tribune*, 10 June 1988.

74. *Tribune*, 17 June 1988.
75. *Independent*, 21 June 1988.
76. *New Statesman*, 22 July 1988.
77. Ron Todd, speech to Tribune rally.
78. *Meet the Challenge, Make the Change*, Labour Party policy document 1989.
79. Peter Kellner, 'State Socialism: an "ism" that became a "wasm"', the *Independent*, 16 August 1991.
80. 'We are the Managers Now', *Director* magazine, September 1991.
81. *Democratic Socialist Aims and Values* (Labour Party, 1988).
82. Peter Mandelson and Roger Liddle, *The Blair Revolution* (Faber and Faber, London 1966) p. 36.
83. *Birmingham Post*, 20 September 1995.

2. THE LONG TRUDGE OF TED GRANT

1. The most authoritative account of Grant's early life is in the introduction by John Pickard to Ted Grant, *The Unbroken Thread – the Development of Trotskyism over 40 Years* (Fortress Books, London 1989).
2. *Independent*, 21 December 1989.
3. Roger Protz, letter to the author, May 1996.
4. Ted Grant, *The Unbroken Thread*, (Fortress Books, London 1989) pp. 8–10 and *passim*.
5. Interview with Tommy Birchall, in Peter Taaffe and Tony Mulhearn, *Liverpool – A City that Dared to Fight* (Fortress Books, London 1988).
6. Roy Hadwin, interview with the author.
7. *Newcastle Journal and North Mail*, 6 April 1944.
8. Ted Grant, *The Unbroken Thread*, (Fortress Books, London 1989) p. 47.
9. *Ibid.*, p. 31.
10. This account is from the unpublished twenty-two-page report drawn up by the ILP Commission of Enquiry, a copy of which is in the possession of the Labour historian, Dr Ray Challinor.
11. Interview with ex-RCP member A.
12. Eric Heffer, *Never a Yes Man* (Verso, London 1991) pp. 334.
13. Information from Dr Ray Challinor.
14. Ted Grant, *The Unbroken Thread*, p. 412.
15. Interview with ex-RCP member T.
16. Interview with ex-RCP member A.
17. John Lloyd, *The History of the EEPTU* (Weidenfeld & Nicolson, London 1990) p. 584.
18. Ted Grant, *The Unbroken Thread*, p. 412.

19. Peter Taaffe, *The Rise of Militant* (Militant Publications, London 1995) p. 11.
20. Ted Grant, *The Unbroken Thread*, pp. 88, 225 and 403. The words quoted in respect of Healy and Mandel are actually those of the book's editor, John Pickard, rather than Grant's.
21. Tony Benn, *Against the Tide – Diaries 1973–76* (Arrow, London 1989), pp. 20–21.
22. David Widgery, *The Left in Britain 1956–1968* (Penguin, Harmondsworth 1976) p. 211.
23. Andy Troke, interview with the author.
24. *Report of the Annual Conference of the Labour Party, 1983*, p. 63.
25. Tony Benn, *Against the Tide – Diaries 1973–76* (Arrow, London 1989), pp. 20–21.
26. Peter Taaffe, *The Rise of Militant* (Militant Publications/World Socialist Books, London 1995) p. 74.
27. *Observer*, 31 August 1975, quoted in Michael Crick, *The March of Militant* (Faber and Faber, London 1986).
28. Tony Benn, *Against the Tide* (Arrow, London 1990) p. 468.
29. Ron Hayward and David Hughes, 'Inquiry into Militant Tendency', *NEC Report 1982*, p. 133.
30. Eric Shaw, *Discipline and Discord in the Labour Party* (Manchester University Press, Manchester 1988) p. 221.
31. Ted Grant, 'The Crisis of British Capitalism' in *The Unbroken Thread*, p. 489 and *passim*.
32. *Ibid.*, p. 501. (Italics as in the original.)
33. Prunella Kaur, *Go Fourth and Multiply – The Political Anatomy of the British Left Groups* (Undated pamphlet, published *c.* 1979, by 'Dialogue of the Deaf', Bristol).
34. Jim Mortimer, interview with the author.
35. *Report of the Annual Conference of the Labour Party, 1983*, p. 60.
36. Information from John Spellar MP.
37. Interview with Anthony Bevins in the *Independent*, 15 December 1986.
38. Derek Hatton, *Inside Left, The Story So Far . . .* (Bloomsbury, London 1988) p. 71.
39. *Militant*, 24 January 1992.
40. *Ibid.*
41. *Ibid.*
42. *Ibid.*

3. THE SHOPPIE ON THE SCOTSWOOD ROAD

1. Joyce Quin, interview with the author.
2. *Report of Conference – Annual Conference 1994* (Labour Party, 1994) p. 114.
3. On 23 February 1983, Murray conducted four hours of taped interview with Hilary Wainwright, for the independent film company Trade Films, of Bottlebank, Gateshead. It took place in the Hydraulic Crane, on the Scotswood Road. The quotation is from pages 2–3 of the unpublished transcript.
4. Len Edmondson, interview with the author.
5. Jim Murray, interview with Hilary Wainwright, 23 February 1983, unpublished transcript, p. 11.
6. On April 4 1985, Jim Murray conducted a brief second interview with Hilary Wainwright for Trade Films. The quotation is from page 1 of the unpublished transcript.
7. Roy Hadwin, interview with the author.
8. Jim Murray, interview with Hilary Wainwright, February 1983.
9. Private information.
10. Alan Plater, *Close the Coalhouse Door*, based on stories by Sid Chaplin, with songs by Alex Glasgow (Methuen, London 1973). This and other Alex Glasgow songs were released on CD in 1994. He himself told me the origin of the final lines of the *Socialist ABC*.
11. Jim Murray, 'Organising the Combines, or Syndicalism Rides Again', unpublished ms, 18 July 1979.
12. Huw Beynon and Hilary Wainwright, *The Workers' Report on Vickers* (Pluto, London 1979) p. 116.
13. *Ibid.*, p. 194.
14. Jim Murray, 'Syndicalism Rides Again', *Tyneside Socialist Centre Bulletin*, No. 19, February 1980.
15. Jim Murray, interview with Hilary Wainwright, 23 February 1983, unpublished transcript, pp. 63–3.
15. *Ibid.*, pp. 46–7.
16. *Ibid.*, pp. 74–5.
18. *Report of the National Executive Committee to the Eightieth Annual Conference of the Labour Party* (Labour Party, 1981) p. 141.
19. *Report of the Annual Conference of the Labour Party*, 1985, p. 120.
20. Jim Murray, 'Take me to Your Leader – Which One?' *Tyneside Socialist Centre Bulletin*, No. 18, January 1980.
21. Jim Murray, interview with Hilary Wainwright, 23 February 1983, unpublished transcript, pp. 74–5.
22. Jim Murray, *Tyneside Socialist Centre Bulletin*, January 1980.

23. *Report of the National Executive Committee to the Eightieth Annual Conference of the Labour Party* (Labour Party, 1981) p. 145.

24. Patrick Wintour and Francis Wheen, 'Enemies of Democracy', *New Statesman*, 5 October 1979.

25. Jim Murray, letter in *New Statesman*, 12 October 1979.

26. Jim Murray, *Tyneside Socialist Centre Bulletin*, January 1980.

27. Hilary Wainwright, 'An Independent Socialist', obituary of Jim Murray, *Guardian*, January 1989.

28. Roy Hadwin, interview with the author.

29. John Evans, interview with the author.

30. Len Edmondson, interview with the author.

4. THE BLIND MAN FROM SHEFFIELD

1. David Blunkett, unpublished letter to Neil Kinnock, 30 November 1989, retained in the Kinnock Archive, Churchill College, Cambridge.

2. David Blunkett, with Alex MacCormick, *On a Clear Day* (Michael O'Mara Books, London 1995) p. 40.

3. *Ibid.*, p. 69.

4. This is a real life example, but to be fair to the staff of Sheffield council, I should say that it was in an officer's report presented to a committee of Northumberland county council in 1976.

5. W. Hamilton, *Democracy and Community* (Oxford University Press, Oxford 1970) p. 86, quoted in Patrick Seyd, *The Rise and Fall of the Labour Left* (Macmillan, London 1987) p. 59.

6. Quoted in Patrick Seyd, *The Rise and Fall of the Labour Left*, p. 60.

7. Hilary Wainwright, *Labour, A Tale of Two Parties* (Hogarth Press, London 1987) p. 108.

8. Patrick Seyd, *The Rise and Fall of the Labour Left*, p. 149.

9. David Blunkett and Geoff Green, *Building from the Bottom: The Sheffield Experience* (Fabian Society, London 1983).

10. David Blunkett, interview with the author.

11. 'The David Blunkett Column' *Tribune*, 5 December 1986.

12. David Blunkett, 'Labour and the Lunacy of Political Correctness' *Daily Mail*, 29 May 1995.

13. *Hansard*, 20 June 1990, col. 1023.

14. *Report of the Annual Conference of the Labour Party, 1984*, p. 140.

15. *Report of the Annual Conference of the Labour Party, 1983*, p. 80.

16. David Blunkett and Keith Jackson, *Democracy in Crisis – The Town Halls Respond* (Hogarth Press, London 1987) pp. 171–2.

17. *Report of the Annual Conference of the Labour Party, 1984*, pp. 103, 129, 130, 134, 137, 138, 295, 296.
18. *Report of the Annual Conference of the Labour Party, 1984,* pp. 140–41.
19. Kenneth Baker, *The Turbulent Years* (Faber and Faber, London 1993) p. 108.
20. David Blunkett and Keith Jackson, *Democracy in Crisis*, p. 171.
21. Peter Taaffe and Tony Mulhearn, *Liverpool: A City That Dared to Fight* (Fortress Books, London 1988) p. 184.
22. *Report of the Annual Conference of the Labour Party, 1984*, pp. 129–30.
23. *Guardian*, 12 March 1985.
24. *Report of the Annual Conference of the Labour Party, 1985,* pp. 176–7.
25. Patrick Seyd, 'Bennism without Benn: Realignment on the Labour Left', *New Socialist*, No. 27 (May 1985).
26. Tony Benn, *The End of an Era, Diaries 1980–90* (Arrow, London 1994) p. 425.
27. *Report of the Annual Conference of the Labour Party, 1985*, pp. 169, 177.
28. David Blunkett, interview with the author.
29. Derek Hatton, *Inside Left* (Bloomsbury, London 1988) p. 159.
30. David Blunkett, interview with the author.
31. Peter Taaffe and Tony Mulhearn, *Liverpool, A City that Dared to Fight* (Fortress Books, London 1988) p. 118.
32. Charles E. Turnock, *Mersey Militants* (unpublished ms, 1986) pp. 32–3.
33. *Guardian*, 19 December 1985.
34. David Blunkett, interview with the author.
35. *Woman's Own*, February 1987, quoted *inter alia* in the *Daily Mail*, 17 February 1987.
36. *Hansard*, 25 June 1987, cols 71, 72–3.
37. *Report of the Eighty-sixth Annual Conference of the Labour Party, 1987*, p. 14.
38. David Blunkett, *Press Release*, 10 June 1988.
39. Colin Hughes and Patrick Wintour, *Labour Rebuilt –The New Model Party* (Fourth Estate, London 1990) p. 122.
40. David Blunkett, interview with the author.
41. *Report of the Eighty-seventh Annual Conference of the Labour Party, 1988*, p. 46.
42. *Ibid.*, p. 49.
43. *Hansard*, 17 December 1987, cols 1272–3.
44. Bryan Gould, *Goodbye to All That* (Macmillan, London 1995) p. 224.
45. BBC Radio 4 *The World this Weekend*, 1 January 1995.
46. David Blunkett, interview with the author.
47. David Blunkett, 'Tables are here to stay', *The Times*, 21 November 1994.
48. *Guardian*, 12 April 1995.
49. David Blunkett, interview with the author.
50. *Diversity and Excellence, A New Partnership for Schools* (Labour Party, 1995).

51. *Guardian,* 27 September 1986.
52. David Blunkett, interview with the author.

5. CLARE SHORT

1. This account is drawn from Alan Clark, *Diaries* (Weidenfeld & Nicholson, London 1993) pp. 29–30; *Hansard,* 20 July 1983, cols 481–3; and contemporary newspaper reports, e.g. the *Sun,* 21 July 1983.
2. Ralph Miliband, *New Left Review,* No. 150.
3. Michael Meacher, Peter Hain, Alan Simpson and Clare Short, *Socialism* (Tribune pamphlet, undated) p.15.
4. *Hansard,* 22 January 1986, col. 126.
5. *Hansard,* 29 October 1990, cols 733–5, 748.
6. *Report of the Eighty-sixth Annual Conference of the Labour Party, 1987,* p. 39.
7. *Hansard,* 24 January 1986, col. 615.
8. For Clare Short's own account, and extracts from letters written to her by women, see Clare Short, *Dear Clare . . . . . . this is what Women Feel about Page 3,* Letters edited and selected by Kiri Tunks and Diane Hutchinson (Radius, London 1991).
9. *Hansard,* 12 March 1986, col. 938.
10. On John Kay, see Peter Chippindale and Chris Horrie, *Stick it Up your Punter! – The Rise and Fall of the Sun* (Mandarin, London 1990).
11. *Hansard,* 3 April 1990, col. 1095.
12. *Hansard,* 18 December 1991, col. 338.
13. *Hansard,* 13 April 1988, cols 168–72.
14. *Hansard,* 14 May 1984, col. 207.
15. *Hansard,* 29 October 1984, col. 1066.
16. *Hansard,* 14 May 1984, col. 70.
17. *Hansard,* 25 January 1989, col. 1155.
18. *Hansard,* 23 January 1991, col. 432.
19. *News of the World,* 27 January 1991.
20. *Daily Telegraph,* 8 August 1991.
21. *Sun,* 19 April 1991.
22. *Report of the Annual Conference of the Labour Party, 1980,* p. 144.
23. *Ibid.,* p. 266.
24. 'Class Rule', *BBC 2,* 26 November 1991.
25. *Hansard,* 24 April 1990, col. 240.
26. *Hansard,* 19 July 1984, col. 555.
27. Information from Clare Short.

28. *Hansard*, 22 February 1984, col. 864.

29. *Hansard*, 15 February 1984. col. 330.

30. I was present at the meeting where this exchange took place.

31. Quoted in Hilary Wainwright, *Labour: A Tale of Two Parties* (Hogarth Press, London 1987) p. 188.

32. *Report of the Annual Conference of the Labour Party, 1985*, pp. 32, 38.

33. *Observer*, 24 March 1991.

34. *Hansard*, 1 April 1985, col. 984.

35. *Hansard*, 13 November 1989, col. 106.

36. *Hansard*, 4 March 1994, col. 1229.

37. This account of the Small Heath selection is drawn from Les Back and John Solomos, *Who Represents Us? Racialised Politics and Candidate Selection* (Department of Politics and Sociology, Birkbeck College, University of London, Research Papers No. 3, May 1992) and from an interview with Muhammed Afzal and a telephone conversation with Roger Godsiff.

38. Clare Short, 'Fifth Column', *New Socialist*, May 1985.

39. Michael Leapman, *Kinnock* (Unwin Hyman, London 1987) p. 153.

40. This phrase appears, for example, in Labour's 1987 general election manifesto, *Britain will win*.

41. *Hansard*, 2 July 1984, cols 93–4.

42. *Hansard* 24 October 1983, col. 90.

43. *Hansard*, 6 December 1998, col. 251.

44. Richard Heffernan and Mike Marqusee, *Defeat from the Jaws of Victory* (Verso, London 1992) p. 189.

45. *Guardian*, 13 March 1991.

46. *Hansard*, 21 February 1991, col. 471.

47. *Guardian*, 13 March 1991.

48. Handwritten note to the author, March 1996.

49. *Hansard*, 18 March 1991, col. 65.

50. Andrew Roth, *Parliamentary Profiles S–Z*, (Parliamentary Private Services, London 1991) p. 1368.

51. Interview with *On the Record*, quoted in John Rentoul, *Tony Blair* (Little, Brown, London 1995) p. 274.

52. *Tribune*, 14 January 1993.

53. Jon Sopel, *Tony Blair: The Moderniser* (Michael Joseph, London 1995) p. 161; Rentoul, *Tony Blair* (Little, Brown, London 1995) p. 344.

54. Nicholas Jones, *Soundbites and Spin Doctors*, (Cassell, London 1995) p. 146.

55. *Labour Party News*.

56. Clare Short, 'Fixing the Fixers', *Fabian Review*, Vol. 104, No. 4 (July 1992).

57. Clare Short, 'In, but Never Of, the Party', *New Statesman & Society*, 13 October 1995.

58. Liz Davies, 'Process of Abuse', *New Statesman & Society*, 2 June 1995.

59. *Hansard,* 21 July 1988, col. 1384.
60. 'Breakfast with Frost', BBC 1, 29 October 1995.

6. THE MYTH OF PETER MANDELSON

1. Brian Appleyard, 'The Third Man' *Sunday Times Magazine,* 1 October 1995.
2. *The People,* 2 September 1990.
3. Conservative Central Office, *Press Release,* 7 June 1991.
4. *Dispatches,* 7 October 1990.
5. Ken Livingstone, *Livingstone's Labour – A Programme for the Nineties* (Unwin Hyman, London 1989).
6. *Observer,* 24 July 1983.
7. *Independent on Sunday,* 10 February 1991.
8. *The Times,* 2 February 1989.
9. Peter Rose, 'Guarding the Good Name of the Rose', *Guardian,* 2 October 1989.
10. Nicholas Jones, *Soundbites and Spin Doctors: How Politicians Manipulate the Media – and vice versa* (Cassell, London 1995) pp. 42–4, 132.
11. Seamus Milne, 'The Leader's Little Helper', *Guardian,* 11 February 1995.
12. *Guardian,* 24 April 1981.
13. *Guardian,* 2 October 1989.
14. *The Backbench Diaries of Richard Crossman,* edited by Janet Morgan (Hamish Hamilton and Jonathan Cape, London 1981) p. 455.
15. Colin Hughes and Patrick Wintour, *Labour Rebuilt – The New Model Party* (Fourth Estate, London 1990) p. 78.
16. *Guardian,* 30 May 1991.
17. Bryan Gould, *Goodbye to All That* (Macmillan, London 1995) pp. 225–6.
18. *Independent,* 11 December 1989.
19. Bryan Gould, *Goodbye to All That* (Macmillan, London 1995) pp. 217–18.
20. Jon Sopel, *Tony Blair: The Moderniser* (Michael Joseph, London 1995) p. 120.
21. Brian Appleyard, 'A Masterpiece in Red by the Party Smirker', *Sunday Times,* 19 May 1991.
22. Quoted in Peter Mandelson and Roger Liddle, *The Blair Revolution – Can New Labour Deliver?* (Faber and Faber, London 1996) p. 328.
23. Wintour is accused of being 'Mandelson's amanuensis' in Richard Heffernan and Mike Marqusee, *Defeat from the Jaws of Victory – Inside Kinnock's Labour Party* (Verso, London 1992) p. 219; and of being 'Mandelson's favourite journalist' in several issues of *Private Eye.*
24. *Guardian,* 30 May 1991.
25. Peter Mandelson, 'Why Labour Lost', *Fabian Review,* Vol. 104, No. 3 (May 1992).

26. *Guardian*, 13 April 1992.
27. Charlotte Raven, 'Tank Boys', *Observer*, 30 July 1995.
28. *Hansard*, 19 July 1994, col. 169.
29. Cleveland county council, *News Release*, 12 December 1994.
30. *Hansard*, 17 June 1993, cols 1096–8.
31. *Hansard*, 25 January 1993, col. 789.
32. *Hansard*, 17 March 1993, col. 369.
33. *Hansard*, 4 November 1992, col. 362.
34. *Hansard*, 24 March 1993, col. 999.
35. *Hansard*, 24 March 1993, col. 1053–4.
36. *Hansard*, 24 March 1993, col. 1041.
37. *Guardian*, 1 January 1994.
38. *Guardian*, 2 February 1994.
39. Tony Benn, *Out of the Wildnerness, Diaries 1963–67* (Arrow, London 1988) p. 508.
40. Peter Mandelson and Roger Liddle, *The Blair Revolution* (Faber and Faber, London 1986) p. 42.
41. Jon Sopel, *Tony Blair: The Moderniser* (Michael Joseph, London 1995) pp. 190–91.
42. Nicholas Jones, 'Blair's Debt to Bobby', *Guardian*, 25 July 1994.
43. Clare Short, 'What's Wrong with Socialism?', in Michael Meacher, Peter Hain, Alan Simpson and Clare Short, *Socialism*, A Tribune Pamphlet (undated) p. 14.
44. The source of this one is the minority of Labour MPs who admire and defend Mandelson. It was given to me in private conversation as an example of how ill-treated he has been.
45. *Today*, 6 October 1994.
46. Peter Mandelson, 'The Rivals who can no Longer be Ignored', *Independent*, 3 August 1993.
47. Richard Burden, 'Time to Renew Labour', *New Statesman & Society*, 11 August 1995.
48. Peter Mandelson and Roger Liddle, *The Blair Revolution* (Faber and Faber, London 1996) pp. 233–4.
49. *Ibid.*, p. 91.
50. Tony Benn, *The End of an Era, Diaries 1980–90* (Arrow, London 1994) p. 422.
51. *Ibid.*, pp. 108, 109.
52. Extracts from the leaked book proposal first appeared in the *Observer*. I am grateful to Barry Hugill of the *Observer* for enabling me to quote from the original document.
53. Will Hutton, 'Left with No Illusions', *Prospect* (March 1996).
54. *Guardian*, 27 February 1996.

55. *Tribune*, 8 March 1996.
56. The first use of the expression 'evil genius' in relation to Mandelson appears to be in the headline of a profile in the *Independent*, 1 July 1989. It has been used numerous times since.
57. Bryan Gould, *Goodbye to All That* (Macmillan, London 1995) p. 229.

7. CALLING TONY BLAIR

1. Interview in *The Times*, 6 July 1994.
2. *Sunday Times*, 28 June 1995.
3. Tony Blair, speech to the Trades Union Congress, 12 September 1995.
4. *Daily Mail*, 27 May 1994.
5. Jon Sopel, *Tony Blair, The Moderniser* (Michael Joseph, London 1995) p. 7.
6. *Sunday Times* Magazine, 17 July 1994.
7. *Hansard*, 18 November 1987, col. 1115.
8. *Mail on Sunday*, 22 June 1994.
9. *Daily Mirror*, 30 September 1994.
10. On Macmurray's influence on Blair, see John Rentoul *Tony Blair* (Little, Brown, London 1995) pp. 41–4.
11. Ian Hargreaves, 'Tony's Best Mate is Back', *New Statesman & Society*, 31 May 1996.
12. I was standing nearby when all this took place, and was recently able to confirm with Tony Booth that his recollection of the incident is the same as mine. Harrison was later posted to South Africa, where he was killed in a car accident.
13. John Rentoul, *Tony Blair*, p. 73–4.
14. Eric Shaw, *Discipline and Discord in the Labour Party* (Manchester University Press, 1988) p. 242.
15. Maggie Rae, interview with the author.
16. Brian Sedgemore, interview with the author.
17. *Hansard*, 6 July 1983, col. 313.
18. John Rentoul, *Tony Blair*, pp. 129–30.
19. *Hansard*, 6 July 1983, col. 315.
20. John Burton, interview with the author.
21. Bryan Gould, *Goodbye to All That* (Macmillan, London 1995) p. 198.
22. Jon Sopel, *Tony Blair: The Moderniser*, pp. 73–4.
23. *Hansard*, 15 November 1983, cols 798, 799.
24. *Hansard*, 8 November 1983, cols 207–10.
25. *Hansard*, 26 March 1984, col. 59.

26. Tony Blair, speech to the Trades Union Congress, 12 September 1995 (transcript issued by TUC).

27. Lord Young, *The Enterprise Years: A Businessman in the Cabinet* (Headline, London 1991) p. 292.

28. *Hansard*, 14 July 1987, col. 986.

29. Alan Clark, *Diaries*, pp. 53–4.

30. *Hansard*, 20 July 1987, col. 79.

31. Chris Mullin MP, 'Why I Will Vote for Tony Blair' (unpublished ms, 1994).

32. *Hansard*, 20 July 1987, col. 45.

33. *Hansard*, 29 January 1986, cols 983, 989–91.

34. *Hansard*, 19 March 1987, col. 1127.

35. *Ibid.*

36. *Hansard*, 13 July 1984 col. 1468.

37. *Hansard*, 8 July, cols 433–4.

38. Chris Mullin MP, 'Why I Will Vote for Tony Blair' (unpublished ms, 1994).

39. *Hansard*, 5 April, col. 269.

40. *Hansard*, 19 November 1979, col. 60.

41. *Hansard*, 12 December 1988, col. 681.

42. *Meet the Challenge, Make the Change: Final Report of Labour's Policy Review for the 1990s* (Labour Party, 1989) p. 15.

43. *Hansard*, 26 June 1989, col. 757.

44. *Hansard*, 26 June 1989, col. 790.

45. This dispute is described in detail in Colin Hughes and Patrick Wintour, *Labour Rebuilt* (Fourth Estate, London 1990) pp. 143–52.

46. *Hansard*, 29 November, col. 727.

47. *Guardian*, 18 December 1989.

48. *Hansard*, 29 January 1990, cols 53–5.

49. *Hansard*, 9 July 1991, col. 796.

50. *Guardian*, 13 April 1992.

51. John Rentoul, *Tony Blair*, p. 269.

52. *Hansard*, 2 March 1993, col. 143.

53. Tony Blair, interview in the *Sunday Telegraph*, 7 April 1996.

54. *Guardian*, 20 February 1993.

55. Toby Helm, 'Blair becomes Labour's Heir Apparent', *Sunday Telegraph*, 28 February 1993.

56. *Hansard*, 10 March 1993, cols 959, 957.

57. *Hansard*, 27 January 1993, cols 1092–3.

58. *Hansard*, 28 January, col. 1187.

59. *Hansard*, 1 February 1993, cols 29, 31, 33–4.

60. Andy McSmith, *John Smith – Playing the Long Game* (Verso, London 1993) p. 239.

61. *Meet the Challenge, Make the Change*, pp. 27–8.

62. *Hansard,* 6 July, col. 315.

63. *It's Time to Get Britain Working Again – Labour's Election Manifesto* (Labour Party, April 1992) p. 12.

64. *Independent,* 27 July 1992.

65. Tony Blair, *'Change and Renewal'*, p. 11. Blair repeated the phrase, virtually word for word, in a speech to the Engineering Employers Federation in Birmingham on 30 June.

66. Tony Blair, *'Change and Renewal'*, Leadership Election Statement, 23 June 1994.

67. BBC Radio 4, *Today,* 22 July 1994.

68. *The Times,* 27 July 1994.

69. Jon Craig, 'Blair Wants to send Son to Tory Flagship Opt-out School', *Daily Express* 21 June 1994.

70. *Observer,* 29 January 1995.

71. *Daily Telegraph,* 13 January 1995.

72. Andy McSmith, 'Can Blair Capture the Soul of the Party?', *Observer,* 29 January 1995. Description of the Gateshead meeting is drawn from my own notes taken that night.

73. The description of the Lewisham rally is from my own notes taken that evening.

74. Figures from the Telegraph Gallup poll, *Daily Telegraph,* 9 June 1995.

75. Brian Mawhinney, speech to Annual Conservative Conference, Blackpool, October 1995.

76. Michael Cockerell, 'Last Grand Old Man Sets New Lease on Power', *Sunday Times,* 19 May 1996.

77. Tony Blair, interview in *The Birmingham Post,* 20 September 1995.

78. Tony Blair, *The Mais Lecture,* given at the City University, 22 May 1995.

79. Tony Blair, speech to the Singapore business community, 8 January 1996.

80. Will Hutton, *The State We're In* (Jonathan Cape, London 1995) p. 326.

81. *Sun,* 16 January 1996.

82. *Guardian,* 25 January 1996.

83. *Daily Mirror,* 26 January 1996.

84. Nicholas Jones, *Soundbites and Spin Doctors* (Cassell, London 1995) p. 153.

85. Gordon Brown, 'New Labour and Equality – The Second John Smith Memorial Lecture', 19 April 1996.

INDEX